Environmental Journalism

Thank you for choosing a SAGE product!
If you have any comment, observation or feedback,
I would like to personally hear from you.

Please write to me at **contactceo@sagepub.in**

Vivek Mehra, Managing Director and CEO, SAGE India.

Bulk Sales

SAGE India offers special discounts
for purchase of books in bulk.
We also make available special imprints
and excerpts from our books on demand.

For orders and enquiries, write to us at

Marketing Department
SAGE Publications India Pvt Ltd
B1/I-1, Mohan Cooperative Industrial Area
Mathura Road, Post Bag 7
New Delhi 110044, India

E-mail us at **marketing@sagepub.in**

Subscribe to our mailing list
Write to **marketing@sagepub.in**

This book is also available as an e-book.

Environmental Journalism

REPORTING ON ENVIRONMENTAL CONCERNS AND CLIMATE CHANGE IN INDIA

D. S. Poornananda

Los Angeles | London | New Delhi
Singapore | Washington DC | Melbourne

First published in 2022 by

SAGE Publications India Pvt Ltd
B1/I-1 Mohan Cooperative Industrial Area
Mathura Road, New Delhi 110 044, India
www.sagepub.in

SAGE Publications Inc
2455 Teller Road
Thousand Oaks, California 91320, USA

SAGE Publications Ltd
1 Oliver's Yard, 55 City Road
London EC1Y 1SP, United Kingdom

SAGE Publications Asia-Pacific Pte Ltd
18 Cross Street #10-10/11/12
China Square Central
Singapore 048423

Published by Vivek Mehra for SAGE Publications India Pvt Ltd and typeset in 10.5/13 pt Adobe Caslon Pro by AG Infographics, Delhi.

Library of Congress Cataloging-in-Publication Data

Names: Poornananda, D. S., author.
Title: Environmental journalism : reporting on environmental concerns and climate change in India / D. S. Poornananda.
Description: New Delhi, India ; Thousand Oaks, California, USA ; London, United Kingdom ; Singapore : SAGE Publications India Pvt Ltd, 2022. | Includes bibliographical references and index.
Identifiers: LCCN 2021057716 (print) | LCCN 2021057717 (ebook) | ISBN 9789354793387 (HB) | ISBN 9789354793394 (epub) | ISBN 9789354793400 (ebook)
Subjects: LCSH: Environmental protection—Press coverage–India. | Environmental degradation–Press coverage–India. | Climatic changes–Press coverage–India. | Mass media and the environment–India. | Mass media and public opinion–India.
Classification: LCC P96.E572.I4 P66 2022 (print) | LCC P96.E572.I4 (ebook) | DDC 070.4/49333720954–dc23/eng/20220124
LC record available at https://lccn.loc.gov/2021057716
LC ebook record available at https://lccn.loc.gov/2021057717

ISBN: 978-93-5479-338-7 (HB)

SAGE Team: Amrita Dutta, Shipra Pant and Anupama Krishnan

Contents

List of Abbreviations

AFEJ	Asian Forum of Environmental Journalists
ANI	Asian News International
BBC	British Broadcasting Corporation
CANE	Citizens for Alternatives to Nuclear Energy
COP	Conference of Parties
CSE	Centre for Science and Environment
DAE	Department of Atomic Energy
DCF	Deputy Conservator of Forest
DDT	Dichlorodiphenyltrichloroethane
DGSS	Dasholi Gram Swarajya Sangh
EIA	Environmental Impact Assessment
ESA	Ecologically Sensitive Area
ESG	Environmental Support Group
FEJI	Forum of Environmental Journalists in India
FIPPAT	Fredrick Institute of Plant and Toxicology
FMCG	Fast-moving Consumer Goods
GM	Genetically modified
GSI	Geological Survey of India
HCCB	Hindustan Coca-Cola Beverages Pvt. Ltd
HLWG	High-level Working Group
IAEA	International Atomic Energy Agency
ICJB	International Campaign for Justice in Bhopal
ICMR	Indian Council for Medical Research
IFEJ	International Federation of Environmental Journalists
IISc	Indian Institute of Science
IPCC	Intergovernmental Panel on Climate Change
IPS	Inter Press Services
ISRO	Indian Space Research Organization
IUCN	International Union for Conservation of Nature
KAPS	Kaiga Atomic Power Station

KAU	Kerala Agricultural University
KBA	Kali Bachao Andolan
KFD	Kyathanur Forest Disease
KIOCL	Khudremukh Iron Ore Corporation Limited
KNPP	Kudankulam Nuclear Power Plant
KSPCB	Kerala State Pollution Control Board
KSSP	Kerala Sasthra Sahithya Parishad
LDF	Left Democratic Front
MAB	Man and the Biosphere
MRPL	Mangalore Refinery and Petrochemicals Limited
MOSOP	Movement for the Survival of the Ogoni People
MSEZ	Mangalore Special Economic Zone
NBA	Narmada Bachao Andolan
NCCL	National Council for Civil Liberties
NCPEPC	National Committee on Environmental Planning and Co-ordination
NDRF	National Disaster Response Force
NGO	Non-governmental organization
NGT	National Green Tribunal
NHRC	National Human Rights Commission
NIOH	National Institute of Occupational Health
NPCIL	Nuclear Power Corporation of India Ltd
NWDT	Narmada Water Disputes Tribunal
PCK	Plantation Corporation of Kerala
PIL	Public interest litigation
PR	Public relations
RERA	Real Estate Regulatory Authority
RML	Ramgad Minerals Limited
RSF	Reporters Without Borders
RTI	Right to Information
SLAPP	Strategic Lawsuit against Public Participation
SPS	Sarvodaya Press Service
SSP	Sardar Sarovar Project
STP	Sewage treatment plant
UCIL	Uranium Corporation of India Ltd
TMC	Tata Memorial Centre
UDF	United Democratic Front

UNCHE	United Nations Conference on Human Environment
UNDRIP	United Nations Declaration on the Rights of Indigenous Peoples
UNFCCC	United Nations Framework Convention on Climate Change
UNEP	United Nations Environment Programme
WCPM	West Coast Paper Mills
WGEA	Western Ghats Ecology Authority
WGEEP	Western Ghats Ecology Expert Panel
WHO	World Health Organization
WSSD	World Summit on Sustainable Development

Foreword

Having grown up in the Western Ghats region of Karnataka, the environment is dear to me. The forests and streams, the birds and animals of my childhood ambiance still fascinate me. The unregulated anthropogenic activities have led to environmental degradation causing serious threats to ecosystems and livelihoods of millions of people. The extreme weather events that we have witnessed in recent years and the unequivocal scientific evidence linking them to climate change have drawn our attention to the urgent need to work towards mitigating environmental deterioration. Assessing the role of media in setting the environmental agenda and examining media framing of causes and consequences of environmental problems assume significance in the context of unsustainable models continuing to dominate the development discourse in India.

For Professor D. S. Poornananda, who has studied and researched environmental issues for over years, the subject of environment has been a passion and a commitment. This book hugely reflects his scholarship and involvement in environmentalism. In these times of environmental emergency, it is a welcome book. The quintessential theme of the book is environmental concerns in India and their reflection in media. Besides drawing information from secondary sources, the author has collected first-hand data and evidence from interviews of environmental activists and media persons and through content analysis of major newspapers. These multiple sources of data give authenticity to the author's inferences and interpretations.

This book traces the evolution of environmentalism and offers a comprehensive overview of various governmental and non-governmental efforts, both in terms of policies and actions, to protect and preserve the ecological system in the last half century. The review seems to suggest that a general awareness as to the need for consonance between development and environment is gradually evolving. Certainly, media have a pivotal role in creating this awareness; but scepticism remains as to how satisfactory is the performance of media in this role. Professor Poornananda rightly identifies the crux of the problem when he says that media coverage of the environment is influenced by the 'political economy of media, professional values and a journalistic sense of what constitutes news'. Further, he highlights the problem of the 'attention cycle' in the agenda-setting process of media and demonstrates how media fail to focus on the environment uninterruptedly. The discussion of Indian media coverage of environmental themes is broad-based and examines the causes for the absence of a sustained campaign for the promotion of the environmental cause.

The analysis of the media coverage of environmental issues based on detailed interviews of activists and journalists delineates exhaustively the inherent problems in the media system which contribute to the present state of environmental journalism. Environmental reporting is hampered by lack of specialization and low salience of environmental news in media. Coverage of environmental news is often event oriented and as the author notes, 'At times, there is only knee-jerk response to disasters ignoring the responsibility of examining the processes that lead to them'. Most of the journalists and activists interviewed by the author know where the shoe pinches but express the helpless media situation in which they are operating. As long as the bane of monopoly control, pressures from interest groups and lack of professionalism haunt the media system, environmental reporting is bound to suffer. Nevertheless, the detailed discourses with committed activists and senior journalists have enabled the author to identify the state of affairs prevailing in the media system and the characteristics of environmental reporting.

The discussion of Narmada Bachao Andolan (NBA) presents a case study of a major environmental movement, its coverage in media and the NBA–media relationship. It is very thorough. The approach of NBA in its media relations is not one of public relations but building relationship with media persons. It is rather unique and provides a useful model for other such movements. As to the media hostility towards NBA, perhaps it is the operation of the 'spiral of silence'. Since a majority of newspapers were anti-NBA, others just followed it. As the spiral of silence theory asserts, 'the perception that one's opinion is unpopular tends to inhibit or discourage one's expression of it, while the perception that it is popular tends to have the opposite effect'.

The analysis of media coverage of floods and landslides in Kerala and Kodagu is both exhaustive and alarming. Although the coverage was marked by sensational headlines and rumours, the newspapers made efforts to bring the attention of the readers to the issues affecting the ecology of the Western Ghats. The silver line in the findings of this analysis is that newspaper articles went into the causes of the catastrophe and highlighted the 'man-made' factors. I presume the newspapers chosen for the study were local editions of the respective papers. It is quite justified. However, the problem is that this coverage may not go beyond the boundaries of their circulation and may not draw the attention of policymakers at the state or national level.

The author justifiably examines the environmental issues in the context of human rights. The interconnection between environmental protection and human rights is discussed extensively, focusing on the impact of climate change on the indigenous people and on the struggles of the tribal communities at Plachimada in Kerala and Niyamgiri in Odisha for their right to access to natural resources. Again, the inadequate media performance in highlighting this connection is made abundantly clear. Comparatively, the media performance in this country is even more appalling than what it is elsewhere in other parts of the world.

I have the satisfaction of reading a well-documented monograph on media and the environment. Much of the data comes from primary sources, namely environmental activists and media persons with years of experience in the field. Issues bearing on media and environment alliance are conceptualized and explored threadbare. A noteworthy point is that the individual journalists support the environment movements, but media institutions have not bothered to protect the interests of the people. It suggests that there is a gap between reporters and editorial decision-makers. Taking the position of a devil's advocate, one may question: Does the narrative here portray the full story or is it one-sided? The inferences and interpretations are reflections of the perceptions of active participants in environmental movements and protagonists of environmentalism among journalists. Could there be an alternative perspective by media owners and managers, and by the champions of development? What are the constraints that hold media from engaging in a long-term agenda-setting campaign in favour of environmental protection? This aspect is not given adequate attention, and perhaps, it is outside the purview of the discourse.

In sum, the present monograph on environmentalism and media is a well-written, adequately researched and abundantly documented resource book. It is helpful to students, journalists and even policymakers, if they ever care to look into it.

Professor H. S. Eswara
Former Dean
Faculty of Communication
Bangalore University

Acknowledgements

This work would not have been possible without the support and encouragement of my friends, communication scholars, media persons and environmentalists. I have immensely benefited from their ideas and experiences.

I express my gratitude to Professor H. S. Eswara for writing the foreword and encouraging me to publish the book.

I am deeply indebted to the leader of NBA, Ms Medha Patkar, for her hospitality and for sparing her valuable time to answer my queries on development, environment and media, despite her hectic schedule.

Mr Umapathy D. made it possible for me to travel to Barwani in Madhya Pradesh to have long conversations with Ms Medha Patkar and other activists. I am thankful to him for taking time off for several days from his busy schedule in Delhi to be with me at Barwani.

I would like to express my heartfelt gratitude to Mr Nagesh Hegde for sharing his experience and thoughts concerning science, environment and environmental journalism.

I am grateful to Mr Manohar Yadavatti, who facilitated my visit to Kodagu and Kerala after the floods in August 2018. Thanks to him, I was able to meet journalists, officials, activists and victims from Somwarpet in Karnataka to Alleppey in Kerala.

I thank Mr K. G. Vasuki, for travelling with me to Kodagu and Uttara Kannada districts in Karnataka and helping me interview journalists and activists.

Mr Panduranga Hegde, Sirsi narrated to me the changing nature of environmental struggles and his perception of media attitude towards environmental issues. I express my sincere thanks to him.

I am thankful to all the journalists, activists and project-affected and flood-affected persons who helped me in many ways.

Introduction

Droughts, floods, heat waves, super storms, wildfires and crop failures have been happening with a higher frequency in recent years, raising concerns about the long-term impact of environmental degradation and climate change. The year 2020 recorded an unprecedented rise in extreme weather events even though there was a dip in emissions because of the COVID-19 pandemic (*The Hindu*, 2021). The Sixth Assessment Report of the Intergovernmental Panel on Climate Change (IPCC) released in August 2021 says that the global temperature is likely to reach or exceed 1.5°C benchmark in the next 20 years if drastic measures are not taken to reduce greenhouse gas emissions. There is overwhelming evidence to show that human activities have substantially altered ecosystems and the climate of the planet earth. Despite the growth of environmental awareness in the past four decades, visible and sustained long-term measures to prevent the catastrophe that looms large are lacking. As developed nations have shown their lack of commitment to international agreements aimed at reducing pollution levels, the developing countries have embarked on a development path which has led to overexploitation of natural resources pushing themselves to the brink of a disaster. Extreme weather events which have increased exponentially in the past two decades and have claimed thousands of lives in India are yet to be fully acknowledged as the consequences of pursuing a destructive development model. Depleting groundwater levels, deforestation, water and air pollution, perennial rivers turning into flood streams, and dwindling biodiversity in India have affected the livelihoods of millions of people. Despite such stark realities, environmental and climate change issues have not been adequately addressed at the political and policy levels. Although there have been frequent references to sustainable development in several policy documents, the discourse on the environment and climate change has not been on the agenda of mainstream politics. The 'development vs environment' frame dominates the environmental discourse. The dilution of environmental laws in recent years with the proclaimed purpose of promoting faster economic growth has been a disturbing trend.

In the early 1970s, environmentalism was rejected as a fetish born out of Western post-materialist societies which emerged in the period following the Second World War (Guha, 1992). It was argued that environmental concern was irrelevant to India, as the country had to work towards meeting the basic needs of an increasing population, unlike the West which had the problem of plenty. The Indian representatives had forcefully argued in several international forums that for a developing country like India, 'development' was more important than the 'environment'. However, it was realized later that the environment was an issue to be addressed. Several legal measures were taken for the conservation of forests, wildlife and water. In contrast to the belief that environmental concern is a feature of the affluent society, the Indian environmental struggles have mostly been led by the poor whose livelihoods were threatened by environmental degradation. The rising awareness about environmental problems partly due to some disasters witnessed in the 1980s led to the consolidation and institutionalization of the environmental movement in India. The environmental movement was aimed at not only influencing policy and political argument but also changing the underlying culture (Smith, 2006).

The media have played an important role in not only creating environmental awareness but also influencing policies related to environmental conservation. They have the ability to move the environmental problems from conditions to issues to policy concerns (Hannigan, 1995). Without media coverage, environmental problems may not enter the arena of public or political discourse. The environmental movement in India has been able to make a considerable impact on environmental policy partly because of the role played by media in influencing public opinion about environmental issues.

The agenda-setting theory and framing provide the broad theoretical background in this book for analysing issues related to media and the environment. The agenda-setting theory holds that the media play a significant role in how certain issues gain public attention. Media coverage influences the importance the public attaches to the issues. The idea of agenda-setting began with the Walter Lippmann's (1922) classic book *Public Opinion*. The book began with a chapter titled 'The World Outside and the Pictures in Our Heads'. His thesis was that the newspapers were the bridge between the world outside and the pictures in the minds of the readers. The pictures were the reflection of what the media reported but not necessarily what was happening in the real world. Only those elements which are emphasized and given prominence in media are regarded by members of the public as important. It was Bernard Cohen who developed the ideas of Lippmann into a theoretical frame. Cohen (1963, p. 13) said, 'The press may not be successful much of the time in telling people what to think but it is stunningly successful in telling its readers what to think about.' By selecting, emphasizing and priming, the media draw the audience's attention to some issues. Going beyond the focus of attention, media may tell people how to think and what to do by shaping their attitudes and opinions.

Maxwell McCombs and Donald Shaw (1972, p. 176) empirically confirmed Cohen's perspective and said:

> In choosing and displaying news, editors, newsroom staff, and broadcasters play an important part in shaping political reality. Readers learn not only about a given issue, but how much importance to attach to that mass media may well determine the important issues—that is, the media may set the agenda of the campaign.

During the 1968 US presidential elections, they found significant correlation between issues considered important by the voters and the priority given to issues by the media in terms of space and time. People are likely to pay attention to and discuss only those issues which receive prominent coverage in media. Agenda-setting hypothesis has provided the framework for several scholars who have studied coverage of environmental issues in media. That the media have played the agenda-setting role with regard to environmental problems has been demonstrated by several scholars (Ader, 1995; Atwater et al., 1985; Kwansah-Aidoo, 2001; Reinert, 2020; Scheufele & Tewksbury, 2007).

In a typical process, the media agenda influences the public agenda, which in turn impacts the policy agenda. In other words, media coverage of environmental issues creates awareness among the public and exerts pressure on the government and the industry to take measures to address those issues. However, as indicated by several studies, the media may play a greater agenda-setting role with regard to some issues and lesser agenda-setting role with regard to some other issues. By choosing not to report certain issues, media may attempt to keep them out of the public discourse.

Media not only report but also frame issues through selection, emphasis, exclusion, interpretation, evaluation and treatment (Entman, 1993; Gitlin, 1980; Tuchman, 1978). As a concept adapted from Erving Goffman's (1974) work on small group interaction, framing has been used by media scholars to understand media construction of social reality. It is closely related to the agenda-setting theory, which refers to how media package and present news to the audience. Frames are abstractions which help journalists organize a story. A frame is a 'central organizing idea for making sense of relevant events, suggesting what is at issue' (Gamson & Modigliani, 1989, p. 3).

Frames restrict how audiences interpret events. They highlight some aspects and omit others, influencing how audiences read stories and make sense of them. Even when the environmental events are not disputed, they can be framed in different ways. Environmental issues are often framed differently, depending on the political and ideological orientation of the media. Environmental news coverage in Indian media has grown in the last four decades. The changing trends in the media market have affected the choice and framing of environmental content. At a time when the dominant national discourse in India is development, it is important to reflect on how media have covered environmental consequences of what is generally understood to be development. Media may frame environmental issues as mere events, conflicts, personality clashes, natural occurrences or processes which are man-made or as those which have resulted as a consequence of unsustainable use of resources. Frames which are manifest in media texts may affect learning, interpretation and evaluation of issues and events.

The way in which media frame issues may have an effect on individual's attitudes and play a vital role in collective decision-making and action. Although frames may not determine what people think, they highlight certain aspects of a problem through selection and salience.

Gatekeeping, agenda setting and framing are also related to professional values and practices of journalism. News sources, reporters, editors and publishers work as gatekeepers in selecting the environmental content and fitting it into the routines of news production practices. There are also advertisers, investors, pressure groups and governmental agencies which exert considerable influence on agenda-setting with regard to the environmental and climate change issues.

This book is aimed at giving a broad understanding of the practice, possibilities and constraints of environmental journalism. It is an attempt to understand the growth of environmental concern and its reflection in media; to analyse the media coverage of environmental news; to examine how media report environmental movements; to enquire into whether media debate environmental issues associated with disasters; and to see if environmental problems are reported in the context of human rights and environmental justice.

For the purpose of this book, interviews and content analysis, both quantitative and qualitative, have been used besides analysis of information drawn from secondary sources. In-depth interviews were held with senior journalists who have specialized in the area of environmental journalism and those who have not been specialists but have written on environmental issues in their long career spanning decades. They have been keen observers of media trends over the years in the context of changing media business models and professional values. Environmental activists, project-affected persons, experts/scientists and victims of environmental disasters have also been interviewed. One owner of a media group, who took part in an environmental movement and ensured that the publications of his group gave adequate attention to the environment and climate change, was also interviewed.

Environmental reporting often involves covering environmental struggles and disasters. A case study of NBA, one of the iconic environmental movements in India, has been carried out to understand how environmental movements are covered and framed in media. Interviews were held with the leader of NBA, Medha Patkar, and her associates in Barwani and Dhar districts of Madhya Pradesh. An unprecedented environmental disaster struck Kerala state and the Kodagu district of Karnataka in August 2018. The floods and landslides claimed thousands of lives and destroyed homes and infrastructure worth thousands of crores. According to environmentalists, this extreme weather event was associated with climate change. To understand how such an environmental disaster was reported in media, a content analysis of four English and four Kannada newspapers was carried out. Journalists, activists, officials, and victims of floods and landslides in Kerala and Kodagu were interviewed to know their perception of media coverage of the disaster and its links with environmental factors. In Dakshina Kannada and Uttara Kannada districts of Karnataka, where several environmental struggles have been active, journalists and activists were interviewed to understand media construction of environmental issues.

The first chapter describes the growth of environmental concern, the environmental movement, and its impact on media coverage of the environment as an issue. It also provides a theoretical understanding of the role of media in covering environmental issues and the growth of environmental journalism.

The second chapter analyses the factors associated with low salience of environmental issues and event orientation in environmental reporting. A critical perspective with regard to the 'development vs environment' frame often found in Indian media coverage of the environment is presented. The chapter also examines different levels of concern and the amount of importance given to environmental issues in the local, state and national media.

Whether media should remain neutral to play the advocacy role vis-à-vis environmental issues is the question discussed in the third chapter. The standard professional practices and the possibilities and limitations of the activist role of journalists are brought into focus from the conflicting perspectives of journalists and activists. The values of truth and fairness in reporting and activists donning the role of journalists leading to blurring of the line between activism and journalism are examined. The potential of the alternative media as a tool of advocacy and the attempts to control them are explained.

The fourth chapter deals with the pressures on the publishers and journalists and the ways in which they have responded to them given the political economy of the media and professional norms. The pro-establishment and pro-industry biases which are noticeable in the coverage of environmental issues and the constraints associated with them are analysed. The cases of publishers standing up to the threats of industries and advertisers and defending their reporters are narrated in the context of media attempts to preserve their editorial independence.

The problems involved in dealing with scientific uncertainties and the consequences of lack of specialization and training in environmental reporting are discussed in the fifth chapter. Conflicting evidence about the environmental impact of aerial spraying of endosulfan on cashew plantations in the Kasaragod district of Kerala and the questionable claims in media about radiation-induced cancer in the areas around the Kaiga Nuclear Power Plant in the Uttara Kannada district of Karnataka are presented from the perspectives of experts and journalists. The reluctance of the publishers to appoint journalists with specialization in environmental reporting, lack of assistance to journalists in getting in-service training and independent efforts to train journalists at the grassroots level are also explained here.

The sixth chapter places in perspective the source–media relations with an emphasis on the role the dominant sources play in shaping and framing of environmental news. It pays particular attention to the official sources which are considered authentic and provide a narrative that justifies the dominant paradigm of development. It also examines how activists and environmental non-governmental organizations (NGOs) are not fully trusted as reliable sources despite their work at the grassroots level and their involvement in environmental struggles. The chapter also brings into focus importance given to different sources as definers of environmental news and marginalization of the project-affected persons as sources environmental news.

The seventh chapter discusses how the media have covered the movement in the Narmada Valley led by NBA and the questions it has raised on the issues related to development in general and big dams in particular. It also focuses on the challenge of the hostile media, movement–media relations, personality-centric coverage and event orientation in reporting the issues in the valley. The change in media attitude towards the movement over the years has also been looked into. The analysis in this chapter is based on content analysis and interviews with the leader of the movement Medha Patkar, activists, volunteers and journalists.

The eighth chapter analyses the media coverage of unprecedented floods and landslides in Kerala and Kodagu in August 2018. The debate on the man-made and natural causes of the disaster in newspapers has been presented through content analysis and interviews. Since the floods and landslides took place in the Western Ghats region, media attention to the recommendations of the two expert panels on conservation of the Ghats has been examined.

The ninth chapter is focused on the media recognition of environmental rights as human rights or lack of it and the extent to which media have gone in treating environmental issues as human rights issues. The chapter also examines from the point of view of environmental justice, denial of right to information, coverage of the problems associated with displacement and media construction of violation of the rights of the communities to have access to unpolluted resources.

The book, overall, is structured to cover what is needed for the students of journalism and mass communication. Historical and theoretical perspectives are presented along with cases, experiences and perceptions of journalists, activists, project-affected persons, and experts in the context of professional practices and the political economy of media.

CHAPTER 1

Environmental Concern and the Media

From Scepticism to Cognizance

The environment as an issue has been a part of the public discourse only in recent decades. As it is generally understood today, the term 'environment' broadly refers to the physical environment that includes animals, plants and their habitats, climate, resources of water, land and air. Environmental concern reflects an attitude towards nature that assumes that the human society has the ethical responsibility of preserving the ecological balance and making rational use of all natural resources (Rosenbaum, 2019).

The environmentalist perspective emphasizes that the limited resources of the world be used with wisdom, taking into account potential scarcities. Ecological balance, which means a harmonious coexistence of all forms of life with their environment, has been at the centre of the environmental debate. Environmentalism is a modern phenomenon which came as a dynamic response to the ecological consequences of the industrial revolution. It is an ideology and a movement aimed at protecting the environment by reducing the human activities on the earth. Environmentalism rejects the idea that man's knowledge of science and technology places him above nature and questions the logic of economic growth as the prime goal of modern society.

Modern societies have been at war with the environment for a long time and have 'treated nature as little more than a resource to be tapped and as a sink into which to dump their wastes' (Foster, 1999, p. 13). Even though environmental degradation was one of the major factors that caused the collapse of some of the great civilizations that had flourished for thousands of years, the massive exploitation of natural resources began with the European colonization of America, Africa and Asia. The coming of the Industrial Revolution in Europe and North America led to unprecedented extraction and burning of fossil fuels. Large-scale felling of trees, which are a link between the natural world and the material world, began at an alarming pace after the Industrial Revolution.

Several writers and thinkers of the 19th century who had witnessed the environmental consequences of the Industrial Revolution in England responded by not only writing about the destruction of nature but also embarking on a programme of action aimed at preventing it. Prominent among them were William Wordsworth, John Ruskin, William Morris and Edward Carpenter. Their philosophy and programme had their influence on the formation of environmental societies[1] in the late 19th century (Guha, 2014). The ideas of Ruskin and Carpenter are reflected in Mahatma Gandhi's book *Hind Swaraj*, which has been described as the 'Gandhian manifesto of ecological living'[2] (Khoshoo & Moolakkattu, 2009, p. 77). In this book published in 1909, Gandhi opposed industrialization, consumption-driven growth and stressed the revitalization of villages. The well-known quote attributed to Gandhi 'The world has enough for everybody's need but not enough for one person's greed'[3] (cited in Guha, 2014,

[1] The environmental societies saved some parts of England from industrial pollution as they exerted pressure on the government to enforce pollution laws (Guha, 2014).

[2] Ramachandra Guha disputes this claim and says that there is nothing about ecology in *Hind Swaraj* (Devschooluea, 2016).

[3] In a lecture on 'Was Gandhi an environmentalist' in 2018, Guha said that Gandhi did not coin such an aphorism, although the sentiments expressed in it undoubtedly reflected his thought (Ragi Kana, 2018).

p. 30) emphasizes that natural resources be used only to meet people's needs. In the journals he brought out, Gandhi wrote about unsustainability of the Western model of economic development. Writing in *Young India* in December 1928, he said:

> God forbid that India should ever take to industrialism after the manner of the West. The economic imperialism of a single tiny island kingdom (England) is today keeping the world in chains. If an entire nation of 300 millions took to similar economic exploitation, it would strip the world bare like locusts. (*Young India*, 1928)

He was prophetic about how industrialization would lead to excessive consumption of resources and deprive people of their necessities. The independent India did start industrializing after the manner of the West and adopted the resource-intensive and capital-intensive economic model. The model remained unquestioned until the 1970s when environmental movements inspired by the Gandhian ideals began raising questions on the consequences of mega industries, big dams and the destruction of forests. These movements have remained committed to Gandhian values of sustainable consumption and non-violence.

Even as environmental movements started emerging in different parts of India, the national discourse continued to be focused on industrial and economic growth. Very little attention was paid to the impact of overexploitation of natural resources on the livelihoods of the marginalized communities. Economic liberalization of the 1990s further worsened the environmental situation in India as it started vigorously promoting development without adequate regulatory mechanisms in place. Despite extreme weather events occurring more frequently, hardly any measures were initiated to deal with the problem of climate change.

Growth of Environmental Concern

Even though people had become aware of the environmental problems in the late 19th century and resistance to environmental degradation began in the early 20th century, environmentalism grew into a movement only in the 1960s. The growth was due not only to an increase in environmental problems but also to new scientific evidence indicating the dangers of the reckless use of fossil fuels. The media began paying greater attention to the environmental problems and their causes. In June 1962, *The New Yorker* magazine published in a three-part series[4] marine biologist Rachel Carson's book *Silent Spring* which has been described as the 'Bible' or the 'founding event' (Guha, 2000, p. 3) of modern environmentalism. The book popularized the concepts of 'food chain', 'ecology', 'web of life' and 'balance of nature' and provided a simplified understanding of what is generally referred to as 'environmental crisis' (Rubin, 1994, p. 30).

People had generally been unaware of the toxicity of pesticides and their effect on ecological interrelationships until the publication of this book. She argued that human beings were poisoning themselves as they went about poisoning the earth with chemicals. According to Carson, chemicals sprayed on plants and trees entered the human body through the soil, water and food chain. She documented how chemical pesticides such as dichlorodiphenyltrichloroethane (DDT) were poisoning wildlife and contaminating the food chain. She had discovered that chemicals sprayed on elms had led to a drastic decline in the population of robins as the poison had travelled through the elm leaf–earthworm–robin cycle. The spring would arrive with no birds to welcome it with songs. Carson (1962, 59) wrote:

> Spring now comes unheralded by the return of the birds, and the early mornings are strangely silent where once they were filled with the beauty of bird song. This sudden silencing of the song of birds, this obliteration of the color and beauty and interest they lend to our world have come about swiftly, insidiously, and unnoticed by those whose communities are as yet unaffected.

She discovered that between 1950 and 1962, the DDT found in human tissue had nearly tripled. Her book led to the banning of DDT and other pesticides. Carson showed that environmental degradation

[4] The series appeared on 16, 23 and 30 June 1962. Even as the magazine published the second part of the series, a Chicago-based chemical company threatened to sue the magazine if it continued with its publication (Lytle, 2007).

anywhere would have consequences elsewhere.[5] Stories about pesticides began appearing in media after the publication of *Silent Spring*, raising the level of people's awareness about the effect of poisonous chemicals on the environment (Jackson, 1991).

Six years after the publication of *Silent Spring*, UNESCO held its first Intergovernmental Conference for Rational Use and Conservation of the Biosphere in Paris in 1968. More than 300 delegates from 60 countries representing a wide variety of scientific fields, management and diplomacy took part in the conference. The conference was an important step in establishing international environmental politics. The term 'biosphere', which was being used only by a few scientists, got international recognition because of media coverage of this conference. The conference adopted a series of recommendations concerning environmental problems and highlighted their growing importance at the global level. The highlight of the conference was the declaration that utilization and conservation of land and water resources should go hand in hand rather than in opposition and that an interdisciplinary approach should be promoted to achieve this aim. Following the conference, UNESCO launched the Man and the Biosphere (MAB) programme in 1970 which had the objective of protecting the biosphere reserves.

The modern environmental movement is said to have begun when 'Earth Day' was celebrated on 22 April 1970. The growth of the movement led to the realization that collective action at the international level was needed to address the environmental problems. The United Nations Conference on Human Environment (UNCHE) held in Stockholm in 1972 brought the attention of the world to the reality of environmental degradation. As the first major conference of the United Nations on environmental issues, it marked a turning point in the development of international environmental politics. Before Stockholm, people in many parts of the world saw the environment as something divorced from humanity. The Stockholm Conference led to a fundamental shift in environmental thinking. After Stockholm,

[5] Despite its remarkable contribution to science, Guha (2014, p. 94) laments that *Silent Spring* is 'not much read anymore'.

there was a growing realization of the basic and indestructible links between what humans do in one part of the world and what they do in another (Eckholm, 1982).

The Stockholm Declaration on the Human Environment constituted a new principle of behaviour and responsibility by nations. It was the first acknowledgement of environmental ethics on the international level to govern the relationship of man with his environment. On 16 June 1972, the UNCHE adopted a declaration consisting of a preamble and 26 principles, embodying a common principle to inspire and guide the people of the world in the preservation and enhancement of the human environment (Khanna, 1993).

Stressing the need to create environmental awareness throughout the world, principle 19 of the declaration said:

> Education in environmental matters, for the younger generation as well as adults, giving due consideration to the underprivileged, is essential in order to broaden the basis for an enlightened opinion and responsible conduct by the individuals, enterprises, and communities in protecting and improving its full human dimensions. It is also essential that mass media of communication avoid contributing to the deterioration of the environment, but on the contrary, disseminate information of an educational nature on the need to protect and improve the environment in order to enable man to develop in every respect.[6]

The declaration recognized the critical role mass media could play in educating people about the environment. The conference was rightly called the United Nations Conference on Human Environment. The slogan 'Only One Earth' emphasized the need to see the earth as the common home for everyone and to take collective responsibility in preserving the environment. The conference established a United Nations Environment Programme (UNEP) so that the world's governments embarked on a programme of sound environmental management.

Following the Stockholm Conference, many developing countries created environmental ministries or agencies and passed laws to

---

[6] https://www.un.org/ga/search/view_doc.asp?symbol=A/CONF.48/14/REV.1

regulate the use of natural resources and to prevent environmental degradation. An analysis of the expected environmental impact of major projects became mandatory in many countries.

The developing countries were initially sceptical about concern for the environment shown by developed countries during the UNCHE at Stockholm in 1972. The representatives of the developing countries argued that they needed industries for their development and that some amount of pollution was a price they were ready to pay for economic development. India and Brazil were vocal in their defence of development over the environment. Indian Prime Minister Indira Gandhi delivered a rousing speech and argued that if pollution was the price of progress, India would want more of it. The conference was termed as a sinister conspiracy to hinder industrial development in the developing world. Despite such a stance taken by the Government of India at the Stockholm Conference, there was a gradual realization that environmental problems had to be addressed.

One of the first steps the Indian government took was to establish the National Committee on Environmental Planning and Coordination (NCPEPC). The committee suggested several measures including legislation for preventing environmental degradation. The Wildlife Protection Act of 1972 extended protection to several endangered mammals and birds. The conservationists had strongly argued for the protection of the tiger in the general assembly of the International Union for Conservation of Nature (IUCN) held at Delhi in 1969. In 1972, a trustee of the Worldwide Fund for Nature urged the then Prime Minister Indira Gandhi to save tigers from extinction (Narain, 2017). Project Tiger was launched in 1973 and nine tiger reserves were set up. The tiger, being at the top of the food chain, came to symbolize the wild wealth of India, and if the tiger could flourish, it would mean the well-being of all wildlife in India. This was followed by the Water (Prevention and Control of Pollution) Act of 1974. Indira Gandhi is credited with ushering in several environmental laws that led to the acceptance of a range of transnational legal principles which would be reflected in newly added constitutional provisions (Sridhar, 2021).

The necessity to introduce an environmental dimension into the development planning process was felt during the Fourth Five-Year

Plan. The proposal of the Planning Commission of India (1975, p. 275) said:

> It is an obligation for each generation to maintain the productive capacity of land, air, water and wildlife in a manner which leaves its successors some choice the creation of a healthy environment. The physical environment is a dynamic, complex and inter-connected system in which any action in one part affects others. There is also the interdependence of living things and their relationships with land, air and water. Planning for harmonious development recognises this unity of nature and man. Such planning is possible only on the basis of a comprehensive appraisal of environmental issues, particularly economic and ecological. There are instances in which timely specialised advice on environmental aspects could have helped in project design and in averting subsequent adverse effects on the environment leading to loss of invested resources. It is necessary, therefore, to introduce the environmental aspect into our planning and development. Along with effective conservation and rational use of natural resources, protection and improvement of human environment is vital for national well being.

This was the first official statement concerning environmental policy in India. Planners in India recognized the importance of protection of the environment in the long-term interest of national development. The basic approach was to bring about sustainable development in harmony with nature. The feeling that development was what life was all about and that the environment was of peripheral interest began to change in the mid-1970s.

The Forty-second amendment to the Constitution of India made it obligatory for the state and every citizen to protect and improve the environment. The Amendment Act of 1976 added two Articles in Part IV and Part IV-A of the Constitution. Article 48A says, 'The State shall endeavour to protect and improve the environment and to safeguard the forest and wildlife of the country'. Under this Article, the state may not only adopt the protectionist policy but also provide for the improvement of the polluted environment. Article 51(G) states, 'It shall be the duty of every citizen of India to protect and improve the natural environment including forest, lakes, rivers, and wildlife and to have compassion for living creatures.' India was the only country to impose a constitutional obligation on the state and citizens to protect and improve the environment as one of the prime duties. To what extent the state and citizens have shown a commitment to this obligation has been a matter of debate. The state which has the dual role as a promoter of economic development and environmental regulator often resorts to environmental managerialism (Redclift, 1986) so that it is seen to be acting against those harming ecological balance. Despite the existence of several environmental laws, the commitment that governments have shown in promoting economic development is lacking in preventing environmental degradation.

In the years following the Stockholm Conference where India had rejected the very idea of environmental protection as a Western fad, there was a realization that environmental issues deserved government's attention. The study of the environmental problems at the academic level was encouraged with liberal funding from the Central government. Jawaharlal Nehru University started the first School of Environmental Sciences in 1974 and began offering a master's programme in environmental sciences in 1976. Academic programmes in environmental sciences began in several other universities later.

Although policy statements and constitutional provisions emphasized the need to protect the environment, no governmental agency to deal with environment-related matters was set up until 1980. The Department of Environment was set up in that year to serve as the nodal agency in the administrative structure of the Central government for planning, promotion and coordination of environmental programmes. In the same year, the Forest (Conservation) Act was enacted to prevent the fast-depleting forest cover. The Act placed the Central government in the commanding position to refuse permission for non-forest activity in all forest areas. Even though the law was unable to stop deforestation, it saved several thousand acres of forest under threat (Dhawan, 2000). The Air (Prevention and Control of Pollution) Act was enacted in the next year, making polluting air a punishable offence. As the government's responsibilities in environmental regulation increased, the Department of Environment was expanded into a new Ministry of Environment and Forests in 1985.

In the year 1983, the Centre for Ecological Sciences was started at the Indian Institute of Science, Bangalore, with the support of the Department of Environment, Government of India. An eminent ecologist of international repute Professor Madhav Gadgil who headed the Centre for over three decades carried out several studies on ecological issues with the primary focus on the Western Ghats. The Centre played an important role in putting the environmental agenda before the Central and state governments.

The state governments set up environmental ministries following the creation of the new Ministry of Environment and Forests at the Centre in 1985. Clearance from the Ministry of Environment and Forest became mandatory to set up major industries. Although many laws had been made which dealt with matters related to the environment, there was no single comprehensive legislation. The enactment of the Environment (Protection) Act of 1986 was a major milestone in the history of environmental legislation in India. The Act entrusted an overall coordination function to the Union government. The scope of the Act is broad, with 'environment' defined to include water, air and land and the interrelationships that exist among water, air and land and human beings and other creatures, plants, micro-organisms and property. Before the passage of this Act, it was open for each state to lay down its own environmental standards. Two years after the enactment of the Environment (Protection Act), the Central government formulated a new National Forest Policy which had the objective of ensuring environmental stability and maintenance of ecological balance, including atmospheric equilibrium necessary for the sustenance of all life forms, human, animal and plant. The two industrial disasters in the 1980s, the Bhopal gas tragedy of 1984 and the Chernobyl accident of 1986, showed beyond doubt the environmental consequences of industrial and nuclear accidents. The environmental hazards of the nuclear option to meet the rising energy demand became a subject of international debate.

The publication of the report of the World Commission on Environment and Development (1987) known as the Brundtland Commission Report titled *Our Common Future* popularized the concept of 'sustainable development'. The commission defined sustainable development as 'development that meets the needs of the present without compromising the ability of future generations to meet their own needs' (World Commission on Environment and Development, 1987, p. 8). The concept caught the imagination of Indian policymakers and environmental groups and became a mantra for the balance between development and the environment.

In order to promote sustainable development, several measures were proposed including assessment of damage to the environment. The Environment Impact Assessment (EIA) notification issued in 1994 made public hearing mandatory. The project proponent was required to submit an EIA report along with an environmental management plan. Submission of details about the public hearing on the project was made compulsory. The ministry itself became the impact assessment agency. Public hearings provide a forum for non-governmental organizations (NGOs) to voice their concerns to project promoters. As the environmental discourse expanded and the demand for implementing the environmental norms became more louder, the government began to play a greater role as a regulator. Acknowledging the significance of climate change as a major issue, the Government of India renamed the Ministry of Environment and Forest as the Ministry of Environment, Forests and Climate Change in May 2014. The government plays a dual role as a facilitator of economic growth and as an environmental regulator. Although there are questions about the extent to which the government has succeeded as a regulator in protecting the environment, there are several laws that enable the government to hold organizations and individuals accountable for environmental destruction and act against them.

Environmental Movements

Although environmental movements began in different forms and with different ideological orientations in different parts of the world after the Industrial Revolution, it was only in the latter part of the 20th century that they began to take the shape of mass movements. The early 1970s witnessed environmental concern of the previous decades turning into movements not only in the West but also in India.

According to Hannigan (1995, pp. 23–29), there are four explanations with regard to the dramatic growth of environmental consciousness and movements from the early 1970s onwards in Europe and America. Although these explanations look inadequate in the Indian context, some aspects of them look relevant and deserve attention. The first is the reflection hypothesis, which says that environmental movements grew as a direct response to the worsening environmental situation (Dunlap & Scarce, 1990). The depletion of forest cover and pollution of rivers had been highly visible in North America and Western Europe, as a result of which people began collectively questioning industrial development and its consequences on the human environment. In those countries where environmental deterioration was less noticeable, environmentalism appeared to be moderate. The environmental struggles that began in several parts of India in the 1970s and 1980s were in direct response to the deforestation, displacement and threat to livelihoods. Nevertheless, environmental movements have not emerged from all those places where ecological destruction had taken place.

Those who found that the public had ignored environmental deterioration even when it was evident challenged the view that the rise in environmental concern was the outcome of deterioration in the environmental situation. Albrecht and Mauss (1975, p. 573) found that 'public concern' about air pollution had risen at a time when the quantity of pollution had declined. It is possible that public concern may not be related to actual environmental deterioration but may have been shaped by the coverage in mass media. What is perceived as a problem may not reflect reality but a particular view presented in mass media. For the public to show concern about the environment media coverage may become necessary, but that alone is not the only reason why environmental struggles have grown.

The second explanation is provided through the post-materialist hypothesis, which argues that the post-Second World War generation that had financial stability showed a lesser interest in economic growth and greater interest in ideas, individual autonomy and quality of the physical environment in contrast to the previous generation that had suffered from economic worries. Rather than being a mere life-cycle phenomenon, post-materialism, according to Inglehart (1977), was a lasting value change. It was Stephen Cotgrove (1981) who linked Inglehart's post-materialism thesis to environmentalism in Europe. Environmentalists were found to be more committed to post-materialist values as compared to the others. The rise in environmental concern was seen more as a phenomenon emerging from changing values rather than as a response to the reality of the deteriorating environmental situation. In India in the early 1970s, environmentalism was rejected on the grounds that the idea came from post-materialist Western society and that it was alien to a society which was concerned with lifting millions of people out of poverty (Guha, 1992). This was the Indian official position at the Stockholm Conference in 1972.

That environmentalism was not a product of the post-materialist society was demonstrated by vibrant grassroots environmental activism in countries such as India, Brazil, Mexico, Thailand, Nigeria, Thailand, Kenya and Uruguay (Brechin & Kempton, 1994; Guha, 2014). Environmental movements in these developing countries had Adivasis and backward classes participating in large numbers, as their livelihood were threatened. In contrast to the environmentalism of the affluent, there has been 'environmentalism of the poor' in Asia and Africa (Martinez-Alier, 2002). Poor peasants and women have been at the forefront of environmental struggles in Indian, including the Chipko movement and the Narmada movement. Despite the existence of grassroots movements against environmentally destructive policies, the media in India ignored environmentalism as they thought that it was a product of the post-materialist societies of the West unrelated to Indian realities. However, there has been a significant change in the attitude of the media towards environmental issues in the last four decades.

The third explanation which is put forward through the new middle-class thesis says that environmental ethics are likely to be adopted by those who work in creative or public service–oriented professions, such as teaching, social work, medicine, journalism and art (Cotgrove & Duff, 1981; Kriesi, 1989). The middle class which these occupations represent has time, skills and resources to participate in environmental movements. Although it is very difficult to say why people in these occupational groups have shown greater environmental concern than those in other occupational groups, a possible explanation that can be offered is that they have been first-hand witnesses to the impact of environmental degradation on the marginalized sections of the society. Those who enter these professions are probably guided by their post-materialist values. If their goal was to make money, they would have chosen other professions such as management and engineering. Journalism is seen more as a public service than as an employment opportunity. Most members of the urban environmental groups and climate activists are from the middle class. Many of the Indian journalists who come from the middle class have been witness to the environmental deterioration, and some of them have also donned the activist role.

The fourth explanation is the 'political closure' hypothesis which says that environmental movement began rising when the state in its corporate-style political arrangement began circumventing democratic procedures in making key political and economic decisions (Scott, 1990). Without going through the legislative process, the states have entered into collaboration with the private corporations without placing the details of the processes in the public domain. This kind of political closure led to the rising of environmental issues outside mainstream politics. With mainstream political parties ignoring environmental issues, it was left to the civil society groups to raise them in the public arena. Ecological movements become active when political debate is restricted as a result of a nexus between the state and the private industry. Environmental issues have rarely been the subjects of debate either in the Indian Parliament or in state legislatures. When debates do not take place there, protests and media coverage become crucial for a problem to be publicly debated.

While the post-materialist hypothesis was used to reject what was seen as Western imposition of environmentalism on India in the early 1970s, the reflection hypothesis, the middle-class thesis and the political-closure hypothesis are helpful in explaining the rise of the environmental consciousness and movement in India.

The first popular environmental movement in India, the Chipko (hug the tree) movement, began nine months after the first UNCHE was held in Stockholm where India had rejected environmental concern as a Western fad. Contrary to the view in India that environmental movements were the phenomena observed only in the Western post-materialist societies, poor peasants launched a movement in the Himalayan region of India to protect trees in the early 1970s. On 27 March 1973, the peasants of Mandal village in the Alaknanda valley of Uttar Pradesh (now Uttarakhand) prevented lumbermen from felling trees by threatening to hug them. The peasants were outraged when the Uttar Pradesh government allowed an Allahabad-based sports goods company to cut down a large number of trees while at the same time denying them access to trees for making agricultural tools. The direct action of the peasants at Mandal set off protests in several other villages where contractors were prevented from cutting down trees for the external market. All these protests constituted the Chipko movement. It remains the most significant step towards the growth of the environmental movement in India (Weber, 1987).

Dasholi Gram Swarajya Sangh (DGSS) founded by Chandi Prasad Bhatt led the Chipko movement with a significant number of women taking part in the direct action of hugging trees to protect them from loggers (Guha, 1989). The peaceful Gandhian methods of protest employed by the Chipko movement became a benchmark for other similar struggles. With the state government, commercial loggers and development planners as its opponents, the movement demonstrated indomitable courage to question the policies which were detrimental to the people of the Garhwal hills. The people of the region had begun to see a link between deforestation, floods and landslides, as they had been witness to the death and devastation caused by the floods and landslides during the monsoon of 1970.

Anil Agarwal, a Delhi-based journalist who was working with the *Hindustan Times*, wrote a comprehensive report on the movement. His report introduced the unique Chipko movement to urban readers. He later founded the Centre for Science and Environment (CSE) and the *Down to Earth* magazine. It was a movement of the poor peasants for whom the environment was a survival issue. The movement inspired several environmental struggles in different parts of India. The launching of Project Tiger, enactment of water pollution law and the

Chipko movement have been important milestones in the history of environmentalism in India (Narain, 2017).

Far away from the Himalayan region, a struggle by areca growers in the Uttara Kannada district of Karnataka began in the late 1970s against the proposal to construct a dam across the Bedti river. When the environmental impact assessment of major projects became mandatory in 1978, the proposed hydroelectric project on the Bedti river came up for review. A committee which was appointed to make the impact assessment recommended environmental clearance despite minority protest. The committee had deliberately underestimated the adverse impact. A farmers' cooperative carried its own assessment and a seminar was held to discuss the possible consequences of the project and a programme of action which was necessary to stop the project. Shivaram Karanth, a giant literary figure in Karnataka and winner of the Jnanpith Award, presided over the seminar which had representatives from Chipko movement and Kerala Sasthra Sahithya Parishad (KSSP), an organization which had made a significant contribution to popularizing science education in Kerala. The proceedings and resolutions of this first-ever public hearing on a development project in India were widely reported in newspapers. Held in January 1980, this seminar succeeded in presenting various aspects of the problem both to the people and to the government (Gadgil & Guha, 1995). The project was shelved, and repeated attempts to relaunch the project have failed.

In the early 1980s in Kerala, a movement led by KSSP succeeded in stopping the Silent Valley Hydroelectric Project. The project would have submerged one of the best surviving patches of rain forest in peninsular India. This movement involving school and college teachers built up collaboration with wildlife conservationists (Zachariah & Sooryamurthy, 1994). The involvement of the national affiliates of the World Wide Fund and the International Union for the Conservation of Nature ensured international attention and pressure on the Indian government (D'Monte, 1985). KSSP, which spearheaded the movement against the Silent Valley Project, convinced M. G. K. Menon who was the chief scientific advisor to Prime Minister Indira Gandhi that the project was going to cause enormous damage to the environment. Eventually, in 1983, Prime Minister Indira Gandhi ordered that the project be shelved.

After the success of Chipko, organized resistance to the felling of trees emerged in different parts of India. The Appiko (hug the tree) movement that began in Karnataka a decade later was inspired by the Chipko movement. The large-scale monoculture teak and eucalyptus plantations had replaced the tropical forests, leading to loss of biodiversity and depletion of water sources in the Uttara Kannada district of Karnataka (Hegde, 2010). The forest officials had defended clear felling of the natural forest and converting it into monoculture plantation as scientific forestry. The villagers led by environmental activist Panduranga Hegde decided to act to the felling of trees and invited the leader of the Chipko movement Sunderlal Bahuguna to be with them. Bahuguna, Hegde and the villagers including women and children walked to the Kelase forest in the Sirsi taluk of Uttara Kannada district on 8 September 1983 and prevented the felling of the trees by hugging them. The peaceful protest continued for weeks, forcing loggers to withdraw from the site. The positive coverage in Kannada newspapers and magazines helped the movement gain popular support. After 38 days of protest, the government withdrew the order to cut trees. The Appiko movement later succeeded in bringing pressure on the government to declare a moratorium on cutting down of green trees in all natural forests of the Western Ghats. It also launched a programme of action to save forests, restore denuded areas and make rational use of the forests. The slogan of the movement has been *ulisu* (save), *belesu* (grow) and *balasu* (rational use) aimed at establishing a harmonious relationship between people and nature.

In the state of Odisha, the struggle by the Adivasis succeeded in stopping the construction of a missile test range at Baliapal in the Balasore district of Odisha. The project would have displaced about 70,000 people from the fertile land with a highly developed agrarian economy based on betel leaves, coconut and fishing. The peaceful agitation that had begun in 1984 went on for 12 years. With the support of the Odia media, the movement succeeded in forcing the government to shelve the project (Raj, 2017). The state of Odisha also witnessed a movement against the Kalinganagar industrial complex in the Jajpur district. On 2 January 2006, when the construction work of the Tata Steel Plant began, a large number of Adivasis who were opposing displacement assembled there. The situation turned violent, resulting in the gunning down of 14 tribal protesters. While the company got the land it wanted, the victims of firing are yet to find justice (Padhi & Negi, 2018). The tribal and non-tribal communities carried on a long struggle against POSCO India steel plant at Paradip. A village which was the epicentre of the struggle was left out of the land acquisition plan. But the Korean company withdrew from the project after 12 years because of several factors including its inability to have its own captive mine and port (Sahu, 2017b). Although the project did not take off, the ecology of the region has been damaged and the displaced persons have lost their livelihoods.

The late 1980s witnessed a significant growth in the Indian environmental movement. This growth is partly attributed to the awareness created by media coverage of the Bhopal gas tragedy in 1984 and the Chernobyl disaster in 1986. The disaster caused by the leak of methyl isocyanate gas from the Union Carbide in Bhopal claimed around 8,000 lives. More than half a million people still suffer from side effects of that exposure (Centre for Science and Environment, 2014). The victims are still fighting for justice. At the time of the Chernobyl disaster, India had begun to see nuclear power as a panacea for its energy crisis. Public protest against such a programme of the government began, as the Chernobyl accident raised questions on the safety of nuclear power plants. Anti-nuclear groups sprang up in many parts of India. Many environmental groups in Karnataka formed an umbrella organization, Citizens for Alternatives to Nuclear Energy (CANE), to oppose India's nuclear energy programme. The focus of CANE's campaign was on the proposed plan to build a nuclear power plant at Kaiga in the Uttara Kannada district of Karnataka state. When the movement against the Kaiga nuclear power plant began in the mid-1980s, students, workers, farmers, writers, film stars, artists, religious leaders and the village folk took part in protests, demonstrations and debates held at many places. Over 100,000 people signed a petition opposing the Kaiga station (Bidwai, 1987). Calls by organizations through newspapers got hundreds of people to participate in the anti-Kaiga protests. Protest marches were held in cities, small towns and villages. Although the struggle created tremendous awareness about the hazards of radiation, it could not prevent the government from going ahead with the project.

One of the significant movements launched in the late 1980s was the 'Save the Western Ghats March' of 1987–1988. Volunteers representing 150 organizations from Tamil Nadu, Kerala, Karnataka, Goa and Maharashtra walked from both ends of the Ghats—Kanyakumari in Tamil Nadu and Navapur in the Dhulia district of Maharashtra—and met at Ponda in Goa after covering the 1,600-km-long mountain chain. The volunteers who took part in the three-month-long march, from 1 November 1987 to 3 February 1988, covered a total of 4,000 km and interacted with people in 600 villages and drew their attention to the threatened ecosystem. The march was widely covered by national and international media, with some of them comparing it to Mahatma Gandhi's Salt Satyagraha.[7]

According to Gadgil and Guha (1995, pp. 101–102), the march inspired similar marches in Tamil Nadu (Save the Nilgiris), Jammu and Kashmir (Save the Sivaliks), Andhra Pradesh, Odisha (Vany Pranty Chaitanya Yatra), Gujarat, Rajasthan and Haryana (Aravali Chetna Yatra), which had brought people's attention to the issues of deforestation, illegal mining and displacement.

Some of the struggles at the grassroots level were subjected to state repression, whereas some others made compromises with their original demands. Only a few of the environmental groups continued their sustained campaign. The anti-nuclear energy groups, which were active in the late 1980s in the wake of the Chernobyl disaster, almost became silent till the 1998 nuclear test at Pokhran. The one movement that grew stronger in the 1990s was Narmada Bachao Andolan (NBA), which has been carrying on a long battle against big dams and displacement of lakhs of people in the Narmada valley. Although the movement's anti-dam campaign has been highly visible, its broader concern has been environmental degradation and social and economic injustice, particularly in relation to lopsided development planning and state oppression.

[7] Official handbook of the Save the Western Ghats Movement, n.k., p. 3.

Dakshina Kannada is one of the three coastal districts of Karnataka which has witnessed vibrant environmental struggles since the 1990s. The mega industries that came to this eco-sensitive district promising the development of the region and jobs for the youth posed serious threat to the environment and to traditional economic activities like fishing. A movement against Mangalore Refinery and Petrochemicals Limited (MRPL) began when the work to lay a pipeline to release effluents from the plant to the Arabian Sea was started in 1995. The fishermen feared that the effluents would pose a serious threat to marine life which was the source of their livelihood (Sitaraman, 1996). The agitation ended in December 1995, when the state government directed MRPL to install a modern recycling plant and build an open canal for discharging effluents into the Arabian Sea. People in the villages around the MRPL plant have been protesting against the company for causing air, noise and water pollution (Kulkarni, 2014; *The Hindu*, 2018). A movement against the proposal to build a thermal power plant at Nandikur succeeded in stopping the project for some time but could not prevent the establishment of the thermal power plant in the Udupi district. The farmers displaced by MRPL and Mangalore Special Economic Zone (MSEZ) are still fighting for justice.

The people of the Uttara Kannada district in Karnataka protested against the proposal to construct a seventh dam across the Kali river in 2000. Six major hydroelectric dams had been built across the river which has a length of only 132 km. After protests and public hearing, the project was stalled. Later in 2003, Kali Bachao Andolan (KBA) was launched to protest against the discharging of toxic effluents into the river by the West Coast Paper Mills (WCPM) Limited. The people's movement succeeded in forcing WCPM to install a water treatment plant.

The introduction of genetically modified (GM) crops became a raging controversy in the late 1990s. Despite prolonged protests by farmers and NGOs, Bt cotton entered the Indian fields in 2002. Consumer rights activists, environmentalists and farmers' organizations stoutly apposed introduction of Bt brinjal to the Indian fields, leading to the declaration of a moratorium in 2010 on its release until scientific studies established that it would pose no threat to human life. The movement against GM crops got wide support from the media.

An anti-nuclear movement began in Tamil Nadu when a proposal to build a nuclear power plant at Kudankulam with the assistance of the Soviet Union was announced in 1988. People living close to the project site opposed the diversion of water for the reactors from the Pechiparai dam in Kanyakumari district. The fishing community had also expressed its apprehensions regarding the threat to their livelihood from the project (Venkat, 2016). The construction work of the project which was in limbo for many years because of the collapse of the Soviet Union began in 2002. It was in 2011 that the People's Movement Against Nuclear Energy led by S. P. Udayakumar began an agitation against the plant in the wake of the Fukushima disaster in Japan. In one of the repressive measures in the history of the environmental movement, over 1,800 protesters were arrested with some of them being charged with sedition. With some notable exceptions, the media carried stories with the intention to malign the protesters and leaders of the movement such as S. P. Udayakumar (Basu, 2012). For a majority of the national newspapers and television channels, nuclear energy was a holy cow. Both the government and the media have been hostile to anti-nuclear activists because they are seen as anti-nationalists, attempting to hold back the nation from developing as an industrial economy. Despite protests, the first unit of the 6,000 MW Kudankulam Nuclear Power Plant (KNPP), the largest of the 21 nuclear power plants in India, attained criticality in 2013.

On 22 May 2018 in the Thoothukudi district of Tamil Nadu, the police fired at a crowd of 20,000 protesters who marched towards the district collector's office, killing 13 and injuring 102 of them. The protest was against the Vedanta group-owned Sterlite Copper factory which was causing soil, water and air contamination (Sangomla, 2018). Protests had been going on against the factory since 1999 for causing health problems in people who were residing in a radius of 5 km from the factory. During 2006–2007, the Tirunelveli Medical College had conducted a study which showed high prevalence of problems associated with respiratory system and ear, nose and throat. After the Sterlite Copper factory announced its expansion plan, people in the villages around it launched a protest that continued for more than 100 days. The firing took place when the protesters started marching towards the district collector's office to submit a petition. The factory was shut down after the firing took place but the National Green Tribunal allowed the reopening of the plant in December 2018. The media coverage was more on the violence than on the issues the protesters were raising (Phadke, 2018).

Only a few of these struggles were able to stop the potentially harmful projects. Many of these struggles did not succeed in stopping the projects but played a significant role in creating environmental awareness and in forcing the government and the industry to take some measure to minimize the environmental impact.

It was these movements, built on the traditions of peasant struggles, that made the educated people aware of deforestation, biodiversity loss, air and water pollution, soil erosion and water depletion. The protesters at times have opted for methods of direct action instead of patient petitioning of government officials and the judiciary. The professional middle class was reactive and responded slowly and at times unwillingly to the environmentalism of the peasants and tribes (Gadgil & Guha, 1995). It was the failure of the mainstream environmentalism in the West that led to direct action and grassroots mobilization to protect communities (Foster, 1999). Organizations like Greenpeace, the Earth Island Institute and the Earth First increasingly distinguished themselves from the other environmental groups by taking a more radical stand on a host of environmental issues. The methods of protest and the strategies for the sustained campaign chosen by the environmental groups in India and the West appear to be similar, if not the same.

India's social, economic and cultural diversity is reflected in the diverse ideological approaches and strategies in the environmental movement. Despite the differences in their values, attitudes and beliefs, environmental activists and leaders are united in their opposition to dominant political institutions which they think can be reformed to reflect the public interest. The leaders of the movement have often emphasized decentralized political power, participatory democracy and greater role for the communities in deciding their own course of development. Of the three ideological streams that Gadgil and Guha (1995) identify in the Indian environmental movement—Gandhian, Marxist and appropriate technology—the Gandhian stream has been the most dominant one. The Chipko, Appiko and the Narmada movements are known for their Gandhian ideals and for their belief in non-violent and peaceful forms of protest.

Environment and the Mainstream Politics

Since the early 1970s, the environmental movement has grown in terms of the number of organizations, diversity of membership and programmes of action. Despite the existence of a wide variety of environmental movements, environmental issues have never been on the agenda of mainstream politics in India. There are still many people in India who are unaware of the environmental problems and there are also people who dismiss it as a fringe concern. In some of the West European countries, there are green parties with considerable political support. They have won seats in national legislatures in Belgium, Luxembourg, the Netherlands, Germany, Sweden and Switzerland and also in the European Parliament. In the year 2017, Iceland elected Katrin Jakobsdóttir, a 41-year-old environmentalist and chairperson of the Left-Green Movement, as its prime minister. She appointed an environmental activist as the minister of environment. The government has promised its people that by 2040, the country is going to be carbon-free. This is a rare example of the environment becoming the main plank of mainstream politics.

Although political parties in India make some reference to the environment in their manifestos, it has never been an issue on which elections have been fought. The two major political parties, the Indian National Congress and the Bharatiya Janata Party, talked about climate change for the first time in their manifestos for the 2019 general elections, but it did not figure in their core election campaigns. Evidence from the past suggests that no major political leader has got involved in any of the major environmental problems affecting voters. There is no example of a politician winning an election either to the Parliament or a state legislature on an environmental issue. Shivaram Karanth, a well-known literary giant and environmentalist, lost the elections in the Karwar Parliamentary constituency in Karnataka in 1989 as an independent candidate. He had played a crucial role in stopping the Bethi project and had also campaigned against the construction of the

Kaiga Nuclear Power Plant in the constituency. Despite overwhelming support for him during the movement, voters did not see environmental issues as election issues. Medha Patkar, an internationally known environmental activist and leader of NBA, unsuccessfully contested the parliamentary elections in 2014 as an Aam Aadmi Party candidate from the North East Mumbai constituency. M. P. Veerendra Kumar, the chairman and managing director of Mathrubhumi Group, who had played a significant role in the struggle against pollution and water depletion caused by the Coca-Cola plant at Plachimada village in Kerala's Palakkad district during 2002–2005, lost the 2014 Lok Sabha elections (Sreejith, 2014).

These examples of election losses suffered by those who had fought for environmental causes are an indication that if political leaders get involved in environmental struggles, they may not benefit politically. When there are no members in the Parliament speaking on behalf of those suffering from environmental degradation and displacement, the only way to get the public attention to the problem is to resort to some direct action through civil society groups. When the political arena is closed for any discourse on the environment, a movement becomes necessary for articulating critical views (Hannigan, 1995).

All major political parties have been supporters of big projects, especially irrigation and power projects, which have raised environmental questions. Gadgil and Guha (1995) have found that the interest of politicians in environmental issues is, by and large, inversely proportional to the size of their constituency. They say, 'In our experience, Members of Parliament appear to care the least, members of the state legislatures a little more, members of district councils a little more still, and members of the *mandal panchayats* emphatically the most' (Gadgil & Guha, 1995, p. 190). What is ironic is that those who have a greater interest in the environment are not involved in the decision-making process. The state governments and the Centre ignore the opinions of the lower-level political bodies. For example, both the Centre and the Government of Karnataka went ahead with building the nuclear power plant at Kaiga despite unanimous resolutions adopted by all panchayat bodies including the zilla panchayat of Uttara Kannada district opposing the construction of the power plant.

Environmental activists have been making efforts to put the environmental agenda before the media and the politicians by issuing green manifestos at the time of elections. During the Lok Sabha elections since 2009, the activists of the 'Save the Western Ghats Movement' have been releasing a Western Ghats Manifesto to the candidates who contest from the 32 parliamentary constituencies that fall under the Western Ghats region. The manifestos have demanded protection of the forest, help for local economies, empowerment of gram sabhas, sustainable tourism and public hearing on Madhav Gadgil and Kasturirangan reports on the Western Ghats to avoid politicization and spread of rumours about the reports (Pinto, 2014). During the 2019 Lok Sabha elections, they demanded increasing the forest cover in the Western Ghats from the present 30 per cent to 66 per cent (Sethunath, 2019). These manifestos have not made any significant impact on the politicians and the MPs Forum for the Western Ghats which had been formed on the demand of the activists as a lobbying group in 2014 has not been revived.

During the 2019 general elections, environmental activists in Delhi expressing their concern over the evasive behaviour of political parties called upon the voters to consider climate change and air pollution as issues on which they would vote (*The Pioneer*, 27 April 2019). Greenpeace and YMCA had organized a programme called 'Green Samvad' (green discussion) on 26 April 2019, in which environmental NGOs and residents participated. They also signed a document titled 'Green Charter'. The residents decided to urge the candidates to fulfil the demands listed in the charter and to ensure clean air, safe food and clean energy access if they wanted their votes. Although the media gave fair coverage to the efforts of the environmentalists, there was no significant impact on the voters which indicates that environmental issues are still not election issues in India. If they become political issues, their coverage is likely to increase, as much of the media content in India is related to politics.

Attempts to get the attention of the politicians to the environmental issues have got activists into trouble. Fifteen MLAs of Karnataka once went to Sirsi in Uttara Kannada district to evaluate the use of Kannada at all levels of the administration. Environmental activist Panduranga

Hegde issued a sarcastic statement that said that the MLAs were so well looked after when they visited the district that they did not say anything about the environmental issues in the district. He was issued a notice to appear before the officers of the Karnataka Legislative Assembly or face action for infringing the privileges of the MLAs. He avoided going there for about six–seven months, but later he was forced to admit that he had issued an inappropriate statement (personal communication, 26 February 2019). Politicians have often looked at environmental activism with suspicion and sometimes with disdain. They tend to take note of a problem when a sustained campaign involving a large number of people is carried on for some time. However, the participation of the people in direct action programmes has been declining over the years. Since political content dominates news media, environmental issues receive media attention when politicians speak about them.

While environmental organizations and media have succeeded to a considerable extent in influencing individual and family lifestyles that include opting for recycled materials and eco-friendly products, mobilizing a large number of people for massive campaigns has not been possible in recent years. Lack of political discourse, growth of consumerism and declining communitarian social relations may have contributed to the weakening of the environmental movement in recent times. Commenting on the loss of vibrancy of the environmental movement activist and the founder of the Appiko movement, Panduranga Hegde says,

> The Chipko or Appiko kind of movement is out of the question today because of the socio-political context. There is a lot of awareness today but the action part is missing. In order to categorize a movement as successful in today's context, you need a community. There is no community left today. Individualism and consumerism dominate our society. To expect Appiko's kind of movement today is a dream. The environmental movement can survive and succeed only in those places where community links are very strong. In the context of the market forces, the individual becomes important not his community. Even when air pollution is putting the lives of children at great risk in Delhi there is no movement there against pollution. The market forces are so strong that Individuals will have air-conditioners in their cars and air purifiers at home but will not

think about any collective action. Consumerism has broken the community links. You can carry on a movement on Facebook but actual movement on the ground is not possible today. (Personal communication, 26 February 2019)

Realizing that protests that were carried on decades ago are no longer possible, environmental groups today are trying to link activists who are doing exemplary work at the grassroots level. The efforts of the individuals are being linked to macro issues. One person may be trying to save turtles or bears, and another may be trying to revive a dried-up stream or well. Building a link between these individual efforts has become the focus of environmental groups today. They are trying to create a network through which community action can be initiated.

The primary objective of any environmental movement is to gain the attention of the wider public through media so that it finds enough support to influence a change in attitude among the people and to bring about policy change at the level of the government. However, it cannot be claimed that victories and defeats of the environmental movements can be attributed to mass media alone. But they have become an important ingredient in the activities of almost all social movements. Despite several struggles across the country against projects with potential for environmental risks, less than 3 per cent of the projects have been rejected on environmental grounds (Narain, 2017). Although environmentalism in India has succeeded in preventing the construction of a few projects, forcing some industries to minimize pollution and stopping the felling of trees in some areas, it has not been able to influence the national development policy in a big way. But its role in placing environmental issues on the agenda of the public and the media despite 'political closure' cannot be ignored.

Media and the Environmental Agenda

For a problem to become a part of the public discourse, sustained media coverage becomes essential. The mass media play a major role as a forum for public debate where 'various social groups, institutions, and ideologies struggle over the definition and construction of social reality' (Guruvitch & Levy, 1985, p. 19). Although people had been aware of environmental degradation to a limited extent for some decades, it was the media that played a key role in broadening that awareness and making it an issue for public debate. Problems experienced by people were redefined as part of a more general problem of the environment (Hannigan, 1995). Media coverage became vital in defining and framing a problem as an environmental problem.

The media were initially slow in grasping the essence of environmentalism, leaving it to 'issue entrepreneurs' who tried to get public attention to the issues outside media (Schoenfeld et al., 1979). In the early years of the environmental debate, the media were unsure about the increasing number of claims by scientists that normal human activities were posing a threat to the environment (Keating & Gallon, 1997). Some journalists would spend a lot of time on the ground and speak to researchers to understand a problem but they would not succeed in convincing their editors to carry their stories.

Covering environmental issues, which are at times extraordinarily complex, requires a sophisticated understanding of science, ethics, law, economics politics, history and international relations. Environmental concerns usually involve a long and tenuous string of interrelated concerns. To a large extent, media coverage of environmental issues is constrained and shaped by the political economy of media, professional values and a journalist's sense of what constitutes news. Since what happens makes news, it seems that news is always or mainly concerned with the unusual and the unexpected. Tuchman (1973, p. 117) argues that 'news organisations routinize the processing of seemingly unexpected events by typifying them along dimensions that reflect practical tasks associated with their work'. While the construction of news may be influenced by cultural or political factors, it is generally seen as the result of organizational routines within the newsroom itself. Instead of digging for information, reporters opt for routine news which is usually a mixed account of scheduled events and pre-formulated accounts of events to meet the deadlines and story quotas (Fishman, 1980). News that fits into the standard formats is preferred to lengthy and more nuanced stories. This means that environmental issues are often framed by journalists within an event orientation. Event orientation not only results in sources controlling story frames but also allows news sources to control the establishment of story frames. Event orientation also keeps journalists free from the obligation of presenting a comprehensive picture (Dunwoody & Griffin, 1993). Event-centred reporting requires journalists to see environmental hazards such as global warming, ozone depletion and acid rain as the results of events rather than the inevitable outcomes of a series of political and social decisions (Wilkins & Patterson, 1990).

The power of the press is usually associated with its ability to set the agenda. The agenda-setting hypothesis suggests that the way the media highlight or de-emphasize issues affects the public perception of the salience of these issues, influencing what people think about them (McCombs & Shaw, 1972). By selecting and displaying certain environmental issues, media can construct a reality. The audiences not only get to know about a particular environmental issue but also learn how much importance is to be attached to it. Selection of environmental issues and giving them prominent space and time consistently over a period of time demonstrate that the media set the environmental agenda (Scheufele & Tewksbury, 2007). Studies have shown that the media can play a potentially powerful role in setting the agenda with regard to environmental issues (Ader, 1995; Atwater et al., 1985; Reinert, 2020; Soroka, 2002). Studies have also shown that public concern about the environment may grow because of the sustained media coverage, even though environmental deterioration may not be so severe (Hannigan, 2006).

The public perception of environmental problems may not necessarily reflect the reality of actual problems but rather the particular narrative portrayed by the media. For a problem to be perceived as important, it is essential that media consistently report about it over a long period with news stories, articles, investigative reports, features and editorials. Otherwise, public attention may not remain focused on an issue for a long time. How long the public attention remains on an environmental issue may be determined by the media coverage of that issue. The media may pay attention to an issue for some time and then move on to other issues ignoring their agenda-setting role.

According to Downs (1972, pp. 38–40), 'Public attention rarely remains sharply focused upon on any one issue for very long.' A problem may get prominence in media, continue to be written about for some time and then gradually fade away. He says that public attitudes and behaviour towards an issue may be strongly influenced by the 'issue-attention cycle'. The issue attention cycle has five stages. The first is the 'pre-problem stage', where a problem exists but it has not yet got public attention. The second stage is 'alarmed discovery and euphoric enthusiasm', where the public suddenly becomes aware of the consequences of a particular issue. The third stage is 'realizing the cost of significant progress', where people become aware of the complexity of the problem and the price they have to pay for solving the problem. The fourth stage is the 'gradual decline of intense public interest', where the intensity of the public interest in a problem declines as more and more people begin to realize that it is difficult to solve the problem. The final stage is 'the post-problem stage', where an issue remains for a long time without much public attention.

Downs demonstrates that media could accelerate or decelerate the cycle of a movement by covering it in a certain way. Like other social problems, the environmental problem also loses its attraction for the media and the public, though it remains unresolved. Uninterrupted reporting about environmental risks over time may lead to waning of public interest. In an environment of competition, media tend to shift their focus on some new and more attention-grabbing problem. Bowman and Hanaford (1977) had shown that the environment as an issue did not receive constant attention of the media but went through the cycle of rise and fall. The issue attention cycle is an indication that the media may not play the agenda-setting role concerning environmental issues. The cyclical nature of media coverage renders particular issues vulnerable to being squeezed out of the public debate, but that does not necessarily mean that the underlying problem has been solved (Gregory, 1972).

The attention span of the audiences has been decreasing over the years, and the complex environmental issues unfold over an extended period. It is really hard for reporters to find news pegs for their stories. The protests against the building of the Tehri Dam in an eco-sensitive area hogged the headlines for a long time. The newspapers became the voice for the people who were going to be affected by the dam. When the construction of the dam continued despite the campaign, the newspapers lost their steam (Mazoomdar, 2006). By the time the old Tehri town got submerged in the dam waters, the media had reconciled to the fact that the dam was going to be completed. They moved on to other issues. In order to continue to get media attention, the International Campaign for Justice in Bhopal (ICJB) has often organized dramatic events. Since hunger strikes were no longer attracting the media attention, the ICJB used direct action methods such as *padayatra* (journey on foot), *dharna* (sit-in protest), die-in,[8] burning of the effigy of Warren Anderson (CEO of Union Carbide), 'Mir Zafar award' for treachery and 'Hall of Shame' award to bureaucrats, politicians, lawyers and corporate heads to engage the media directly (Sharma, 2014a). In December 2020, on the eve of the 36th anniversary of the disaster, the victims held a torch procession to draw the attention of the public and the media to the justice that is yet to be delivered to them (Sahay, 2020). The purpose was to create spectacle through the images, stories and actions that capture media attention. All these forms of protest helped ICJB bring the attention of the national and international media to the plight of the survivors of the Bhopal gas tragedy.

While the event-centred coverage has the potential to raise public awareness of otherwise ignored environmental topics, it also has a negative side. By focusing on discrete events rather than on contexts in which they occur, the media tend to give news consumers the impression that individuals or errant corporations rather than institutional politics and social developments are responsible for those events (Smith, 1992; Wilkins & Patterson, 1990). Media do not often hold powerful institutions accountable for environmental destruction but focus on actions of individuals. Instead of capturing the complexity of the problem, they tend to highlight only one cause and ignore others.

Individuals and institutions as sources of information greatly influence what appears as environmental news. Sources as providers of the raw material of news set the tone and frame of environmental discourse in the media. The role of the journalist is to refine and change the material made available from these sources and turn it into a product suitable and familiar for his audience. Gans (2004, p. 237) views news

---

[8] Bhopal survivors lying down on the ground covering themselves with either white sheet or with the picture of the iconic Bhopal child (Sharma, 2014a).

as 'information which is transmitted from sources to audiences, with journalists—who are both employees of bureaucratic commercial organisations and members of the profession—summarising, refining and altering what becomes available to them from sources to make the information suitable for their audiences'. He sees a tug of war between journalists and their sources. While sources want to 'manage' news, putting the best light on themselves, journalists concurrently 'manage' the sources to extract the information they want. News is finally the outcome of the relationship between the newsmen and their sources (Sigal, 1973). Despite the growth of environmental journalism in the last three decades, conventional sources still dominate the environmental news (Beder, 1998). Government officials are by far the major information sources in most environmental stories not only because they are seen as credible and authoritative but also because they are easy to reach (Herman & Chomsky, 1988).

Even though environmental groups play a key role in framing environmental problems as social or political, they are often unable to influence the news agenda (Valiverronen, 1992). Even those environmental groups that are considered to be reliable sources of information do not generally figure prominently as primary definers of actual coverage. While environmental pressure groups may be playing an important agenda-setting role, their ability to shape the resulting coverage may be limited (Hansen, 1990). When environmentalists are used as sources, they tend to be leaders of the 'mainstream' environmental groups, which are known for their comparatively moderate position on issues. Those groups that ask fundamental questions on the development models as the sources of the problems are often ignored. In recent years, the mainstream environmental groups have developed sophisticated strategies for getting media attention. Some of them have communication units that provide information on regular basis to the media and arrange site visits for the reporters. But many of the smaller environmental groups lack resources to reach out to the media.

Widespread recognition of the environment as an issue by the media was noticed in the early 1970s. When Earth Day was celebrated in 1970, the mass media afforded the environmental issue 'instant and widespread recognition' (Gottlieb, 2005). The interpretation of Earth Day as 'day one' of the new environmentalism was widely embraced by the media. As the public began to see the environment as an issue of importance, the media began paying attention to it.[9] In the same year, newspapers in the United States and Europe created environment beats, which ensured that the environmental issues were covered on a regular basis (Rubin & Sachs, 1973). Television networks broadcast special programmes on pollution, newspapers hired environmental reporters, advertising agencies emphasized ecological features of products, book companies published environmental paperbacks and magazines devoted entire issues to the protection of nature (Bowman & Hanaford, 1977). By the time the UN Conference on Environment was held in 1972, there was a considerable rise in the press coverage of the environmental issues. An information explosion occurred in the mass media, leading to a rise in public concern for the environment.

Several factors had forced even reluctant media managers to treat environmental stories as mainstream news. Irrefutable damage to the environment and frequent protests from citizens groups had put environmental concerns on the public agenda. What was more important was that the environment had begun to be treated as a political story. Pollution and protection were being hotly debated in legislatures, and opposition politicians found that they could score points in the media by attacking governments for failing to protect the public from environmental decline (Keating & Gallon, 1997). More and more media began to take the environment seriously. Media interest in the environment seemed to grow till the late 1970s, after which a declining trend became visible.

But by the early 1980s, there was already a decline in environmental reporting in the United States and Europe (Hannigan, 1995). In most newspapers, environmental beats disappeared and became part of general news or science reporting. Reporters who continued to

---

[9] In contrast to the popular belief, Neuzil (1996) has argued that journalists were conscious of local and regional environmental controversies from the early 18th century to the 1950s when dialogues about air and water pollution emerged. He found that much before the Earth Day in 1970, serious concerns about environmental issues were closely and hotly debated in the media.

write on environmental issues were often starved of space and time (Friedman, 1991, p. 20). The environmental movement was also on the decline. Only 10 per cent of those specialized environmental periodicals that had come into existence during 1969–1975 remained by 1983 (Schoenfeld, 1980).

Media reporting of environmental problems increased at the end of the 1980s, reaching a peak in 1989–1990 in many countries around the world and declining steadily after that (Hannigan, 1995). The amount of coverage given to the environment in media and the level of environmental concern are not positively correlated, indicating that a higher level of concern is not always the direct result of media prominence the environment has received. In the early 1990s, media coverage of environmental issues in the United States was less than 2 per cent, despite the high level of concern among the public (Beder, 1998). In recent years, not only media coverage of the environment has increased, but the focus has also shifted from individual environmental problems to the larger issues like climate change. Longitudinal studies have found ample evidence to demonstrate that the media agenda can exert considerable influence on the public and policy agenda (Hansen, 2015).

Environment and the Indian Media

The Indian media for a long time did not consider the environment as a serious issue, generally reflecting the views of the political leaders and policymakers whose concern was development rather than the environment. When the UNCHE was held at Stockholm in 1972, very few correspondents of the Indian newspapers covered it (Guha, 1992). The environmental concern was dismissed as a Western fad irrelevant to the Third-World countries. The attitude of the press was in line with Prime Minister Indira Gandhi's defence of development over the environment at the conference. Environmentalism was brushed aside as a value associated with post-materialist societies. But a gradual change in the attitude of the press was noticed after the conference. The press began taking interest in the environment after the Chipko movement began in the Himalayas for the protection of forests (Gadgil & Guha, 1995). It was the first popular struggle against the destruction of the environment in independent India that received international recognition. When environmental news began appearing in the media in the 1970s, it was seen as part of a broad area of development journalism. One of the objectives of development journalism was to create awareness among the people about the need to protect the environment. Journalists who did development reporting also wrote on environmental issues.

While a widespread recognition of the environment as an issue by the Western and European media was noticed in the 1970s, such a trend became visible in the Indian press in the 1980s. The decade witnessed many environment-related events that attracted the attention of the press. The government took several measures aimed at protecting the environment beginning with the Forest (Conservation) Act of 1980. As the environmental movement grew into a significant force, newspapers began paying attention to issues related to environmental degradation. Environmental groups brought pressure on the government to stop some projects and review some of its development policies. Protests of various forms launched by environmental groups against environmental destruction provided dramatic news to the press (Krishna, 1996). The struggle for the protection of the Silent Valley in Kerala made headlines in the local and national press as the KSSP intensified its campaign to mobilize people's support in the early 1980s. After the Chipko movement of the 1970s, it was the Silent Valley movement that received prominent media coverage.

The Bhopal disaster of December 1984 proved to be the turning point in environmental reporting (Akhileshwari, 1989: Kovarik, 2020; Mishra, 2020). The magnitude of the disaster shook many newspapers out of their indifference to environmental problems. Thousands of correspondents descended on Bhopal to cover the worst-ever industrial disaster. Accessing reliable information was the biggest challenge for journalists (Centre for Science and Environment, 2014). The disaster continued to make news for years, as the victims carried on a long struggle for justice.

The dramatic increase in the number of environment-related events following the disaster indicated growing awareness among the people about the environment. More environment-related events meant more environmental news. With the increase in awareness, several campaigns were launched against environmentally destructive projects. Anti-nuclear campaigns intensified in the wake of the Chernobyl disaster of 1986. The involvement of writers, artists, film stars and religious leaders in the protest against the building of nuclear power plants provided dramatic news for the newspapers. Environmental pressure groups that realized the importance of publicity began interacting with the pressmen by providing them information and taking them on a tour of to the controversial project sites. Writing on environmental politics in India, Krishna (1996, p. 258) has observed that 'no other pressure group has used the press as devastatingly as environmentalists have done'. There was a healthy cooperation between the press and the activists with regard to the coverage of the disaster (Akhileshwari, 1989).

The English press appeared to be slow in picking up environmental stories (Guha, 1992). The reports about people's action for environmental protection appeared first in local Indian language newspapers and then in the major Indian language newspapers and later in the English dailies (Krishna, 1996). The leading English newspapers demonstrated greater interest in environmental issues in the 1980s. According to environmental historian Ramachandra Guha (1992, p. 17), Indian journalists have, since the 1980s, drawn public attention to the environment and have provided a 'critical analysis of state policies for environmental practices and rehabilitation'. Newspapers have contributed to the beginning of an informed public debate on environmental issues. An explosion of investigative journalism in the 1980s made its impact on the reporting of issues and events. Newspapers attempted to dig out information about controversial projects that were likely to cause environmental hazards.

The Centre and the state governments enacted legislations and launched several plans for protecting the environment, leading to an increase in the number of environment-related activities. The newspapers found environmental intervention, to a limited degree, by the government necessary to stop the unregulated exploitation of natural resources. Such a role of the government made it a major source of news for the newspapers. But the information governmental agencies gave to the media was insufficient to write comprehensive stories. There was very little information available about those projects that posed a serious threat to ecological balance. The government built an iron curtain around the projects and prevented the newspapers from gathering technical details. The Official Secrets Act was used to deny information about controversial projects to the press. Lack of access to information has been considered as one of the reasons for the very low coverage of environmental news.

With the growth of the environmental movement in the 1980s, the media coverage of environmental issues increased. As the environment-related events began occurring more frequently, environmental frames became more noticeable in the news stories. The 1980s saw a sudden spurt in the number of public interest litigations (PILs). Once the Supreme Court started admitting PILs to tackle matters of public interest that were otherwise neglected, it was ineluctably drawn into issues concerning the environment. Environmental controversies that were brought to the court began making headlines in the newspapers. Since reporting court is a regular beat in most major newspapers, environmental issues, which come up before the court, receive good coverage in newspapers. The Supreme Court took up a huge number of issues, including deforestation, pollution in Delhi, pollution of Yamuna and Ganga, and garbage disposal. The pro-environment judgments and increased use of PIL provided a lot of material that had news value (Dhawan, 2000).

By the beginning of the 1990s, newspapers had realized that the environment was one of the issues that the nation had to address. When the Earth Summit was held in Rio de Janeiro in 1992, a huge contingent of Indian media persons covered it. Almost every major newspaper in India sent its representative to cover the summit. It was in total contrast to how the Stockholm Conference was covered two decades before. It indicated a realization by the Indian media that a global policy was needed to address environmental problems and that they were not the concerns of people in the developed countries alone. Even those newspapers that had dismissed environmentalism as a Western fad during the Stockholm Conference in 1972 sent their correspondents to cover the Rio Summit in 1992. The summit received wide coverage in the newspapers, with some newspapers bringing out special supplements. Many newspapers introduced special sections and columns on the environment, as environmental awareness among the readers increased. Some of the environmentalists wrote columns in newspapers, analysing problems and offering solutions.[10] However, specialization in environmental reporting did not grow to the extent it had grown in Northern America and Europe. Although Gadgil and Guha (2007, p. 411) argue that there was a 'virtual explosion of environmental writing in English and Indian language newspapers and magazine', there is no adequate evidence to suggest that there was an 'explosion'. Ramachandra Guha (Devschooluea, 2016) says that Indian media uncritically celebrated economic liberalization of the 1990s and accused all those who were critical of liberalization of holding up development. According to him, if there is one agency that has been complicit in the anti-environmental movement in India in the 1990s, it is the Indian media. He argues that in contrast to the liberalization era, newspapers in the 1970s and 1980s did outstanding environmental reporting and wrote detailed reports about depletion of ground water and the impact of chemical fertilizers on fishing downstream. Because of the grassroots pressure from below, every major Indian newspaper in the 1980s began carrying environment-related stories. Guha says that it is very rare that serious and reflective environmental reporting is found in Indian newspapers. In his view, once newspapers embraced liberalization in the 1990s, they became so hostile to the environmental movement that they either laid off environmental journalists or asked them to cover stock markets.

Specialization in environmental journalism is lacking in India. Much of the reporting in the daily newspapers is done by non-specialists (Chapman et al., 1997). However, specialization has developed in magazine journalism. Many environmental magazines were launched in the 1990s. The fortnightly magazine *Down to Earth*, published by CSE, provides in-depth analysis of issues related to environment and development. The magazine provides scientific, social, political and economic perspectives on key environmental issues. However, since specialized magazines reach only those who have a special interest in

---

[10] Sunderlal Bahuguna and Chandi Prasad Bhatt, the two key leaders of the Chipko movement, and Panduranga Hegde, the leader of the Appiko movement, have written columns/articles in newspapers.

environmental issues, the role of daily newspapers and television is vital in informing the public about environmental issues. Public opinion about environmental problems and policies can only be built through the daily press and the broadcast media, as they reach all sections of society.

Environmental activists as 'claims-makers' have (Hansen, 2015, p. 33) always tried to put the environment on the agenda of the media. However, they have not succeeded most of the time (Wilkins, 1987). Despite the phenomenal growth of television and the new media in the past two decades, the print media continue to be prime channels of environmental information. Environmental stories on television channels routinely cover the way all news is, in small quantities, for short amounts of time, and cyclically. The values that emphasize progress, technology, production and materialism which are not consistent with environmentalism dominate television content. There are now television channels that are completely devoted to nature and wildlife but they do not report on environmental issues. Television news channels occasionally cover environmental issues, although they lack depth and perspective because of several constraints including time and resources. Some scholars have shown a negative correlation between television-viewing time and the degree of environmental concern (Dunlap & Van Liere, 1984). Since radio news broadcasting is still the monopoly of All Indian Radio, controversial environmental issues rarely come up for analysis except reporting of events and messages which come from government agencies. But All India Radio in general has been broadcasting various types of environmental awareness programmes.

Although environmental coverage in media has increased over the years, a large part of it has been on disasters and dramatic developments. Activists and civil society groups may be involved in creating awareness among the people for years, but an issue becomes newsworthy only when there is a controversy or confrontation. Although media frequently cover environmental issues, they seldom take initiative in reporting environmental issues on their own. Newspapers tend to report on environmental issues only after activists and pressure groups have taken them up and highlighted them through some events. They are usually reported after the grassroots campaigns have taken off (Kumar, 1996). Another trend noticed is that the media focus on personalities who lead the environmental movements rather than on the innumerable men and women who contribute to the movement (Guha, 1995). Notwithstanding these trends, media coverage of environmental issues seems to have grown over the years in both volume and scope.

The new media have become the new tools for the youth to fight the environmental battle. The alternative media display a great deal of involvement and freshness, and the mainstream media often take the cues from them to come up with broad-based articles. Digital and social media have democratizing influences, as these channels of communication often offer a platform for an unlimited number of people to become content producers and therefore have the potential to more readily shape the public agenda (Boykoff, 2011). However, the unlimited choice in social media has led to the shrinking of circles of information because only those with similar ideological orientations, interests and tastes form groups and communicate within their own networks. Despite interactive technologies, people are more divided and disconnected today than before. Only those with environmental concerns form groups, but their ideas do not get across to those who have very little understanding of the relationship between man and the environment. Although environmental pressure groups and activists use social media to create awareness and to set the environmental agenda, their influence is limited, as digital activism is a kind of proxy participation. Social media discussions may not result in any concrete action, but they have unlimited potential in mobilizing public opinion in favour of a cause.

Conclusion

Environmental concern in India began growing in the 1970s despite India's official rejection of environmentalism as a phenomenon of the affluent West at the Stockholm Conference on Human Environment in 1972. The Chipko movement, which marked the beginning of the modern environmental movement in India, became a torchbearer of the 'environmentalism of the poor'. Several environmental struggles in the country drew inspiration from the Gandhian non-violent methods of resistance to environmental degradation. Only a few of the struggles were able to achieve their objectives, while a majority of them were unable to stop ecologically harmful projects. However, the activities, campaigns and debates associated with the environmental movements made their impact on people's awareness and policy. Several legal measures of the 1970s and 1980s to protect the environment reflected the growing environmental concern in India. However, environmentalism did not become a part of the mainstream political discourse. In the absence of political discourse, media played an important role in building a public debate on environmental degradation, its causes and consequences. Although Indian media were slow to respond to the rising environmental concerns, there was a considerable increase in coverage of the environmental issues by the 1980s. Environmental disasters and people's struggles in different parts of the country led by Adivasis, peasants and women were too visible for the media to ignore. The Bhopal disaster became a turning point in Indian environmental reporting to the extent that media coverage of the environment could be examined in terms of 'pre-Bhopal, post-Bhopal, post-1991 and post-2000' phases (Mishra, 2020, p. 296).

As the environmental struggles intensified, the media had to shed their deep scepticism about environmentalism and report ecological destruction. The very fact that hundreds of Indian journalists were sent to cover the Earth Summit at Rio de Janeiro in 1992 was an indication of the amount of importance the media gave to the environment as an issue. Even though the media have made significant contribution towards increased environmental awareness, they are lacking in setting the agenda with regard to environmental issues. The media coverage has often seen a rise and fall in relation to the frequency of occurrence of environment-related events. Environmental activists and groups have organized dramatic events to keep the media attention throughout their long campaigns. With the emergence of overwhelming scientific evidence linking climate change to temperature rise and extreme weather events, it is imperative for the mainstream media to play a proactive role in turning the attention of the people and the government towards assuming greater responsibilities in reducing greenhouse gases. Even though the new media have shown the potential to shape the environmental agenda, there is much to be desired.

CHAPTER 2

Covering the Environment
Framing of Environmental Issues in Media

The environment has generally been a subject of low priority in media which accord prime space and time to politics, crime, business, sports and entertainment. Although media coverage itself does not guarantee either social or political action in terms of helping resolve problems, it is crucial in setting the agenda (Hansen, 2015). The quantity of coverage depends on several factors including the media's own perception of the significance of the issue, claims-making activity and the perceived impact. While there was an upsurge of environmental coverage in the late 1960s and early 1970s in European and American media (Hannigan, 1995; Hansen, 1993), it took another decade for the Indian media to give attention to the environment as an issue. A significant increase in coverage of the environmental issues in the Indian media was witnessed in the 1980s, the decade that witnessed major environmental disasters (D'Monte, 2010). The Bhopal gas tragedy, Chernobyl disaster, enactment of the Environment (Protection) Act and growth of environmental movements in different parts of the country contributed to the increase in coverage. International efforts to understand the impact of climate change, frequency of occurrence of extreme weather events, increasing pollution levels and struggles for livelihood began to appear in media as news in the 1990s. Increased industrial activity as a result of economic liberalization without adequate concomitant regulatory measures led to higher levels of pollution (Joshi, 1999). Rapid expansion of energy and transport sectors contributing to worsening air quality in urban areas attracted media attention. Although the total volume of environmental news increased in the last two decades, the overall coverage remained low as compared to other major topics of news. The coverage came to be largely focused on events and lacked depth and analysis, as the media houses did not provide enough manpower, space and time. These constraints within a media organization forced reporters to follow the routine and produce stories that fall into conventional frames (Tuchman, 1973). A considerable volume of news in media comes from the news agencies that tend to focus more on conflicts than on the long-term processes (Hachten, 1992; Hestler, 1973; Kariel & Rosenvall, 1984; Rosenblum, 1979).

Covering the environment has been a more complex affair as compared to covering the other topics. At times, environmental reporters feel that they are caught between the professional canons of journalism on the one hand and of ecology on the other (Schoenfeld, 1980). News-making practices that are firmly grounded in occupational and organizational norms influence how journalists interpret environmental issues over time (Dunwoody & Griffin, 1993). The newsworthiness of the issues and the routines of the news production process may prevent journalists from seeing problems in bigger and more conceptual frames.

Competition from the rival media, expectations of the advertisers and editor's disposition about key issues influence the selection of news. The constraints of the deadline, at times, may prevent journalists from filing a story, as environmental stories generally require more time and sometimes more resources when compared to other news stories. Inadequate resources, lack of time to piece together facts, lack of space and lack of encouragement from the management are some of the major problems reporters encounter. Journalists who are occupied with their routines find no time to investigate and write about environmental issues. Dealing with editors who have little interest in the environment is also a major problem for the reporters. The amount of interest the editor has in environmental issues may determine the volume of environmental news in a newspaper. Priorities, trends, orientations, limitations, frames, sources, biases, challenges, uncertainties, pressures, threats, professional and social responsibilities associated with coverage of environmental issues deserve closer examination.

Low Salience of Environmental News

Several studies have revealed that the percentage of environmental news is less than 2 per cent of the total editorial content (Adiga, 2017; Biswas, 2009; Friedman, 2015; Varna, 2020). Environmental issues generally don't make front-page news unless there are dramatic events, conflicts or disasters. The mainstream media, which are filled with stories of politics, crime and sex, have little space for environmental stories. Those who cover politics mostly become editors as the political content in media gets precedence over other types of content. Because of the preoccupation of editorial decision-makers with political issues, the environment as an issue is rarely a priority for the media (D'Monte, 2010). Environmental stories are complex, and a serious pursuit of issues might displease big advertisers who enjoy enormous political and economic power. Newspapers that are dependent on the advertising revenue tend to be cautious when it comes to the business interests of the advertisers who may be the owners of the polluting industries. In their zeal not to antagonize advertisers, editors may either avoid stories or carry them in an insignificant place in their newspapers.

Senior environmental journalist and former assistant editor of *Prajavani* Nagesh Hegde, who has been writing on science and environment for over three decades, says that environmental issues are not often reported or given prominent space because commercial media organizations do not promote serious kind of journalism (personal communication, 12 October 2018). He says,

> *The Times of India* group, for example, has clearly shown that they are in the business of advertising and in the business of journalism. They don't provide resources or encourage journalists to report on serious issues affecting people. Naturally, the media coverage of environmental problems is very low.

Independent environmental journalist and the president of the Forum of Environmental Journalists in India (FEJI) Keya Acharya says that it is very difficult to convince editors of mainstream newspapers to carry environmental stories because they prefer political or conventionally current news (personal communication, 11 September 2020). In their competition for space in newspapers, environmental stories lose out to stories on politics, crime, business and entertainment.

Meera Bhardwaj, special correspondent, *The New Indian Express,* who has been writing on environmental issues for over two decades says that many of her stories on environmental issues have been killed wherever she has worked so far because they would affect the revenue of the publishers (personal communication, 27 March 2019). These were the exclusive stories not reported by any other newspaper but still, they were considered as stories of low salience. She says that when an issue is an isolated one and a single reporter is trying to pick up an investigative story, it is very difficult for a newspaper or a television channel to kill such a story. But when an issue is widely reported in newspapers and television, it would be difficult for a newspaper to kill such a story. Collective efforts among the journalists, she believes, can increase the possibility of environmental stories receiving greater prominence in media. However, that is something that rarely happens as every newspaper or television channel wants to run exclusive stories.

According to Umapathy, a Delhi-based journalist who has worked for leading Kannada dailies *Kannada Prabha, Vijaya Karnataka* and *Prajavani,* if the environment receives low coverage it is also because of the dearth of talent in media (personal communication, 26 June 2019). He explains why the environment is a low salience issue in newspapers.

There are very few journalists today who have the ability to understand public issues in their wider contexts. Journalism is no longer attracting good talent as the salaries are low and insecurity is very high given the reality of contractualization and casualization of employment. Moreover, a journalist today is made to work with digital devices and is forced to perform the job of four–five journalists. The environment is the first casualty of downsizing the workforce. Journalists end up doing too many regular stories and have no time to write about environmental issues as they demand more time. The conditions with which journalists are forced to work today do not encourage them to investigate issues of public interest. There is a need for journalists who can explain the impact of environmental degradation on the daily lives of people, the way P. Sainath does.

Working conditions and demands of the profession provide very little incentive for the journalist to go after environmental stories. The newsmen are forced to cover several stories in a cursory manner, rather than covering one story intensively. They skim the surface of many stories than digging down a potential blind alley to provide intensive coverage of one event as news (Tuchman, 1973). With the newsrooms becoming more and more understaffed, journalists become so preoccupied with their work that they have no time to attend a workshop or a training programme to get educated about environmental issues. In several other professions, there are opportunities to take part in programmes which are helpful in updating one's knowledge. Such opportunities are very rare in media. In Umapathy's view, the environment is the last priority when the primary goal of a media organization is profit.

According to Ramnath Shenoy, State Bureau Chief, Press Trust of India, Bengaluru, low salience of environmental issues in media is like chicken and egg story (personal communication, 11 May 2021). While publishers try to wriggle out their responsibility by saying that there are not many readers for environmental stories, readers say that the newspapers are not giving due importance to environmental issues. A major factor for low coverage, Shenoy says, is that the consequences of environmental problems are experienced over a long period of time, and for the people who are concerned about livelihood, the environment is not an imminent issue.

Manohar R. Yadavatti, Zonal Editor, *Hindustan Samachar*, who has worked in print and electronic media for over three decades, says that although environmental issues have been given fair coverage in media, it is far from being satisfactory because environmental news becomes major news only when it becomes a subject of political debate in the country (personal communication, 26 June 2019). Most political parties in the country today have no clear policy towards environmental issues. In his experience, political parties that oppose certain projects make all efforts to complete them when they are in power, and the media with political leanings shift their positions too. He cites the case of Dabhol power project in Maharashtra as an example. In the early 1990s, the opposition party Shiv Sena opposed setting up of naphtha-based power plant by Enron, a United States-based company, at Dabhol in Ratnagiri district of Maharashtra, on the grounds that it would pose a severe environmental risk. But when Shiv Sena itself formed the government in alliance with the BJP in 1995, the project was given clearance within a few days. And the newspapers that were pro-Shiv Sena changed their stand in line with the change in the position of the party. Since many of the newspapers are linked to political parties, they carry only those stories that are in some way connected to politics. The Dabhol project became a subject of debate in media because political parties were involved, although they did not have a clear environmental policy on which their opinions were based. Media give wide coverage to environmental controversies when political parties get involved in a fierce debate. The salience of the issue depends on the extent to which it is politicized.

Some journalists who pursue environmental stories have faced backlash for critical reporting. In order to avoid backlash, some journalists resort to metaphors without directly referring to individuals and institutions. The 'spiral of silence' within the media has been expanding as forces which reject environmental concern as a fringe concern dominate political discourse (Noelle-Neumann, 1974). While the diversity of opinion and interpretation is the hallmark of journalism, drowning out critical voices can seriously imperil scientific approach to understanding environmental problems.

At times, opposition to exposing environmental issues is couched in the garb of nationalism and patriotism. There have been several instances of environmental activists being branded as 'anti-development', 'anti-national' and 'anti-people' for raising questions on the environmental consequences of 'development' projects. The perceptions of journalists about what constitutes an environmental problem differ when their ideological orientations are strong. There is polarization to the extent that if a particular newspaper or news channel presents an environmental issue as an issue of great concern, another newspaper or channel may dismiss it as a non-issue.

According to Hunasavadi Rajan, Group Editor, *Samyukta Karnataka*, when there is a cut-throat competition among the media, survival becomes the order of the day, leading to a preference for the content that sells (personal communication, 26 March 2019). He says:

> Irrespective of whether it is Indian language newspapers or English newspapers, the marketing department controls what should be the approach to content selection. When newspapers carry serious articles on issues of public interest the readership decreases. This in many cases has forced editors to select the content that may get more readerships. Most readers today like the content that is entertaining and sensational which means facts need not be reported as facts. That is why serious issues like environmental issues do not get the kind of importance they deserve in media, more so in newspapers. It is very rare that you find a meaningful and serious discussion on culture, literature, and even on politics in visual media. There is so much of noise that is produced for the polarized audience, especially in visual media. Public taste is also a major factor.

In his view, between environment and entertainment, the editor today is forced to choose the latter, as it means more readership and more advertising revenue. The business model on which the media operate today provides very little space for analysis and debate on vital issues.

In Umapathy's view, the media have become so much market-driven that the editor has been pushed to a corner in the newspaper organization (personal communication, 26 June 2019). In recent years, the CEO has become the super boss with marketing and circulation departments calling the shots. For the non-salience of the environmental issues in newspapers, Umapathy explains:

> It is the marketing people rather than the editor who decides what kind of content should be carried and should not be carried. The institution of the editor is nearing extinction. Journalists who are occupying the positions of editors are those who function according to the expectations of the marketing people. Independent-minded editors who want to pursue their own editorial policy are shown the door.

The market-driven media cannot be expected to prioritize environmental stories that question the very logic of the market.

In the last few years, what is heard in the newsroom is that reporters have to sell their stories to the desk. They are hammered day in and day out about what they should write about and how they should write. If reporters package their stories in such a way that they please the desk, they will get prominent space on the front pages with their bylines. All that is taken into account for the evaluation of the performance of a journalist through 'self-appraisal', which has a bearing on the renewal of a journalist's contract. According to Muralidhar Khajane, deputy editor, *The Hindu*, a reporter today is asked to give graphics, visuals and bullet points before he gives the story (personal communication, 26 June 2019). This is the impact of the visual media on print journalism. Environmental stories that are connected to science, economics, society and culture demand greater depth and analysis, which may not always provide dramatic visuals. Depletion of ozone layer, increase in greenhouse gases, air pollution and water pollution cannot often be presented visually but require analysis and data that may not be entertaining.

According to K. S. Dakshina Murthy, Associate Editor, *The Federal*, and former editorial consultant, *The Hindu*, people are vaguely aware of issues like global warming. Explaining the difficulty in making people understand and act with regard to certain issues, he says,

> It becomes very difficult to tell people what they should do at the individual level. Should they walk or ride a bicycle? Should they stop using their vehicles? Should they reduce carbon footprint? If you look at it from that point of view, it is not possible for the individual to do anything about it. The problem is a complex one. (Personal communication, 26 June 2019)

For journalists explaining certain environmental issues to the readers is an arduous task as compared to the other issues. Moreover, the editor's disposition towards the environment is a major factor in certain issues getting media space and time.

An editor's narrow understanding of an issue and his assumption about who reads his newspaper may result in the spiking of stories which deserve prime space. Muralidhar Khajane, once travelled to the tribal areas in Kodagu and Chamarajanagar and produced four stories on how effectively the Scheduled Tribes and Other Traditional Forest Dwellers (Recognition of Forest Rights) Act, 2006, was being implemented. His chief in the Bengaluru bureau did not allow his story to be published on the grounds that tribes did not read *The Hindu*. He was told to write for the readers of *The Hindu*. Khajane told the editor that the story was written to educate the readers about the rights of the tribes and that the tribes did not even read local Kannada newspapers. He has not been able to write a single story on the tribes even to this day. The tribes have been the worst victims of deforestation, mining and displacement. However, their problems rarely find space in newspapers. He feels that the market has ruined the very values of journalism.

The polarization of media in the country has had its effect on what is selected and what is rejected as news. When environmentalist G. D. Agarwal passed away in October 2018 after 111 days of fasting demanding action against pollution of the Ganga river, the media in India ignored his sacrifice. 'Leave alone common people, even the reporters themselves did not know what Agarwal wrote in the three letters he sent to the Prime Minister. Many of the journalists do not even know that Agarwal wrote letters to the Prime Minister,' says Umapathy. Some issues are written about in media because of the prevailing political climate. When the interlinking of rivers was proposed two decades ago, there was a debate in media about its environmental consequences. But today when the *river linking project* is again on the agenda of the government, there is virtually no media discussion on it.

That the environmental issues are low-salience issues in media is also reflected in who in a media organization is assigned to cover them. Usually, junior journalists are asked to cover environmental issues. The experience of the environmental NGOs has been that the junior-most journalists are sent to cover their press conferences, whereas the senior-most journalists are sent to cover political press conferences. Environmental activists feel that many of the junior journalists lack training and thorough knowledge and do not ask analytical questions that put the NGOs on the defensive. That the junior-most journalists are asked to cover environmental issues is an indication of their low salience.

Event-orientated Coverage

Much of the content in the daily press and television channels is event-oriented. While event-centred media coverage may help raise public awareness about environmental topics, it is focused on discrete events rather than on the contexts in which they occur. The media tend to give news consumers the impression that individuals and institutions are responsible for a problem rather than the processes. Reporting on the environment tends to be dramatic and event focused and once the event is over, the issue is forgotten until it emerges with another event (Einsiedel & Coughlan, 1993; Friedman, 1991; Wilkins & Patterson, 1987). Events are the principal diet of a journalist and account for the overwhelming majority of stories. Journalists usually file reports when irate citizens protest against pollution, when a government announces a decision, when a lawyer files a suit, when individuals go on fast, when clashes occur between the protesters and the police, and when courts deliver judgments. When the stories are based only on events, it is likely that the sources influence the story frames. Besides, event orientation gives very little scope for the journalists to interpret and absolves them from the responsibility of presenting comprehensive and analytical stories.

Event-oriented environmental news coverage is often characterized by conflict between individuals or institutions or nations. Because 'the media still value people and ideas in conflict more than conditions and trends that are omnipresent', environmental coverage is often reduced to a conflict of authorities and even personalities quoted in the media (Dennis, 1991, p. 60). Unable to explain the scientific and political complexities associated with a given environmental problem (Wilkins & Patterson, 1987) and similarly unable to investigate the intercorrelations between issues, the environment becomes a personality conflict, and environmental stories become little more than informational dumps into which the reporter unloads quotes (Stocking & Leonard,

1990). Journalists with short attention spans fail to report the historical context or long-term implications of the issues and focus on conflict and controversy rather than long-term trends. Environmental news items tend to be centred on the relationship between personalities and environmental events (Triandafyllidou, 1996) rather than focusing on the substance of environmental problems or the consequences of environmental problems.

Most journalists are of the view that events should be reported because they are indicators as to what is happening in the world, but then follow-up stories are needed to provide greater depth to the issues related to the events. When disasters happen, they make front-page news, but an analysis of factors that caused them and how such disasters can be prevented in the future is necessary. At times, there is only a knee-jerk response to disasters ignoring the responsibility of examining the processes that lead to them.

Mohit Rao, special correspondent, *The Hindu*, who has been writing on environmental issues, says that writing on a single event connected to one controversial project is necessary but not enough (personal communication, 21 February 2019). According to him, highlighting the felling of 2.5 lakh trees for the Hubli–Ankola railway project needs to be linked up with infrastructure development throughout the Western Ghats giving a comprehensive account of what has been happening in the Western Ghats over the years to make an impact. He says:

> Long-term effects of projects and policies are rarely presented to the readers. Journalists do lack training in reporting complex issues but at the same time, the activists who take extreme positions will also not be helpful. A bigger and broader picture is always helpful in putting everything in a perspective. Writing about protecting the forest and natural resources is of no use unless the specific cases are presented to the people. I have always written about specific cases with all the details needed to understand them comprehensively and I feel that is the responsibility of a journalist.

Going deep into the specific cases invariably means starting with an event and connecting it to a larger issue which may involve facts and figures explained in proper perspectives.

According to the Delhi-based science and environmental journalist T. V. Jayan who works with *The Hindu Business Line* as its senior deputy editor, event-orientation is a product of the very nature of the media (personal communication, 11 September 2020). Going deeper into things is not possible when reporters are asked to file two–three reports a day. There is hardly any time left for investigating issues and preparing analytical reports. When someone starts investigating an issue for several days the newsroom bosses think that he is whiling away his time. Jayan says that Indian language newspapers, especially Malayalam newspapers, have carried a lot of in-depth stories as compared to national media. Those who are doing serious journalism and are free from reporting daily occurrences produce analytical stories. Some editors allow reporters to pursue an environmental story and give them time off from their regular work. But that rarely happens. The environment is a minor beat in most newspapers, and therefore it is difficult for the reporter to go into the details of an issue.

Environmental and human rights activist Vidya Dinker who is the convenor of the Citizens' Forum for Mangalore Development says that the argument of some of the editors that they focus mostly on events because their readers are not interested in anything that is too serious and analytical is indefensible (personal communication, 5 May 2021). She says that this argument usually comes from those who do not want to invest in resources and time in covering complex environmental issues. She says,

> The readership you get is the readership you cultivate. If the reporters are capable of looking deeper into issues and putting them across to the readers they will gradually begin to appreciate it. Then you will have readers who want more informative and analytical pieces.

If the journalists don't try to dig deeper into issues, put facts in perspective, write their copies better and challenge themselves professionally, they do not grow at all. Dinker says that when the processes are not important to journalists, environmental groups have to keep on creating events for them. Much of the work carried out by environmental groups goes unnoticed by the press because the work involves dealing with processes. Journalists have often asked her 'Where are you? You are not to be seen'. According to her, this remark only confirms journalists' expectation of events all the time from the NGOs and activists. Journalists in her experience, generally do not show interest in the work the NGOs and activists do on the ground and the documentation they do about the impact of projects with environmental consequences.

Dinker also holds activists partly responsible for this as some of them feel they are activists only if they are written about or quoted in media. For that, they focus their attention on creating events, which may not serve the cause of the environment but puts them in the media spotlight 'conferring' a kind of 'social status' (Lazarsfeld & Merton, 1948). The activists' desire to be in the limelight and the journalists' preference for undemanding newsgathering results in greater event-orientation in environmental news coverage. Journalists do not often take personal interest in seeking information, evidence and ideas from different sources including activists to analyse complex issues. Some of them may be interested in looking for those stories that give them bylines and space on the front page.

Independent environmental journalist and activist Shivananda Kalave who has been writing for the last three decades on environmental and developmental issues argues that the media which helped the environmental movement grow should have moved beyond events by presenting analytical articles including those that are critical of the movement (personal communication, 27 February 2019). He strongly feels that one of the serious limitations of the media is that they have not been able to provide a critical discourse to their audiences. The media have focused more on the number of participants in a movement and what visuals they provide rather than on the issues involved.

According to Kalave, much of the reporting in media is still event-oriented because the habit of reading and researching is lacking in the present generation of journalists who are dependent on internet-based information. They do not go to the field; instead, they ask someone in a village to send a photo or a video of an incident or an event. If some trees have been felled illegally in some remote village, journalists ask someone to send the photos through WhatsApp and write a story based on whatever information they get. Over the years, field-based reporting has become very rare irrespective of whether the media are local, regional, or national. Kalave observes:

> The media are becoming vehicles of expression for those who have the ability and opportunity to talk. Journalists are mostly involved in networking and any opinion or information on anything that comes from their own network. The voice of the voiceless is not being heard. To do this one has to work hard by travelling, witnessing, and listening to the people who have been affected by a project.

Many journalists he has known do not want to travel, speak to people, understand their problems, get reactions from the authorities and produce meaningful reports. The easiest thing for them to do is to report an event because it doesn't demand either skill or hard work.

Environmental activist and the leader of the Appiko movement Panduranga Hegde has found that much of environmental reporting is based only on events and stresses the need for journalists to go beyond mere events (personal communication, 26 February 2019). He has always asked journalists to dig into the events and write the truth according to their conscience. He does not want journalists to wait for the events to happen but to start working on saving the planet by placing the truth before the people. He says,

> Nature is truth and I would want journalists to understand nature. Nature cannot speak and the journalists who have the capacity and inclination should give nature a voice. Wherever the journalists have the opportunity, they should speak for nature. Journalists are, after all, products of society.

In contrast to the Indian journalists, he has found foreign journalists, especially those from the BBC, making serious and concerted efforts to understand the issues in their broader contexts of polity, science and society. For him, the processes are much more important than some dramatic developments.

Some journalists see events as bases on which longer, deeper and analytical stories can be constructed. For Dakshina Murthy news reporting is invariably connected to the events as they drag the reporter into a story (personal communication, 26 June 2019). Insisting that that is the way stories are written he says if sparrows have disappeared from Bengaluru city it should become a trigger for a journalist to dig deep into the environmental factors that caused such disappearance. If there are more layers to the news, it depends on the ability of the reporter to find out. If someone is protesting against the pollution of a river' then the event has to be covered but at the same time a reporter has to find out what led to the pollution and what can be done to clean up the river or prevent pollution in the future. According to Murthy, unless analytical reports are connected to events that evoke curiosity among the readers they would lose their relevance. For him, more than any other topic the environment requires an event through which it can be explained.

Regular events themselves can be turned into great opportunities to bring about pro-environment behaviour among the people. With regard to pollution and accidents caused by the burning of firecrackers at the time of Deepavali, Nagesh Hegde (personal communication, 12 October 2018) says that newspapers can bring out a series of articles to create public opinion against the burning of crackers. He is of the view that even while covering the events depth can be provided to the stories if the journalists plan for them. He says:

> There could be stories about the quantity of firecrackers that are going to be in the market and the possible pollution they can create. The possibility of rain and fog during the Deepavali time which makes pollution more severe can be explained in relation to weather predictions. What happened in the past years in other cities and how people, especially children, suffered due to the pollution caused by firecrackers can be explained. Injuries caused during the burning of crackers and the suffering of the asthma patients can be explained with the easily available statistics. It is also important to explain how harmful pollution is to cows and pets. Over several weeks preceding Deepavali, public opinion can be built against the burning of firecrackers with these kinds of stories. Slowly people will understand the harm caused by fire-cracker pollution. By the day of the Deepavali, about 50 per cent of the people may have decided not to buy firecrackers. People can be encouraged to celebrate and enjoy a better, cleaner, and peaceful Deepavali.

He suggests that the regular events associated with the environment including those found in the United Nations calendar of events be used to write about themes they represent. According to him, if there is International Disaster Reduction Day celebrated on 13 October, journalists have the responsibility to speak to the people concerned and ask them what they have planned for the day. By doing so, they will be alerting the authorities concerned about what they can do. When the authorities celebrate a day, its coverage can go beyond an event and provide context and depth. The celebration of Earth Day, according to Hegde, can be an opportunity to reflect on the threats to the planet. According to independent environmental journalist and the President of the Forum of Environmental Journalists in India (FEJI) Keya Acharya, the mainstream media look at only the events but not the layers of facts connected to them (personal communication, 11 September 2020). 'The background knowledge the journalists in the mainstream media have about some important events is very poor. Even when they are reporting a cricket tournament' it is possible to connect it to the amount of water used and the waste generated,' she says.

Many analytical articles, which are not connected to events, appear on the editorial pages but very few people read them. The editorial page is the most expensive page for a publisher because it carries no advertisements and those who are in charge of it are the highest-paid journalists in newspapers. Most of the common readers run through the news stories based on events and do not read the contents on the editorial page. The contents on the editorial page are too heavy and serious for them to spare their time. The real dignity of a newspaper is reflected in what it carries on its editorial page. Some newspapers have not allowed the editorial page to be commercialized. According to Nagesh Hegde, if good and analytical reports on environmental issues are allowed to be published people will start reading them and the demand for such stories will grow. If the beginning itself is not made it would be difficult to know whether readers are interested in issues related to the environment.

Media are event-driven, but narrating only events to the readers all the time without depth and analysis is irresponsible journalism. Reporting events is needed to get the audiences interested in an environmental issue, but to provide them with a comprehensive understanding of the issue, follow-ups and investigative stories are necessary.

Development vs Environment Frame

Although politicians, bureaucrats and policymakers have been talking for decades about the right kind of balance between development and the environment, in reality, there has always been a tilt towards development. Rewriting of green laws to make way for industries, curtailment of powers of statutory bodies like Forest Advisory Committee and National Board for Wildlife, speeding up of environmental clearances indicate that in the development agenda environment has got the short end of the stick. When a cabinet minister charged with protecting the environment and forests refers to his own ministry as 'roadblock ministry' (Thekaekara, 2015), it reflects how the government deals with environmental questions.

The media have broadly reflected the development vs environment debate in the political arena. Environmental journalist and conservation biologist Bahar Dutt (2014, p. 5) says that every time she tried to pitch an environmental story, the editor of a leading media house would say 'environmentalism is stalling growth; all I am interested in is double-digit growth for this country'. The moment a question is raised on the environmental consequences of a project, the response, most often, centres around how stopping the project is going to harm development. There is a belief that priority right now is development and that the issue of environment can be dealt with later as if development and environment are mutually exclusive.

Guha (2008) says that environmentalists came under severe attack by the national press from the mid-1990s. They were not only branded as CIA and KGB agents but also as those who were suffering from the hangover of the bad old days of socialism. These arguments were palatable to politicians, bureaucrats and technocrats who had been critical of environmentalists for allegedly opposing development.

Environmentalists feel that the entire development vs environment debate is a false debate brought up to defend development at the cost of anything. They argue that development is not a substitute for the environment and that media have the responsibility of not promoting the false narrative. The real issue they believe is buried between the two faces of the same coin because the two are not opposites. In environmental journalist Nagesh Hegde's view, the development vs environment frame was created by the big corporations because they want all those who raise questions on the environment to be seen as 'anti-development'. These kinds of binaries, in a way, help build sensationalism into the environmental stories shifting the focus away from the real issues. Most pro-establishment media that use the development vs environment frame focus on only the positive impact of a controversial project and play down the harmful consequences. They have attempted to portray those who raise questions on environmentally harmful projects as 'anti-development', 'anti-progress' and 'anti-national' (Sethi, 2015, p. 131).

Rohin Kumar, Media Specialist, Greenpeace, argues that the entire development vs environment debate is a propaganda being carried on by the governments around the world to justify unsustainable and destructive development (personal communication, 20 May 2021). 'If the forest cover is depleting, how can that be development. Development should be judged by how much forest cover has increased in the last five years and how many people got green jobs,' he says.

Activists often point to Article 39 of the Indian Constitution which serves as the guiding principle for journalists when they write about development and environment. The Article says (a) that the citizens, men and women equally, have the right to an adequate means of livelihood; (b) that the ownership and control of the material resources of the community are so distributed as best to subserve the common good; and (c) that the operation of the economic system does not result in the concentration of wealth and means of production to the common detriment.

There is deep humanism that is built into this Article. The core idea here is that the wealth of the country should not get concentrated in a few hands. If this principle becomes the basis of all policies, development would not cause any harm to the environment. Leo Saldanha who heads the Environmental Support Group (ESG), a Bengaluru-based NGO, and has fought battles with industrial houses and the government on several environmental issues, feels that a close reading of this Article will guide journalists towards what is the right thing to do (personal communication, 21 February 2019). In the frequent interactions he has had with journalists, he has found that most journalists do not have a proper understanding of the constitutional provision about the environment. There is a lack of reference to this Article in policy documents and media debates. In the absence of such debate in academia and the media, a person who raises questions about who the beneficiaries of a project are going to be is portrayed as 'anti-development'.

Environmental activist Vidya Dinker who is the convenor of the Citizens' Forum for Mangalore Development is of the view that development vs environment frame dominates media coverage of the environment because of their uncritical acceptance of the discourse shaped by the government and the industry (personal interview, 5 November 2018). Journalists, she says, rarely search for a narrative that is different from the narrative that the government and the industry consistently promote.

According to environmental activist and the leader of the Appiko movement Panduranga Hegde, there is a misconception about what is development (personal communication, 26 February 2019). He says:

The three basic needs of mankind are air, water and soil. Development means developing all the three but instead, we are destroying them. This is a straightforward truth. If you take Delhi or Bengaluru, the air is highly polluted. Almost all rivers are polluted and you can't question. People in distant places are promised water from river diversion projects, even though it is not going to be a reality. Soil is getting contaminated because of fertilizers and pesticides with only a pep talk about organic farming. Unless you develop water, air and soil, there is no development. My entry into government programmes has been blocked because I fought against the proposal to lay Hubli-Ankola railway line cutting across the Western Ghats. The project will destroy 2,000 acres of forest and 3–4 lakh trees. The forest cover which was 80 per cent a few decades ago has come down to 10 percent in Uttara Kannada district, and if you take away 2,000 acres of the forest what will happen to the water and soil? The government and the industries think that laying the railway line is development. If you look at the way media reported it, it is worrying. They argue that the railway line should be built for the development of the region. They were reflecting the view of all political parties which want the railway line whatever may be the ecological cost. The highly commercialized media cannot take a pro-people stand when the interests of the industries are involved.

Hegde finds it disturbing when some media argue that the Hubli–Ankola railway line will bring development and prosperity to the Uttara Kannada district. This is one of the keenly debated issues in the district today. In contrast to the view of the journalists, the common people in the district think that connecting Ankola with Hubli will lead to the development of the district. Decades ago the people of the district associated construction of roads and railways with the destruction of forest and the ecology of the Western Ghats but today they link the development of the district to such infrastructure projects. Even though the district has been the worst victim of development in Karnataka and has witnessed a vibrant environmental movement, the economic aspect of the railway line has taken precedence over environmental destruction.

Senior journalist Narasimha Adi, who works for PTI news agency, *Samyukta Karnataka* and *Rajasthan Patrika* at Sirsi, says that people are now demanding railway networks even though there has been a severe water crisis in the district (personal communication, 27 February 2019). However, most of the journalists in the district are opposed to cutting down lakhs of trees to build the railway line. It is disturbing that the Shalmala river that fills life into the Bedti river completely dried up two years ago for the first time. While the common people want roads and railway lines which they think will boost the development of the district, journalists want no further damage to the ecology of the Western Ghats.

According to development journalist Shivananda Kalave, the media should move away from the development versus environment frame to 'development with the environment' frame to put the issues in proper perspective (personal communication, 27 February 2019). He feels it is important to give due importance to those who are questioning the environmental movement because only when it is confronted with questions it will become sharper in its focus and clear in its approach. The media have the responsibility of giving space and time to opposing views to make the process of resolving any issue more democratic.

Science and environmental journalist T. V. Jayan is of the view that the 'development versus environment' paradigm has changed now (personal communication, 11 September 2020). That narrative has now shifted to a more realistic approach that gives equal importance to the development and the environment, he says. There are no journalists today who would argue that development should happen at the cost of the environment. Jayan sees greater sensitivity among the senior journalists who may be holding key positions in media.

Dakshina Murthy sees rural–urban divide when it comes to the perception of what is development (personal communication, 26 June 2019). He says:

> For rural people, it is the question of livelihood and improvement in the quality of life. Journalists in rural areas who reflect the view of the people there tend to be in favour of development even when there is a possibility of environmental degradation. For the people who migrate to cities in search of livelihood, setting up industries and cutting down the forest for the construction of railway line and roads look like great opportunities. The rural people aspire to be like urban people. And the journalists in rural areas broadly reflect this hope when they write about the development projects. There is a need for awareness among both the journalists and the rural people about the environmental costs of development.

For people whose concern is their livelihood, the issue of the environment may look irrelevant. But in the long run, their livelihood is also going to be affected by mindless development. A journalist, Dakshina Murthy feels, should try to understand the complexities involved in the development vs. environment debate. In India, the environmental question is so intertwined with the development that it is difficult to isolate it as a category that has independent meaning (Chapman et al., 1997). The English newspapers and Indian-language newspapers differ in their approach to understanding environmental issues. The English newspapers seem to be more concerned about environmental issues than the Indian language newspapers. While the Indian language newspapers tend to be pro-development, the English newspapers tend to be pro-environment.

When Nagesh Hegde wrote a column in *Prajavani* about the environmental consequences of the proposed construction of the railway line between Ankola and Hubli in Karnataka, he was bombarded with hate messages from the local journalists who wanted the railway project because they thought that would give a boost to the development of the region (personal communication, 12 October 2018). The local journalists believed that people like Nagesh Hegde were coming in the way of development by raising environmental questions. At times, it is livelihood vs protection of the environment. That the livelihoods are going to be affected in the long run if the environment is not protected is a reality that journalists should be aware of. Environment should actually become India's development agenda; otherwise the very concept of development becomes meaningless (Narain, 2017).

A general view expressed by both journalists and activists is that media coverage of environmental issues should go beyond 'development vs environment' frame and focus on sustainable development that would make responsible use of the resources in such a way that livelihoods of people in the long run are not affected.

Coverage in Local, State and National Media

When it comes to covering environmental issues all media play important roles whether they are local, state level or national media.[1] However, their orientations, priorities and perspectives may differ in significant ways. Local newspapers usually report events that happen

---

[1] The term 'local media' is used here to refer to the media whose reach is limited to a district or a few taluks in a district. They are usually newspapers in the local language and the content they carry is mainly about the district, taluks and the villages. All Kannada newspapers which have circulation across the state are referred to as state newspapers. Kannada television channels are also state media, as their content is mostly about the affairs of the state. The national newspapers are the English newspapers which have circulation in two or more states. The English television news channels are also considered as national media.

within districts and taluks where they have their readership. Proximity is considered an important element that determines the news value of an event. Events that occur in places close to the newspaper's place of publication are likely to receive greater attention than those taking place in faraway places. In the districts where environmental movements have been active, the local newspapers have played an important role in shaping the discourse on environmental issues. The state newspapers usually report issues that have consequences across the districts, but the district editions they have brought out have blurred the distinctions between local and state newspapers.

Some researchers have found a tendency among the newspapers to focus on problems in places far away from the community they serve. In the United States, this attitude of the newspapers is referred to as 'Afghanistanism' (Hungerford & Lemert, 1973). The newspapers draw the attention of the people to the problems in distant places instead of bringing the local problems into the notice of the community. The American media audiences tend to think that human rights violations take place only in African, Asian and Latin American countries because their media report about violations only in those countries ignoring such violations within the country (Taleb, 2004). Chapman et al. (1997, p. 67) who interviewed journalists of Indian newspapers reporting on the environment found that some of them saw environmental problems as those happening 'somewhere else' but not in their own community.

Hegde (2010, p. 273) says that during the Appiko movement in the early 1980s, the local media were 'initially supportive but played a negative role in the later stages' and saw 'forest protection as an impediment to the development of the region'. While the local people might see a development project as one that would provide them livelihood, people living far away from there might see it as a serious environmental issue.

One explanation that Mohit Rao provides for local media ignoring local issues is that journalists working for local newspapers at the taluk or district levels may be under pressure from local groups or influential individuals who would not want certain issues reported (personal communication, 12 February 2019). But those who work for state and national newspapers may not have such pressures. Moreover, a local journalist would be concerned with the livelihood of the people of his community rather than environmental issues. Rao says that despite mining operations in the Bellary district of Karnataka causing enormous environmental destruction, people there want mining operations to continue because they provide employment and local newspapers may be reflecting that view.

Well-known lawyer, journalist and activist of Uttara Kannada district Ajit Nayak was murdered on 27 July 2018 (Bhat, 2018). He was involved in the Kali Bachao Andolan, a movement to safeguard the river from damming, rampant sand mining and industrial pollution. He had been campaigning against the releasing of effluents by the West Coast Paper Mills into the Kali river. The local media did not delve much into the circumstances of his death. Ajit Nayak was a vocal campaigner for the Kali Bachao Andolan and had demanded action by the Real Estate Regulatory Authority (RERA) against corruption. Leo Saldanha of the ESG decided to bring the issue to Bengaluru because he felt the local journalists were embedded in the welfare system created by the corporations.

The ESG organized protests in Bengaluru to get the attention of the state and national media so as to bring pressure on the government. According to Saldanha, the West Coast Paper Mills had so much influence on the Dandeli town that no journalist dared to write against it. The issue needed coverage by the national and state-level media. Without media support activists like Ajit Nayak become vulnerable. The ESG went after the West Coast Paper Mills and questioned its operations with national media writing about it. Because of the efforts of the ESG, the death of the activist lawyer and also the questionable operations of the mill got the attention of the state and national media. The group did succeed in preventing the expansion of the paper mills. The expansion would have meant more pollution of the river in which the lead level was far above permissible levels. Saldanha says media must not just be a watchdog but should be a fraternity of solidarity for dissenters. What could not be done through the local media could be done through the state-level media that did not have the kind of constraints that the local media had.

This may not be the case all the time. In some of the cases, the local media first reported about the threats posed to the environment while the state-level and national-level media had ignored the same. The editor of *Lokadwani*, a Kannada daily published from Sirsi, P. S. Sadananda, says that local newspapers gave a voice to the Appiko movement in Uttara Kannada district (personal communication, 27 February 2019). Even with regard to Kaiga nuclear plant and Seabird naval base, newspapers carried stories about the benefits and environmental consequences. But the state and national-level newspapers did not give the needed attention. These projects were national projects with environmental consequences that would affect lakhs of people. The protests against these projects were mostly covered by the local press. Sadananda explains with an example: 'When a group of senior journalists came here from Bengaluru to know about the role of media during the movement against the Kaiga nuclear power project and the Seabird naval base, they were surprised to see newspaper cuttings of well-known writer Shivram Karanth and Pejawar Swamiji of Udupi taking part in protests. The press in Bengaluru was not aware of the popularity of the movement and public figures taking part in it. The state and national media have not covered several such significant movements.'

A clear divide between vernacular media and national media can be seen in the way the recommendations of the Madhav Gadgil Committee were reported in the media. According to Leo Saldanha of the ESG, the vernacular media were embedded in local politics and were managed in such a way that accepting the Madhav Gadgil report was presented as detrimental to the livelihoods of the people in the Western Ghats region (personal communication, 21 February 2019). The media at the rural and district levels created a false impression among the people of the Malnad region that they would lose everything if Gadgil's recommendations were implemented. The media had failed in cultivating a rich and textured understanding of what was recommended in the Gadgil report. Saldanha emphasizes that the media did not make sincere efforts to protect the fragile nature of the planet as the real reason as to why sometimes people should say a definite 'no' to the abuse of nature like they say 'no' to sexual abuse. The vernacular media did not take up the responsibility of explaining the key features of both Madhav Gadgil and Kasturirangan reports which are still not available in regional languages.

Saldanha gave another example of how local media did not cover a serious health issue related to declining forest cover in the Western Ghats region. A tick-borne viral disease known as Kyathanur Forest Disease (KFD) has been claiming several lives every year in the Western Ghats region. Large-scale destruction of forests is a major reason for the spread of the disease as a variety of animals which carry the virus start moving towards human habitation in search of food (Korse, 2019). Saldanha says that the local media have not adequately reported about the link between the destruction of forest and the spread of KFD. Virologist Dr P. K. Rajagopalan (2017) who had worked with the Indian Council of Medical Research (ICMR) has said that the exploitation of the forest and the probable increase of interfaces could have led to the spread of KFD virus. According to him, long-term changes in the ecology can bring about signifi- cant changes in the fauna and flora affecting human lives. Cutting the forest down, making roads and building houses can increase the chances of the virus spreading faster and wider in the Western Ghats region. However, the media attention has been more on the treat- ment of the disease than on factors that have caused it and ways of preventing it. The state and national media, according to Saldanha, have given a better coverage to the issue. Implementation of the Kasturirangan report or Gadgil report on conserving Western Ghats can help prevent the spread of such diseases. But, the local media have not paid serious attention to this aspect.

In Saldanha's view, it was a partial and wrong reading of the Kasturirangan report that led to protests against its implementation. He feels the local newspapers had the responsibility of presenting the key recommendations of the report to the readers but they did not do so. The national media according to him gave positive coverage to the key recommendations of both Gadgil and Kasturirangan reports. Dr Vasudeva, professor of forest biology, College of Forestry, Sirsi, Uttara Kannada district of Karnataka, is also of the view that the national media have a better understanding of the broader environ- mental issues as compared to the local media (personal communication,

27 February 2019). As a member of the Western Ghats Task Force, Government of Karnataka, he found that the local media did not give due importance to the issues of the Western Ghats. According to him, there is ample evidence to show that the priorities and concerns of the local and state/national media are different.

As an environmental activist, Vidya Dinker says that local newspapers understand the problems of their communities better than the state or the national newspapers (personal communication, 5 May 2021). The nuances of what people think and experience are better described in local newspapers. Most environmental stories, she says, are reported by the local language newspapers first and later picked up by the English newspapers. Local language newspapers are usually free from big advertisers and therefore enjoy a greater freedom than national/state dailies that are cautious about offending their advertisers.

On the coverage that the environmental movement in Dakshina Kannada district received in the local press, Dinker says:

> In our struggle, the first newspaper that started giving a lot of coverage was Karavali Ale, a Kannada daily published from Mangalore. It was later that the English newspapers took notice of our struggle. English journalists would not come on their own to witness what we were doing. I had to talk to them and invite them. An active engagement with them was necessary to see that our struggle was covered. When the pressure from the advertisers came, the English newspapers stopped carrying stories of our struggle first. Because the visibility of the English press is more the industry and authorities are slightly more sensitive about negative stories in the English press. It can go to a wider audience and to the higher ups in the government. So they try to influence the English newspapers a lot more. The pushback is stronger with English newspapers, therefore that kind of coverage also dries up faster. The window of opportunity to get our issues highlighted in the English press is a lot smaller.

Local newspapers in both Dakshina Kannada and Uttara Kannada districts of Karnataka have covered environmental issues in-depth and have initiated the debate on them but the industry and the authorities are more concerned with what is reported in national/

state dailies. For greater visibility and to reach people across the state, coverage of issues in national/state dailies is important. However, with the national/state dailies bringing out their own district editions the stories of environmental struggles do not reach the readers in the other districts. Building a wider network for carrying on their struggle on a larger scale has become very difficult for the activists. What used to become state-level news is now restricted to the districts. Readers in Uttara Kannada would not know what is happening in Dakshina Kannada.

Panduranga Hegde who sees the launching of district editions of state-level newspapers as a negative development says:

The news that emerged from Uttara Kannada during the Appiko movement in the early 1980s would reach the entire state because newspapers then had only single editions. People from all over Karnataka used to write to us and express their solidarity with us after reading about our programme in Sirsi. Newspapers helped us a great deal. Among the editors, Khadri Shamanna of *Kannada Prabha* and Jayasheela Rao of *Munjaane* took interest in the movement and gave so much of importance to the issues we were raising. The movement received front-page coverage in newspapers. The scope of news has shrunk so much that if I give a press release in Sirsi no newspaper in Bengaluru will report it. Some newspapers in Sirsi might carry it because they know me. Even when an event of national importance is held here in Sirsi, it becomes local news. District editions of newspapers have done a lot of harm to the cause of the environment because people in the neighbouring district like Shivamogga would not know what is happening here unless something tragic or sensational happens. (personal communication, 26 February 2019).

For those who want to gain support for their causes and influence policymakers, coverage in state and national media becomes crucial. Both journalists and environmentalists are of the view that carrying even the most significant news only in the district editions is not fair, as it keeps people in one district unaware of what is happening in other districts. Even when environmental NGOs and activists travel all the way from districts to the capital city of Bangalore to hold press conferences with the purpose of reaching out to a wider audience the state and national newspapers still carry the story in district editions (Vidya Dinker, personal communication, 5 May 2021). This practice is ranged against environmental activism based outside of the capital. Giving a state-level perspective to local issues is considered important as it is likely to get the attention of political leaders and officials. Local issues appear on state pages only when Bengaluru-based NGOs take them up. Destruction of forests in Kodagu should be a matter of great concern for the people of Bengaluru as they are dependent on Kaveri river for their drinking water. However, such events are usually treated as news that deserves space only in the local editions of the state newspapers. The district editions are not only keeping people unaware of the problems in the other districts but they have also prevented environmental movements from spreading to other districts. This is a big disadvantage to the environmental activists who want to mobilize support for a cause across districts.

Social media can be used to get messages to people in different places but they will not have the same kind of influence as printed newspapers. For those who want to build an environmental movement across the state, the district editions have become obstacles.

Conclusion

Although media coverage of the environment has increased over the years, it has remained an issue of low salience. Environmental issues have not been given their due space and time in media but there are journalists relentlessly writing about them. A variety of factors have contributed to the low salience of environmental news. Preference for conventional news, inadequate resources and downsizing of the staff has led to decline in coverage. Journalists who are burdened with loads of work lack of time to dig for facts and piece together a story. Lack of encouragement from the management, pressure from the advertisers, absence of collective efforts and aggressive competition among the media are also other factors for the low salience of environmental news. The environment not being a part of the political discourse is also a factor as politics dominates the front page and the prime time in media. If the environment is on the agenda of the political parties there would be more coverage to it.

Much of the environmental reporting is event-oriented and focuses more on dramatic developments rather than on the processes that are associated with environmental problems. Event-centred reporting is also the result of journalists being left with no time to investigate and prepare analytical reports. Journalists see events as inevitable for news media but want follow-up stories with greater depth and analysis. They suggest that the events can be used to create awareness and to offer ways of dealing with environmental issues. In-depth reporting requires that the background and the consequences of events are interpreted in broader contexts. Even though environmental issues are complex and are related to science, economics and society, they are often presented in the development vs environment frame. Environmentalists as well as journalists are of the view that the very 'development vs environment' debate is a propaganda which the government and the industry have launched to justify unsustainable development. They want media to move away from this frame as it limits the scope of environmental discourse. The local, state and national media play significant roles but they may not be on the same side of an issue. While the local media usually pick up local environmental problems that may not always be the case. The issues that are ignored by the local media are sometimes picked up by the state and national media. For the local media the livelihood issues may become more important than environmental issues that have consequences over a long period. The claim that local media are pro-development whereas the state and national media are pro-environment or local media are pro-environment whereas the state and national media are pro-development is not sustainable. The local media may set the agenda by consistently reporting about certain issues but they may not report certain other issues at all. Local industries, groups and individuals may bring a lot of pressure on the local media not to report certain issues. Such a pressure may not be there on the state and national media. The state and national newspapers carry stories about environmental struggles in the districts only in their district editions. By doing so, they keep the readers in one district unaware of the problems in the other districts. District editions have made it hard for the activists to find support from across the state.

Even though there are limitations in covering the environment, the media have made a significant contribution to constructing it as an issue. The media coverage alone may not have led to the shelving of some of the environmentally harmful projects but when a balance sheet is made about their performance in the last four decades, the overall constructive role they have played becomes perceptible.

CHAPTER 3

Advocacy in Environmental Reporting
Activism and Professional Practices

There has been renewed interest in the advocacy role of media in recent years because of the proliferation of media channels and the expanding reach of the new media. In its simplest meaning, advocacy is expressing support for a cause. Advocacy in journalism is a combination of activism and professionalism that goes beyond reporting, pushes a narrative and presents a perspective. Advocacy reporting is focused on an issue or some injustice that needs to be addressed. It is aimed at engaging citizens and offering them a means through which they can solve problems. It pleads on behalf of those who want to build support for a cause. Although advocacy is not very widely practised in the mainstream media, journalists who believe in it feel that journalism is a calling and passionately try to influence public opinion in favour of a cause. They express their opinions on certain issues and editorialize their reports. While editorializing may be very subtle in some newspapers, it may be obvious in others. Advocacy is more often found in the alternative media and special interest publications than in conventional and general interest publications. It is rarely visible in the mainstream media because media corporations have, over the years, established norms and routines that rarely give journalists the freedom to campaign for a cause. However, advocacy in the mainstream media is considered important because of their wider reach, acceptability and influence on policymakers.

Advocacy is fact-based but supports a specific point of view on an issue. The focus is on stories dealing with corporate business practices, government policies, political corruption and social issues. Many journalists reject objectivity as a practical impossibility. Even though advocacy journalism follows an agenda, there is an implicit suggestion of neutrality and fairness. Media may play an advocacy role with regard to some specific causes and remain neutral on other issues.

Objectivity vs Advocacy

The concept of objectivity emerged during the 19th century as part of the intellectual movement that stressed scientific detachment and separation of fact from the value (Gitlin, 1980). Journalism is believed to be an empirical information-gathering activity, with reporters making a dispassionate observation of events that happen around the world. Objectivity stresses scientific detachment and separation of fact from value. A scientific approach to newsgathering and reporting means that journalists believe that through observation, the world can be perceived and interpreted objectively. A reporter with strongly held values and opinions challenges the traditional system of journalistic practice. A journalist is expected to be value-free and present social reality in an objective and balanced way. The ideal of objectivity rests on the assumption that the facts are ultimately knowable and the journalist is capable of transmitting a truthful account of 'what is out there' (Reese, 1990, p. 394). As a golden rule of journalistic practice, objectivity is something like the Hippocratic Oath that doctors take to uphold ethical standards. Adherence to objectivity supposedly gives respectability to journalists. However, the ideal of objectivity has remained more an ideal than a fully realized goal of journalism.

One of the major criticisms against the ideal of objectivity is that it denies freedom of interpretation and subjectivity to a journalist

(Mattelart, 1980; Tuchman, 1972). If the subjectivity of the journalist is eliminated, it means that the very personality of the journalist is lost. When a journalist denies individuality to himself he becomes a mere transmitter of information. Objectivity alienates the journalist from the very product he produces. The way a factory worker is alienated from the product he produces, a journalist is alienated from the story he produces because of the norms of professional practice imposed upon him. On the one hand, he is denied recognition of himself in the product and on the other, he is forced to act as an agent of the dominant forces in society (Mattelart, 1980). The word 'objectivity' is used defensively by reporters as a 'strategic ritual' for protecting themselves from mistakes as well as critics (Tuchman, 1972, p. 661). Journalists use objectivity as a strategy to meet constraint of time, to avoid defamation cases and to avoid flak from seniors. Since the stories are only records of information and opinions that the sources provide, the responsibility for the consequences of the stories is transferred to the sources.

The ideal of objectivity in a way sanctifies the ideology of the dominant forces in society as a universal value. The media audience receives a reality which has already been given an interpretation. The interpretation is 'that of the ruling class and its mode of false consciousness' (Mattelart, 1980, p. 38). Interpretation is implicit in the selection itself as journalists select some events and ignore others. Events are reported in terms of the dominant system of values. When a media report describes a reality, it has inherent ideological meaning. Mattelart (1980) says even a photograph which is considered as a mirror of reality is ideological not only because of selection of themes but also because of choice of framing, background, foreground and colour filters that give a particular meaning. What is generally seen as objective is not objective at all but imbued with subjective meaning. The notion of objectivity allows dominant social and economic forces to determine what is important and what is not. The interests and values of the dominant groups in society are projected as if they are universal and ubiquitous.

Whether media should practise objectivity or play an advocacy role concerning environmental reporting has been a subject of debate for decades. While most media organizations want to address environmental problems through objective reporting, some of them have proclaimed themselves environmental advocates. Objectivity is still viewed as the cornerstone of the journalistic profession although there has been an emphasis on the perspectives of the reporters in recent years (Sachsman & Valenty, 2015). Objectivity in environmental reporting means that 'reporters often attempt to distance themselves and their readers from the environmental struggle to effect a shift in the public consciousness, taking refuge instead in the objectivism of science' (Killingsworth & Palmer, 1992, p. 149). A journalist sees himself as a neutral voice that is willing to report on an environmental issue only when there is adequate and indisputable evidence. However, very few reporters have the ability to understand how scientific is the evidence about an environmental issue (Friedman, 1991). Unlike scientists who are guided by theories, journalists are guided by the reality they observe. Therefore, what journalists observe can be described differently or can even be disputed (Tuchman, 1973).

Environmental stories are rarely presented in explicitly political terms but in relation to consumerism, conservation and civic responsibilities. One of the reasons why environmental issues attract media attention is that they can be presented in non-partisan terms even while fostering environmental protest subversively (Lowe & Morrison, 1984). While the stories may appear to be politically balanced, they may be promoting an environmental cause without conspicuously deviating from the principle of balance. However, maintaining balance in news stories means that environmentalists and their opponents are given equal space or time in the media without making any judgement as to who is right or who is wrong. In such a situation, environmentalists would find it hard to 'convince the public that an issue in fact is a problem' (Hannigan, 1995, p. 68). Those who argue that journalists should take an active part in environmental protection say that reporting should go beyond what the sources say and place the issue in a proper perspective. It is believed that objectivity as a principle of reporting encourages uncritical reporting of what officials and those in positions of power say. In this way, 'the individual biases of journalists are avoided but institutional biases are reinforced' (Beder, 1998, p. 204). Reports that appear to be objective in reality represent the dominant values in society. The government, industry and other institutions including media agree as to what constitutes objectivity.

A reporter who challenges the dominant values and openly espouses a point of view on an issue is seen as violating the norms of journalistic practice. The public and media professionals have different perspectives on how the media function in a society. While the public tend to see media in relation to profits, political influence and sensationalism the media professionals tend to see them as impartial communicators who separate fact from opinion (Dennis, 1991).

Because of the concern expressed by some activists and scientists that the media are not doing an adequate job with regard to covering environmental issues, a few have called on the media to abandon their traditions of 'objective' reporting. They argue that journalists must become 'advocates' if society is to prevent climate change, depletion of the ozone layer, deforestation, soil erosion, degradation of oceans and loss of biodiversity (World Resources Institute, 1989). In their view, the time is running out and that one cannot afford to wait for the audience to come to their own conclusions. Stressing the pro-active role of media, Rubin and Sachs (1973, p. 7) argued that the education system would not be able to keep pace with social problems and that would leave the 'burden of educating the public about scientific and technological challenges squarely upon the mass media'. What they suggested was that the media had to do something more than mere reporting to move people to action. Lester Brown, the founder of the environmental research organization Worldwatch Institute who emphasizes the role of media in environmental education, says:

> We don't have time for the traditional approach to education—training new generations of teachers to train new generations of students—because we don't have generations, we have only years. The communications industry is the only instrument that has the capacity to educate on the scale needed and in the time available. (Cited in Detjen, 1991, pp. 93–94).

Advocacy is strongly recommended, as the media have the ability to educate millions of people in a short span of time. It is considered as an important means through which further damage to the environment can be prevented with a sense of urgency.

But, Detjen (1991) who was the founder president of the International Federation of Environmental Journalists (IFEJ) argues that though the media coverage of environmental issues is often lacking, advocacy journalism is not an answer. He says:

> I believe that advocacy journalism if it means one-sided and unfair reporting, is misguided and in the long run counterproductive. If major newspapers, magazines, and broadcast stations adopt an advocacy philosophy, the media will be treading on dangerous ground that could alienate readers and viewers and cause them to stop trusting the media. Journalists who have spent their careers establishing reputations for fairness and accuracy could suddenly find their credibility evaporating. (Detjen, 1991, p. 94)

He prefers traditional approaches of media such as investigative reporting, agenda setting and mass education to advocacy. Although it is hard for a journalist to be free of value judgement, Detjen argues that it is important for journalists to be balanced and fair even when they report views with which they do not agree.

Keya Acharya says that she too does not believe in advocacy (personal communication, 11 September 2020). She says:

> What I do believe in is doing serious research and placing the facts before the readers. It is through our investigation and through writing that we can help bring attention to the problems. If you take for instance the present issue of laying a railway line between Ankola and Hubli. What I would do is to present the harm it is going to do to the Western Ghats. I would write about the economics of the project and the impact on water, health, biodiversity, and ecological balance. I would also write about possible alternatives. I would put it in such a way that people will think of doing something about it. You will have to argue it out. You can't scream or protest as a journalist. You have to battle it out differently.

She believes that doing research and placing facts before the people are more important than advocating a cause. A journalist is expected to be different from those who shout slogans on the streets while holding a protest demonstration. According to her, consistent and sustained coverage of certain issues with evidence will certainly help the cause of environmental protection.

Science and environmental journalist T. V. Jayan says that he has no problem with advocacy provided those who advocate have a scientific outlook and present their arguments with evidence and without biases (personal communication, 11 September 2020). As a person from the science background, he feels that it is important to ask uncomfortable questions to even those who are advocating a cause. According to him, environmental journalism today has gone much beyond reporting about nature. 'If you are saying that big dams are bad you will have to provide adequate evidence and if you are saying that nuclear energy is bad then you need to provide a scientific explanation,' he says.

Explaining the problems associated with advocacy in environmental reporting, he says that those who believe in advocacy tend to produce one-sided stories that do not include views of those who do not agree with them. He illustrates it with his experience of working with the *Down to Earth* magazine 15 years ago.

I was doing a 4000-word story about nuclear energy for the Down to Earth magazine with arguments mostly against the nuclear option. Though this was a special story on which I had spent a considerable amount of my time I refused to take a byline until the last moment because I had not got any response from the Department of Atomic Energy (DAE). The questions I had sent to the officials at the DAE were difficult to answer. I was under pressure to let the story go to print without their response. Since I was not comfortable with a one-sided narrative I had decided that I wouldn't use my byline unless I had the response from the DAE. The response which was delayed because of the bureaucratic process was faxed to me at the last moment. I decided to take the byline only after I included the statements of the DAE officials. You have to have a balance of this kind. We should allow the other person to express his opinion even if we think he is wrong.

Jayan says that many activists have become journalists and, in turn, journalists have also become activists and many of them do not take the arguments that the other person is putting forth. In specialized magazines like the *Down to Earth*, the coverage can be one-sided because it is brought out by an organization that is involved in advocacy. But professional values in journalism, according to him, demand that there is balance in the story in the sense that opposing voices are not excluded.

Journalists consider it important to maintain their tradition of healthy scepticism, questioning the government, corporations and even environmental groups. The code of the Asian Forum of Environmental Journalists (AFEJ), adopted in 1998, says,

> The journalist should not be influenced on environmental issues by vested interests—whether they are commercial, political and governmental or non-governmental. The journalist ought to keep a distance from such interests and not ally with them. As a rule, journalists are expected to report all sides of an environmental controversy. (Asian Mass Communication Bulletin, 1998, p. 2)

Reporting all sides of an issue suggests that the reports only provide news from diverse sources but do not provide a perspective.

Many journalists use terms like accuracy, fairness and balance instead of 'objectivity' as they find it hard to claim that they are fully objective in producing stories (Reese, 1990). Many argue that the media embrace of professional objectivity leads to a lack of public debate and may result in inadequate information reaching the audience. Chapman et al. (1997) who interviewed journalists reporting on environmental issues in India and the UK found that while the Western reporters claimed to be neutral, the Indian reporters associated with the English press claimed to be campaigners.

Environmental activists argue that there is no objectivity in journalism at all. Within the profession too they say advocacy is rarely encouraged and journalists are criticized by their own professional colleagues for being activists and not following standard professional practice. Activists say those who go out of the way to cover some environmental stories receive a lot of flak. They see a tendency among many journalists to see advocacy in reporting as violation of the principle of objectivity because of which they refuse to go beyond their conventional mindsets. Environmental activist Vidya Dinker says journalists like any ordinary citizen see everything through their own lens, their own viewpoint, their own experience and what they value in their lives (personal communication, 5 May 2021). She rejects the entire claim about objectivity in reporting and argues that there could be some objectivity only when robots begin to write stories. However, she emphasizes that one cannot be certain about even robots because they are designed by individuals who have their own ideas, biases, likes and dislikes. According to her a subjective view is inevitable in any story that is analytical. Dinker says:

> So long as there are individuals going out, witnessing something and writing a story involving emotions and mental processes there cannot be any objectivity. There is nothing wrong in calling out something that seems to be wrong environmentally, constitution-ally, legally or from the perspective of rights. The job of the journal-ist is to highlight that and take it to the people or the authorities. I think that is the inherent job of the journalist. A journalist is not some rarefied creature who does not breathe oxygen and sits in ivory tower where he does not eat or drink. If the food is poisoned by the chemical that farmers are forced to buy the journalist should write about it. If you are doing it, you are not an activist but a good jour-nalist. If MRPL is spewing out toxins into the atmosphere beyond the legally permissible limits, you must write about that because it is going to affect the health of the people living around it. If the government has not done anything and has failed to put systems in place between the first wave and the second wave of corona virus journalist has to write about it. If that is advocacy, we need a lot it.

Dinker feels that for an environmental movement to grow and to push people to act against environmental degradation, advocacy in reporting is essential. She found local Kannada newspapers showing greater concern about pollution and displacement than the English newspapers. Local newspapers relentlessly covered the struggle against MRPL and MSEZ highlighting the impact of their impact on the livelihoods of the people while the coverage in the state level newspapers was sporadic and sketchy. The advocacy role played by the local media helped the environmental cause in Dakshina Kannada district but they could not make a significant impact on political leaders and bureaucrats in the state capital who were the decision-makers.

Activists Leo Saldanha of the ESG and Rohin Kumar of Greenpeace also strongly argue that the media should play an advocacy role so that people become aware of the environmental issues that would otherwise be ignored. They reject the very idea of objectivity in journalism and argue that it is no longer in practice in many media because of their links with the dominant economic forces. They feel that advocacy is necessary to bring pressure on the government to desist from giving clearance to unsustainable projects and to act against those who violate the environmental law.

Reporter vs Journalist

Media commentators make a distinction between reporting and journalism and the nature of work reporters and journalists do (Greenslade, 2009). While reporting is gathering information, writing reports based on facts, journalism is going beyond facts and digging deeper into the news. Journalism involves going into the depth of an issue through investigation, analysis and thoughtful commentary (Snells, 2009). It is also time-consuming and expensive as it involves piecing together of pieces of information and placing them in a proper perspective. A reporter is one who gathers and transmits information while a journalist attempts to educate people and influence their lives. There has been a debate about the decline of journalism in the context of electronic and social media almost instantly reporting events. Environmental activists expect the media to go beyond reporting of environmental issues and produce analytical reports based on investigation. They do not want media persons to be reporters of events and speeches but advocates of environmental causes.

Leo Saldanha of the ESG makes a distinction between a reporter and a journalist based on his own experience with media. He says a journalist is an analytical creature, whereas a reporter only narrates what happens in a press conference as it is. When a journalist moves from a formative stage into an analytical frame, he is supposed not to accept information as it is but test it himself and re-narrate it based on his understanding and experience. Journalism should not be mistaken as a neutral thing at all. It is a position where a journalist puts forward his understanding and experience. It is an argumentative position that can keep shifting in the context of changing realities. When a journalist goes beyond reporting what someone said into the depth of issues, he is certainly moving closer to advocacy.

According to Saldanha (personal communication, 12 October 2019) the audiences want a journalist to argue and present a perspective. A journalist has to take a stand and argue his position because he has seen something happening. He should report not only what he sees but also what he thinks. Saldanha suggests that NDTV India's Ravish Kumar could be a model journalist for those who want to report on environmental issues because he presents facts in a meaningful context and appeals to his audience to see, think and act. 'Ravish Kumar takes on people on what their claims are and tears them apart. Whatever he says is based on evidence. He helps us understand issues,' he says. Journalists are expected to put forth a sound argument before their audience, not just pieces of information. While Ravish Kumar, according to Saldanha, is an advocacy journalist, many in the journalistic fraternity are only reporters because they neither go into the depth of an issue nor take a stand on it.

Most of the journalists when asked about advocacy in environmental journalism say that activism is built into the practice of environmental journalism. They are of the view that the bias in favour of an environmental cause is the responsibility of public-spirited journalists and they must make all efforts to push the government and the people into action. India has had a long tradition of advocacy in journalism. Gandhi and Ambedkar were advocacy journalists who brought out journals that had political and social reforms as their agenda. They were more views papers than newspapers. During the Indian freedom movement in the first half of the 20th century, there was nothing like a journalist being neither with the British nor with the Indians. It was a calling for the cause of the nation. They were freedom fighters as well as journalists attempting to mobilize people's support for freedom and social reforms. 'A journalist has to be biased towards the future of this planet. Journalists reporting on the environment invariably become pro-environment,' says senior environmental journalist Nagesh Hegde (personal communication, 14 October 2018).

Hegde's firm belief is that activism or advocacy is at the very core of environmental reporting. After he wrote articles about the Kaiga nuclear power plant, the Western Ghats and the Kali project in Uttara Kannada district of Karnataka in *Prajavani* daily and weekly magazine *Sudha,* many institutions and citizens' groups began inviting him to give lectures. Sometimes after the lectures were over, the groups would take out marches and would give him a banner to hold. He found it difficult to say no to hold the banner when someone handed it over to him. The other newspapers began saying that he had become an activist. 'The management probably heard about all this and felt that I was a biased person', he says. While he was asked to write editorials on various issues, he was not asked to write editorials on energy and environment as he was seen as a biased person. However, there were absolutely no restrictions on what he wrote in articles and features. *Prajavani* is now more open and asks Hegde to write one or two editorials every month on environmental issues (personal communication, 9 August 2021). There is a realization that a lot of damage has been caused to the environment and that there is nothing like natural calamity and that all calamities are man-made. What was once seen as activism is now being accepted as a necessity.

Mohit Rao, who has been reporting environmental issues for *The Hindu,* is of the view that journalism always has an angle of advocacy (personal communication, 21 February 2019). If smoking is bad for health, he says, the media should not hesitate to say that. Health hazards always outweigh economic benefits. The industrial lobby and the bureaucracy would not want the media to do the advocacy job. It is important for the journalist to be on the side of the truth. When it comes to the forest rights of the Adivasis, the newspapers must advocate the rights of the tribes to have access to the resources of the forest. According to Rao, until recently the newspapers took a middle course with regard to the benefits and environmental consequences of large dams but now with indisputable evidence before them that the dams have caused large-scale destruction, most media are opposed to the building of large dams. They advocate non-conventional ways to meet the needs of irrigation and power.

While passionately defending the advocacy role of the media, Meera Bhardwaj says that journalism is bigger than mere reporting and that media should play the advocacy role with regard to environmental issues (personal communication, 27 March 2019). As a citizen, she feels, it is the responsibility of a journalist to remain committed to preventing environmental destruction 'I am first a citizen and then a journalist. It is everyone's duty to protect the resources of this country. Even in the residential layout where I live I always fight with those who cut down trees or cause pollution,' she says. Bhardwaj has been doing environmental reporting out of her own interest, not because her editors assigned to her environmental news. She says it is to everyone's knowledge that development has been unsustainable but the politicians and bureaucrats do not pay attention to it. It is the responsibility of the media to bring pressure on them to act to prevent further degradation of the environment. Depleting natural resources, especially water, has been a matter of great concern for her. She is of the view that journalists have to go beyond the confines of traditional reporting and actively push for immediate action to halt further depletion of natural resources.

Journalists, according to her, can also work as catalysts in dealing with environmental issues. She explains with an example how a pro-active role played by a journalist can help address a problem of water contamination. Every year, lakhs of people visit Male Mahadeshwara temple located in the MM Hills Wildlife Sanctuary in Chamarajanagar district of southern Karnataka. A natural water source upstream of the temple known as *antaragange* used to get contaminated with sewage, plastic debris and faecal matter. People and wild animals used to consume the same water as it flowed down. The temple located in the ecologically sensitive area was supposed to follow the guidelines of the Ministry of Environment and Forests and construct a sewage treatment plant (STP). Despite the fact that the forest officials sent several letters to the temple authorities, nothing had been done. As she began piecing together detail about the issue, the forest officials themselves requested Bhardwaj to write about it. After her story appeared in the *New Indian Express*, different authorities of the government like revenue, forest, police came together and held a meeting leading to the formulation of guidelines as to who should do what during the festival to protect wildlife and forest. Following Bhardwaj's (2018) report in *The New Indian Express* on 30 November 2018, the temple authorities cooperated with the other authorities in taking measures to prevent contamination of the natural water source. The newspaper played the role of a catalyst in moving officials to act to contain pollution of a water source.

On the impact of her reporting of environmental issues, she says sustained coverage of an issue in the public interest will bring some positive results. If reporters simply report and do not take up a public cause when necessary, the purpose of journalism is not served. Bhardwaj says, it is the responsibility of the media to report from the point of view of the poor, the marginalized and the politically alienated people who have been victims of environmentally destructive development. Even while trying to preserve the forest and wildlife it is also important to ensure that the livelihoods of people who had been inhabitants of the forest for generations are not disturbed. However, there have been several cases of people being displaced from the forest and not being properly compensated and rehabilitated. Twenty-five people who were displaced by the Bhadra Tiger Reserve in Karnataka had been waiting for compensation for over five years as part of their relocation programme. They were unable to use their land inside the reserve and at the same time, they were unable to move out of the forest. Their livelihood had been affected. *The New Indian Express* carried a story detailing the desperate situation of these people who had voluntarily agreed to leave the Reserve. She took all their names and the amount of compensation they were to be given and wrote a story in the *Indian Express*. A day after the story was carried in the newspaper, compensation was paid to them.

In the Bhimgad Wildlife Sanctuary in Belagavi district a resort had been built in violation of the Wildlife Protection Act. Bhardwaj wrote a series of stories on how the Soutira Mini Water Park and Resort had gone about constructing luxury cottages and a swimming pool without obtaining necessary permission from the Forest Department and the National Board for Wildlife. Her first story appeared on 26 November 2016, and as she continued to write on the illegal construction there was pressure on the Forest Department to act. The resort was ultimately demolished on 27 December 2016. Newspapers usually boast about the impact of their stories but Bhardwaj feels no newspaper should gloat over its own professional work. Strongly defending advocacy in reporting she says, 'A responsible journalist has to serve the public because if the society is benefited the journalist is also benefited'.

Environmentalist and leader of the Appiko movement Panduranga Hegde sees only a thin line of difference between advocacy and objectivity in media (personal communication, 26 February 2019). He argues that advocacy should be based on facts and indisputable evidence but complete neutrality is not at all possible.

Some journalists have been associated with civil society groups that are involved in advocacy but to what extent their involvement in such groups has influenced their coverage of environmental issues is difficult to say. India's well-known environmental journalist Darryl D'Monte was an advocate of citizens' involvement in caring for neighbourhoods. He was the president of Bandra West Residents Association, a trustee of Mumbai Waterfronts Center, a member of Apna Mumbai Abhiyan, Chair of the Celebrate Bandra Trust and a convener of Celebrate Bandra festival (Babu, 2019).

According to the journalists and activists interviewed here, journalists' engagement with environmental movements and civil society organizations should not be seen as something that interferes with their professional work so long they base their arguments on facts. Nagesh Hegde took part in the public hearing on the proposed expansion of the Kaiga nuclear power plant held on 14 December 2018 and argued that the environmental impact assessment (EIA) had not said anything about how the nuclear waste from the plant was going to be disposed of (Sadashiva, 2018). He also said at the meeting that the radiation from the plant would last over 20,000 years affecting several generations. At the public hearing, Hegde was speaking on behalf of those who were protesting against the expansion plan. He has participated in such programmes as he feels they are necessary to create awareness. In situations where preventing an environmental hazard appears very urgent, journalists have taken part in protests and public hearings along with advocacy groups.

Truth and the Fairness

The principle of fairness, which gives equal importance to both sides of an issue, is valued as a standard practice in journalism. While reporting events and issues, professional norms require journalists to keep their stories free of their own biases. They are expected to present facts as they are and opinions as they come from sources. Fairness in reporting means that a journalist provides all sides of a story without making any judgement himself. The readers are expected to arrive at their own conclusion based on the information and opinions given in the news stories. The standard journalistic practices that might work well with reporting of events and speeches many not always work with covering environmental issues.

Environmentalists argue that an environmental reporter has to be on the side of the truth and the victim. If he gives equal importance to the polluter and the victim, the readers may not be able to arrive at their own judgement, which is considered necessary in addressing an issue. If a serious threat to life appears a possibility, a journalist is expected to be on the side of those whose lives are threatened. Environmental activist Panduranga Hegde explains why balance in a news story is problematic with the example of a polluting paper mill. The West Coast Paper Mill in Dandeli of Uttara Kannada district, which has been releasing effluents into the Kali River, poses a serious threat to the lives of three lakh people who depend on the river. If a journalist takes the version of the company and the Karnataka State Pollution Control Board (KSPCB) then everything is fine according to their online monitoring system. A journalist will understand the truth only when he goes to the ground and sees the dead cows that drank the contaminated water in the river. In such a situation a journalist has to use his analytical ability and reveal the truth.

In Nagesh Hegde's view, when the truth is exposed it does not become advocacy but a revelation of truth and if advocacy means exposing the truth, Indian media need more of it. 'The truth has to be presented but unfortunately, it is suppressed in the name of maintaining balance. The dominant forces in the society want the truth always suppressed and that's why they often talk about balance in news coverage,' he says.

In many places, the local activists who have been part of the long environmental struggles have become journalists. Activism and environmental journalism have become inseparable. When the activists feel that mainstream media with wider audiences do not do their job, they decide to play the role of the journalists themselves. Development journalist Shivananda Kalave says that out of necessity there has been an intermixing of activism and journalism in the Uttara Kannada district of Karnataka, where the environmental movement has been active for nearly four decades (personal communication, 27 March 2019). Beginning with the protests against the Bedthi hydel power project in the late 1970s, the activists themselves became writers because they had discovered that the information they had provided was not being reported correctly in media. If the activists had focused on something in their statements and petitions, the journalists would focus on something else. The activists wanted certain aspects of the issues to be highlighted and decided that they must themselves explain the problems to the people. When they started writing, they began forcefully arguing against the projects that were detrimental to the ecology of the Western Ghats. They set the trend for advocacy journalism in the district. While the truth was strictly adhered to, the balance had tilted towards the people who were going to lose their land and homes for the hydel project.

Ashok Hasyagar, chief editor, *Janamadhyama*, a daily published from Sirsi, says that one of the distinctive features of the environmental movement in the Uttara Kannada district has been that many of those who participated in the movement have been journalists and writers (personal communication, 27 February 2019). They know how to explain the effect of deforestation with the example of the felling of a single tree. They ask questions to the politicians as if it is their responsibility to protect the environment. Advocacy has been a feature of journalism in the Uttara Kannada district of Karnataka. When the so-called development project itself is unfair and unjust, how can someone demand balance in a news report? Should one talk about benefits of destruction to achieve balance in a story? Hashyagar asks.

Journalists have not only reported possible harm a project would cause but have also been instrumental in bringing public personalities and the people into the environmental movement. Muralidhar Khajane wrote a series of articles in *The Hindu* in 2007 about the proposed 1,000 MW coal-fired thermal power project at Chamalapura in Heggadadevenakote taluk of Mysore district. After writing the series, he met well-known writer, thinker and Jnanpith awardee Professor U. R. Ananthamurthy who was then residing in Mysore and explained to him the harm the proposed plant was going to cause to the environment (personal communication, 26 June 2019). The proposed plant that was to come up on 2,000 acres of fertile land would displace 20,000 people and pollute the air putting at risk the lives of the people in Mysore city only 15 km away from the proposed plant. He succeeded in convincing Ananthamurthy to get involved in the movement against the project. By making consistent efforts to get a public personality involved in an environmental struggle, he had crossed the boundaries of traditional journalism. Khajane says:

> You may call it activism, but I convinced Ananthamurthy that some immediate action was needed. He promised that he would write a letter to the chief minister about the consequences of building the power plant and if the proposal was not withdrawn he would join the movement. When media, people, and public intellectuals like Anantamurthy work together it is possible to strengthen a movement. His involvement and the resistance by the villagers with the support of the newspaper ensured that the project was dropped.

Khajane's conviction is that a journalist has to go beyond mere reporting to push people into action especially in matters related to the environment. Sticking to the notion of balance would not have brought the pressure on the government to shelve the thermal power plant. K. G. Vasuki special correspondent, *The Pioneer*, Bengaluru, says that the so-called balance in a news story would not be useful when a threat to an ecosystem has to be removed (personal communication, 26 June 2019). Besides reporting about the dangers of the Chamalapura thermal power plant for the news agency Asian News International (ANI), he made a documentary film titled 'Death Knell to Nilgiri Biodiversity' in 2008 in collaboration with another journalist Maya Jaideep. In his report for the agency and in his film, Vasuki says there was no balance but support for the protesting villagers (personal communication, 25 June 2019). The film showed the threat the plant would pose to the biosphere and the livelihoods of the farmers and at the end gave a call to the people to support the movement. The film also contributed to the strengthening of the movement and calling off the project.

Muralidhar Khajane says that beyond the larger narratives of liberalization, industrial interests and management of media channels there are micro-narratives through which issues can be brought before the public (personal communication, 25 June 2019). Construction work for a 100 per cent export-oriented dye and pigment manufacturing industry promoted by Highland Pvt. Ltd, a joint venture between the US-based M/s Engelhard and India-based M/s Highland Pvt. Ltd, began in December 1996 at Kadandale village in Dakshina Kannada district of Karnataka. The plant was to manufacture pigments and dyes to be used to colour the United States' currency.[1] The project was approved by the Government of Karnataka despite the fact that it was only 10 meters away from the Shambhavi river. Questions were raised as to whether it was a case of a developed country dumping a hazardous industry in the Third World. People began protesting against it under the banner of the Shambhavi River Protection Committee. *Prajavani* carried a detailed report with the views of the experts, environmentalists and the local people. *Prajavani*'s report was discussed in the Assembly and several members demanded that the proposal be dropped (Poornima R., personal communication, 26 June 2019).

[1] https://esgindia.org/new/campaigns/engelhard-highland-coloring-us-dollar-bills/

An expert committee was sent to visit the site and submit a report. When the committee held a meeting with the representatives of the industry but refused to listen to the views of the people of the village, *Prajavani* carried a report criticizing the committee for violating the right of the villagers to be heard. Despite the newspaper's campaign against the project, it was not dropped. Since the newspaper's efforts did not produce any positive results it was decided to try other means of building a strong resistance to the project.

The people of the Kadandale village had a strong faith in *buta kola* (spirit performance), a ritual where local spirits channelized by a ritual are asked to deliver judgement on disputes. To get the strong support of the community, Muralidhar Khajane who was then a correspondent of *Prajavani* at Mangalore reported about the impact of the industry and spoke to the local political leaders about the possibility of holding *buta kola* to ask the *buta* whether the industry could be permitted. The leaders of the community accepted the suggestion and arranged for the *buta kola*. During the *buta kola* the question as to whether the factory should be allowed near the Shambhavi river was referred to the *buta* and the *buta* decreed that no such factory be allowed. Once the decree came from the *buta*, people of the community living in places as far as Mumbai rushed to the village. The movement against the project was energized with the involvement of more and influential people. A lot of political pressure was brought on the government leading to the dropping of the project. A newspaper's correspondent was not only reporting what was happening in the village but played an important role in helping the village community come up with strategies to ensure that the project was scrapped. According to Khajane, these are micro-level cultural narratives that can be used to deal with issues of the environment. The activist role of a journalist in making use of a ritual to mobilize people against the project, solidarity among the people of the village and the critical reports in the newspapers had made a combined impact.

Cultural and social assertions do play an important role. But playing on faith can be very tricky because certain religious practices cause pollution and it is difficult to reason with those who cause such pollution. According to independent journalist B. S. Nagaraj who works with

ThePrint, although immersing the idols of Durga and Ganapathy in lakes and rivers during the annual festivals has been causing pollution, it is hard to question such practices as that would be seen as hurting the sentiments of the people. When he put up a flyer in his apartment asking the residents not to immerse the Durga idol in the nearby pond, there were angry reactions. He feels the media should play an advocacy role with regard to educating people about the harmful consequences of immersing idols in water and the burning of crackers during the Deepavali festival, but trying to use the beliefs and emotions of the people can be risky and at times can be counterproductive.

One of the ways to find out if newspapers are playing the advocacy role with regard to an issue is to look for mobilizing information in environmental stories. Mobilizing information is information found in the news that helps people act on attitudes they already hold (Einsiedel & Coughlan, 1993; Hoffman, 2006; Lemert, 1981; Lemert et al., 1977; Nicodemus, 2010). Mobilizing information is useful to the people who get involved in political or social movements. The news stories give information to the readers about what to do, where to go, whom to contact, whom to send a petition, etc. with regard to an issue. By providing such details, newspapers try to get people involved in a programme of environmental action. Frequent appearance of mobilizing information in a newspaper is an indication that it is playing an advocacy role. Mobilizing information helps environmental groups or civil society organizations to get people to participate in protest demonstrations or rallies. It is rarely found in mainstream media but often seen in the alternative media including the digital media. Even when newspapers give a favourable coverage to an issue they may hardly provide any mobilizing information (Adiga & Poornananda, 2012).

Unlike political reporting where balance is a key element, environmental reporting requires analysis of harmful consequences and a call for action. When there is stark injustice so visible, the principle of balance is not so important, and the journalist should be on the side of justice. A journalist needs to be the voice for the voiceless. When the forest in which Adivasis live, is being destroyed endangering their livelihood the journalists must speak on their behalf. The presence of a strong environmental movement, as in the case of Uttara Kannada district of Karnataka, is likely to influence environmental advocacy in media.

Rohin Kumar, the media specialist of Greenpeace India and an independent journalist, says that media often play the advocacy role during the times of crises (personal communication, 20 May 2021). In the context of COVID-19 pandemic of 2020–2021, he says that media have played the advocacy role. The media appealed to the people to wear masks and stay safe. They not only gave valuable information about how people should protect themselves from the virus but also urged them to take vaccine. The media, according to Kumar, can play the same kind of advocacy role with regard to the environmental crises. He says,

> The advocacy role of the media deserves appreciation. They are doing it because people's lives have to be saved. If the media are playing advocacy role with regard to some environmental issues what is the problem. It is about saving life. I am also a reporter and write for some independent publications. I would not be satisfied with reporting about death or injuries. I would go into how they were caused and how they can be prevented in future. I must ensure that the victims have got relief and justice. I do not agree with this 'objectivity' argument. When the media are playing advocacy role with regard to the pandemic why can't they do the same with regard to an environmental problem? Media should ask questions on behalf of the people. Are media objective when they take the side of the government or the corporate houses? If you are running your newspaper on the money of the corporations how would you be objective? Is there any single channel, left, right or centre that is objective? They are trying to escape from their responsibility. Nothing is objective. Where are the objective reports about the industries that have posed serious threat to the lives and liberties of the people? Many publications have vested interests in industrial projects. Are there objective reports about large-scale environmental destruction taking place in the north-east? The people would have been happy if the media had played their role properly and dug out the truth. It is not fair to object to reporting the truth by insisting on objectivity. (Personal communication, 20 May 2021)

Kumar also finds the term 'balance' problematic. If the media are funded by the government or by a corporation and if there are tribes who are protesting to save their lands from acquisition for an industrial plant how is a journalist supposed to strike a balance? He poses this question and says that most of the media houses in the country including the English and the regional press are biased towards the government. When only a small publication reports the truth while a majority of the major media produce stories after stories defending the government or a corporation, the principle of balance loses its meaning. Often the governments and corporations demand balance in media stories even when they spend huge amounts of money on advertising and publicity. In such a scenario, it is important for the media to hold the polluting industries accountable and demand answers going beyond balance in their stories. In a way all environmental reporting is advocacy because it raises awareness (Neuzil, 2008, p. 128). One of the key questions has been whether reporters' advocacy role harms the business of a newspaper. While it may attract more readers and boost the circulation of newspapers, it may harm the businesses of those who either have invested in the newspaper or have been advertising in it.

Advocacy in Alternative Media

Activists and environmental groups involved in environmental advocacy have their own publications, blogs, websites and social media platforms. They put out lot of information and persuasive messages through the alternative media to move their audience to action. Alternative points of view that are not often seen in mainstream media are found here. The technology has lowered the barrier to publishing today as it provides an opportunity to NGOs and activists to present their own news and opinions to the public. It has also helped them engage the audiences in a conversation. They have realized the power of technology in engaging their audiences and spreading their stories to influence the public debate in a way they could not have done before.

As many big media houses began downsizing the staff due to the financial trouble they were facing in recent years, many journalists moved to digital platforms. They began presenting their own analysis of environmental issues which might not have been possible in the publications for which they worked earlier. Some of them became transparent about their own political and ideological orientation and began writing despite the fact that they had limited audiences.

Some of the advocacy journals brought out by nongovernmental organizations have adopted professional journalistic practices thinning the line between activism and journalism. The *Down to Earth* magazine, brought out by the CSE, an environmental NGO, has been involved in advocacy ever since it was established in 1992 but a closer look at the contents and the narratives presented in the magazine reveals that journalistic norms and practices have not been ignored. In the inaugural issue of the magazine dated 31 May 1992 the founder-editor Anil Agarwal wrote, 'We intend to report all those things that a regular magazine or newspaper will report—finance, economics, politics, markets, diplomacy, conflicts, development. But we will look at all this with two eyes, the eyes of science and of environment' (cited in Narain, 2003). Explaining the purpose for which the magazine had been launched and the advocacy it would play, Agarwal said,

> Information is useful only if it leads to action. We hope the information we provide will not just be used by individuals in their daily work but also provide opportunities for networking, by the concerned to get to know each other and build bridges and partnerships. (Cited in Narain, 2003)

Providing accurate information and pushing the government, corporations and people to action have remained the major objectives. With a blend of advocacy and journalistic practices, the magazine enjoys high credibility because of its adherence to science and accuracy in coverage of environmental issues.

Comfort (2020) who conducted a study on the three magazines[2] brought out by three environmental NGOs found that the magazines

---

[2] The Sierra Club's *Sierra*, National Audubon Society's *Audubon* and Wilderness Society's *Wilderness*.

despite being advocates of environmental issues maintained the journalistic standards followed in commercial media. Those who came as editors to these journals with their experience in mainstream media introduced 'hybridity' of the journalistic and advocacy fields' (Comfort, 2020, p. 1094). Even while they were committed to advocacy, these magazines tried to uphold journalistic practices including accuracy, fairness and neutrality.

Their websites provide interactive content too. Environmental NGOs to a considerable extent rely on their own dissemination strategies as they are not always able to reach people through the mainstream media. With the increased use of electronic media for communication, NGOs feel that there is lesser scope for distortion or misinterpretation. Nagaraj believes that social media and online media have been putting out a lot of content on development and environmental issues. Some of the online media are not market-driven but are run through subscription and donations because of which they enjoy greater freedom. Advocacy, according to him, has moved from the mainstream media to the online media. Analytical reports on deforestation, mining, threats to wildlife and water pollution have appeared in the online media. However, digital platforms do not enjoy the kind of credibility that mainstream newspapers have. Lack of credibility seriously limits the possibility of any medium emerging as an effective tool of advocacy.

During the lockdown in 2020 and 2021 the environmental movement has gone digital. Social media usage has significantly increased since the beginning of the pandemic (Iqbal, 2021). The number of twitter users went up by 27 per cent in 2020 (Tankovska, 2021). The governments, corporations and the users keenly watch what people are saying on the social media. The hashtags play an important role in spreading awareness on issues related to the environment and climate change. In the summer of 2020 conversations in social media turned into mobilization of people that forced the Brazilian government to act against illegal burning and deforestation of the Amazon forests (TED, 2020). The young people around the world created powerful graphics to ease their audiences' data-heavy information. They used hashtags and memes to make their conversation on climate change more visible. The digital media brought young climate activists together. When the Ministry of Environment, Forests and Climate Change released a draft EIA notification in March 2020, environmentalists were up in arms arguing that the draft notification would dilute the procedure for EIA.[3] The climate action group 'Fridays for Future India' used its digital media platform *fridaysforfutureindia.com* to mobilize two million people to send suggestions and objections to the draft notification.

Despite the considerable impact, the digital platforms have made in mobilizing people for environmental action, the digital movement has been characterized as 'clicktivism' and 'slacktivism' suggesting that the participation is 'impulsive' and 'non-committal' (Finnegan, 2020). However, at a time when real world protests are not possible the digital platforms provide the forum for expressing voices of dissent, bypassing the traditional media controls.

Several digital publications provide in-depth and comprehensive analyses of environmental issues. The environmental and conservation news platform, *india.mongabay.com*, is published in English and Hindi. The website states that it is dedicated to 'evidence-driven objective journalism' and to play a role in shaping the media discourse around key environment-related topics. *Thethirdpole.net* publishes news and analysis on environmental issues concerning South, Central and Southeast Asia in six languages, including Hindi, Bengali, Urdu, Nepali and Russian.

There are also websites[4] that provide resources for activists looking to use digital technologies to increase their impact.

Despite the fact that the alternative media have the potential of reaching a wider audience, they have not been as influential as the print media. Environmentalist Panduranga Hegde is of the view that online and social media are not of much use as tools of advocacy because they do not reach the people who need to be reached. As several recent

---

[3] Among others, the draft EIA notification granted 'post-facto clearance' for projects and exempted 'strategic' projects from the assessment process. Environmentalists argued that public consultation process would be weakened.

[4] https://movements.org

surveys have shown, printed newspapers, irrespective of the quality of the content, are still seen as reliable sources of information and opinions. Although online newspapers carry a lot of content, they only reinforce what the printed newspapers have reported (Hoffman, 2006). Therefore, activists and NGOs value the advocacy role of print media with regard to environmental issues. One of the major problems with using new media for advocacy is that they can be censored easily. Many activists have complained about their Facebook posts and YouTube videos being taken off for allegedly posting objectionable material. Even while using the internet one has to constantly fight for the freedom of expression. In a real sense, no medium is free.

Conclusion

Whether media should play advocacy role with regard to environmental issues or stick to objective reporting of events has been a subject of debate for decades. While most media organizations want to address environmental problems through objective reporting, some of them proclaim themselves environmental advocates. The standard professional journalistic practice requires that news reports about the environmental issues are objective and free from opinions and biases of journalists. Objectivity essentially means separation of facts from value. A reporter is expected to provide a truthful account of an event or an issue without interpreting it subjectively. Advocacy in journalism is going beyond reporting and pushing a narrative and presenting a perspective. It also means that a reporter takes sides and expresses support for a cause. Advocacy in environmental reporting does not have universal acceptance among journalists as it is believed to be in conflict with professional journalistic practices. It goes beyond mere reporting and attempts to influence the readers to act so that an environmental problem is addressed. One of the criticisms against the ideal of objectivity is that it denies freedom to the journalist to interpret the reality and alienates him from the very report he produces. He is expected to work as a mere transmitter of information without delving into the causes and consequences of an environmental problem. Another criticism against objectivity is that what is presented as objective in media is in reality the ideology and the interest of the dominant forces.

Environmental activists have been arguing that journalists must abandon their practice of objectivity and become advocates if environmental degradation has to be prevented. Most of the journalists who have been reporting on environmental issues say that advocacy is at the very core of environmental journalism. They also say that advocacy should be based on facts but facts should be presented in a perspective that fully explains a problem to the readers. They also believe that balance in an environmental story that presents both sides of an issue may leave the readers with no clarity as to what the problem is. Going beyond facts and the notion of balance is considered important to ensure that an environmental threat is prevented. Environmental activists argue that there is nothing like objectivity in reporting as there are several factors that influence construction of news including the political economy of the media. While a majority of the journalists interviewed by this author do not find any problem with advocacy, some of them say that doing research, producing evidence and adhering to the professional values are more important than advocacy as that would make environmental stories more authoritative and credible. Some of the environmental journalists have gone beyond the bounds of journalism and have helped activists bring in public figures into the movement and mobilize the masses for the movement. They claim that they are first citizens and then journalists and feel that advocacy is needed to create awareness and to push the bureaucracy and political leadership into action.

In recent years, there is a lot more advocacy happening in the alternative media than in the mainstream media. Digital technology has allowed several organizations and individual activists to carry on environmental campaigns online. Some of the websites exclusively devoted to environmental issues have been publishing in-depth and comprehensive reports with audio and visual material. This has been immensely helpful to the organizations involved in advocacy. The environmental movement has gone digital with several digital platforms including social media carrying on sustained campaigns against environmental degradation and climate change. Despite many advantages of the digital media, they still lack the kind of credibility that traditional media enjoy. In recent years, frequent internet shutdowns and coercive restrictions have made the digital media unreliable as promoters of advocacy.

CHAPTER 4

Pressures on the Publishers and Journalists
From Resistance to Acquiescence

The media are frequently under pressure to publish or, most often, not to publish stories on certain issues. The government and the industry exert pressure in several ways directly not only on journalists but also on individuals and corporations that either own media or have made substantial investments in them. The government has legal provisions that can be selectively invoked to place restrictions on the media when they raise probing questions or when they provide space and time for dissenting voices. With the breaking down of the media revenue model in recent years, the internet being a major contributor, the mainstream media are being pushed to the limits of prioritizing revenue at the cost of their editorial independence. The government and private corporations as advertisers can choose only those media that give favourable coverage to them. Many of the major projects in which the government[1] is directly involved as a promoter, investor and

---

[1] A study conducted by Vidhi Centre for Legal Policy, an independent think tank, found that a majority of the environmental cases in the Supreme Court were against the government (*The Times of India*, 2021).

operator including large dams, thermal power plants, nuclear plants, mining, etc., are at the centre of the environmental debate. Some of the environmental movements are against polluting industries operated by private corporations. Both the government and the corporations would not want environmental issues associated with their 'development' projects given prominence in media. The media may self-censor their content as falling into their disfavour might mean losing huge advertising revenue.

Government agencies and big corporations shape the environmental discourse by regulating, prioritizing, foregrounding and disseminating information and opinions of their choice and marginalizing those that contradict them. The kind of environmental discourse that is prevalent in the country is largely influenced by the institutions that control political and economic power. Some of the media groups that are directly owned by big corporations cannot be expected to objectively write about environmental hazards associated with the industries owned or controlled by these corporations. Even when the corporations have no link with the media, they still influence the editorial content through their advertising support. They may stop advertising in those media that carry content that has the potential of harming their interests. The profit-driven mainstream media that are dependent on advertising revenue coming from big corporations would not want to offend the advertisers with stories about pollution caused by those corporations (Roy, 2014). Legal action is another way of exerting pressure on journalists, editors and publishers. There are many cases of defamation filed against journalists and publishers claiming huge damages. The legal process itself becomes a punishment and a deterrent as it takes a lot of time and money which many publishers can ill afford. Long legal battles sap the energies of journalists and serve as a disincentive for those who work with a missionary zeal in defending the public interest. In spite of all these pressures, some publishers have strongly asserted their independence and have defended their reporters. Some editors have also fought against all odds, stood by their colleagues and upheld the core values of journalism in holding government agencies and corporations responsible for environmental degradation.

Pro-establishment and Pro-industry Bias

Pro-establishment and pro-industry bias in media is visible when information and opinions of the officials and industry representatives are treated mostly as facts in news stories. What activists and NGOs say about an environmental issue is often taken with a pinch of salt. Both the government and the industry exercise a lot of influence on the mainstream media content because it is very hard for the media to survive without their support. The present business model of the media exerts a lot of pressure on them to toe the government line. According to Leo Saldanha of the ESG,

> Media have been told that they have to be pro-establishment; otherwise, their revenue streams would be turned off. There have been several cases where newspapers have been told that because they wrote a particular story they would not get government advertisements. That is a serious threat to the independence of newspapers. The editor is obviously under pressure to ensure that salaries are paid to his staff and has to work according to the revenue model of the newspaper. This has reached an alarming level in the last few years. (Personal communication, 21 February 2019)

When people have been fighting for the rights of the people it is essential that the media lend their support by reporting the truth. Saldanha says when the government took harsh measures in 2015 against international environmental group Greenpeace for raising environmental issues the media mostly put out pro-government reports. The raids conducted on the offices of Greenpeace by the Enforcement Directorate were portrayed as those that were necessary to ensure that there were no roadblocks to development projects in India. There were probably some issues with Greenpeace but it was clear that the organization was being deliberately targeted, says Saldanha and adds that because of the actions against Greenpeace an impression was created that all environmental organizations were the same. Many of those who work for various media lack a fair understanding of the complexities of the problem. According to Saldanha bureaucrats, politicians, journalists and even judges do not have a good understanding of what environmental issues are. He argues that when the ESG organized a protest to express its solidarity with Greenpeace the media turned up but played down the issue by parroting the government line.

In contrast to the view of Saldanha, the representative of Greenpeace Rohin Kumar finds no strong pro-government bias in media with regard to restrictions placed against the NGOs including Greenpeace (personal communication, 20 April 2021). He says most of the media understood that Greenpeace was involved in genuine work and that restrictions were not only on Greenpeace but also on the larger landscape of NGOs and civil society. According to him, Greenpeace was highlighted because it is an international organization but there were smaller grassroots organizations facing the heat from the government. The action against Greenpeace was also a tacit message to the media that they were not expected to report from the perspectives of the Greenpeace but barring a few newspapers, the media coverage was overall favourable, he says. He did not see a strong pro-government bias in the media coverage about restrictions placed on Greenpeace.

Pro-government bias was evident in some Hindi newspapers that carried lead stories on Greenpeace without even talking to anyone in the organization. Rohin Kumar says,

> *Dainik Jagran*, a leading Hindi daily, published a front page story on Greenpeace alleging that it was funded by foreign money despite the fact that we were not funded by any foreign company. The newspapers' journalists did not even bother to get in touch with us and take our quotes.

As a keen observer of media affairs, he says there are instances of the higher-ups in the government calling up the editors and objecting to the reports about certain environmental issues and demanding publication of reports highlighting their version. It is possible that some editors acquiesce to their demand as they face the prospect of losing the advertising revenue and other concessions.

Although Rohin Kumar does not see a strong pro-government bias generally in media, he sees a clear pro-industry bias in the coverage of environmental issues. He says,

The influence of the industry on media coverage of environmental issues is huge. The corporations make an impact on the editorial line. It is not just with small publications but all kinds of publications. Even those alternative media, which are now running on subscriptions, will come under pressure from corporations if they begin to depend on advertisements. Their digital platforms have to find alternative financial models. Otherwise, they might also end up in the same crisis as the conventional media.

According to Kumar, it is not only the mainstream media but even the alternative media are likely to come under the pressure of the corporations. In the absence of sure-fire business models for the alternative media there is uncertainty about how long they will remain free from the influence of financial forces, he says.

During the protests against Kudankulam nuclear power plant in 2011, a majority of Tamil newspapers were in support of the project. A couple of newspapers, which dared to write what they wanted, faced action. The Jayalalithaa government issued notices to 60,000 persons for joining the protest. Sedition charges were filed against the activists and every attempt was made to neutralize the movement although some media supported the activists. Leaders of the anti-nuclear movement were discredited and branded as anti-national. According to Leo Saldanha, there was no protest from the media houses that were completely under fear (personal communication, 21 February 2019). This is one example of the media becoming pro-establishment and pro industry despite overwhelming evidence on the harmful effects of the plant. When a German national[2] who went to Kudankulam was deported for allegedly funding the anti-nuclear movement a debate was held on *Times Now* with the sole purpose of defending the government action. Participating in the debate Leo Saldanha argued that just because a German national was there it did not mean that he was a spy. His voice was drowned out in the

---

[2] In an email interview to *The Hindu* after he was deported to Germany on 28 February 2012, Hermann Rainer Sonntag said that he was not affluent enough to fund any organization in India and that he was only a passive member of an ecological awareness group without any political orientation. He also claimed that he was in India as his savings were too small to live comfortably in Germany (Kolappan, 2012).

din of aggressive arguments in government's favour. They were not asking any questions on what the nuclear establishment was saying. The media were simply swallowing whatever the industry gave. The media did not pay attention to the argument of the protesters that what had happened at Fukushima in Japan could happen in India too. The details of the disaster that were available did not figure in the media reports that took the pro-nuclear stand. The point here is not that they must have supported the movement but they did not allow the views of the protesters to be heard. Only some online publications and a few newspapers that put out some critical stories. The extent of government and industry influence on the media content is a matter of concern when a large section of the population is facing a possible environmental crisis.

Giriprakash, Chief of Bureau, *The Hindu BusinessLine*, Bengaluru, is of the view that the policies that have long-term consequences are rarely enquired into by the media (personal communication, 26 June 2019). On the face of it, he says, a policy looks positive and innovative but a closer look into its effects tells much more. He describes how the policies take shape and how the media, because of their pro-government bias, ignore details:

> One of the justifications for introducing electric vehicles is that the pollution level will come down. But automated vehicles account for only four percent of the air pollution in India. What is the reason behind this? Why do they want to immediately convert all oil-run vehicles to electric vehicles? Is it possible at all? Since India does not manufacture lithium-ion batteries required for electric vehicles where will the batteries come? There was a small clause in the interim budget of February 2019 which said that the incentive for manufacturing lithium-ion batteries in India would be withdrawn. The batteries are going to be imported from China and the cost of electric vehicles is going to be three times more? At a time when auto sales have come down by 26 percent which is unprecedented who will be able to buy expensive electric vehicles? Unfortunately, media have not been questioning whether it is possible to bring down the total pollution level by focusing only on automobile industries. Media are simply parroting the government version without any critical view of their own.

He sees a total lack of analysis of the policy implications in media. The media have been uncritically reporting what the government and the industry have been saying without looking deeply into what electric vehicles mean to the common man and to the environment. Another issue he considers very serious is the 100,000 crore bullet train project between Ahmadabad and Mumbai that is going to destroy 53,000 mangroves. The media are so silent about it that there is not even a discussion on cost–benefit analysis. Some of the newspapers have praised it as a great project without taking into account the environmental cost. The development discourse has become so strong that it does not even allow a debate on the environmental consequences. 'If people talk about the environmental impact of the bullet train they are attacked and branded as anti-national. Journalists are being arrested and booked under sedition law for publishing articles critical of ministers and chief ministers,' says Giriprakash. The pressure the government and the industry exert on the media is evident in the absence of analytical stories on major policies concerning the transport sector.

The efforts of the activists in different parts of India to save trees have gone down the drain. In response to a question in Lok Sabha the Minister of State for Environment, Forests and Climate Change revealed on 26 July 2019, that between 2014 and 2019 the ministry had permitted cutting down of 1.09 crore trees for development purposes (Prasad, 2019). There was neither public outrage nor adequate media coverage about the cutting down of such a large number of trees and its consequences. Only brief statements of opposition parties questioning the government for permitting the felling of trees appeared in media. They seemed to believe in the government's explanation that trees had been cut for the purpose of development.

Industries influence media policies towards the environment either through ownership or through advertising (Althoff et al., 1973; Beder, 1998). A pro-industry bias about environmental issues is linked to the fact that big corporations that have high stakes in big projects control big media houses. Whether the rivers have water or not, the dams built across them are presented as symbols of development because they require massive investments running into thousands of crores. Corporations try to manipulate public hearings on projects by using the newspapers they own. A writ petition was filed in the Chhattisgarh High Court in 2011 against the DB Power Ltd, a subsidiary of the DB Corporation that owns 59 newspaper editions in 13 states including *Dainik Bhaskar* and *Daily News and Analysis* (DNA). The DB Power Ltd was accused of using 'deliberate, illegal and manipulative' measures to influence the public hearing on the proposed open cast coal mine (Sethi & Jebraj, 2011). On the eve of public hearing the Raigarh edition of *Dainik Bhaskar* carried two stories with the headlines 'Black diamond to lend sparkle to Dharamjaigarh's destiny' and 'Villagers move forward in support of DB power'. The stories had been carried with the intention of creating an impression among the readers that villagers were in favour of the mine. At the public hearing held on 28 February 2011 not a single project-affected person gave his or her consent. The affected persons had protested against the project as they feared that the mine would pollute their air, water and land. This is only one example of how big corporations try to use their media to influence public opinion in favour of their controversial projects.

Many environmental movements are against projects that are promoted by big corporations that control media either directly or through advertising. Journalists with concern towards the environment have to fight two battles at the same time; one against norms, routines and restrictions within the media organizations they work for and the other against the corporate interests. While editorializing is allowed in the case of political, crime and sports stories the same kind of freedom is rarely allowed in the case of environmental stories. Writing generally about the environmental issues in the Western Ghats or in the Himalayan region is not a problem but when it comes to a particular company building a harmful project or launching mining operations, there would be a lot of constraints on journalists.

Science and environmental journalist T. V. Jayan did a story on a chemical plant of a well-known Indian industrial house polluting Lake Natron in Tanzania a decade ago (personal communication, 11 September 2020). The lake became so polluted that the flamingos had stopped coming there. The story that was prepared after several days of investigation to gather accurate information was spiked.

No major Indian newspapers carried any critical story on the plant. Jayan says,

> Given the compulsions under which the editors work today my editor probably had strong reasons to reject my story. I too would probably have done the same had I been the editor because there are proprietors who have their own notion of what is good news and what is good for their business. I asked the editor three or four times bud he did not give any answer as to why my story was not carried. This is how things work in media when big corporations figure in news stories. If the company had been a different company not as well known as the Tata Company the editor would have carried the story. It is not that the company had bribed the editor or something but he made that decision probably on the basis the track record of the company over the decades. This was the only story that was held back and I never had a similar experience with any other story before or after that.

The reputation of a company and the editor's decision as to what meets the requirements of a story may determine whether a story is published. The editorial decisions are so complex and, at times, not explicable.

While newspapers express concern over environmental degradation, they tend to remain silent when an industrial unit of a big corporation is polluting the environment. Besides silencing media through their advertising money, corporations use their corporate social responsibility (CSR) programmes to influence the opinion of the people. The pressure on the media works in many ways.

There are several cases of corporations preventing the publication of stories about their environmentally harmful projects by threatening to withdraw advertisements. Most journalists deny any pressure by the industry on what they write but the advertising executives of the media organizations keep checking if stories critical of the big advertisers are being carried.

Mohit Rao who reported for *The Hindu* from Mangalore for some years, says,

> In Bengaluru, no corporation has tried to influence me with regard to publication of stories on environmental issues. But when I was

working at Mangalore the advertising people used to ask me if I wrote anything about Mangalore Refinery and Petrochemical Limited as it was one of the big advertisers in Mangalore. From the editorial side there have been no pressures on what to write or what not to write but there are some benchmarks. You can't write about one polluting company. For example, we can write about the sugar industry but not one particular sugar factory. On mining, we can write anything. We don't carry stories on individual companies causing pollution. If you take industries causing pollution in Penya in Bengaluru it is not one company that is causing pollution but all of those small companies. (Personal communication, 21 February 2019)

Instead of blaming a single industrial unit, he believes, it would be better to contextualize the problem by presenting a larger picture involving several industries.

Vidya Dinker who has been in the forefront of the environmental movement in Dakshina Kannada district says that *The Hindu* stopped carrying stories about the violation of environmental norms by Mangalore Special Economic Zone (MSEZ) and Mangalore Refinery and Petrochemicals Ltd (MRPL) because of the pressure from the advertising section (personal communication, 12 December 2018). A reporter of *The Hindu* would give only the company version and would become judgemental about the information provided by the activists. The newspapers would not carry anti-real estate stories even when they were blatantly violating environmental law. If the activists raised any question about the violation of environmental norms by any of the industries, journalists would go to the industry sources and put out their version that there was no violation and that all allegations against them were false.

There are also situations when reporters write stories with a lot of evidence showing violations of environmental norms but the editing desk cuts off certain parts that point to the accountability of the industries. This happens more often with the journalists who report from district centres to the state or national level newspapers. Journalists have told Vidya Dinker, who has often asked reporters about leaving out key aspects of issues related to industries in coastal Karnataka in their stories that the editing desks cut off parts of their stories (personal communication, 5 May 2021). She feels that reporters should write to their editors, and insist on carrying their complete stories. However, editing stories and even rejecting well-researched stories has been part of the professional practice. If the gatekeepers above the reporters do not allow stories that show industries and the government in poor light, the reporters have no other options.

When it comes to industrial, irrigation, energy and infrastructure projects, usually the government is involved in acquiring land, giving clearance and imposing conditions. Therefore, the government tends to tread with caution when there are charges of pollution against industries or project promoters. In several cases when environmental NGOs raise questions on certain projects, the response of the government and the industry tends to be the same. However, pollution may be the result of government inaction and defiance of the environmental law but reports that blame either of them are rarely to be found in media.

Since NGOs are not seen as authoritative agencies, it is difficult for them to get their version into the news stories. When CSE, an NGO, released a report in August 2003 which said that the soft drinks marketed by PepsiCo and Coca-Cola companies had pesticide residues several times above permissible limits, the companies' version defending the colas was prominently carried by the media. Newspapers carried PepsiCo chief's articles, which argued that the freedom of speech was being misused and that there was a need to impose 'norms and codes of conduct on NGOs' (Narain, 2017, p. 57). As companies that had pumped in a huge amount of advertising money into newspapers, they had easy access to space in newspapers to explain their version to the readers. It would not be possible for the NGOs to get that kind of space in newspapers. Besides, the companies had Hindi film stars Shah Rukh Khan and Aamir Khan[3] in their advertisements telling the

---

[3] Ironically, Aamir Khan launched a television show titled 'Satyamev Jayate' which had episodes on environmental pollution including chemical pollution. The experts he had in Episode 8 of Season 1 (23 June 2012) showed substantial evidence to point to the fact that pesticide industries were violating safety norms and poisoning the food chain.

audiences that the soft drinks were safe. The media provided time and space for the corporate houses to defend themselves against charges of violating safety norms.

There are several instances where the media have succumbed to the pressure of the big corporations. Nagaraj says that the companies like Jindal and Vedanta (personal communication, 26 June 2019) have hounded journalists in Chhattisgarh and Jharkhand, especially those who work for the local newspapers. In the coal belt that has witnessed a blatant violation of environmental law, there have been attacks on journalists with an attempt to silence the media. Senior journalist Umapathy who has been the Delhi correspondent for three major Kannada newspapers for nearly three decades says:

> There is no doubt that the media have played a supplementary or complementary role with regard to the environmental movement but they would not allow their reporters to file stories if they raise issues that are in conflict with their business interests as well as political interests. Many of the companies that own media are linked to the companies that have been carrying on mining operations in deep forests and other areas where mostly tribals live. We can see a clear change in the media attitude towards the environment in the post-liberalization era. The kind of zeal with which the media reported environmental issues during the pre-liberalization era is rarely to be seen in the later years. (Personal communication, 26 June 2019)

Umapathy sees a clear pro-industry bias in media coverage of environmental issues in the post-liberalization era dominated by a market-oriented neoliberal ideology. Journalists are free to write environmental issues so long as the business interests of the media owners are not affected. Once there is a conflict of interest, even well-researched stories are blocked.

The media ownership pattern is a major factor that has affected coverage of the environment. When a single corporate house controls a major share of the media market, it is hard to find views that question the very development model that has facilitated the growth of such a monopoly. Several media organizations are owned by multinational multi-billion corporations that are involved in several businesses such as forestry, pulp and paper mills, defence, real estate, infrastructure, oil wells, agriculture, steel production, water and power utilities. Given such a reality is it possible for a journalist to write about a polluting industry that the publisher owns or has invested in?

In the annual appraisals of journalists, the heads of newspaper editions are asked about the number of events they have organized in a year and the revenue they have generated. Giriprakash of *The Hindu BusinessLine* says that it is not unusual for business journalists to face pressure from a variety of people while writing reports about companies, especially those which are critical of their practices. Hence, it is important for them to be extremely careful while reporting about the corporate houses. He says 'facts need to be checked repeatedly to ensure that they are not targeted by vested interests both inside and outside their organisations. The sooner they realise the risks involved in practising this profession, the better for them' (personal communication, 19 July 2021).

Media organizations in which big corporations have neither ownership nor investment, advertisers greatly influence the content. The editors who allow stories on polluting industries owned by the advertisers run the risk of losing their advertising revenue. When news is selected based on the revenue it generates, taking on the big polluting industries which pump in a lot of advertising revenue into the media every day is a rare possibility. The bias in media coverage of environmental issues is often the outcome of the pressure the industries exert on media through ownership, investment or advertising.

Pressure on the Management

For any journalist who covers environmental issues support from the management is very crucial because of the pressure people with political and financial power exert on the media houses. If the managers of media organizations think that environmental stories do not have a readership and that they do not attract advertisements, they may discourage journalists from reporting on environmental issues. Advertising executives attending editorial board meetings have now become common in many media organizations. Their opinions matter in deciding what is to be reported in the newspapers. However, there are media managers who have thrown their full weight behind reporters doing investigative stories on environmental controversies.

According to senior journalist Poornima R. who worked for *Prajavani* as its assistant editor says that the newspaper's management has not buckled under corporate pressure when it came to environmental issues (personal communication, 26 June 2019). When the findings of the Delhi-based CSE about pesticide residues in soft drinks were reported in *Prajavani* and *Deccan Herald* in 2003, a six-member team of marketing executives from Pepsi and Coca Cola visited the office and told the management that all soft drinks sold by them were safe. The visit of the executives of the cola companies did not result in the newspaper going soft on the soft drink companies. The newspaper continued to carry stories based on the findings of the CSE.

When the Bhopal Gas Tragedy took place in December 1984 *Prajavani* called upon its readers not to buy Eveready batteries until the Union Carbide company gave compensation to the victims (Nagesh Hegde, personal communication, 12 October 2018). At that time, there were no clear laws with regard to compensation for the victims of such a massive industrial disaster. The *Prajavani* group decided that it was the responsibility of the citizens to teach the company a lesson by not buying its products. Unlike several countries in the West where people boycott products when there is such an appeal, the products of the Union Carbide company in India continued to sell. Within three weeks after the disaster, the company came up with an aggressive campaign with the slogan 'give me red'. The *Prajavani* group's campaign calling upon the readers not to buy *Eveready* batteries was muted by the loud and massive campaign by the company with a series of advertisements. Big corporations have the money to buy space and time and drown out critical voices. It is very rare that a media group stands up to a multinational company with an enormous amount of advertising budget at its disposal.

Nagesh Hegde, who wrote on environmental issues in *Prajavani* for over three decades, says the management of the newspaper gave him full freedom to write on any environmental issue. When Hegde was a young journalist, the chief editor of *Prajavani* K. N. Harikumar called him and asked him to explain to him about nuclear power and its environmental consequences before writing an editorial about it. The owner-editor of a newspaper group asking a young journalist to explain a problem to him before writing an editorial on it was something unique in journalism. This is a reflection of the extent to which the management valued the specialized knowledge of a journalist. Although *Prajavani* published innumerable stories on environmental controversies, journalists in the newspaper took enough precaution to ensure that no legal complications arose as a result of reporting on environmental issues.

Sticking to the facts and presenting analyses based on accurate information helps journalists avoid legal complications. Polluting organizations often use litigation as a means of harassing editors and their reporters. In recent years, journalists heading editorial sections of many newspapers are insulated from legal complications as the owners/ publishers are themselves the editors.

When Cogentrix Energy Inc., a United States-based company, wanted to establish a thermal power plant jointly with China Light and Power near Nandikur in Dakshina Kannada district of Karnataka in 1995, several organizations representing different sections of the society opposed the project. *Prajavani*, which published a series of articles on the environmental consequences of the thermal power plant in the ecologically sensitive area, was banned from the company's press conferences. Ron Somers, the Managing Director of Cogentrix, met the editor of *Prajavani* K. N. Harikumar and complained against Poornima R., the newspaper's chief of bureau in Mangalore, for writing against the project (Poornima R., personal communication, 26 June 2019). The editor not only defended the journalists but also encouraged them to write such stories. To gain the support of the local people, Ron Somers began giving funds to youth organizations liberally and sponsoring sports events for students. Poornima had written about how the company was trying to prevent lakhs of students from opposing the project through sponsorships. However, the company protested saying that the newspaper was trying to find non-existent motives behind the sponsorship, which was being done to only benefit the people of the district. In spite of all these attempts, opposition to the project became louder with newspapers covering every small event. *Prajavani's* publishers stood by their journalists and encouraged them to dig into the environmental situation in coastal Karnataka.

In 1997, a news editor at *Prajavani's* central desk in Bengaluru was blocking stories about the possible environmental impact of the mega industries that were coming up in Dakshina Kannada district of Karnataka. The frustrated journalists informed Tilak Kumar, one of the owners of the Prajavani group, about it when he visited the Mangalore bureau. He immediately told the news editor to clear all stories from Mangalore without editing (Muralidhar Khajane, personal communication, 26 June 2018). The owners' unconditional support encouraged journalists in Mangalore to file a series of stories on the environmental situation in Dakshina Kannada district. *Prajavani's* campaigns against polluting industries in coastal Karnataka would not have been possible without the freedom the correspondents had to write on any issue. The environmental movement in the district was gaining momentum around that time. The Cogentrix company was finally forced to withdraw from the thermal power project because of protests, media campaigns and prolonged litigation.

According to Khajane, another instance of *Prajavani's* management standing by its journalists was when it carried in July 2000 a series of stories about a family erecting a fence around 13,000 acres of forest near Karkala in Dakshina Kannada district. The family, was so powerful and connected to people in power that even a minister of Karnataka was denied entry into the forest it had occupied. The tribes who lived in the forest had to seek the family's permission. The journalists who went to the forest were not allowed to take either photographs or videos. All those who wanted to enter the forest had to take the family's permission. *Prajavani's* article exposed how the family had taken possession of the forest that belonged to the government. The chief reporter of *Prajavani* then encouraged the journalists at the Mangalore bureau to write about the illegal occupation of the forest. In response to the stories that appeared on the front page the family filed a ₹101 crore defamation case against *Prajavani*. It is significant that the newspaper management solidly stood by its journalists and defended their stories. *Prajavani* too filed a defamation case of ₹102 crores against the family for damaging its reputation. Reporters feel encouraged to probe such issues when newspaper managements defend their freedom and their reports even when cases are filed against them.

The Indian Express has also defended its journalists when they wrote on environmental controversies. Ernst and Young (E&Y), a multinational consulting firm had done an Environmental Impact Assessment study of the proposed mini hydel power project at Dandeli in Uttara Kannada district of Karnataka. The report was a plagiarized version of a report prepared for another hydel power project in the same area. No independent assessment had been carried out. The impact of one project on the environment cannot be the same as the impact of another project. Nagaraj who was a senior correspondent at *The Indian Express* wrote a lead story that was carried by all editions of the newspaper on 27 August 2000 (personal communication, 26 June 2019). There was pressure on the *Indian Express* to publish the firm's version of the story but the editor refused to do so as the story had been written with irrefutable facts. The E&Y made several attempts to first of all stop the story and then demanded that the story be not published until its representative gave Nagaraj the agency's version. The *Indian Express* did not succumb to the pressure from the firm. Because E&Y was a multinational firm, there was a lot of interest in the story overseas also. Following *The Indian Express* story, *The Times of India*, *Outlook*, *India Today*, *Business India*, *The Guardian* of the UK, *The Times of Singapore*, *International Rivers Journal* and *Earth Island Journal* carried reports about the fraud committed by this international consulting agency. Because the management and the editor stood by the correspondent, there was no compromise with the independence of the newspaper.

The environmental impact of mining had become a major issue in Karnataka, especially in the Bellary district, around 2005–2006. A Lokayukta enquiry had been ordered into the illegalities in mining but the report was yet to be submitted. Muralidhar Khajane collected massive data running into thousands of pages and wrote a 10-piece series on the issue for *The Hindu*. The resident editor Parvati Menon and the Editor-in-Chief N. Ram gave full freedom to their reporters to probe into how illegal mining was destroying the economy and the ecology of the district. Before writing the last piece on mining an email was sent to Janardhana Reddy, a mining magnate, and a senior BJP leader, for his reaction. A former employee of *The Hindu* who had started working as a public relations (PR) agent of Janardhana Reddy threatened that a defamation case would be filed if the story was published. *The Hindu* carried the story with Janardhana Reddy's quote. His name was used in the story for the first time and he was pinned down with facts about his illegal mining operations. Despite the solid support from the management, there was fear of backlash as a result of which the stories were carried without any byline. When the Lokayukta inquiry report on mining was released at 10 PM on 27 July 2011, three correspondents who were following the issue along with the resident editor went through the 11-volume report till 1 AM and took out the key findings to produce a report for the next day's issue. The story made a huge impact with politicians, bureaucrats and the public talking about the fallout of the report. Journalists at *The Hindu* would not have been able to follow the mining story without the management standing by them.

The Karnataka Government in 2007 proposed to construct a thermal power plant near Chamalapura village in Heggadadevena Kote (H. D. Kote) taluk of Mysore district. The proposed 1,000 MW coal-fired thermal power plant was to be located on the fertile land between Kabini and Cauvery rivers. There were 80 lakes in the region that irrigated a variety of crops. Around 3,000 acres of land including 600 odd acres of the forest was to be acquired for the project that would displace 13,000 people. If completed, the project would cause air pollution, water pollution, biodiversity loss, food insecurity, soil contamination, deforestation and soil erosion. The people of Chamalapura and the surrounding villages launched an agitation against the project. *The Hindu* carried several articles in its 'District Plus' weekly supplement about the harm the proposed thermal power was going to cause to the biodiversity of the region. The supplement brought out from Mysore gave a lot of space and freedom to the correspondents based in Mysore to present a detailed account of the issues affecting the lives of the people in the region. Since there was no limit on the length of the articles and the choice of topics a lot of facts, figures and opinions appeared in the supplement (Khajane, personal communication, 26 July 2019). Bowing to pressure from the farmers, intellectuals and the media the government shelved the project although there was no official announcement.

The Delhi-based English newspaper *The Pioneer* carried stories on the impact of uranium mining in Karnataka despite the risk of losing advertising revenue from the Department of Atomic Energy. K. G. Vasuki, who has worked for both television and print media for nearly three decades, says he had the full backing of the management when he did stories on iron ore mining in Bellary district in 2006 and on the proposed thermal power plant near Mysore in 2007. For *The Pioneer*, he wrote a report in November 2011about how uranium mining by the Uranium Corporation of India Ltd (UCIL) at Gogi village in Yadgir district of Karnataka had caused radiation-related health problems among the residents of the village (personal communication, 1 August 2019). In response to his report, a senior official from the Department of Atomic Energy called him the next day and asked 'are you not patriotic? India needs uranium for which we are dependent on other countries. Don't you want development in your country?' The senior scientist asked Vasuki not to write any such stories. But Vasuki went ahead with another report on how effluents generated in the process of mining uranium were being discharged into a nearby tank. The villagers and the cattle had suffered serious health problems after consuming the water from the tank. The news editor at the central editorial office in Delhi did not want to carry the story. Vasuki spoke to the editor Chandan Mitra who directed the news editor to clear the story as it was written. The report had an impact. The newspaper did not get a single advertisement from the Department of Atomic Energy after the publication of the report.

The resistance to publishing the story comes not only from the sources who allegedly cause pollution but also from the senior journalists managing the editorial sections of newspapers. There are hurdles for journalists in getting their stories into the newspapers. For daring to publish an environmental story, a newspaper needs to be prepared to face the consequence of losing advertising revenue.

Very few newspapers come to the defence of their reporters and take the risk of losing advertising revenue. According to Vasuki, there has been a radical change in the media situation in recent years. It is very difficult to get stories on big industries polluting the environment on the front page. The space and time for stories that expose environmental destruction are sinking. In his view, environmental stories have become insignificant for the national media in recent years.

The newspapers rarely tell the reporters to do environmental stories. Most of the stories are written with the personal initiative of reporters (Meera Bhardwaj, personal communication, 27 March 2019). However, the newspapers do tell the journalists not to write on certain issues. There have been instances of officials and other organizations making journalist-specific requests to the management to ensure that nothing critical is written about them. When a report on the power situation in Karnataka prepared by a top bureaucrat was to be released, *Prajavani*'s management was told not to send Nagesh Hegde for the programme because he would ask uncomfortable questions. Even when the report was sent to the newspaper office the management was again asked not to give the report to him for review. The newspaper management refused to yield to the pressure of the bureaucrat and gave the report to Hegde to do a review.

There are instances of media groups cautioning the reporters about writing on environmental controversies. Some newspaper groups refuse to carry stories if they conflict with their marketing strategies. Meera Bhardwaj, who has done a lot of stories on environmental issues, was asked to tone down her stories by many of her editors (personal communication, 27 March 2019). She was also advised to do just one story a week. The editor would tell her no one would read such stories. The management would advise the editors that her anti-corporate stories were affecting the newspaper's revenue.

When media managements come to know that environmental stories are going to affect their market, they in fact, put pressure on the editors to drop such stories. The market-driven newspapers ignore serious issues if they are likely to have any impact on their revenues. However, even those newspapers that are editorial-driven would not allow stories that are likely to interfere with their revenue. It is very rare that a newspaper provides monetary support for doing investigative reporting. 'I spend a lot of my personal money on investigating environmental issues. I do my own investigation because it is my interest and passion. I feel it is my responsibility to make people know about how the environment is being destroyed', says Bhardwaj.

She narrates how her attempts to expose a poaching case went down the drain: Once two persons were arrested in the Hebri range of Kudremukh Wildlife Division between Shivamogga and Udupi districts of Karnataka for poaching but the case was not allowed to be registered as the forest minister brought pressure on the officials to protect the poachers. No newspaper carried the story because a minister was involved. In her attempts to get the story published she tried to present the story in different ways but still failed. Several such stories may go unpublished because the managers do not want to get into trouble with people in power.

Bhardwaj wrote a series of stories in 2017 based on her investigation into the encroachment of 1829 acres of forest in the Masagali area of Chikkamagaluru district of Karnataka but her stories were dropped once the names of the ministers figured in the 15-part series. The then Deputy Conservator of Forest (DCF) in charge of Chikkamagaluru district was trying to follow the Supreme Court order about taking back encroached forest land. The government had submitted an affidavit before the court that it would take back all the encroached forest land by December 2017 and would provide details about how much of the encroached land was taken back. She wrote about how the forest officer had been trying to take back the forest from these encroachers. As she started digging out the facts she discovered that the top politicians including the cabinet ministers were involved in the encroachment. The forest official was transferred, and false affidavits were filed in the Supreme Court. Besides the threat calls she received, there was pressure on the management and the editor not to carry her stories. The encroachers succeeded in stopping Bhardwaj's stories from being published but this was not new to her.

There have been cases where environmental activists have swung into action when the newspapers have dropped stories under pressure. In 2015, the well-known educationist in Dakshina Kannada district of Karnataka who owns several educational institutions had built a health resort inside the mining area in Khudremukh National Park (Bhardwaj, 2015). The Supreme Court, which had ordered the closure of all mining activities by Kudremukh Iron Ore Company Ltd (KIOCL) by December 31, 2005, had asked them to hand over the land back to state government. But KIOCL went on to lease this 'government' land to the educationist. Bhardwaj asked KIOCL how could it lease out the land when it did not own it. Without heeding to any warnings the educationist went ahead with the construction and spent ₹3 crore on it (personal communication, 27 March 2019). She wrote two stories on how the luxury resort had come up in violation of the environmental law and the Supreme Court order. However, as usual if one story was used, the second story was dropped, bowing down to pressures of revenue earnings. To ensure that her stories were accepted she had not revealed the identity of the violator. Later, Wildlife First (conservation advocacy group) went on to file a case in the high court so as to get the lease cancelled. The court asked the additional chief secretary (forests) to take immediate action and thus, the health resort project was immediately shut down. Bhardwaj's stories and the activist's efforts helped stop a health resort from coming up in a precious area in the Western Ghats. Many wildlife organisations, conservationists and activists had fought for years to stop mining by KIOCL.

Independent environmental journalist Keya Acharya wrote an investigative story for the global news agency Inter Press Service (IPS) on land grabbing in poor African countries like Kenya and Ethiopia by the cut-rose industry titled 'India's Cut Rose Sector Pushes Past Barriers'. The story that appeared on the agency's website on 18 July 2014[4] was

---

[4] For details, see Ghosh & Thankurta (2016).

based on facts and documents about the business practices of Karuturi Global, which had rose farms that were polluting Naivasha Lake in Kenya affecting the livelihoods of the poor people. Two weeks after the story was published, Karuturi Global served a legal notice to Keya Acharya, IPS, and two businessmen who were quoted in the story demanding an apology and ₹100 crore as damages for defamation. Immediately after the notice was served the IPS capitulated and took the story off its website. The IPS notice on its website said: 'We are suspending the contents of this article to ensure their veracity and that of the sources on which it draws and, therefore, request our subscribers not to republish or use it in any way'.[5] The news agency for which she had worked for more than 15 years did not stand by her and left her to defend herself. Acharya asserts that every word that she wrote was based on solid evidence. The case was not pursued because the company was beset with its problems and declared insolvency in 2019. Acharya says,

> Defamation cases like these make other journalists in the field wary of reporting on such issues. This is called the chilling effect. Several journalists face this kind of challenge in their careers when the management does not support them. When the very organizations journalists work for wash their hands off a case they are virtually pushed to the wall. This is where the Press Council of India becomes important but it is a toothless body. There should be some kind of a system for stopping such frivolous cases so that journalists are not harassed. The entire work schedules of journalists and their careers get disturbed because of legal actions. Very few media houses provide full support to legal cases that are initiated against their journalists. (Personal communication, 24 September 2020)

Although there are several examples of the newspaper managements refusing to carry stories painstakingly written by the journalists, there is a belief among some journalists that it is possible to push their stories into the newspapers.

---

[5] http://www.ipsnews.net/2014/07/indias-cut-rose-sector-pushes-past-barriers/

Poornima and Muralidhar Khajane are of the view that if a journal-ist is committed to exposing the truth and if he is able to convince the management about his thorough knowledge of an issue and the public interest involved, it would be possible to get the stories published (personal communication, 26 June 2019). So long as a journalist remains committed to revealing something in the interest of the public, they believe, it is not difficult to find space for stories on environmental issues. Despite the limitations in the media organizations, it is pos-sible to write about environmental issues if the journalist has a rapport with the publisher. Khajane believes getting space in the newspaper also depends on how a journalist tells his story because if the story is written most convincingly it is unlikely to be rejected. However, as Bhardwaj has narrated, attempts to write stories in different ways to avoid rejection by the desk do not always succeed. When the environ-mental stories are going to affect the commercial interest of the big advertisers, no efforts or strategies of the reporters might work. As Keya Acharya says many media organizations succumb to the pressure from corporations and do not come to the defence of their journalists who would have produced a story after several weeks of investigation to dig out facts.

Threats and Inducements

Threats to environmental journalists are on the rise throughout the world. Environmental journalists have been threatened, harassed, sued, fired, arrested, assaulted and killed while covering logging, mining and encroachment. Logging, deforestation and mining are dangerous zones in environmental reporting. According to Reporters Without Borders (RSF), 15 per cent of the cases of threats registered against journalists are linked to environmental issues. At least 10 journalists covering the environment have been killed in the last five years, an average of two journalists per year.[6] There were 53 press freedom violations that were linked to environmental journalism during the period between 2015 and 2020. In India, the threats to environmental

---

[6] https://rsf.org/en/news/red-alert-green-journalism-10-environmental-reporters-killed-five-years

journalists have only increased over the years. Some journalists have risked their lives to investigate violations of environmental law by the mining mafia, big corporations and politicians. The RSF report says that all four environmental journalists murdered in Asia in the last five years were from India.

On 1 June 2015, a gang entered the house of Jagendra Singh, an independent journalist, in Shahjahanpur, Uttar Pradesh, doused him with petrol and set him on fire. He died of injuries later in a hospital. Jagendra Singh had been investigating land encroachment and illegal sand mining in the Garra River. Although a video showed Singh saying 'Why did they have to burn me? If the ministers and his goondas had a grudge, they could have beaten me instead of pouring kerosene and burning me' (*DNA*, 13 June 2015)' the Uttar Pradesh police concluded that he had killed himself.

Karun Misra, who was the Ambedkarnagar bureau chief of the Hindi daily *Jan Sandesh Times*, Uttar Pradesh, was shot by three gunmen on motorcycles in Sultanpur as he was driving home, on 13 February 2016. He died on the way to the hospital. He had written about illegal mining by two local contractors in his newspaper and had refused to accept bribes from them (https://www.thenewsminute.com). Misra had ignored repeated threats to his life and paid a price for his commitment to professional values.

Sandeep Misra, a television journalist, who was probing the police-sand mafia nexus in Madhya Pradesh, was crushed to death by a speeding truck that ran over him on 26 March 2018. Misra had filed a complaint with the police about a threat to his life after he conducted a sting operation in which a police officer was shown receiving bribe from the sand mafia (https://www.deccanchronicle.com).

On 19 June 2020, Shubham Mani Tripathi who worked for the Kanpur-based Hindi daily *Kampu Mail* was allegedly killed at the behest of a sand mafia and land grabbers in the Unnao district of Uttar Pradesh.[7] Tripathi had written to the state authorities that he had been

---

[7] https://thewire.in/media/shubham-mani-tripathi-journalist-killed-unnao-sand-mafia

threatened by the sand mafia. He had also said in a Facebook post, shortly before his murder, that there was a threat to his life because of his investigation into the illegal sand mining and land grabbing.

With the phenomenal growth in the construction industry, the demand for sand is increasing which has been taken advantage of by the sand mafia in several states. The four journalists probing sand mafia had been threatened before they were killed. In two of the cases, there was the involvement of the police too. In such an environment, very few journalists can ignore the threats and continue to investigate illegal mining. That none of these reporters worked for a large mainstream media organization indicates greater vulnerability of journalists who work for smaller media organizations. These attacks would not have taken place if several other journalists had also reported the nexus between the sand mafia and the police.

Nagesh Hegde (2015) had written an article on 12 March 2015 about the proposal to construct a new port at Tadadi in Uttara Kannada district of Karnataka in *Prajavani* explaining what problems would arise once the port became operational with examples of other countries. He had said that the port would only benefit the contractors and the millionaires and that the underworld activities, bars, pubs would lead to more incidence of crime. He had also said that those who work in ships for months together and return to the ports get hungry for sex and that would lead to prostitution in the port area. He gave the examples of some ports in other countries, which were notorious as sex ports. Soon after the article was published, some groups began circulating a message accusing Hegde of suggesting that the women in Tadadi would become prostitutes. Protests were held calling for action against Hegde. In Kumta town, 5,000 people gathered and burnt an effigy of Hegde. An FIR was filed and the police went to Hegde's house to conduct an enquiry. *Prajavani* was also served a notice but the paper stood very firm and argued that there was nothing wrong in what Hegde had written. It said no one had been defamed in the article (personal communication, 9 August 2021).

Hegde says local political groups who wanted the port to be established circulated the false message. The reference to prostitution, that too in other countries, was only an excuse to silence criticism against the port project.

Threats to journalists also come from groups involved in illegal timber trade, mining, encroachment of forest land and poaching. Meera Bhardwaj followed the sambar deer poaching case in Tanigebailu Wildlife Range for *The New Indian Express* for almost one year (personal communication, 27 March 2019). Each sambar deer is worth lakhs as its meat is sold at a very high price in the illegal market. As she went on investigating she discovered that poaching had a huge network across the country and links went up to terrorists in Afghanistan. Her own sources advised her against following the case as there was a threat of being targeted by the poaching mafia. She stopped writing on the case much against her will because there was a possible threat to her life. The poachers had links with the politicians in Shivajinagar of Bengaluru. Her stories led to the jailing of as many as 11 hunters for 102 days. They were all released as the forest department did not build a strong case against them. Each of them had links with politicians. The hunters included doctors and software engineers from Bengaluru and other cities. 'Reporters alone cannot go on highlighting such cases in the media. Environmental activists and wildlife groups should do their part of the job mobilizing public opinion against such illegal activities and further go to the courts', says Bhardwaj.

When Muralidhar Khajane went to write about the encroachment of 13,000 acres of forest by a powerful family in Dakshina Kannada district in July 2000 he was threatened that he would not be allowed to go out of the forest (personal communication, 23 July 2019). He was allowed to go only after he told the family that he had informed the superintendent of Police, Dakshina Kannada District, about his visit and that if he did not go out of the forest by 5 PM the police would come looking for him.

The mining lobby tried to offer bribes to the editor of *Samyukta Karnataka* daily for not carrying stories on mining in a green hill range in northern Karnataka. One of the correspondents of *Samyukta Karnataka* in the Gadag district of Karnataka told his editor Hunasawadi Rajan about the biodiversity and the geographical significance of Kappattagudda, a lush green hill range located in the district (Hunasawadi Rajan, personal communication, 26 June 2019). Since mining for gold and iron ore had been allowed on this eco-sensitive hill range Rajan asked his correspondent to talk to all the stakeholders and send 10 stories, each carrying 500 to 600 words describing the destruction mining was going to cause. This was surprisingly leaked and three days later a person from a steel company came to the Samyukta Karnataka's office in Bengaluru and invited Rajan to a hotel for dinner. Despite Rajan's rejection of his invitation efforts continued to woo him. After a few days, a senior professional from the steel company came with three others to Bengaluru and tried to convince him about the benefit of mining gold in Kappatagudda. Rajan says:

> The company representatives tried to pressurise me not to carry the stories on Kappatagudda. They offered to help the newspaper financially through advertisements or any other means in installments. They invited me to their guest house in Hospet for a 'discussion' but I rejected their offer. When they failed to influence me they met the members of the Lokashikshana Trust that runs the newspaper and tried to bring pressurise on me not carry the series. A senior executive from the group tried to work out a kind of a business transaction with the trustees. The trustees gave a clear message that they would not compromise on their newspaper's editorial independence. They expressed full faith in the freedom of the editor to decide the content.

Three more persons tried to bring pressure on Rajan not to carry the stories. They demanded that if the stories had to be published then a story written by their expert should appear first. They offered to arrange for a trip to Gadag for interaction with the people they would choose. They insisted that the stories could be published only after talking to the people and seeking their opinions. Their plan was to present a selected group of people before Rajan to ensure that they gave the company's version of the issue. Rajan rejected all their inducements and demands and went ahead with the publication of the stories. Three days after the paper began publishing the series another newspaper published the version given by the company's executive. *Samyukta Karnataka* did not yield to any of their offers of bribe and continued to carry the series. This is how many of the mining companies try to induce journalists to present a glorious picture of their mining projects.

Resisting pressures and incentives requires a commitment to the core of professional values.

When the Malayalam newspaper *Mathrubhumi* was carrying on a campaign against the Coca-Cola Company for causing water depletion and pollution in Plachimada in 2003 the company approached the chairman and managing director of the *Mathrubhumi* group M.P. Veerendrakumar with an offer of crores of advertising revenue if the newspaper stopped campaigning against the company (personal communication, 18 September 2018). However, Veerendrakumar rejected the offer and continued to carry investigative stories about how the company was polluting the environment and deceiving the people by giving away solid waste from its plant as fertilizer to the farmers. He said,

The company's agents came to me with a deal in the thick of the Plachimada struggle. They told me I would get five percent of the revenue from their plant at Plachimada if I did them a favour. They wanted me to appoint a lawyer picked by them to fight the case in the court. I told them I was not for sale. I lost a lot of advertising revenue but I have the satisfaction that we succeeded in stopping the project that would cause a lot of harm to the land and the people of Plachimada.

Veerendrakumar did not succumb to pressures and remained committed to the environmental cause. Journalists in his group were free to investigate into environmental issues and write stories based on facts. The environmental cause was dear to him and he would go to any extent to defend it as a publisher.

One of the potent weapons the polluting industries use against the media has been dragging them to court on defamation charges. When Sunita Narain of the CSE wrote an article in the *Business Standard* (16 March 1999) about how the diesel cars were polluting the air, Tata Motors filed a ₹100 crore defamation case against her (Narain, 2017). Holding corporations accountable involves the hard work of putting together a lot of vital data together and the formidable risk of litigation which can be a huge drain on the sparse resources of an organization. Filing legal cases against critics to intimidate, harass and silence them is known as Strategic Lawsuit Against Public

Participation (SLAPP) in Europe and America. The purpose is not to win the lawsuit but to threaten the critics into silence. The most often used form of threat is the defamation suit in which millions of rupees are claimed as damages.

The possibility of threats is higher when a journalist comes with an exclusive story. When Meera Bhardwaj wrote a series of stories on encroachment of forestland for the *The New Indian Express*, a powerful minister refused to answer any queries on encroachments by his family and in turn, threatened her. The series was dropped and never saw the light of the day (personal communication, 27 March 2019). If only one journalist does a special story on a particular issue, the other newspapers do not take it. It is very difficult for an individual reporter to do a series of stories on an environmental issue and expect it to be telecast or published. Bhardwaj says,

> When the commercial interest of the newspaper is affected environmental stories get buried. Most environmental stories are against government authorities and industries who are the major advertisers. If there is some collective effort on the part of conservation groups or activists to expose the ongoing destruction of the forests or environment, there would be more published stories and lesser threat to journalists.

Reporting environmental issues involves risk because it often requires a journalist to travel to remote communities and confronting those who wield political power and control bureaucracy. The risk can be reduced if journalists make a collective effort to write about environmental issues without looking for exclusive stories. In the absence of such a collective effort, the industry and the bureaucracy continue to exert pressure on the media to abstain from investigating environmental issues.

Conclusion

Although media are generally under pressure with regard to news and opinion they carry, it is more so in case of covering environmental issues. The government and the corporations exert pressure on the media in several ways, including advertising through which they influence the choice of content and framing of stories. There is a tendency among the media to treat information that comes from the government agencies and corporations that operate polluting industries as a fact. The representatives of the environmental NGOs are of the view that the pro-establishment and pro-industry bias is often found in the stories that media carry. They believe that editors and reporters are under pressure to reflect the view of the government and the industry because of the risk of losing financial resources that might lead to their own professional insecurity. Though most journalists say that their own organizations have stood by them and have not curtailed their freedom they admit that there is a lot of perceptible pressure while reporting some specific environmental issues.

Corporations use the newspapers they own to create an impression that people have welcomed their projects despite questions on their environmental impact. Even when corporations are not owners or investors, their influence on the content comes through advertising. The editing desk sometimes cuts off parts of stories filed by reporters if they are found to be offensive to the advertisers. Reports blaming a particular industry for pollution rarely appear in media and when they do appear the claims of the industry are given prominence. The reports may begin with the statements of the industries denying any wrongdoing on their part. Journalists say that in the post-liberalization era the zeal with which the environmental stories were reported in the pre-liberalization is missing, not because of lack of commitment on the part of the journalists but because of increasing pressure from both the industry and the management. Journalists, especially those who write for business newspapers become extremely careful about offending any of the major advertisers.

Some of the newspaper managements have not buckled under corporate pressure to not to carry stories on pollution. Even when they faced the risk of losing huge advertising revenue from big advertisers, they continued to carry stories based on facts and scientific evidence. Reports calling upon the readers not to buy products from a polluting company have also appeared. However, this kind of boldness in appealing to the readers to influence their attitude towards a polluting company is very rare. Journalists think that what happened two decades ago might not happen today. A reporter needs full backing of the editor and the management to investigate issues and name the individuals, agencies and companies in his stories to hold them accountable. In some cases, a sustained media campaign contributes to closing down of harmful projects. However, there are also cases in which the editors and the management have refused to carry stories that would include the names of influential corporations and individuals. The painstaking efforts made for weeks in unearthing the blatant violation of environmental norms have gone down the drain. Threats and attacks on journalists reporting environmental issues, especially mining, have increased in recent years. The murder of four journalists probing illegal mining in the last five years is a disturbing trend. While some media houses have solidly stood by the journalists who produced investigative stories exposing big industries for causing pollution, others have blocked such news stories when they found them in conflict with their interests.

CHAPTER 5

Scientific Uncertainties and Lack of Specialization in Environmental Reporting

One of the key challenges journalists face when they report about environmental issues is scientific uncertainty. They often confront individuals and groups that either 'amplify or downplay uncertainties' (Painter, 2013, p. 8). Sometimes, they have to deal with contradictory evidence produced by groups that hold diametrically opposite views on certain environmental issues. They have the arduous task of understanding how much of that evidence is actually scientific. The way common people see science is different from the way scientists see it. The common people associate certainty with science, whereas scientists may consider uncertainty as an opportunity to explore further and provide new explanations (Painter, 2013). The common person wants conclusive statements about issues rather than indications, hypotheses, suggestion or propositions. Since a majority of the news consumers are the common people, the media have the responsibility of bridging the gap in knowledge between scientists and common people so that some of the key issues related to the environment and climate change are properly explained and understood. However, highlighting uncertainties in media may lead to audiences perceiving an issue as less serious and not exerting adequate pressure on the authorities to take mitigating action. Media debates on uncertainties may also confuse the audience about science, economics and politics, leading to justification of inaction (Moser & Dilling, 2007).

There are claims and counterclaims on the causes and consequences of issues and measures needed to deal with them. There are disagreements between scientists and activists, and there is a lack of unanimity among scientists themselves about some issues. Experts disagree about interpretations and applications of research or how to manage environmental trade-offs. Besides, unlike many other topics, environmental issues are highly complex as they are connected, apart from science, to economy, society, culture and politics. Scientists have often accused the media of carrying poorly researched articles and sensationalizing environmental issues by blowing certain aspects out of proportion and ignoring key concerns. Science is necessary to explain and legitimize claims about certain issues, but one often hears of misuse of science by pressure groups, corporations and public authorities (Taylor & Nathan, 2002). In their zeal to gain public attention, pressure groups tend to oversimplify complex issues, highlighting only those aspects of a problem that the public understands, thereby making the job of a reporter harder. A journalist has the responsibility of presenting a problem in the frame of science and at the same time making it understandable for the common person.

The Challenge of Conflicting Claims

One of the challenges of environmental reporting is dealing with issues on which there are conflicting views. While scientists speak in terms of evidence, activists speak in terms of how people are going to be affected and how the problem is perceived at the poplar level. There are very few areas on which an overwhelming majority of scientists do not agree. However, even when there is adequate scientific evidence to establish causal link between pollution and diseases, there are still some people who do not agree. For example, although there is substantial evidence to link tobacco to cancer, radiation to cancer, air pollution to lung infections, water contamination to several diseases, there are still some individuals and lobbies questioning the evidence and pointing at several other factors.

One controversial area on which there has been an international debate is climate change (Taylor & Nathan, 2002). Some studies have shown that the media in their reporting of climate change have spread scepticism about the issue among their audiences by giving undue importance to the minority opinions that dispute the causes of climate change (Grundmann & Scott, 2014; Olausson, 2009; Painter & Ashe, 2012; Painter & Gavin, 2015; Schmid-Petri et al., 2017). When the Intergovernmental Panel on Climate Change (IPCC) says that it is 'very likely' that human activities cause global warming, there is a possibility of it being interpreted as 'unsure' (Ekwurzel et al., 2012). Those who are opposed to climate action have often used some experts to articulate doubts about climate science despite overwhelming consensus on the causes and consequences of rise in global temperatures (Moser & Dilling, 2007). Because of the overwhelming evidence there is high certainty that the rate of temperature has accelerated since the beginning of the 20th century and that it is the result of human activity (Harrison, 2013; Painter, 2013).

There is also high certainty that if the warming is more than 3°C above preindustrial levels it will have negative impact on humans, animals and plants. However, there is uncertainty about the robustness of climate models, about how the earth is going to respond to higher temperature and about what will be the response of the governments and society. Climate sceptics who are well-organized and well-funded often pick out uncertainties, amplify them through media and use them to spread doubts and delay action aimed at reducing greenhouse gases (Oreskes & Conway, 2010; Painter, 2013). Painter and Ashe (2012) found that newspapers in Brazil, China, France and India gave lesser space to climate sceptics compared to the newspapers in the United States and United Kingdom.

Climate change has never been a contentious subject of debate among the people in India. A Yale University survey in India showed that a great majority of the people (72%) believed that climate change was happening (Leiserowitz & Thaker, 2012, p. 18). A majority of them also believed that climate change was caused by human activity and that protecting the environment was much more important than economic growth. The survey also found that people with higher levels of education were more worried about global warming than those with lower levels of education.

In the Indian media, there has almost been no debate on whether climate change is happening. The argument that there is no climate change is almost absent. Jogesh and Painter (2013) in their of analysis of coverage of climate change in three Indian newspapers—*The Times of India*, *The Hindu* and *Business Standard*—found that only 1 out of 56 articles had a sceptical voice. However, the consensus in the article was that climate change was man-made. Dutt et al. (2013) who analysed articles on environmental issues in 31 English dailies in India found that a majority of the articles were about climate change and global warming. There were no articles that challenged the existence of the climate problem. No major scientist or institution in India has challenged the claims climate scientists and activists have been making about the causes and consequences of climate change.

Climate scepticism does not exist in Indian political debates and there has been no example of a member of parliament raising questions on the science of climate change. The parliamentary debates on climate change are usually about how much India is going to gain or lose because of its international commitments. However, there are questions about gaps that exist between India's active involvement in global efforts in addressing the issue of climate change and action on the ground on the domestic front (Singh, 2021). As the third-biggest emitter of greenhouse gases India is under pressure to improve its climate commitments by shedding its dependence on coal. When the process for auctioning 41 coal blocks for commercial mining was launched in June 2020 the opinion in media was that it would seriously compromise India's stated climate commitment (Jaffrelot & Ganesh, 2020; Koshy, 2020; Roy, 2021). The print media in India are more focused on the politics of climate change than the climate science–related issues (Jogesh & Painter, 2013).

The challenge for a journalist in reporting risk and uncertainty is to work towards a balance between scientifically accurate information and journalistic norms about what makes something 'newsworthy'.

Consulting scientists to explain certain contested claims is important. Authority and credibility in environmental reporting can be achieved only by sourcing information from scientists and scientific institutions of good standing. The evidence available needs to be looked at from various angles. The polluting industries always try to present and interpret the evidence in such a way that it supports their claims of no link between pollution and health issues. They want 'conclusive' and 'incontrovertible' evidence that there is cause and effect relationship whenever questions are raised about pollution (Narain, 2017, p. 67).

Keya Acharya says that scientific uncertainties are a big challenge to any environmental journalist (personal communication, 11 September 2020). When some activists and journalists see a problem from one perspective those who are going to be affected by it might see it from a different perspective. They may understand a problem differently based on the pieces of evidence they have come across. When she went to the villages to talk to farmers about Bt cotton a decade ago they told her that they knew very well what to do and asked her not to give them any advice. They said they would know whether it was good for the soil or not and they would decide about what seeds to use. She saw this argument as an eye-opener. They were not willing to listen to the arguments against Bt cotton despite the possibility of a decline in productivity and chemical poisoning. Since the extension officers of the agriculture department were not going to the field but sending sales representatives from the seed and fertilizer companies, the farmers had been given incorrect and misleading information. While the activists were telling farmers about the harmful consequences of Bt cotton, the representatives of the seed and fertilizer companies with the tacit support of the officials were telling them that there were great benefits. There have been arguments in favour of it and against it with no final answer. Only a thorough investigation can reveal realities on the field.

T. V. Jayan says that a reporter has to provide all arguments in favour or against an issue and allow the readers to arrive at their own judgment (personal communication, 11 September 2020). However, presenting both sides of case is possible only when writing a full story running into thousands of words. If a journalist has to write a 300-word story there is no way he can do that.

The media audience not only need unambiguous reports on issues but also specific information about how those issues are to be addressed.

There are times when journalists themselves are confused about how to present an issue before the people. There may be two or more ways of presenting a problem but a journalist has to choose the one that helps him explain the issue in the best way within the deadlines. When a journalist is faced with questions that are not fully answered he does not have the luxury of holding back the story until it is fully understood. However, no story that is likely to create confusion in the minds of the readers should be carried. If possible, the publication of a story can be postponed by a day or two to consult experts, gather more information and to decipher the nuances of the problem. When a journalist is not sure of the causes and consequences of an environmental problem, he should not send off his report but should go deeper into the issue by conducting an investigation and by consulting experts. He should also look at the weight of the evidence if there are arguments on both sides of an issue. Rohin Kumar, media specialist with Greenpeace, who has also been a journalist, says it is important for journalists to speak to as many experts as possible to know how an issue is understood and interpreted differently (personal communication, 20 May 2021). If they are still confused and uncertain they should wait to investigate more and find out and then come out with a story, he says. Journalists need to have critical faculties to seek evidence from the experts for the conclusions they have arrived at.

Rohin Kumar says that uncertainties, claims and counterclaims are not only associated with environmental stories but also with the other stories that frequently appear in newspapers. Any story, including a political story, has claims and counterclaims. Any crime story will also have claims and counterclaims. However, what is special about environmental stories is that they are related to scientific evidence, which is often challenged. The NGOs, activists, the affected people and the government may be talking about different indicators about an issue. All stakeholders including the government tend to defend their positions as the right ones. When officials, scientists, activists and the affected people are saying different things expressing conflicting opinions it is essential for a journalist to put all those views in a proper perspective and let the audience know all their positions. It is also necessary to prioritize those views that are based on sound scientific evidence.

Stressing the need for including different points of view in reports, Rohin Kumar says,

> I understand that none of the publications have the space to look into whether every source is saying something right or wrong from the point of view of science. However, they try to take all the viewpoints of all the persons involved to let the audiences know what the issue is about. They should also talk to the oppressor and the oppressed because that is the way to understand a problem scientifically. The right kind of evidence may not have been gathered systematically because of which there would be no follow-up stories. If I have visited a site of controversy, I would file the first report with claims and counterclaims. If the reporter is doing a follow-up after fifteen days more can be said about the processes that are happening. A journalist has to report the facts, claims and counter claims but he often presents the perspective of a company. (Personal communication, 20 May 2021)

According to him, the business model of media and their close links with the industry may prevent them from presenting a narrative based on science. He says there was never a serious debate in Indian media on the consequences of using chemicals fertilizers, hybrid seeds and pesticides, during the green revolution. The media mostly carried shiny stories about it and overlooked the harmful impact on soil, health and people's livelihoods. But, of late, they seem to have realised the long-term effect of the green revolution. The 'cancer train', Kumar says, is the best example of the harm the green revolution has caused. The problem has become so visible that media cannot ignore it. The train that goes from Bathinda in Punjab to Bikaner in Rajasthan carries an average of 100 cancer patients every day for treatment at Acharya Tulsi Regional Cancer Hospital and Research Centre (Singh, 2021). Although some studies have shown that the high incidence of cancer is linked to high use of pesticides in the Malwa region of Punjab, the results have not been conclusive (Zwerdling, 2009). Even in the absence of conclusive evidence, the media reports have linked high incidence of cancer to pesticide use. An article in *The Pioneer* said, 'In fact, the epidemic created by the Green Revolution is bigger than the Covid pandemic. The vaccine of Covid-19 has been prepared, who will make the vaccine against diseases spread by the Green Revolution?' (Singh, 2021). Despite studies and media coverage, uncertainties remain and there is no official acceptance of the link between pesticide and cancer. Even when a reporter bases his story on plain facts without his own analysis there is still sufficient information for the readers to arrive at their own conclusion amidst conflicting claims.

Scientific Evidence and the Media: The Case of Endosulfan

The issue of aerial spraying of pesticide endosulfan and its impact on the health of the people in Enmakaje gram panchayat of Kasaragod district in Kerala is a classic example of conflicting claims and contradictory conclusions that could pose a serious challenge to journalists. The Plantation Corporation of Kerala (PCK) had been spraying endosulfan on cashew plantations on the hills around Padre village for over two decades despite people's protests against it. Mohan Kumar, a doctor in the area, had noticed disorders of the central nervous system, cerebral palsy, retardation of mental and physical growth, epilepsy and congenital anomalies among children of some families in Padre village. He discovered over a period of time that health conditions he had noticed among the children of the village were related to endosulfan. Teachers in a local school had also noticed mental retardation among the children coming from the Padre village. Some young people of the village and school teachers protested against aerial spraying of endosulfan but in vain. Local newspapers and television channels began reporting about the effects of endosulfan. The images of physically and mentally retarded children brought the attention of the readers to the seriousness of the impact of chemical pollution. The PCK began issuing press statements saying that aerial spraying of endosulfan and the health issues were not at all related. However, the local media were not convinced. The largest circulated Malayalam newspaper *Malayala Manorama* carried the picture of a boy suffering from cerebral palsy (Joshua et al., 2006). Several newspapers and television channels reported about health problems that the people of Padre were suffering from. There was circumstantial evidence, but the scientific evidence to link the health problems to endosulfan was lacking.

CSE released the results of its laboratory analysis[1] of the samples collected from Padre village of Kasaragod district of Kerala on 21 February 2001. The samples had been collected on 29 December 2000, three days after the aerial spraying of endosulfan. The laboratory tests showed that samples from human blood, soil, water, human milk, bovine milk, vegetables and fish had extremely high levels of organochlorine pesticide endosulfan. The test showed that in one woman's blood the amount of endosulfan was 900 times more than the permissible level in water. The CSE's report received wide coverage in the media. The evidence very clearly linked the physical deformities and mental retardation to endosulfan (David, 2001). That all victims were young and born around the late 1970s and 1980s meant that there were no such problems before the aerial spray of endosulfan began. Three months after the CSE released its report, the Pesticides Manufacturers and Formulators Association of India (PMFAI) issued an advertisement (in May 2001) in a Bangalore-based daily with the headline 'A Clarification of Endosulfan' (*Down To Earth*, 2001) claiming that endosulfan was not responsible for the health problems in Kasaragod district. The advertisement argued that endosulfan was safe and that the media had created an incorrect impression in the minds of the public. The advertisement, issued as part of the damage control exercise, had very little impact because

---

[1] https://web.archive.org/web/20110601035556/http://www.cseindia.org/userfiles/CSE_report-1.pdf

every newspaper and television channel gave extensive coverage to the issue. The Director of the National Research Centre for Cashew wrote an article titled 'First Convict the Suspect then Conduct the Trial' in the June 2001 issue of *Agriculture Today* magazine. The article was aimed at creating the impression that CSE's report had been unfair and judgemental without producing convincing evidence. A former head of the division of agricultural chemistry at ICMR, in another article, alleged that CSE's findings were 'pseudoscientific'. However, they could not point out any inaccuracy in the procedure and results of tests conducted by the CSE.

The pesticide industry went on demanding a scientific study to counter the findings of the CSE's study. Several committees[2] were set up to investigate whether the health problems were the result of endosulfan. Dealing with different conclusions of the committees was a gruelling task for the journalists.

Soon after the CSE's report was released, a committee was constituted by the Kerala Agricultural University (KAU) which said in its report, submitted in February 2001, that there was no evidence to fix endosulfan as the cause of the problem. The Tamil Nadu–based private laboratory the Fredrick Institute of Plant and Toxicology (FIPPAT) released a report in June 2001 that concluded there were no residues of endosulfan in any of the blood, milk and water samples. The *India Today* magazine published a report titled 'Spray of Misery' on 23 July 2001 which said a series of reports had appeared in the media about the issue. Following the *India Today* report the National Human Rights Commission (NHRC) took suo moto cognizance of the problem and asked the Indian Council for Medical Research (ICMR) to submit a report. A team of the National Institute of Occupational Health (NIOH) submitted a report in July 2002 that concluded that the health problems in Enmakaje village panchayat were due to continued exposure to endosulfan.

Another committee set up by the Kerala government (Achyuthan Committee) found no direct evidence to link health problems to

---

[2] https://www.cseindia.org/endosulfan-industrys-dirty-war-a-chronology-of-events--1927

endosulfan in its report released in November 2001, but at the same time, it said that there was no evidence to completely deny the link either. An expert committee (Sivaraman Committee) set up by the Health and Family Welfare Department of Kerala said in its report submitted in August 2003 that it found high content of endosulfan in blood samples of schoolchildren, soil, water and flora and recommended banning of areal spray. Another committee was set up by the centre under the chairmanship of Dr O. P. Dubey, Assistant Director General of Indian Council for Agricultural Research to examine the reports of NIOH, Achuthan Committee, KAU and FIPPAT. The Dubey Committee that submitted its report in August 2003 found no link between use of endosulfan and health problems in Padre village. Since there was no unanimity among the members of the Dubey Committee the Central government formed another committee under the chairmanship of Agriculture Commissioner C. D. Mayee, in September 2004. In December 2004, the Mayee Committee concluded that there was no link between health problems and aerial spraying of endosulfan.

There were conflicting findings, contradictory conclusions and questionable recommendations in the reports of these committees. The results of the studies conducted by the CSE and NIOH which linked the health problems in Padre village to endosulfan received favourable coverage in the media. Several media reports questioned the tests and procedures adopted by the committees that had found no connection between the pesticide and the health problems. Senior journalist K. G. Vasuki who had reported about the issue for ANI says that media played a significant role in making people aware of the harmful pesticide and in building pressure on the government to ban it (personal communication, 26 June 2019).

The Endosulfan Manufactures & Formulators Welfare Association (EMFWA) claimed that the NGOs like CSE were a part of the conspiracy against India. A defamation case was filed against the CSE. Booklets and obscene cartoons were distributed at CSE's gate in Delhi to discredit it and the investigations it had carried out (BEDROC, 2011). A section of the media also carried advertisements, interviews and articles that claimed that endosulfan was a safe pesticide (*Down To Earth*, 2002). Interviews and advertisements began appearing in the media that claimed that endosulfan was a safe pesticide. Veerendrakumar, the Chairman of the *Mathrubhoomi* group, says that the media in Kerala were not carried away by the campaign of pesticide manufacturers (personal communication, 23 October 2018). They gave sustained coverage to the issue from the perspective of the victims and activists. The overall opinion in media, according to him, was that there was mounting evidence against endosulfan and that banning it was very much necessary to prevent further harm to the people in Enmakaje gram panchayat.

Although the newspapers reported the claims made by the pesticide manufacturers, they did not give much credence to them. The evidence that heavily weighed against endosulfan found positive coverage in almost all media despite their divergent political leanings. Not only that the issue was given prominence in Kerala newspapers, it also became the subject for a film, a novel, short stories and textbooks. The media agenda became the public agenda, which in turn led to policy agenda. The pressure began mounting on the authorities to ban the chemical.

Nagesh Hegde says that newspapers in the endosulfan case upheld science and rejected the arguments of the pesticide companies that tried to use some of the laboratory reports to their advantage (personal communication, 9 August 2021). He says the false claim by the pesticide industry that marriage between close blood relatives was causing physical and mental deformities was rejected because such problems did not exist in the region before spraying of endosulfan began although such a practice was common. Moreover, such problems were not found among the people elsewhere who had the same practice.

The claims of the pesticide industry and the questionable results of some of the enquiry committees could not make any impact on the media audiences, as the evidence against the chemical was overwhelming. Although Kerala banned endosulfan in 2005, it did not become effective until the Supreme Court of India banned its use in India in 2011. Even after the ban, the pesticide company sought permission to sell its stock amounting to thousands of tons but its request was rejected. This is one of the few cases in which the media played the agenda-setting role and helped set the process for ending chemical contamination of the environment.

Nagesh Hegde is of the firm view that there is an indisputable link between pollution and diseases and that journalists must not be misled by the kind of evidence that the polluters come up with (personal communication, 14 October 2018). Although there is a link between pollution and diseases, the polluting companies argue in the court pointing at those who have not been affected by pollution. It is possible that 70 per cent of those who drink the same water are not affected but the 30 per cent who belong to the poor communities are affected. When such cases are presented before the court, it is important to explain them to the readers. 'Even if you take tuberculosis which claims a large number of lives every year throughout the world it is again the poor who are affected. The rich are rarely affected', Hegde says. Only those who are aware of such findings read deeply into them and interpret the result so that the issue in question can be presented in a proper context. The industrialists and bureaucrats try to interpret the data in such a way that contradictions become more visible so that claims of risks can be rejected. Therefore, it is a challenge for the journalists to explain how uncertainties are created through selective use of evidence.

Nuclear Power Plant, Cancer Risk and the Media

The media in the Uttara Kannada district in Karnataka have been reporting about the increased incidence of cancer in the villages around the Kaiga Atomic Power Station[3] (KAPS). In 2010, a survey conducted by the Karnataka state's Bio Fuel Task Force in 68 villages around Kaiga found that there was a steep increase in cancer cases (*The Times of India*, 2010). The task force had conducted its own

---

[3] The station located 56 km away from Karwar was commissioned in 1989 and became operational in 2000. The station currently has four units that produce 220 MW each.

survey after the nuclear establishment rejected its request to conduct a health survey in the Kaiga area on the grounds that there was no radiation in the area. It also claimed that the users of Kali river water would become prone to cancer as it was contaminated with tritium, a by-product of nuclear reactors. Stories about increasing cancer cases began appearing in local and state dailies (Ashok Hasyagar, personal communication, 27 February 2019). The arguments of the activists and the complaints of the villagers dominated the stories although official denials did appear in the leads of some of them.

Continued media coverage given to rising cancer cases near Kaiga forced Nuclear Power Corporation of India Ltd (NPCIL) to undertake a damage control exercise as a part of which a seminar was held at Kaiga with experts from the Mumbai-based Tata Memorial Centre (TMC) and assured the villagers that there was no increase in cancer cases (*The Times of India*, 2012). They were told that cancer cases were three times more in the USA as compared to India and that as many as 70 per cent of the cancer cases were related to obesity, lack of hygiene and chewing of tobacco. However, the environmentalists, villagers and journalists were not convinced.

Environmentalist and the chairman of the Western Ghats Task Force[4] (WGTF) Ananth Hegde Ashisara[5] held a press conference on 13 March 2013 and charged that the power plant was causing cancer among the residents of the nearby villages (*Deccan Herald*, 2013). The statement was reported widely in the media. When the members of the task force visited the villages, the residents told them that the number of cases had increased after the plant was established. Ashisara had also claimed that the increase in the number of cancer cases had been borne out by medical tests. He cited a survey of 10,000 people living around the Kaiga plant carried out before the plant was established

[4] The task force was set up by the Government of Karnataka in 2008 to study the issue of conservation and sustainable development in the Western Ghats region of Karnataka.

[5] Anantha Hegde Ashisara, presently the chairman of the Karnataka Biodiversity Board, has been the leader of Vriksha Laksha Andolana, an environmental movement active in the Western Ghats region of Karnataka.

by the Bengaluru-based environmental organization Citizens for Alternatives to Nuclear Energy (CANE) which had found that there were only three cases of cancer. But after the plant became operational, the number of cases had crossed 35–40 in the villages with populations of around 3,000. A report in *Deccan Herald* quoting the deputy commissioner of the district had said that radiation from KAPS was not the cause of cancer as per the findings of the TMC. (*Deccan Herald*, 2015). However, newspapers continued to report the frequent claim of the environmentalists that radiation from the plant was causing cancer among the people living in the surrounding areas.

A report in *The New Indian Express* on 21 June 2018 said that according to a study by the TMC in the 16 km radius of the plant, the number of cancer cases had gone up by 200 per cent over a period of three years between 2010 and 2013 (*The New Indian Express*, 2018). The headline and the lead of the news story suggested a direct link between radiation from KAPS and the increase in cancer cases. However, the report of the TMC had only recoded a rise in cancer cases but did not link the increase to radiation from the Kaiga plant. According to the report, the number of cases had increased from about 70–80 in 2010 to 316 in 2013. It also said that lung, mouth, oesophagus, tongue, hylpharynx, cervix uteri, ovary, thyroid and corpus uteri cancers were found among the patients. The TMC's report did not say that the cancer cases had any links to radiation. However, the last paragraph of the news story quoted a cancer expert who said that it would not be possible to say whether there was increase in the number of cancer cases because of KAPS, unless studies were conducted in other areas also. While the newspaper headline talked about KAPS causing cancer, the cancer expert wanted more investigation. Following the publication of the newspaper report the *Journal of the Scientific Society* wrote an editorial on the suggesting a careful examination of the results of the study conducted by the TMC (Nerli & Ghagane, 2018). Further research was suggested instead of spreading false information. The editorial said that increased tobacco consumption, environmental pollution, food habit and lifestyle could be the contributing factors. Better awareness and diagnostic facilities could also have been the reasons for higher number of cases being detected.

When environmental clearance was given to the expansion plan of KAPS to add two more units to the existing four despite opposition by the environmentalists and the people from the villages around the plant, a massive public protest was held at Mallapur, a town close to the nuclear plant on 17 November 2019. At this protest too the issue of radiation from KAPS causing cancer was raised besides deforestation and threat to wildlife (Bhat, 2019). The protesters referred to the TMC's report and argued that the spurt in cancer cases in the past two decades in Kaiga was because of the radioactive pollution caused by KAPS (Vasuki, 2019).

Whenever a protest was held against KAPS, the media highlighted the issue of radiation-induced cancer even though there were many other issues which the protesters had spoken about. A popular perception emerged that the increase in cancer cases was caused by the radioactive pollution. However, scientists reject any link between KAPS and increase in the number of cancer cases. Dr Kamalaksha Shenoy, consultant radiation oncologist at AJ Hospital in Mangalore who has been visiting Karwar for over three years to treat cancer patients says that increasing incidence of cancer are multifactorial and cannot be solely attributed to nuclear plant at Kaiga (personal communication, 7 June 2021). He has closely interacted with the TMC which has been making a registry of cancer cases. He says in India the primary causes of cancer are mainly tobacco, alcohol abuse, lack of awareness and life style changes including unhealthy food habits. Oral, throat, oesophageal, stomach, lung, tongue, cervix uteri, ovary, thyroid, corpus uteri, and breast cancers which are called solid tumours are commonly found among the people of the district. Dr Shenoy says:

> Radiation induced cancers have not significantly increased compared to the other cancers induced by tobacco chewing or alcohol abuse. Therefore, it is difficult to arrive at a conclusion unless rate of cancer incidence after the nuclear plant was set up is compared to the incidence of cancer before the plant was set up. Also, the data should be compared to incidence of cancer in other areas.

Some of his patients from Uttara Kannada district told him about people blaming the KAPS for the rise in the number of cancer cases. According to him, attention should be paid to the consequences of spraying of pesticides, use of chemical fertilizers and plastics in areca plantations, which also could be contributing factors for the rise in cancer cases. The registry maintained by the TMC rules out any type of radiation-induced cancer. Shenoy says, the media are creating misconceptions among the people by carrying the statements made by people who have not understood the environmental impact of radiation. His advice to journalists is that they should collaborate with doctors and medical institutions to understand the causes of cancer and to create awareness among the people.

Professor Vasudeva believes that the media have been largely pro-ecology but faults them for not considering the views of the scientists about linking the increasing cases of cancer to the radiation from the nuclear power plant (personal communication, 27 February 2019). He argues that if radiation from the Kaiga plant had caused cancer then many of those who work inside the plant should have been affected. Except for one person who died after mistakenly drinking titanium at the plant, no one has suffered any disease because of radiation, he says. According to him, domestic burning of plastic could be a major contributor to increase in cancer cases than the radiation from nuclear power plants. Dr H. M. Somashekarappa, professor of nuclear physics at Mangalore University, who had conducted the baseline background radiation in and around Kaiga before the nuclear power plant was established, says that the claims about radiation causing cancer among the people in the surrounding areas are not based on scientific evidence (personal communication, 26 January 2020). He also says radioactive contamination of the environment happens only when there is an accident or an explosion at the plant. Although there are issues with regard to processing of uranium and decommissioning of the nuclear power plants, he says, journalists should speak to the scientists and report objectively without causing any fear among the people.

Journalists Narasimha Adi and Ashok Hasyagar who have been covering environmental issues for decades in the district say, based on their interactions with the people, that the incidents of cancer have increased after the nuclear plant became operational (personal communication, 28 February 2019). Journalists are in a way caught between the people who complain that the cancer incidents have increased and the scientists who deny that there is any link between the Kaiga plant and cancer. When there are claims and counterclaims about causes of cancer one way of reporting the controversy is to give both sides of the argument but at the same time stress on the argument which is supported by overwhelming evidence. A journalist is expected to present before the readers what the experiences of the people are and also what the scientific community's views are without creating panic among the people by highlighting questionable evidence. It is essential that different points of view are presented in their proper contexts and an indication is provided as to on which side of an issue a greater weight of scientific evidence lies. While deforestation, mining of uranium and decommissioning of the nuclear plants are not often contentious issues the radiation-cancer link has been a highly contested subject. Dr Vasudeva and Dr Kamalaksha Shenoy say the media have not played responsible role in allaying the fears about cancer.

However, senior environmental journalist Nagesh Hegde justifies the media coverage of radiation-cancer link as there has been no sufficient scientific evidence to reject it (personal communication, 9 August 2021). He says the survey conducted by the TMC was not scientific as it was conducted only in one area. According to him, the survey should have been conducted in another area with similar agricultural, economic and cultural practices to compare the cancer cases in both the places. He feels that a comparative study has not been done deliberately to keep on misleading the people. Those who refute the link between the nuclear power plant and increase in cancer cases do not talk about the studies in other countries which have found substantial evidence to show that cancer cases had increased in the areas close to the nuclear power plants. He found fault with the way questions were asked while conducting the survey as they were focused more on the food habits of the people including chewing of areca nut and betel leaf rather than on other factors. Hegde says officials always come up with readymade answers and refuse to see the other side of the story and it is the responsibility of the media to report the genuine apprehensions people have about radiation-induced cancers.

Despite pressure from the environmental groups and the media, no comparative study has been conducted. In such a situation, environmental reporting requires a lot of research and legwork to ascertain the validity of the claims the environmentalists make and the evidence that scientists have produced. It involves checking and rechecking facts in their contexts and not being influenced by pressure groups that may have their own strategy of building an agenda. People's experiences with the consequences of environmental degradation cannot be rejected outright only because they lack evidence. Proper investigation and interpretations of evidence are necessary to promote scientific understanding of the issues among the media audiences.

Nagesh Hegde says if there is a controversy about industrial pollution causing diseases, factors like individual immunity levels are not given adequate importance (personal communication, 14 October 2018). Poor communities that have lower levels of immunity are always at higher risk. He says he conducted a survey several years ago in Rajasthan, which revealed that skin disease, cataract, infertility and reproductive dysfunction among women of poor communities were caused by exposure to radiation. In case of fluorosis, it has been noticed that although everyone drinks the same water only the poor people are afflicted by the disease. In a case of chemical contamination those who are healthy and genetically strong are not affected. Since the nutrition levels among the poor are very low they are vulnerable to diseases caused by pollution. However, Hegde says, the media do not make adequate efforts to present these realities to the people. Hegde says that when chemical companies claim that only a few families are affected and that if the disease had been caused by the chemicals, then everyone would have been affected, the media rarely highlight the effect of pollution on the poor people who have low immunity levels. He says it is the responsibility of the media to provide that kind of analysis to the readers. Otherwise, the media audiences may be left with the impression that there is no direct link between chemical/radiation contamination and diseases.

Lack of Specialization and Training

Non-specialists do much of environmental reporting in Indian newspapers although there are a few specialists. One of the questions often asked is whether journalists reporting on environmental issues have the necessary knowledge, training and the skill to understand, investigate, analyse and present environmental issues. In most parts of the world, specialization in environmental reporting is lacking while there are specialists reporting on civil aviation, lifestyle, travel and food (Koop, 2020; Mercado & Chavez, 2020; Motta, 2020). There are no designated environmental reporters in the Indian media, although many newspapers have some reporters who regularly write on matters related to the environment. Training and orientation to young people entering the profession is lacking in most media. The orientation programmes run by some newspapers for the young recruits seldom include a component that sensitizes them to environmental issues. Media houses that have been downsizing their staff strength do not send their reporters for short-term training programmes and workshops on environmental reporting. Even when there are journalists with master's degrees in subjects related to the environment, they are assigned to cover subjects unrelated to their areas of specialization.

Many universities, which have been offering bachelor's and master's programmes in journalism and mass communication did not have a course in environmental journalism until recently. There are now several journalism schools in India that teach environmental journalism as a paper or a course but a specialization in the subject is not offered while specialization is offered in broadcast journalism, online journalism, print journalism, new media, business journalism and development journalism. Specialization in postgraduate programmes actually means offering a certain number courses/papers in a particular subject. Specific courses on some key aspects of the environment and climate change are needed not only to raise the level of awareness about causes and consequences of major issues but also to impart the skills of writing and presenting them to the media audiences.

Even in those schools where environmental journalism is taught as a course, no serious attention is paid to equip the students with necessary tools to investigate, gather evidence and analyse the problems. Rohin Kumar of Greenpeace who took a course in environmental journalism as part of the diploma programme in journalism says students studied that paper only for marks, and not with the purpose of acquiring skills to report environmental issues (personal communication, 20 May 2021). 'If you ask students who are their favourite journalists they will name some anchors but not a journalist. If you ask them what was the last environmental story they read, the students would have no answer,' he says. That may not be the case in all schools of journalism as some of them have well-known environmental journalists regularly teaching them, bringing their rich experience from the field to the classroom.

Generalists and Specialists

In media organizations it is mostly generalists who move to higher positions and become editors, not the specialists who may have spent years gaining deeper knowledge in a particular area. There are exceptions like Derryl D'Monte who brought recognition and respectability to environmental journalism. His death in March 2019 was a massive loss to environmental journalism in India. He was the only environmental journalist in the mainstream Indian media who rose to the position of editor. He became the editor of the Sunday magazine of *The Times of India* and later the resident editor of the *Indian Express*, Mumbai. He was also the founder president of both FEJI and IFEJ. Derryl D'Monte and Nagesh Hegde have made an outstanding contribution to environmental journalism in India as specialists. Several journalists who worked with them have been writing on science, environment and development.

In the late 1980s, some journalists and concerned citizens in Bengaluru would hold informal discussions on every Sunday with noted environmental scientist Madhava Gadgil, environmental historian Ramachandra Guha and nuclear scientist D. P. Senguptha at Kumara Park in Bengaluru (Nagesh Hegde, personal communication, 14 October 2018). These discussions would help journalists understand issues related to science, the environment and society. Some complex issues used to be discussed threadbare so that journalists had a comprehensive picture before they wrote their stories. But the number of persons attending these sessions decreased as the teleserial Mahabharata began to be aired on Sundays. A highly useful and insightful programme of discussion ended ultimately because of the lack of interest among the journalists themselves. They would rather watch Mahabharata than listen to scientists and scholars. Regular interaction between scientists and journalists no longer exists but consultation with scientists does happen when complex and controversial issues are reported.

According to Nagesh Hegde, journalists do not make efforts to help themselves gain deeper knowledge about environmental issues (personal communication, 12 October 2018). He once suggested to the journalists in the Sagara taluk of Shivamogga district in Karnataka that they form an association of journalists in the Western Ghats region so that they got a better understanding of the environmental problems in the Western Ghats but, no attempts were made in that direction. Hegde says,

> When there are state level, district level and taluk level journalists' associations, an association of this kind will help journalists know what is happening in the entire stretch of the Western Ghats. It would also help journalists enhance their level of awareness about the threats to the Western Ghats and conservation measure needed.

However, no such association has been formed in either Karnataka or any other state in the Western Ghats region.

Leo Saldanha, who often holds interactive sessions with journalists reporting on environmental issues, believes that orientation towards reporting the environment, if not formal training, is necessary to ensure that the media present issues in proper perspectives. He says,

> In media, there is a lot of untrained writing by and large. Whenever we send press releases it is very rare that a journalist calls back to seek clarification or to express disagreement. I don't expect them to parrot what I say but would want them to come up with critical comments. There is no pushback from the media. Very few journalists who know the issues will ask us to talk about them in some detail. Most journalists are content with what we give and do not interpret the facts before them. In order to keep the democratic

space alive, journalists need to be critical and analytical in what they write. When we put out the information, we expect debate and discussion in media. Without debate and discussion, there cannot be any change. It is not the case in other countries where I have some experience of working with the media. There is always contestation and debate in media in the US and Europe. Sometimes the questions journalists ask here are deliberately provocative, not even intelligently provocative. (Personal communication, 21 February 2019)

According to him, more than the lack of specialization there is an acute lack of awareness because of which journalists do not do any research for their stories. The Karnataka government converted 28,000 acres of land into a solar park in Pavagada Taluk in 2018. On the ecological consequences of the park and the absence of media coverage about it, Saldanha says:

If you look through any of the newspapers there is hardly any coverage. The scale of displacement is so bad. It is a sea of glass stretching to 20–30 km. Where did the cattle go? Where did the villagers go? Nobody knows. It is just two hours from Bengaluru. Just because it is solar, it does not mean it is benign. Solar power is good when it comes from rooftop panels but in Pawagada a large area is covered with glass. Thousands of acres covered with glass is an ecological disaster. After we started investigating one or two write-ups have appeared in 'The Wire'. The mainstream newspapers completely neglected it. We are not opposed to solar energy but against solar park consuming vast expanse of land.

The popular perception created in media is that solar power, whatever may the way of producing it, is good and that the opposition to it is illogical. It is important to critically examine the environmental consequences of creating solar parks. Millions of farmers are being displaced around the world for building solar parks. The media are yet to see this as an issue. Saldanha believes the issue was not adequately reported because of a lack of awareness among the journalists. According to him, most journalists lack basic knowledge about the environment. They do not know how environmental problems are caused and what environmental laws exist. Even those who sit in higher positions in the editorial sections of newspapers, from the resident editor to those who work on the desk, have very little awareness about environmental issues. The problem with the journalists who lack a deeper understanding of environmental issues is that they do not conduct an investigation into issues but try to sensationalize them. This can harm those journalists who want to do serious reporting.

Rohin Kumar, who frequently interacts with journalists has found that most of those who write on the environment and climate change are not familiar with the key issues involved (personal communication, 21 May 2021). Talking about poor knowledge of journalists about climate-related issues, he says:

> They have no idea what IPCC is or what climate agreement is about. Even those who work for the Delhi media, which are considered as the national media, have no understanding of what climate change is. I don't know about the people in the regional press. Some of them might know about it. I have not yet met a general reporter of any media who is interested in climate change and knows what carbon neutrality is or what net-zero emission is or what IPCC is or what is climate change commitment is or why President Trump pulled US out of the Paris Agreement and why Joe Biden brought the US back to the agreement. They are all alien topics to them. Their low level of awareness is evident in their coverage of the issue. How will these media make their audiences understand how this global issue is going to affect their own lives in future? Many a time when we do air pollution stories I have to actually tell them how to write. Sometimes I ghost-write for them. I have been doing so for some journalists who work for the reputed media houses. Of course, they are not at fault because the structure of the newsroom and the structure of the digital spaces are such that the reporter who is working on a climate change issue is also assigned to write a political story.

For Rohin Kumar, the low awareness is a cause for concern because the consequences of climate change have become more visible in recent years in the form of frequently occurring floods, droughts and cyclones. Despite the fact that the world is already in a climate emergency, awareness about it among the journalists is lacking. He says even when a journalist is not a specialist writing about the environment, it is important for him to know about climate change because it is not only going to affect the economy and health of the people but also their very existence. Even editors, sometimes, do not know how to approach the problem of climate change and how to present its impact. Kumar says the Indian press does not have the language to write such stories. The media follow some general guidelines as to how to write on certain sensitive issues like communalism and rape, but the vocabulary to write about climate change is lacking. 'It is important for a journalist to develop an appropriate language to narrate to the public issues associated with climate change. The media should treat climate change as seriously as they have treated corona virus pandemic,' he says.

Leo Saldanha, who frequently holds media conferences, says that many journalists are not even exposed to environmental issues leave alone training. He says,

> Journalists attend press conferences without knowing the abcd of the problems being presented. They come to the press conference without any homework. If a press note is given there are hardly any questions coming from the journalists on the issues in focus. The analytical ability is lacking even among the senior journalists who look after some specific pages of newspapers.

Nevertheless, he says, a few journalists pay careful attention to every bit of information the activists provide and ask searching questions.

On the lack of knowledge about environmental issues among the journalists, activist Panduranga Hegde (personal communication, 26 February 2019) agrees with Saldanha and argues that even the core recommendations of the Madhav Gadgil and Kasturirangan panels on conservation of Western Ghats have not been fully understood. Fearing displacement and restrictions on developmental activities some groups of people in the Western Ghats region have been protesting against the implementation of the recommendations since 2013 (Coastal Digest, 2014; *Deccan Herald*, 2018; *The New Indian Express*, 2020; *The Hindu*, 2013). Newspapers and television channels have been reporting about the protests without going into to the details of what the recommendations are and their implications. Hegde tried for 2–3 years to bring journalists for a one-day discussion on what the two reports say. It was a frustrating exercise for him because even the district and taluk level journalists were not interested. They continued to present some aspects of the reports in such a way that implementation of the reports would be detrimental to the lives of the people living in the Western Ghats region.

Panduranga Hegde says the Madhav Gadgil report empowers the *gram sabhas* (village committees) to make crucial decisions that the media never tried to understand. Hegde says,

> Journalists who have no vision and no training do not understand the complex environmental issues. There is not even a 2-page note on the report, which could be helpful to journalists. In the absence of reading of those reports, they are influenced by the opponents of the reports.

Journalists who have very little knowledge about the processes that cause environmental problems often ask him to speak about the issues in the Western Ghats in two minutes. 'What can be said in two minutes about the Western Ghats spread across six states and with such diverse flora and fauna,' he says. Well-informed journalists would not be insisting on opinions in two sentences or two-minute bites about a complex issue. If there are pointed questions on specific aspects of a problem, it is possible to obtain short responses. If only media had trained journalists to cover environmental issues there would have been greater awareness among the people.

While activists say that many journalists are not fully aware of the issues related to the environment and climate change there are some journalists who have struggled hard to educate themselves on those issues spending their own time and resources. In the absence of environmental beat, it is the personal interest of the journalists who have concern for the environment that matters. For Meera Bhardwaj, a senior journalist with decades of experience, it was self-education that made her familiar with the nuances of some of the key environmental issues (personal communication, 28 October 2018). She says, 'as a journalist, I am so busy with my routine work that it is hard to find time to update my knowledge. I have always tried to update myself against all odds'. She does not submit or publish any story unless she has done her investigation and collected all documents. She has sat on stories for several months looking for evidence. Since facts and claims need to be checked it will take several days for a journalist to produce a story that provides authentic information about issues and policies.

Environmental activist Vidya Dinker has found that journalists from the rural background have a better grasp of the environmental issues as compared to those who come from urban background despite the fact that they have had no formal training in environmental reporting (personal communication, 5 May 2021). When it comes to acquisition of agricultural land for industrial purposes, the journalists from rural background seem to understand the problem better. Some journalists who have parents still depending on the land for their livelihood empathize with those who are facing eviction. They understand what it means to be losing one's land and common property resources. While formal education in environmental journalism would make coverage much more efficient, journalists' own commitment and experience do matter.

Even though coastal Karnataka has witnessed rapid industrialization and consequent environmental degradation in the last three decades, there is not even a single specialist from any media groups reporting on environmental issues. With the number of reporters working for state-level newspapers decreasing in recent years they are assigned to file two-three stories every day. When journalists are under such tremendous pressure, they have no time to investigate environmental issues.

There are no specialists reporting on climate change except in niche publications like the *Down To Earth* and *India Climate Dialogue*[6] (Newslaundry, 2019). There are no dedicated people covering climate change in the mainstream media. Covering climate impact is not an easy task unless the journalist has a good knowledge of the factors that have led to the accelerated rate of increase in global temperatures.

---

[6] The India Climate Dialogue has now merged with thethridpole.net, a multilingual platform for information and discussion about Himalayan watershed and rivers.

One needs to understand several questions. What does expansion of coal mines mean? Why are floods happening? Are these the result of misgovernance? What do international and national policy changes mean on the ground? It is important for a journalist to speak to all stakeholders to determine if disasters being witnessed are the results of misgovernance or climate change.

There are no budgets to investigate and find answers to these questions. Reporters who used to be posted to places that had seen rapid industrialization have been shunted out. In the absence of support from media houses, what specialists should have done is left to the freelancers and a few committed journalists. Sustained and comprehensive coverage of climate change is not possible when a media house has transferred its responsibility to freelancers. Moreover, comprehensive coverage of the environment and climate change is possible only when a team works in coordination as many of the anthropogenic activities are connected and interlinked. Only a team can cover the climate story as it is a multidimensional problem, otherwise the crucial aspects of the story would be left out. It requires journalists covering business, agriculture, politics and science and technology to work together to make an impact. Efficient coverage of environmental and climate problems cannot be achieved unless energy systems, global finance and complexity of the climate science are understood. When journalists are reporting climate change, they are not reporting a single issue but a bunch of issues that need to be examined in relation to each other. It is important to find whistle-blowers in the system who provide information about violation of norms and misuse of public funds. A journalist has to work with active watchdog groups at the community level as well at the intellectual level but all of that requires dedication and hard work of a specialist. It is a complex challenge. Journalists have to skill up themselves to understand the other aspects like industry, finance and health that are linked to climate change.

Grassroots Training

Most of the training programmes for journalists outside the formal academic programmes are usually focused on technical and production skills including newsgathering, interviewing and using of advanced technology. Some aspects of environmental journalism are included in those programmes but it is very rare that exclusive training programmes are held to help journalists report environmental issues. However, outside formal educational institutions, attempts have been made to impart training in development and environmental reporting. Environmental journalist Shivananda Kalave has been conducting short-term courses in journalism for nearly two decades (personal communication, 27 February 2019). One of the objectives of the courses is to sensitize young people to environmental issues. Around 1,700 people have attended the short-term courses conducted in development journalism. All of them have been taught about rainwater harvesting and sustainable methods of agriculture. The participants who attend the courses realize their ignorance about the environment and start exploring the problems. Nearly a hundred of those who participated in short-term courses have actively involved themselves in writing about development and environmental issues. They have also become activists in their own way. It is hard to find journalists from big newspapers attending such grassroots-level programmes.

On the question of newspapers appointing specialists to write on the environment, senior journalist Poornima feels it is very difficult to find journalists who have a sound knowledge of the impact of economic development on nature (personal communication, 26 June 2019). She says it is better to first produce such specialists and then ask the management of a media group to create such beats. She believes that specialization and training will lead to better journalism. Dr R. Vasudev, professor of forest biology, College of Forestry, Sirsi, who has been closely working with local journalists is of the view that reporting on issues related to science and environment becomes meaningful only when the reporters deep dive into the subject. (personal communication, 26 February 2019).

Environmental organizations like the Delhi-based CSE have been conducting workshops and training programmes for the journalists from diverse media channels. The CSE offers media fellowships for journalists from Africa and Asia. The publications brought out by the CSE are of immense value to journalists in understanding the depths and dimensions of the key environmental problems.

One of the challenges today is bridging the gap between specialists and generalists as there are fewer and fewer specialist in media. Specialists are the first to be laid off whenever there is downsizing of a media organization. The business model with which media are run today is beset with problems that have far-reaching consequences on the quality and goals of professional journalism. When generalists are assigned to cover specialized areas like the environment or climate change, accuracy becomes a serious challenge. Efficient and professional coverage of the environment and climate change issues requires specialization and prioritization in media so that it helps build a discourse necessary for addressing those issues.

Conclusion

Scientific uncertainties are a big challenge to any environmental journalist. While scientists speak about an issue in terms of indicators, hypotheses, propositions, links and correlation the public who constitute a vast majority of the media audience seek definite answers. Journalists have the responsibility of bridging the gap in knowledge between the scientists and the common person, so the issues of science that relate to the environment and climate change are adequately understood. Sometimes journalists are faced with the challenge of reporting claims and counterclaims with regard to some major issues. Even when there is overwhelming evidence that has shown that climate change has accelerated in the last century due to human activity there are climate sceptics who have been challenging it with their own data. However, in the Indian media, there are hardly any questions on climate change but a lot of discussion on what India should be doing as a key participant in the international climate dialogue.

In order to strike a balance between scientifically accurate information and journalistic norms, a consultation with scientists who have divergent opinions is necessary because the available evidence has to be looked at from various angles. Conclusions about several complex environmental issues are elusive and are rarely expressed in a tone of finality making the journalists' job harder. While the media audiences seek unambiguous reports on issues with specific information about how those issues are to be addressed, simple and straightforward answers do not come from either scientists or officials. This leaves media audiences unsure of what they should be doing.

There are times when media have consistently covered an issue despite conflicting evidence emerging from committees that have conducted investigations into it. In the case of endosulfan issue, the media were not carried away by the results of biased investigation and the campaign of the pesticide company. Consistent media coverage played a key role in building a strong public opinion in favour of banning endosulfan as there was sufficient evidence to show that it had caused serious health problems. The media gave a wide coverage to the link between radiation and cancer but did not make any efforts on their own to investigate and demand answers from scientists and activists about the factors responsible for the rise in cancer rates. According to scientists and doctors, the high incidence of cancer reported from areas around the Kaiga nuclear plant was not related to radiation, but the activists and the media have pointed to the absence of a comparative study.

The focus in media often tends to be on the consequences rather than on the contributing factors. Scientific explanation remains incomplete when contributing factors are not fully investigated. The corporate media may not provide critical and comprehensive reports because of their links with the industry. Scientific uncertainties related to environmental issues can be understood and explained better if there are reporters specializing in the area. Courses in environmental journalism at journalism schools will not only sensitize students to the key issues but also help them develop deeper knowledge and skills that are needed to analyse issues in broader contexts. Orientation programmes, workshops and short-term courses that several intuitions offer are of immense value to journalists. Media houses have not been investing enough in covering environment and climate change. In order to enhance the quality of environmental journalism, it is important to provide necessary resources and opportunities for journalists to upgrade their knowledge and skills.

CHAPTER 6

Building the Environmental Agenda

The Role of Sources

Sources are individuals or representatives of organized or unorganized groups who, with their knowledge or expertise, provide information, the raw material for news. A journalist refines and changes the material gathered from the sources and turns it into a meaningful story for the news audience. Gans (2004, p. 80) views news as 'information which is transmitted from sources to audiences, with journalists—who are both employees of bureaucratic commercial organisations and members of a profession—summarising, refining and altering what becomes available to them from sources in order to make it suitable for their audiences'. What is seen as news in media is the outcome of the interaction between the newsmen and their sources (Sigal, 1973). Sources become 'surrogate observers' when journalists themselves are unable to observe everything that occurs in places they are reporting from (Roshco, 1975, p. 84). Sources are not merely conduits of information to journalists but providers of perspectives. The perspectives the sources offer may be the main criteria for their selection among various competing sources. Despite journalists' claims to objectivity, studies show that there are biases in the selection of sources (Brown et al., 1987; Hoynes & Croteau, 1989; Sachsman & Valenti, 2015;

Soley, 1992; Whitney et al., 1989;). While some sources are given prominence, others are marginalized. Representatives of civil rights, human rights and labour groups are usually underrepresented as sources, whereas government officials are overrepresented.

Many a time, sources themselves contact reporters to tell them their story ideas. They are not always neutral conveyors of information but attempt to promote their own interests or construct their own discourse about events or issues. The reporters decide whether the sources are suitable, authentic or reliable. Most of the times, reporters seek out sources who can throw light on issues they are investigating. There are sources that are eager to provide information and sources that are uncooperative and evasive. Reporters try to gather information suitable to their stories as quickly as possible from the sources that are easily accessible within deadlines. Gans (2004, p. 116) says,

> The relationship between sources and journalists resembles a dance, for sources seek access to journalists, and journalists seek access to sources. Although it takes two to tango, either sources or journalists can lead, but more often than not, sources do the leading. Staff and time being in short supply, journalists actively pursue only a small number of regular sources who have been available and suitable in the past, and are passive toward other possible news source.

While sources generally play an important role in what is reported as news, some sources that have greater access to the media influence story frames. These groups are often engaged in agenda building, which refers to influencing what issues journalists report on and how they cover them (Cobb & Elder, 1972). Although agenda building is seen as a 'process in which media, government and the citizenry reciprocally influence one another', it is the government that influences the media the most as a major source of information (Lang & Lang, 1983, pp. 58–59). Hall et al. (1978) argued that powerful 'accredited' sources such as government departments or the courts enjoy privileged access to the media. They command greater access to the media by virtue of their claims to expert knowledge, their powerful position in society, or their representative status. They suggest that powerful sources become over-accessed by the media, and as a result, they become 'primary definers' of key issues.

Sources try all possible strategies to get their ideas across to the people through the frames they prefer. They tend to believe that they understand the problems better than anyone else. If a reporter is a specialist and has a deeper knowledge of an issue, he may not allow one particular source to dominate the story. However, under the pressure of time and limitations of resources to pursue the long trial of a story, a reporter may not be able to access all sources.

Because of reluctance among the officials to disclose unfavourable information, reporters turn to anonymous sources who may not give accurate information. However, the stories that are based on anonymous sources or those who do not want to be identified would be less convincing to the readers.

Sources play an important role in influencing story frames and constructing the environmental agenda (Dunwoody & Griffin, 1993). If the story frames are to be decided by the reporters, a sustained effort is needed to dig out information from the sources and use them in appropriate contexts. When a reporter lacks knowledge about the environment or climate change, he is unable to tap the full potential of sources in terms of gathering information, ideas and opinions. Instead of delving into layers of information surrounding an issue or an event, a reporter ends up obtaining superficial information and an angle, which the source prefers. In some cities there are only single reporters reporting not just for one publication but also for all sister publications of a media group. When events related to sports, politics and the environment are covered by the same reporters, only those sources they have easy access to get quoted. The limited number of sources with whom they interact frequently influence their perceptions about certain issues. For an issue to be reported comprehensively, a wide variety of sources are needed, otherwise sources try to use reporters to get their message across to their adversaries and their allies.

Hansen (2020, p. 43) says that the sources play such a dominant role in the construction of news that the 'balance of power between environmental journalists and their sources is shifting significantly towards the latter'. At times, more than the journalists the sources define and frame events. Powerful sources often dominate the news but environmental activists and other independent sources also influence the news content as 'claims makers'.[1]

The most common sources of information found in environmental stories are officials, industry representatives, environmental NGOs and activists. Environmental reporters tend to receive more PR material than the reporters on regular beats do. The influence of the PR material is often more visible in the stories that the reporters on environmental beat produce than the stories that other reporters produce. A lot of pre-packaged material comes from the state agencies and corporate houses or through their front groups/think tanks (Hansen, 2020). A typical reporter spends much of his time covering breaking stories, attending routine meetings and press conferences and rewriting press releases (Anderson, 2017; Davis, 2013; Gans, 2004; Gitlin, 1980). The reliance on sources that are considered authoritative sources and overreliance on promotional materials from PR firms influence story frames.

Readers' perceptions about the credibility of sources may be in variance with the degree of credibility attached to them in actual coverage of environmental issues (Varna, 2020). Sources that are most often quoted in news stories may not be the most trusted sources from the point of view of the media audiences. The perception of trustworthiness of sources may change according to the type of environmental issues. While officials may be trusted more in case of one issue, activists and affected persons may be trusted more in case of other issues.

In a survey carried out by Yale University in November–December 2011 in India, it was found that scientists were the most trusted (73%) sources of information about global warming (Leiserowitz & Thaker, 2012, pp. 29–30). The media were the second most trusted sources (69%), followed by environmental organizations (68%). It is interesting that family and friends were trustable sources (67%) on global warming. The state governments (56%) were found to be more trustworthy than the local governments (54%) and the Central government (54%).

---

[1] Claims makers are those who are involved in animating, legitimating and demonstrating a problem. They package their claims in a novel, dramatic and succinct form (Hannigan, 2006, p. 66).

Corporations as sources (52%) were trusted more than religious leaders (46%) and community leaders (50%). Religious leaders who play an important role in social and cultural lives of the people were the least trusted of all the sources.

Although newspapers show a lot of concern for the environment in general terms, they take 'development first' position when it comes to specific issues. The position they take with regard to environmental questions is not very different from those of the mainstream political parties. Independent sources that have no links with either the government organizations or corporations have not always succeeded in putting their point of view across as their acts and positions are not seen in positive frames. Official and industrial/business sources receive more favourable coverage than environmental groups. The very rules, which grew out of the media's desire for greater professional neutrality, also serve powerfully to orientate them in the definitions of social reality which their accredited sources provide. If non-institutional sources and activists are to attract quality coverage in media that have larger audiences, they need to be seen as credible and legitimate sources.

Officials as Primary Definers of News

Agencies of the state tend to enjoy the most privileged access to the media. Several studies have shown that in the media coverage of environmental news, government officials are the predominant sources (Beder, 1998; Dunwoody & Griffin, 1993; Freedman, 2011; Nisbet & Newman, 2015). They are regarded as authoritative and reliable sources that provide accurate information. Although environmental groups and activists often raise environmental questions and attempt to garner media attention, official sources are quoted much more often than environmental groups or activists (Adiga, 2017; Anderson, 1993; Einsiedel, 1988; Einsiedel & Coughlan, 1993; Gooch, 1996; Greenberg et al., 1989; Hansen, 1991, 1993; Nohrstedt, 1991; Wang, 1988). What officials say is usually taken as a fact, while any information given by other sources is looked at with a lot of scepticism.

An analysis of environmental news in four English newspapers— *The Hindu, The Times of India, The Indian Express* and the *Deccan*

Herald—from 1984 to 2004 showed that during the 20-year period, the officials accounted for an average of 35.37 per cent of the quoted sources (Poornananda, 2008). Scientists and experts were the second most often quoted sources (22.27%) followed by environmental NGOs (17.90%). Although officials dominated environmental news stories as sources throughout the two decades the percentage of NGOs quoted went up from 2.99 per cent in 1984 to 20.21 per cent in 2002.

Adiga (2017), in her analysis of environmental news coverage in two English and two Kannada newspapers between 2002 and 2011, found that 37.3 per cent of the sources quoted were official sources. Environmental NGOs were the second most often quoted sources (20.8%) after official sources. Only 8 per cent of the quoted sources were scientists. Surprisingly, industrial sources accounted for only 1.7 per cent of the total sources quoted. Official sources dominate environmental stories and the absence of a diversity of sources is an indication that officials are the primary definers of news.

Environmental groups receive lesser importance as sources of environmental information as compared to officials and experts. Although scientists, diplomats, politicians, activists, affected persons, and individual citizens are found in environmental news stories, it is the officials who occupy the prime position as sources. Chapman et al. (1997) who examined the relationship between sources and journalists found that both environmental pressure groups and politicians in power were setting the media agenda with regard to environmental issues. In India, they argue, the struggle to attain economic development places environmental issues low on politicians' agenda. Hence, politicians are not frequently quoted as sources in environmental stories. Although environmental groups have been able to influence media coverage of some environmental issues, their use as sources, when the total volume of news devoted to the environment is considered, is lesser than the use of official sources.

According to Nagesh Hegde, official sources in India did provide good stories to the newspapers a decade ago (personal communication, 12 October 2018). There were some officers in the government who would bring several environmental issues to the notice of the media. Several stories were written based on the inputs provided by the concerned officers. That kind of concern among the officials, Hegde says, is almost non-existent today. The decline in coverage of environmental issues is not only because journalists are not taking the initiative to probe environmental issues but also because the officials who work in the departments related to the environment do not keep journalists informed about issues of public interest. The information that the officials provide to the media today presents all that the government and the industry do in a positive light. Decades ago, officials used to reveal some information about the environmental consequences of certain projects to make sure that some measures were taken because of the media and public pressure. Hegde says it is almost impossible today to get the officials to speak on any environmental issue.

Many journalists still believe that what the officials say is reliable and trustworthy. They are sceptical about the facts and views the independent sources and non-governmental sources present before the media. Scientists who speak on behalf of the government are seen as more knowledgeable and trustable sources than those who are independent and have opinions in variance with the official opinion. Nagesh Hegde who had studied environmental science at IIT Kharagpur says that his colleagues in *Prajavani* wanted an official to be quoted in all his stories (personal communication, 12 October 2019). He says,

> When I wrote about nuclear power, I was asked by a senior colleague if I knew anything better than the nuclear scientist Rajaramanna who was a strong advocate of the Kaiga project. This question was asked even though I had studied environmental science at IIT Kharagpur and Jawaharlal Nehru University. When Rajaramanna went to Kaiga to tell the people there about the benefits of nuclear power, he faced a volley of questions from the people who had read my article on nuclear power in *Sudha* weekly. Unable to answer all their questions, Rajaramanna left the place midway through his dialogue with the people saying that they were biased. In my article, I had explained in the language of the common person the environmental consequences of nuclear energy. However, there is a clear tendency in media to trust only official sources as indicated in the opinion of my own colleagues.

There is a belief among some journalists that only an official or a scientist says is reliable but others argue that official sources are extremely important because readers want to know what they are saying. Keya Acharya (personal communication, 11 September 2020) says that what officials say matters a lot because what they say reflects the official policy about which public awareness is needed.

Rohin Kumar of Greenpeace says that environmental beat in the national capital Delhi has always meant covering the Ministry of Environment, Forests and Climate Change. As a result, information and views coming from the sources in the ministry take precedence over the crucial pieces of information and the opinions that the other sources may have. Kumar says that covering the ministry regularly is necessary, but too much dependence on official sources will lead to narrowing down of the entire coverage to a single frame denying a broader knowledge about an issue to the audiences. According to activist Vidya Dinker, if a journalist does not believe in what the government and the industry are saying he should bring that through in his reports (personal communication, 5 May 2021). She says that journalistic skills are not about juxtaposing what people are saying, what a reporter sees and what the officials are saying, but it is about exposing who is speaking the truth and who is not. A journalist's job is not publicizing the view of the government but presenting environmental news in a context that helps readers understand the reality.

Meera Bhardwaj, who has been writing on environmental issues for over two decades, says she takes information from only trusted sources irrespective whether they are officials or other sources (personal communication, 28 March 2019). She says if someone makes a serious allegation about an issue, she asks the person to give a written statement so that her newspaper is able to defend itself in case the issue is taken to the court. Some people do not want their names to be quoted in the news for the fear of being targeted by the legal agencies or by some pressure groups. She changes the names of those sources who she feels have no support but not the names of the officials, conservationists, experts and activists. While official sources should own up the responsibility for what they say, it is important to protect those sources who are likely to face the consequences of revealing important information to the media. Journalists can be hauled up for the claims the sources make. They normally quote sources only when they are convinced that the information is true and that the claims are factual. Many of the environmental stories have both activists and the officials with the former receiving greater prominence.

Bhardwaj explains her experience of dealing with official sources with an example. In March 2019, a leopard was trapped at Yelahanka in Bengaluru in the morning around 5 AM. It remained there in the cage until 5 PM. An activist who was highly disturbed by the plight of the predator alerted Bhardwaj about it. The forest officials had not followed the standard operating procedures for trapping a big carnivore. The guidelines of the Ministry of Environment, Forests and Climate Change about the norms to be followed as per the Wildlife Protection Act had been ignored. Bhardwaj's (2019) story on the leopard said that the animal had been traumatized because it was in a cage for over 12 hours in high temperatures. The forest official in charge of the area who was annoyed with Bhardwaj for writing about the incident alleged in a tweet that the journalist had not spoken to anyone and that her report was based on hearsay. The official also alleged that Bhardwaj was doing it only for publicity and that the story had demoralized the lower-level staff who tried to capture the leopard. When Bhardwaj brought this matter to the notice of the Principal Chief Conservator of Forest, he advised the officials to delete their comments on the story and reprimanded them for not acting as per the guidelines on capture/relocation of big cats.

The activists and volunteers had given an accurate version (including video evidence) of what had happened to the leopard while the senior official had not only denied the information but had also accused the journalist of filing a false story. That a higher official in the Forest department had come to the defence of the journalist points to the necessity of speaking to more than one official when there are allegations of lapses in acting as per the law. However, questioning what the officials have done requires that the journalist is aware of the legal provisions. If a journalist is writing about forests and wildlife, it is essential that he or she has a fair knowledge of the law and responsibilities of the officials concerned. Otherwise, questioning officials and seeking answers from them would not be possible.

Even though official sources are considered as authentic sources, they may not always provide accurate information and at times, the information they provide might be misleading. A reporter needs to speak to different sources so that facts can be corroborated and issues can be presented in proper perspectives. Environmental stories can be meaningful only when the reporter has drawn facts and opinions from different sources. Not all that activists say may be entirely true but so is the case with officials. A tip-off from an activist can lead to the unravelling of a big story even when the officials continue to avoid answering key questions.

With regard to the credibility of the official sources Bhardwaj, who had worked as a correspondent for Doordarshan for two decades, says usually government officials refuse to commit themselves and avoid all probing queries. Most (excepting a few) try to brush every uncomfortable question under the carpet and try to avoid the media. They do not answer the phone and are not available at their office. They do not even respond to messages sent through email or mobile phones,' she says. She neither trusts the government nor the NGOs fully but often looks for independent eyewitness accounts and other sources for cross-validating their claims.

Scientists who have specialized in certain areas related to the environment can be sources of immense value to journalists when they deal with uncertainties associated with a problem. Since many of the scientists work in organizations that are parts of the government departments or in research institutions funded by the government, they are seen as government sources. It is very rare that a scientist in a public organization has an opinion that contradicts the statements issued by the government. In the experience of K. G. Vasuki only a very few of the scientists working with the publicly funded research institutions and laboratories volunteer to speak to the media on controversial issues (personal communication, 28 June 2019). Some of them do not want to get involved in the politics of certain issues and therefore do not want to be quoted. Vasuki says it is very difficult to get officials and scientists to answer some key questions on a controversial project. Some scientists who are eager to share information with the public have been valuable sources to environmental reporters.

Frequent interaction with scientists as sources of environmental information can lead a journalist to exclusive stories. Sometimes scientists come to know from journalists about certain issues that deserve investigation. Narasimha Adi (personal communication, 27 February 2019) who works for *Samyukta Karnataka* and PTI news agency from Sirsi in Uttara Kannada district of Karnataka says he has written many environmental stories with the help of Dr Vasudeva, forest biologist in the town. Whenever an issue comes to his notice, he informs journalists and provides them with facts, figures and explanations. Dr Vasudeva who believes that the newspapers have played an important role in creating awareness among the people about environmental issues says he has been co-discovering a lot of things with the journalists (personal communication, 27 February 2019). Whenever journalists notice something unusual, disturbing, mysterious, or something new in the forests they bring it to Vasudeva's notice and they together go to the spot to find out more and to get a scientific explanation. He is a major source for the journalists in Uttara Kannada district as he has been an authentic source on the ecology of the Western Ghats.

Accurate information about the projects located in ecologically sensitive areas is very difficult to find. There is hardly any information in the public domain about controversial projects. However, for every story, a reporter is supposed to provide evidence, which is the job of an investigative agency. One has to struggle very hard to get information and documents. At times, getting information from a proper source is a frustrating experience for journalists. Expressing her anguish over the difficulty involved in getting information about environmental issues from official sources, Bhardwaj says, 'I feel we are not living in a democracy but under a totalitarian regime'. Whenever she gets information about projects that are going to be harmful to the environment, she shares it with other journalists and activists because she feels more than doing an exclusive story for her newspaper it is important to save the environment. When she got some documents about mining in Bannerghatta National Park near Bengaluru she shared them with other journalists and also with an NGO that took the case to the court. It is very rare that a journalist shares the information and documents painstakingly collected from the official sources with journalists representing other media organizations.

When asked about using the Right to Information (RTI) Act to obtain information from the offices and ministries dealing with the environment and climate change, journalists say that they have not used the Act even once and feel that it is not of much help. Obtaining information through RTI takes several weeks when the stories are to be written in hours to be relevant to the audience. Sometimes activists share with journalists the information they have obtained from the public authorities through RTI. Officials dominate environmental news coverage as source but information about controversial projects, which the journalists seek, is difficult to obtain. In a way, the official sources are the primary definers of news and at the same time deniers of information. The government agencies that deal with use and conservation of natural resources place varying degrees of restrictions on access to information. The bureaucratic decision-making process is important when it involves environmental policies but journalists have no access to notings on the files. Even when cabinet decisions are made on key projects that have environmental consequences only the decisions are communicated to the media but the details of how such decisions are made are not available to journalists. Because the official control over information is so enormous, many issues go unreported or inadequately reported.

Environmental NGOs as Sources

Environmental NGOs have been the major sources of information for the media. They orient their campaigns through media to influence popular opinion and to gain grassroots support. They put out a lot of written and visual material to present their perspectives to the media persons and to the public. Environmental groups, which often design their campaigns to appeal to news reporters, aim to bring pressure on the government to take measures to address the issue they are raising. Some journalists who regularly interact with environmental groups tend to use them as sources more often. Environmental groups that are ideologically more neutral are likely to be quoted as sources of news more often than those that are ideologically oriented (Anderson, 1993). Even though journalists and broadcasters tend to regard official sources as the authentic sources, the environmental groups have managed to attain a fair amount of media coverage. However, they are rarely treated as principal definers of the environmental debate.

While journalists are often very sceptical about the claims made by the environmental NGOs as sources of information, NGOs argue that they present reliable and well-researched information to the media. Leo Saldanha says environmental groups always attempt to provide relevant and credible information to the media because they would be judged by the quality of information they provide (personal communication, 21 February 2019). Explaining the relationship between the media and the NGOs as sources of environmental information Saldanha says,

> Media is the vehicle for me, not only to take the message to the people but also to present my critical views. The quality of work that we do is important for me, not just grabbing of the media attention. Because of the quality work that we do, we usually receive healthy criticism although criticism does get unhealthy at times. If we produce some worthless information not founded on facts, somebody will tear us apart. If we make false claims, we not only lose our credibility but the issue that we are trying to explain will also be lost.

He argues that NGOs act with responsibility in taking an issue to the public through the media. Giving information that is inaccurate or making tall claims would be harmful to any NGO in the long run as they can function effectively only when they enjoy public trust. According to him, most NGOs work with the helpless people who go to them because they have been abandoned by the government, academia and civil society.

NGOs conduct their own research on the issues and want their findings to reach people through the media. Emphasizing how the NGOs give a great deal of attention to research before giving information to the media, Saldanha explains that they thoroughly research things and discuss them before they put out their information for the media. They ensure that there are no factual errors in what they circulate to media. For example, in October 2018 Saldanha wrote a critical paper on 'climate-resilient zero budget natural farming'.

The paper was the outcome of a two-month-long debate he had with several people including former union minister for environment and forest Jairam Ramesh, environmentalist Vandana Shiva, academicians, and others who had been associated with the financial aspect of agriculture. When Saldanha circulated the 70-page article among the media representatives, the initial response was cold, as it did not look like a press release.

While the NGOs produce volumes of documents, the journalists want the information in condensed form unless they are specialists. They have no time to read long reports that describe the issues in-depth. For the NGOs, access to media is crucial to reach out to people and to seek their support for a specific programme of action.

Environmental activist Vidya Dinker says,

> We continuously document what we do and also prepare our responses and reports on the basis of comprehensive evidence we have gathered. We spend a lot of our time and resources on compiling complete information about a project so that we can answer any questions coming from any journalists. Unfortunately, very few of them show the patience of going through the document and the information that we provide.

Although activists and NGOs provide facts, statistics and explanations on several issues to journalists, they do not go through the documents completely but look for simplified and short statements. It is not that journalists must believe what is given to them but going through those reports will help them understand the issues better and enable them to ask probing questions to the government agencies and industries. Journalists preoccupied with loads of routine work may not have time to go through lengthy reports. As a result, their reports may not carry in-depth analyses.

For the NGOs with meagre resources, access to media is becoming very difficult. There was a time when only reporters, activists and politicians would go to the Press Club in Bengaluru, but today it is very difficult to get a booking because many corporate houses have taken the space. The NGOs, according to Saldanha, have been priced out because the rent for space has been increased from 300–400 rupees to 5,000 rupees. It is a deterrent cost for the movements and networks to use the space. Everybody who is organizing an event is doing a press conference. When there are so many press conferences held on the same day and in the same place journalists make a choice as to which of them would be newsworthy. Even when international events are held, the press conferences the NGOs hold are not adequately covered. Alongside the Earth Summit at Rio de Janeiro in 1992 the NGOs held their own Global Forum that discussed vital issues concerning sustainability and accountability of the governments and the corporations but the mainstream media scarcely reported it (Beder, 1998). Those radical environmental groups that raised fundamental questions on government–industry nexus at the Forum were ignored as fringe elements.

Media do not consider even those NGOs which are engaged in research, training, education and publication as authoritative sources. The Delhi-based environmental NGO CSE with knowledge-based activism as its objective is well known for its quality of campaigns, research and publications. Based on the findings of an investigation conducted in its laboratory the CSE released a report on 5 August 2003 that revealed that major soft drinks marketed in India contained extremely toxic pesticide residues. While Pepsi brands had 35 times more pesticide the Coca-Cola products had 30 times more than the European Union limits. Though the report made national and international headlines, the credibility of the NGO was in question. Many newspaper reports did not see the laboratory results as facts and continued to describe the findings as 'allegations' and 'charges'. The following are some of the examples:

> NEW DELHI: The arch rivals Coke and Pepsi together unanimously denied the CSE **allegations** and urged an independent scientific probe. (*Deccan Herald*, 6 August 2003)

> NEW DELHI AUG. 7. Parliament was today quick to banish from its premises the soft drinks manufactured by Pepsi and Coca-Cola following **allegations** by a non-governmental organisation on Tuesday that they contained toxic pesticides. (*The Hindu*, 7 August 2003)

NEW DELHI AUG. 6. Coca-Cola India and Pepsico India today refuted the **allegations** made by the Centre for Science and Environment (CSE) about the presence of pesticides in soft drinks of the two cola giants and said they would consider legal recourse if the NGO report tarnished their image. (*The Tribune*, 6 August 2003)

NEW DELHI: TS: The **allegations** of "excessive" pesticide content in soft drink brands of Coca-Cola and Pepsi have hit these companies hard, with sales believed to have plummeted by 30-40 per cent over the last one week. (*The Times of India*, 13 August 2003)

NEW DELHI: An environmental NGO that **claimed** Coca-Cola and Pepsi products contained unusually high levels of toxins Thursday sharpened its attack on the beverage giants, saying its findings were bolstered by data released by the soft drink manu-facturers. (*The New Indian Express*, 8 August 2003)

Of the 58 reports published between 6 August and 12 August 2003 in eight newspapers,[2] as many as 37 of them described the CSE's findings as allegations (Poornananda, 2008). The official and industrial sources dominated the coverage. Some newspapers dumped reports of the CSE's announcement to the inside pages and put the reports of the rejection of the findings by the soft drink companies on the front page. Government sources and industrial sources dominated news coverage. There was a demand for a test by an 'independent' laboratory. In fact, some reports that supposedly presented 'public reaction' about the CSE findings selectively quoted consumers who said they would continue to drink the soft drinks in question as they felt the controversy was sheer politics. The coverage of the findings of the similar tests conducted by the CSE on the same soft drinks three years later (2 August 2006) was similar to the coverage of the first findings. CSE was again described as a group that was still making claims and allegations about the presence of pesticide residues in soft drinks.

The coverage in the international press too was not very different. When the members of the Indian parliament recommended stringent

[2] *The Hindu, The Times of India, The New Indian Express, The Hindustan Times, The Tribune, The Statesman, The Telegraph* and *The Asian Age*.

regulations against the soft drink companies a report in *The Guardian* published on 5 February 2004 said:

> The row between soft drink makers and campaigners erupted last summer when a Delhi-based environmental group, the Centre for Science and Environment (CSE), claimed that Coca-Cola and PepsiCo products manufactured in India contained toxins far above the norms permitted in the developed world. (Ramesh, 2004)

The Coca-Cola and Pepsi companies launched an advertising campaign three days after the CSE released the report of its findings and argued that they had been certified by a laboratory in the Netherlands and that their products contained no pesticide residues (*Hindustan Times*, 2003). Popular film stars Aamir Khan and Shah Rukh Khan who appeared in the ads claimed that the drinks were absolutely safe. The strategy of the cola majors was to discredit the CSE and denigrate the report and the people who worked there (Narain, 2017). The PepsiCo moved the court arguing that an NGO had no right to raise public issues and had no legal authority or recognition. The PepsiCo's chief wrote articles in newspapers and claimed that the freedom of speech was being misused and that there was a need to review the norms and codes of conduct of NGOs (Narain, 2003). When the industry sources question the authenticity of the work carried out by environmental NGOs, it receives prominent coverage in the media. A Joint Parliamentary Committee headed by Sharad Pawar confirmed the CSE's findings and said the soft drinks of the two cola majors did contain residues (Bezbaruah, 2004). It was a vindication of the authentic work carried out by CSE.

While environmental groups may play a key role as claims-makers and draw the attention of the media to particular environmental problems, it is to the forums of 'public authorities', 'formal politics' and 'science' that journalists turn for validation of such claims (Hansen, 1991, p. 451). Media prominence to certain environmental problems depends on the extent to which they become part of the agendas of these other established fora. Journalists' lack of trust in non-official sources is reflected in the way their statements are quoted in news stories. The terms 'claimed', 'argued' and 'alleged' are often used whenever non-official sources are quoted raising doubts in the minds of the readers about the reliability of their statements. In contrast, the statements of officials are quoted as facts. Officials and experts 'say', 'explain', 'assert' and 'clarify' whereas non-official sources 'claim', 'argue', 'allege', 'contend' and 'charge'.

Some journalists argue that one should not read too much into these terms, as they are common in reports of daily newspapers. Mohit Rao says that just the use of terms such as 'claimed', 'alleged', 'contended' and 'argued' does not mean that the story is leaning towards the official sources (personal communication, 21 February 2019). According to him, the claims made by the activists or the victims usually occupy 70 per cent of the space and in the remaining space official or government reaction is given. He asserts that a journalist has to use those words while quoting sources because the statements or information given by the sources cannot be taken as truth. He believes that mere use of terms like 'claimed' or 'alleged' while quoting sources does not mean that sources are not credible. Readers often pay a lot of attention to claims and allegations of environmental activists and do not always believe what officials say or explain to be true.

Science and environmental journalist T. V. Jayan says that NGOs, affected people and independent sources are getting much more space than they used to get two decades ago (personal communication, 11 September 2020). He says one cannot take an individual case and say that only the official sources are quoted because a wide variety of sources are being used today unlike in the past.

Environmental NGOs as sources face the challenge of convincing the reporters with their facts and perspectives. Mohit Rao is of the view that

> Some of the environmental NGOs have extreme views and are not even prepared for a debate. They are not realistic even though they have done amazing work at the grassroots level. Among the NGOs themselves, there are many disagreements on key issues. If there are

three NGOs that are saying something on an issue, I will choose the one that looks more sensible.

Although NGOs claim that information they put out is based on their research, he does not believe everything they say as is truthful.

Ramnath Shenoy, Chief of Bureau, PTI, Bengaluru, says that there is a perception, which may be wrong, that some of the environmental groups have some kind of an agenda and are not true to their cause (personal communication, 15 May 2021). Explaining why journalists take the statement of NGOs with a pinch of salt, he says some times their data is suspect because they do not talk about their modus operandi and do not provide details of their surveys. When they are probed about the claims they make about an issue they may not give a satisfactory answer. Shenoy says, 'Many of them have their own vested interest and agenda. Because of a few environmental groups which do not provide accurate data journalists tend to suspect all environmental NGOs'. At the same time, he says there are also instances where officials and industrial sources plant stories in the media to discredit environmental groups.

Rohin Kumar, who represents Greenpeace, says that environmental NGOs as sources have always been treated with scepticism and at times with suspicion (personal communication, 20 May 2021). According to him, even after investing years and massive resources in campaigns, NGOs are still not seen as credible sources by a large section of the mainstream media. He says,

> Even though NGOs make significant revelations after studying some issues for considerable amount of time and provide news breaks journalists do not want to be seen with a particular NGO or a particular activist because they know the repercussion. Therefore, they use very defensive terminology when they report what the NGOs are saying. Journalists may be writing their entire stories based on the information provided by the NGOs but by using a certain terminology, they raise doubts in the minds of the audience about the facts that NGOs provide. Quoting statements as 'claimed' and 'alleged' when the NGOs are sharing complete information and

are ready to take responsibility for it is not fair. The reporters are unnecessarily getting defensive about it. That is why the language of reporting is very important. That needs to change. That also reflects an attitude that anything the officials say is ought to be true.

While there is difficulty in finding accurate information on environmental issues, the other side of the argument is that very few journalists today go to the field, gather first-hand information and study a problem and report about it. They tend to depend on web-based sources and statistics produced by government agencies rather than on the sources on the ground. Newspaper managements and editors today believe in numbers. They attach greater importance to the stories that carry numbers than the stories written on the spot. If the figures say something, they will believe it. The results of surveys conducted by organizations that contain figures and graphs are given importance although there is a possibility that the organizations may have vested interests. Those who play on those numbers are considered good environmental journalists. Meera Bhardwaj says,

What comes in an excel sheet is considered as gospel truth. Today, some journalists think they can write on anything sitting in their offices because they have access to information and statistics. They do not want to travel to find the truth themselves but depend on others who may not give accurate information. (Personal communication, 28 March 2019)

While the sources on the ground are more reliable than the officials and NGOs, it is essential to verify the information before putting out a story.

For sustained reporting on the environment, tapping diverse sources is important but that demands time, resources and editorial support. Many media houses are reluctant to make that kind of investment in environmental reporting. Activists and environmental groups who feel that the mainstream media do not see them as reliable sources and ignore them even when they provide accurate information have now turned to online media and social media. With the length of the stories decreasing in newspapers, there is very little scope for analysis and presentation of details. Although digital media do not provide the kind of audience that the mainstream media provide, activists see them as the right platforms for comprehensive and in-depth analysis.

Vidya Dinker says journalists who cover environmental issues, as other reporters, generally see officials and politicians are credible sources (personal communication, 5 May 2021). When an official or a politician tells journalists something about a controversial project, journalists often take it unquestioningly but when an activist says something, journalists raise questions and ask for proof.

Dinker says:

> In much of environmental reporting, non-governmental sources are treated unequally. Many of the very good celebrated mainstream journalists also carry this bias. From the junior-most reporters to the senior-most journalists across the media there is visible bias against activists and environmental groups. When a politician or a bureaucrat makes an off-the-cup remark over the phone, it will be taken more seriously than what an activist or a victim of a developmental project says. Even the lawyers representing the victims will not be taken as seriously as the official. Only those who are highly conscious and suspicious of the authority give equal importance to non-governmental sources.

Journalists often suspect that activists or their advocates are trying to push a narrative. 'In reality, authorities are always pushing a narrative that is a deeply flawed narrative, which does not put people or the environment first', Dinker argues. The might of the state or what is called as the eminent domain gets positively covered in media even when the rights of the citizens that the constitution guarantees are violated. When an official or a politician says something that is anti-constitutional that becomes more important than what an activist or an affected person or an affected community leader is saying. Dinker says 'the critical mind of a journalist does not work against the people who hold power. Journalists' notion of what development should be is deeply influenced by the authorities'.

Getting journalists to see and understand a problem has been an arduous task for a person representing an NGO. Dinker says,

First of all journalists refuse to come if the place in question it too far and if the issue is a bit complicated. Unless there is big breaking news coming, they would not be interested. Even when they come they expect a certain kind of treatment.

NGOs and activists often complain about media misrepresenting what they say about environmental issues. Dinker says that many years ago she used to read the newspaper stories that carried the information or the opinion she had given to journalists and call them up if she found inaccuracies and misrepresentations (personal communication, 5 May 2021). Journalists would get irritated when she pointed out some flaws in the copy leading to snapping of communication with them. Next time when she invited them to the sites of protest or meetings, they would not write a word. She no longer tells journalists even if what is reported is divergent from reality and distortion of the truth. 'I stopped reading the stories and began to reconcile with the reality that there would be some misrepresentation all the time. I would not want to waste my time and energy on attempting to tell them about the inadequacies in their reports,' Dinker says. It has not been easy for her to get space and positive coverage in media to put across information that would reach policymakers, politicians and the people.

Rohin Kumar too has come across some instances of media distorting the information provided by him but says that the distortion may not be intentional and that it could be the result of tremendous pressure under which journalists work today (personal communication, 20 May 2021). Greenpeace once said that if air pollution had been prevented, deaths in large numbers could have been avoided. But the newspapers wrote that a large number of people had died because of air pollution. This distortion could have been unintentional but that could cause panic among the public. For the distortions created by the newspapers, environmental groups could end up losing their credibility.

Journalists are generally suspicious about sources of funding for the NGOs. There is a perception that NGOs receive funds from external agencies and conspire to undermine development and keep the country backward. Dinker says decades ago leftists who had a lot of influence on journalists went on charging that the NGOs were receiving foreign money and that percolated into the minds of the young reporters but now such allegations are being made by the right-wing outfits that have considerable influence on the journalists (personal communication, 5 May 2021). She says that is one of the reasons why they are not seen as credible sources.

While the autonomy of the journalists to include or exclude facts and opinions or to write a report in a certain way cannot be questioned, it would be frustrating to the sources when the most important aspect of a problem is completely left out. In such situations, the sources might go to the other journalists and try to communicate in different ways. There are also times when stories are presented far better than what activists expected.

Since the public perception about the environmental struggles is shaped by the media how they present the struggles is a matter of great significance for the activists. To develop a long-term relationship with the media it is essential that the NGOs as claims-makers give information devoid of sensationalism and inaccuracies. It is also important for the journalists to question NGOs, fully understand their claims and report them without misrepresenting facts and opinions.

Marginalized Voices of Affected Persons

While officials and environmental groups are often found as sources in media coverage of the environment and climate change, it is very rare that the voices of the affected people are heard. The sources, which are easily accessible, articulate and hold some positions in an organization or pressure groups, are often quoted in news stories. People who have lost their homes, land, livelihoods and common property resources or those who are affected by pollution are rarely featured as sources in media stories. The participants in grassroots level environmental movements who would have a different understanding of the issue in question are seldom asked for their opinions. Even in cases of deforestation and threat to wildlife, the view of the well-known conservationists receives media prominence, not the experiences of those who have been living in forests for centuries.

An analysis of environmental news coverage in four English dailies between 1984 and 2004 showed that only 4.5 per cent of the sources quoted in the news stories were affected persons (Poornananda, 2008). Varna (2020) who analysed environmental content in three English and three Kannada dailies during 2015 and 2016 found that only 3.7 per cent of the sources were the affected persons. In a study of coverage of issues of displacement in print media between May 2013 and April 2015 it was found that only 4.7 per cent of the quoted sources were displaced persons while the officials alone accounted for 44.2 per cent of the quoted sources (Poornananda, 2017). Marginalization of the affected or displaced persons as sources points to how the powerful and privileged sources become the primary definers of environmental news.

Meera Bhardwaj says that some conservationists who want forests exclusively for animals do not pay adequate attention to the fact that forests are inhabited by both animals and people and that people have played a significant role in conserving both forest and wildlife (personal communication, 28 March 2019). She says,

> Displacing forest dwellers from forests is like throwing fish out of water and denying them access to the means of livelihood. Unfortunately they are seen as poachers and encroachers and hence their opinions have hardly mattered to the authorities and also to the news media.

She has paid particular attention to the problems of the people who have been evicted from the forest for the purpose of conservation and has consistently written about them until proper compensation and rehabilitation were provided to them. The official sources gave her evasive answers and made incorrect claims about the plight of the evictees.

According to Muralidhara Khajane, reporting from the field has declined over the years in state and national dailies (personal communication, 26 June 2019). He says that those who are affected or displaced by projects are hardly found as sources in news stories because of two reasons. One is lack of personal commitment on the part of the journalists to ensure that all voices are represented in the stories they write. Another is that because of the reduction in staff strength journalists have no time to visit distant places and spend time interviewing affected persons who live in places that are not easily accessible. Despite such limitations, he says, some journalists put the affected people in the lead paragraphs of stories as sources. When Khajane reported about the environmental impact of industries in Dakshina Kannada and Mysore districts of Karnataka he spent several days talking to the people who were going to be personally affected in terms of losing their lands or facing the threat of pollution. He says, it is not always possible to spend so much of time as the pressure of work does not allow journalists to travel often to distant places. He has found local newspapers frequently reflecting the voices of the people who are affected by big industrial and infrastructure projects. Journalists who work for local newspapers in Uttara Kannada district say that their stories are usually based on information and opinions gathered from the affected persons. Ashok Hasyagar who has been working for local newspapers for over three decades has rarely seen journalists representing state and national media reporting realities on the ground from the perspectives of the affected person. The sources in those media are mostly those who are easily accessible on the phone and those who are associated with some organizations. The voices of the people who have been thrown out of their traditional occupations and homes have not mattered as sources at all. Hasyagar cites the case of fishermen and farmers who lost their homes and livelihoods because of the Seabird naval base near Karwar, the headquarters of the Uttara Kannada district. According to him, the state and national media did not represent the voices of the affected people but reflected the claims of the officials even though the affected persons had been petitioning the authorities and protesting against poor compensation and inadequate resettlement.

Quoting the affected people as sources in news stories means that journalists have to travel to inaccessible places in forests or in remote areas to listen to their stories. While officials, experts, conservation-ists and representatives of environmental NGOs are only a phone call away, it requires a lot of time and effort to find the affected or displaced people. Taking time off from their regular beats to seek out the views and experiences of the affected people is an onerous task as it requires approval from editors.

Conclusion

Sources play a vital role in constructing and framing of environmen-tal news. Several studies have shown that a majority of the quoted sources in environmental stories are official sources. The government plays a dominant role in matters related to the environment because it has the dual task of promoting development and, at the same time, protecting the environment. The officials, as the primary definers of environmental news, are the key players in building the environmental agenda. A comprehensive coverage of an issue demands that views and claims of non-official sources are also given due importance, if not in equal measure. However, the media see the information and perspectives the environmental activists and NGOs provide with a lot of scepticism despite the evidence they produce through research and documentation of issues. Analyses of environmental news in newspapers have also shown that while the statements of the official sources are treated as facts, giving them legitimacy, the information and observations NGOs provide are presented in words that are likely to raise doubts in the minds of the readers. Scientists who speak on behalf of the government are seen as more knowledgeable and trustable sources than the scientists who are independent and have opinions in variance with the official opinion. Industrial sources are also treated as more reliable sources than the environmental groups. This should be seen in the context of industrial houses either owning media or investing in them besides being major advertisers.

To some journalists, NGOs and activists have been of immense help in understanding certain dimensions of the issues, which the official sources would not want to disclose. All journalists do not fully believe what the government officials say and seek validation of their statements from independent sources. While officials, scientists and activists often find space in newspapers as sources, it is very rare that the voices of the affected persons are heard. The affected persons are more likely to be found in local newspapers as sources than in state and national dailies. The decline in the field-based reports in recent years is a major reason for non-representation of affected persons in environmental news. The overburdening of journalists because of cost cutting and downsizing of staff in media houses has led to fewer attempts to do ground reporting with affected persons as sources. While there is greater willingness to include opposing views in environmental stories, scepticism about activists and environmental groups has also grown.

CHAPTER 7

Environment and the Media
Coverage of the Narmada Movement

The environmental movement in India has played an important role in bringing media attention to the environmental consequence of 'development'. Much of environmental reporting in news media involves writing about environmental movements providing detailed accounts of the issues they raise, the specific demands they make and their programme of resistance. Covering a movement requires a thorough understanding of the cause it is fighting for, the premise on which it is raising questions, its ideological orientation, the support base it enjoys and its long-term goals. A movement that remains active for decades may change its goals, priorities, methods and programmes of action over time to stay relevant and to cope with the challenge of social, political and economic realities. The priorities and orientation of the media also change over time depending on the ideological biases of those who control them and the dynamics of the business model they adopt. The movement–media relations may not remain the same and go through phases from cooperation to extreme hostility. However, the environmental movement and the environmental concern among the public have grown together because of media coverage. Media framing of the movements influences to a considerable extent how the public perceives them. But for the media, most of the environmental movements would not have been known nationally and internationally.

The most iconic of all the movements in India have been the Chipko movement and the Narmada movement. While the Chipko movement led by Chandi Prasad Bhatt and Sunderlal Bahuguna emerged in the early 1970s, the Narmada movement led by Medha Patkar began taking shape in the mid-1980s. Both these movements have derived their strength and inspiration from the Gandhian values and have adopted non-violent methods of protest. This chapter examines the media coverage of the Narmada movement, which has been the only environmental movement in India that has been carrying on a long struggle against large dams and displacement of people for nearly four decades.

There have been hundreds of movements of peasants, tribes, fisher folk, Dalits, urban poor, workers and women, which have raised questions about development projects, policies and ownership of resources. Only a few of them have been able to carry on a sustained campaign like NBA. NBA remains the most popular and visible environmental movement in India. Although Adivasis facing displacement are the core participants in the movement, the city-based middle-class activists have lent their support in bringing worldwide recognition to the struggle. The involvement of public intellectuals—among them social activist Baba Amte and writer-activist Arundhati Roy—helped the movement bring into focus broader issues of development and sustainability. Medha Patkar has been the public face of NBA which has been described as the longest Gandhian *satyagraha* (Sengupta, 2018). For nearly four decades, NBA has been carrying on a peaceful and non-violent struggle against ecological destruction and displacement of people caused by the Narmada valley projects. It did achieve a major moral victory when it managed to convince the World Bank to back out of the Sardar Sarovar Project (SSP) in 1993, but it could not prevent its completion. The dam was inaugurated on 17 September 2017 displacing 32,000 families in 178 villages (Mohan, 2019).

Narmada is the biggest west flowing river in India that originates at Amarkantak in the Maikal ranges situated in the Shahdol district of Madhya Pradesh. From there it flows down mostly westwards and is joined by 41 major tributaries on the way. The overall catchment area of the river is 98,796.8 square km with the Maika ranges in the east, Vindhya ranges to the north and Satpura ranges to the south. The river passes through sal and teak forests, traversing 1,312 km through gorges and broad valleys to merge with the waters of the Arabian Sea in the Bharuch district of Gujarat. Considered as one of the most sacred rivers of India, it is venerated as the epitome of freedom and sanctity. Even pumping the waters of Narmada for any purpose is considered by many as a sacrilege (Patel, 1995). Numerous dams in the Narmada valley that impound water for irrigation and power generation defy such beliefs.

The Narmada basin projects include more than 3,200 dams, of which 30 are major, 135 medium and the rest small. Of these dams, the SSP in Gujarat is the biggest in the basin. These dams have displaced lakhs of people and destroyed several thousand hectares of forest. Therefore, The Narmada Valley Development Project has been termed as India's 'greatest planned environmental disaster' (Roy, 1999, p. 15).

The focus of popular opposition has been the SSP, the largest of the project's schemes. When the foundation stone was laid by Prime Minister Jawaharlal Nehru for a dam at Navagam, the height was fixed at 162 feet, but over the years the height of the dam went on increasing up to the present level of 454 feet. It is a unique project in India because the command area of major beneficiaries lies in one state, Gujarat, while much of the submergence area lies in another state, Madhya Pradesh. The submergence area includes 19 villages in Gujarat, 33 villages in Maharashtra and 193 villages in Madhya Pradesh, where Adivasi communities such as the *Bhils, Bhilalas, Pawaras* and the *Tadvis* live. The first protest against the SSP began in 1972 to save the fertile agricultural land from submergence. Protests against the project organized through Nimar Bachao Kendriya Sangharsh Samiti attracted thousands of protests but could not prevent its construction.

Medha Patkar as a social activist first began working on the rehabilitation of people who would be displaced by the SSP in Maharashtra through Narmada Dharangrast Samiti (Narmada Dam-affected group) in the mid-1980s. Later, several organizations came together to organize a movement to save the Narmada river and to fight for the rights of the people whose lands and homes were marked for submergence by the SSP. This movement—Narmada Bachao Andolan (Save the Narmada Movement)—with Medha Patkar as the key organizer became one of the well-known environmental movements in India and a symbol of resistance to environmental degradation. The early objective of the movement was proper compensation and rehabilitation of the people to be displaced. When it was realized that there was no land available to be given to the oustees under the 'land for land' policy, opposition to the construction of the dam itself began. There was no adequate land available in Maharashtra, Madhya Pradesh and Gujarat to allot to the oustees the same amount of land they had lost to the dam.

Since the beginning of the Narmada movement in the mid-1980s, media response varied as the struggle moved to different phases. Media ownership and the regional political environment had their influence on the debate. Newspapers and magazines published by the same media groups had different perspectives on the environmental movement depending on the linguistic and regional politics they represented. The Indian language newspapers published by *The Times of India* and *The Indian Express* groups had different views about large dams and development priorities. The tendency to see dam construction as the inevitable way to promote development was noticeable among the language newspapers. The media space and time for the movement decreased over the years (Patkar & Sangvai, 2006). It has been a formidable task for the movement to mobilize and motivate media to provide space for the deprived and the suppressed. NBA has recognized the fact that media play a crucial role in making a movement known to the outside world. For mobilizing people and involving them in the decision-making process' access to mainstream and alternative media became necessary for the movement.

Coverage in the Early Years

During the early phases of the Narmada movement, the media responded positively to the questions raised about the issues in the valley. The coverage started with articles and reports written by the activists of the movement. NBA's interaction with media began as part of its objective of using all democratic forums to strengthen the struggle for justice. The press material itself was used as an appeal to seek people's support for the movement. As the Narmada movement clearly articulated the issues through mass struggle and made humanistic appeal regarding development' the media attention increased.

When the Narmada struggle intensified in the 1990s challenging the dam and questioning the World Bank for providing financial assistance to the SSP, the media reports began appearing more frequently. However, the amount and the orientation of the coverage depended on language, readership and political value of the struggle and the media perception of the gravity of the situation (Patkar & Sangvai, 2006).

Extensive media coverage of compensation, resettlement and rehabilitation for the displaced persons helped readers understand the far-reaching and long-term consequences of building large dams. The debate was not confined to the specific issue of SSP but also threw light on the development options and their advantages and disadvantages. Keeping the debate alive was no easy task for NBA. The criticism it received from people through the newspapers helped it reflect on its own paths and strategies. But some of the key programmes including resistance of the *samarpit dal* (dedicated squad) went largely unreported in the Indian language media.

Some committed journalists from major dailies, magazines and television channels covered every phase of the movement. They travelled and stayed in the remote villages of the valley under the scorching sun and rains to experience the conditions of the Adivasis facing displacement. Their first-hand experience made their stories authentic and credible. The forests, the tribal culture, community relations, sustainable agricultural practices and ecological values the journalists had witnessed would all be gone once the waters of the dam submerged them.

Veteran journalists and columnists helped the Narmada movement grow by consistently writing about the issues it was raising (Patkar & Sangvai, 2006). But the coverage in general was both supportive and critical. NBA's campaign that forced the World Bank to withdraw from the SSP in 1993 caught the attention of the international media. Medha Patkar went to the United States and addressed the members of the US Congress asking them to exert pressure on the World Bank to withdraw support to the project. The United States as a major shareholder in the World Bank had the power to influence the decisions of the bank. Patkar says *The Times of India* wrote an editorial criticizing her for appearing before a foreign committee for a matter that it considered as only a domestic problem internal to India. (personal communication, 6 March 2019). That kind of criticism was also reflected in some other newspapers.

> Some newspapers were critical of our demand without looking into the other side of the story. My argument was that the governments were signing agreements with foreign countries or agencies without even going through the process of discussion at democratic fora. The issues were not being discussed in parliament. Since it is the people who are going to be affected by the agreement between countries' they have the right to know what has gone into the agreement. Some newspapers rejecting the demand for public review of the agreements expressed the view that these agreements were in 'national interest' which could not be debated.

From the beginning of the movement some newspapers were biased against the movement and portrayed a band of people working against national interest without even considering environmental consequences. But there were also other media representatives, young and old, who took pains to reach out to the mountainous region too.

According to the experience of NBA, the mainstream media's help is important for any people's movement to get out of isolation and to relate to a larger society (Patkar & Sangvai, 2006). Without the mainstream media coverage, a movement may be regarded only as a local struggle. The coverage in mainstream media also acts as a restraint on the state's attempt to repress and delegitimize movements to push through policies and projects that would not be in the interest of a large majority of the people. When the so-called development agenda of the government is imposed through school curriculum, public relations programmes and advertising campaigns, it is hard for a movement with very little resources to present a counter view without the support of the mainstream media. Movements are faced with an atmosphere where the mainstream media distance themselves from people's struggles that raise fundamental questions on democracy and development. According to the activists of NBA, there have been several instances of the pro-dam lobby exerting pressure on media to ignore the arguments of the movement and to highlight only the benefits of the projects in the Narmada valley.

When the agitation led by NBA reached a new high in March 1993, newspapers in Gujarat published false news that a Maharashtra government official who was visiting the tribal areas of Bamni was kidnapped and that another official in charge of rehabilitation was questioned by a group of anti-dam activists in dense forests. NBA gave a different version and denied the charge of kidnapping and harassment of another official in the forest and described the newspaper reports as a deliberate attempt to malign the agitation (Medha Patkar, personal communication, 5 March 2019).

Some newspapers tried to trivialize the concerns of the people in the Narmada valley highlighting the government's arguments against NBA. They were full of reports that glorified the benefits of the project. The proximity of many journalists and newspaper owners to the political leaders led to the publication of stories that confused the readers in comprehending the enormity of the issue. However, almost all journalists recognized the fact that the SSP was not in the interest of the people of Madhya Pradesh. Among the daily newspapers, *Naiduniya* and *Dainik Bhaskar* covered the news about NBAs programmes continuously. The coverage increased whenever the programmes of mass actions intensified. Although depth was lacking in many of the newspapers, some senior columnists wrote about the questions that NBA was raising consistently.

While there was a fair amount of coverage in the Hindi press, the Marathi press initially ignored the problems associated with the Narmada project as only 33 villages in two remote tribal taluks in Maharashtra were affected (Patkar & Sangvai, 2006). However, as the agitation in the Narmada valley intensified even those newspapers published from non-affected areas began carrying the news of the movement. Although journalists and prominent people recognized the struggle of the Adivasis for their rights, they did not appreciate the opposition to the dam. They would rather support a movement for better resettlement and rehabilitation.

In Patkar's view (personal communication, 4 March 2019) some media persons played an important role in reporting what NBA had been doing.

> They have walked with us through the valley for days together. The 'rally for the valley' in 1999 got huge publicity but thousands of people have taken part in the other rallies too. All our rallies do not receive good coverage in the media. Some of our rallies have been long-term struggles lasting for days and weeks which the media would cover to some extent and leave. We have to be continuously in touch with the media to keep them abreast of the realities in the valley. This was our appeal to the journalists because we knew the constraints with which they worked.

Media attention to the issues in the Narmada valley has not remained the same. There has been a rise and fall in coverage with some events getting highlighted and others being ignored. Despite some criticism, the overall media coverage was encouraging in the early years of the struggle.

Movement–Media Interface

NBA has always made attempts to keep the media well-informed about the issues it has been raising, but it does not go after the media all the time. Talking about NBA's relations with media, Patkar says,

> Our communication strategy has not been focused on media per se. Whether media covers or not we continue our struggle. My experience has been that if you go after media, they dodge you. We should go on genuinely working on our own strategic path and our action plan. The media will reach out anywhere if our actions are powerful in three senses. Firstly, our conceptual contribution should be something special. The issue that we raise should not be just the macro-level issue but it should be rooted at the micro-level. It should have a micro-level impact and conceptual clarity. Secondly, we should have people's power with us. Unless we have people with

us we cannot make an impact, either on the government or on the media. The third thing is we should have political strategizing in the larger sense of the term. What kind of visuals, symbolic action, and what kind of challenge you give and take need to be kept in mind. Non-violent action requires more political strategizing than violent action. It is more of a political understanding than reporting or reacting. (Personal communication, 4 March 2019)

Although the movement needs media coverage and support, it does not organize events with media publicity in mind. For a movement to sustain itself for a longer time, its conceptual clarity, people's power and strategic inputs into the media are necessary. Patkar believes that attracting media attention through some dramatic events will not help any movement in the long run.

NBA does not believe in 'using' media as a strategy and respects the freedom of journalists to select issues and interpret them according to their professional norms. It does not make unreasonable demands keeping in mind the constraints within which journalists work for the mainstream media. NBA thinks of media persons as those whom it has to cultivate and orient. Patkar explains (personal communication, 4 March 2019) about what the movement would expect from the media.

We would start with a simple orientation to make them a part of our struggle. I would always tell them 'you may not publish this. I don't mind but listen to the whole thing and you decide and make your own position clear. That is what we want. We know your editor may not approve or your chief editor or reporter may disapprove and reject it fully or partially or may get it edited. You may not be able to cover everything we give you. We may be giving too many details which you may not be able to use but that does not matter. You still please listen to us. We want to convey to you as our friends the realities that are around us.' This was our appeal to the journalists because we knew the constraints with which they worked.

NBA starts with low-key publicity when programmes to be held for over several weeks are launched. As days pass, media start sending their correspondent to the valley. Sometimes, even when a few journalists write about a programme of action with facts placed in a proper context, it gives a breakthrough to the movement.

Patkar gives an example of how a single article helped a crucial campaign of NBA. On 8 March 2006, the government declared that the height of the dam would be increased to 122 metres. NBA started a *dharna* in front of the Water Resources Ministry in New Delhi. The Adivasis and activists sat on the footpath at the gates of the ministry. There was no response from Saifuddin Souz who was the Union Minister of Water Resources. He was only sending messages that he would look into the issue. There was no coverage in the media but the agitation continued. Then NBA decided to go on an indefinite fast. An article by Amit Sengupta in *Tehelka* on why Adivasis were protesting gave the andolan a breakthrough. All other media, started coming later and when the activists started the fast the coverage got such hype that on several streets there were supportive protests, rallies and fasts. People started talking about the negative effects of dams. One good report gave a big boost to the movement.

Rather than doing public relations with the media, NBA has tried to build a relationship with the journalists based on a genuine approach to the understanding of the issues that affect common people. NBA does not organize media trips as it has no resources. Patkar says, 'Even for a trip to Indore we think twice. We cannot provide journalists with lunches and dinners. The government does all that. But you know the striking difference is that there is no level playing field and fortunately some media have also written about it'. The government often makes it easy and comfortable for the journalists to write about the benefits of the dam by arranging press conferences and tours on which a lot of money is spent. NBA usually invites journalists whenever it embarks on a mass action programme and arranges for their frugal stay and travel in the valley. NBA's office at Barwani has a meeting hall and a computer room from where volunteers help send emails and upload information to the website. NBA has always given equal importance to all journalists whether they reported for local, national or international newspapers. It provides them complete information and tries to convince them with hard facts and socio-political realities and does not push through stories.

Although NBA does not have a mechanism to monitor all the time what is reported in media, it pays particular attention to the reports that are critical of the movement. It is also interested in knowing political orientation of newspapers in order to understand how they generally respond to issues related to development. For the activists of the movement, it is also important to know to what extent a particular newspaper makes an impact on the government, courts and the common people. Because of a lack of resources and time, NBA has not been able to make a complete assessment of the media. NBA activists say that the media generally show a lot of concern for the environment but when it comes to specific projects they do not want the projects to be shelved. They feel this is the strategy of the media to project themselves as promoters of environmental conservation whereas in reality they promote the interests of the corporate houses.

NBA identifies one or two journalists in each newspaper who understand the issues it is raising and continues to inform them about their activities and responses from the government. Those journalists who came to witness and experience the struggle of the people have written illuminating stories that have made the audiences think about the larger issues of development. Their discussions have not only been about the Narmada dam but also about destructive development in general.

Even in the face of media hostility and severe criticism, NBA has always responded with the offer of dialogue. It is this openness to criticism that has made a long-term relationship with the media possible. NBA admits that it might not have satisfied the expectations of the media as media coverage has not been the prime concern of the movement (Patkar & Sangvai, 2006). The primary focus of the movement is to reach out to the people in remote areas so that they take part in the dialogue.

Patkar feels that it is necessary to make journalists aware of the larger issues of people's rights and democracy. The media should be made aware of the fact that people's movements are political but their politics goes beyond parliamentary and party politics. Sustained dialogue with the media is felt necessary to ensure that the movement remains relevant and vibrant. Press releases are sent to the newspapers whenever there is some new development or when certain issues are to be explained to the people. The press releases and documents that NBA prepares are full of facts and figures rather than perspectives. According to Saurav Rajput who has been working as a volunteer with NBA, it is very difficult to break the perspectives and stereotypes of the urban people and one way of doing it is to present them the realities with complete information (personal communication, 5 March 2019). But doing that has been an arduous task.

Sending a press note frequently to the media representatives means a lot of work for NBA as it does not have volunteers exclusively dealing with media. Sanjay Sangvai,[1] who was working as a senior journalist quit his job in 1989 and joined the Narmada movement. He was in regular contact with the media, supplied them timely information and answered all their questions. The articles and books he wrote made issues related to big dams understandable to the journalists. His death in 2007 was a massive loss to the movement.

Despite NBA's efforts to explain, the problems of the displaced people have not received expected response in all phases of the struggle from the media. Patkar says,

Media have fallen short of reporting all that has been happening in the valley. Many media persons think that now that the dam has been inaugurated and 'dedicated to the nation' there are no problems associated with it. When I ask them if they have checked real status of the dam promised by the government they have no answer. I ask them to go and see for themselves what was promised and what has been achieved. There are 32000 families in the submergence area of the Sardar Sarovar dam today. It was 40000 houses that were built for the affected people in the last one and a half years. Media persons seem to think that these issues are no longer important. (Personal communication, 6 March 2019)

---

[1] Sanjay Sangvai taught journalism and mass communication at the University of Poona for several years before he joined NBA. His book *The River and Life: People's Struggle in the Narmada Valley* (2000) analyses destruction of natural resources and the politics of dam-building.

The dam may have been inaugurated but the displaced persons are yet to be compensated, resettled and rehabilitated. The media began carrying stories based on the claims of the government about the benefits of the dam without checking if the benefits had been delivered to the people as promised.

According to her, as media became alienated from people's issues in the mid-1990s they became part of the establishment instead of fighting it. Social movements that used to set the agenda in the 1980s and the early 1990s came under the influence of forces which did not represent a majority of the people. As a result of this shift there was less overage of the struggle and whatever was reported was hardly noticeable. The movement began to be covered only when certain events it organized looked, 'exotic', 'novel' or had some 'entertainment value'.

Devramji, one of the NBA activists from Kaparkhed village of Dhar district in Madhya Pradesh, sees a change in the media attitude towards the movement after the year 2000 (personal communication, 5 March 2019). He says,

> In the beginning of the movement, the media were helpful to us. Until 2000 media were generally reflecting reality to a considerable extent but after that, they have become tools in the hands of the corporate houses which benefit from projects like the big dams. Journalists as individuals have been supporting the Narmada movement but the media as institutions have not bothered to protect the interest of the people. Some English newspapers made our problems known to people nationally and internationally but unfortunately, a majority of the people in this country don't read English newspapers.

Devramji who has been with the Narmada movement for over three decades does not see much of a problem with individual journalists but with corporate houses that employ them. Hundreds of cases have been booked against him despite the fact that he never held a stone or a stick in his hands throughout his involvement in the anti-dam movement. He has been attacked by the pro-dam protestors causing serious injuries. He says that the media do not cover such kind of atrocities on the workers of NBA that happen frequently.

Talking about how the media are partial in covering the issues in the Narmada valley Devramji says,

> Media have become one-sided in recent years. We don't say that they should write only about our problem but they should represent the views of everyone including the government. But what is happening now is that most media are pro-government and ignore the problems of the people in the Narmada valley. If they don't report about the issues that affect people how can they claim to be voices of the people?

Devramji feels that public knowledge about the problems arising from dam construction would have been higher had there been comprehensive media coverage.

Another activist Waheed Mansoor of Chikhalda village in Dhar district agrees with Devramji with regard to how media cover issues in the Narmada valley and adds 'in our communication with the people and other stakeholders media role has not been very significant. Only around 20 to 25 percent of our communication is through the media and much of our focus is on personal contacts, pamphlets and meetings' (personal communication, 5 March 2019). Mansoor, who has been associated with the Narmada movement for over three decades, believes that it is the most democratic, peaceful and secular of all the movements in India. Unfortunately, he feels, such uniqueness of the movement is not communicated to the people through the media.

Mansoor says,

> The media do not report about all aspects of the problem of displacement even though we have tried to explain them to the reporters again and again. While there is some coverage about the money spent on the dams, canals, and compensation given to the displaced persons, there is no coverage of what happens to our temples, mosques, sacred places, and our customs and traditions. We are being forced to move and settle down in different places. For the people of the villages moving to a new place, where their earlier community practices and traditions are absent, has been a traumatic experience. The media have not actually paid any attention to these problems. (Personal communication, 5 March 2019)

According to Mansoor, the media have largely ignored the effect of displacement on the culture and traditions of the people who have lived together for generations. While the economics of dam building and compensation are reported in media, the effect of displacement on the culture and traditions of the people is ignored. Breaking up of communities and the social network that holds the people together are rarely the subjects of public debate because the media agenda is focused on the economics of dam building, compensation and rehabilitation. The problems of the displaced persons are framed as only 'economic' problems focusing more on compensation rather than on the human consequences of displacement.

Challenge of the Hostile Media

Social movements have often found themselves facing the challenge of hostile media which represent the dominant political view. Since the beneficiaries of the SSP are in Gujarat while most of the displaced people are in Madhya Pradesh the Gujarati press has passionately supported the pro-dam dam lobby. NBA faced the toughest challenge in Gujarat as all major political parties were pro-dam and against anyone questioning the benefits of large dams. The media faithfully reflected the position of the political parties thereby encouraging extreme reactions against the Narmada movement. Patkar and Sangvai (2006, p. 171) describe the Gujarati media's response to the movement:

> Using rhetoric, untruth, secrecy, parochialism, intolerance, defamation, and physical attacks they openly instigated or justified violence against the Andolan. The dominant media in Gujarat has always reflected the intolerant attitude of the ruling class against any dissenting or minority voices and encouraged the suppression of their rights. This was borne out by its provocative role during the anti-Dalit and anti-Muslim riots in the 1970s and 1980s, and which again targeted the NBA. A similar pattern can be discerned during the anti-Muslim pogrom of March–April 2002.

The Gujarati media have virtually carried on a campaign to malign the movement. Gujarati newspapers such as *Lok Satta, Gujarat Samachar* and *Sandesh* produced highly biased news and created hysteria against those who questioned the benefits of the SSP (Patkar & Sangvai, 2006). In September 1988, over 100 eminent scientists, environmentalists and social workers sent a petition to Prime Minister Rajiv Gandhi to reconsider the environmental clearance given to the SSP (Tripathi & Singh, 1988). The signatories included well-known space scientist Sathish Dhawan, internationally renowned genetist M. S. Swaminathan and the founder of the Centre for Science and Environment Anil Agarwal. While the petition became a major story in the national media the Gujarati newspapers began a vituperative attack on the signatories forcing some of them to withdraw their signatures (Medha Patkar, personal communication, 5 March 2019).

The activists demanding the review of the dam project were depicted as demons that were out to disturb the development of Gujarat. NBA activists were accused of being 'anti-Gujarat, anti-development, and agents of the CIA, the KGB, and Pakistan' (Patkar & Sangvai, 2006, p. 171). An organization that has always employed peaceful methods of protest based on the Gandhian principle of non-violence was also accused of being a Naxalite group. Newspapers played on the emotions of the readers by equating the SSP with Gujarat's self-esteem. The activists were also accused of conspiring with the Western forces to obstruct India's progress.

In a five-week-long Jan Vikas Sangharsh Yatra from 25 December 1990 to 31 January 1991, the Adivasis led by NBA asserted their right to livelihood as they faced the threat of losing their homes and land without being fully rehabilitated and resettled. Demanding a comprehensive review of the project and halting of all construction work until then, they staged a peaceful *satyagraha* at the site of the dam. The Gujarati press described the *yatra* as a violent move to smash the dam and accused Medha Patkar and the Adivasis of preparing for armed combat with bombs, bows and arrows, spears and other weapons (Kothari, 1991). The reports in Gujarati newspapers about the *yatra* were full of half-truths and falsehood. The participants in the *yatra* were portrayed as a violent mob despite the fact that they had their hands tied as a symbol of non-violent protest. When some differences emerged in an open discussion about the strategies to be adopted by NBA the Gujarati newspapers portrayed it as a division within the movement and that the *yatra* was going to fizzle out (Kothari, 1991).

Attempts were made to discredit the *yatra* through distorted coverage. There were false reports about lakhs and crores of foreign money being spent on the *yatra*. The demand of NBA to prove the charges was ignored. The Gujarati press not only blacked out several events that were held as part of the *yatra* but also ignored the press notes issued by the *yatra* camp. Blatant lies, half-truths and concocted stories filled the pages of all major Gujarati newspapers. All claims of the Gujarat government and the pro-dam organizations were presented as authentic and truthful (Kothari, 1991). NBA complained to the Press Council of India regarding biased coverage of the *yatra* by the Gujarati newspapers. *Gujarat Samachar* which accused Medha Patkar of receiving foreign funds had to apologize unconditionally as the allegation was completely baseless. *Sandesh* and *Gujarat Samachar* were censured by the Press Council of India for scurrilous and distorted reporting.

Patkar and Sangvai (2006) argue that the obsession with the SSP was so much that it drove journalists and editors, who were otherwise sensible, to take a fascist stand. The news about NBA was either suppressed or distorted. The editor of *Loksatta Jansatta* gave a call on 8 August 1993 to boycott all the eminent supporters of NBA describing them as traitors to Gujarat. A well-known columnist claimed that the anti-dam protestors 'would have been shot dead like mad dogs' if they were to be in China (Patkar & Sangvai, 2006, p. 172). The view that was dominant in the media was that the Adivasis were leading miserable lives in their villages and that their development lay in displacement.

A nexus among industrialists, businessmen, builders, politicians and religious fundamentalists built a narrative that Gujarat would be destroyed if the SSP was not completed. The newspapers suppressed information and opinions that were critical of the project. NBA became a victim of a disinformation campaign by some of the Gujarati newspapers. They distorted the statements of NBA and tried to discredit its programme of action.

On 8 April 2002, two dozen reporters representing the national media were attacked when they went to cover a peace meeting at the

Sabarmati Ashram where Medha Patkar was present. The Gujarat political readership charged that journalists from the national media had been writing against the interest of the state of Gujarat (Sardesai, 2004). While the 'local' media were seen as those that worked for the development of Gujarat, the 'national' English media were seen as those trying to hinder Gujarat's development. The local newspapers called Medha Patkar all kinds of names, the mildest of them being 'anti-Gujarati' (Sharma, 2002). All those who were either seen as supporting her or speaking in favour of NBA became the target of attack by the local newspapers.

The local media criticism was so aggressive and abusive that even those who usually voiced their concern about human rights violations chose to be silent. The organizers of the peace meeting at Sabarmati Ashram including artiste Mallika Sarabhai and Gandhian Chunnibhai Vaidya made a statement under pressure that Medha Patkar had gone there uninvited, although invitations had been emailed to people across the country. Medha Patkar who was also attacked by a mob at the meeting told a local court hearing the case in Ahmedabad on 5 September 2013, that it was a conspiracy to kill her. The anger against NBA had been whipped up by the local newspapers.

The hostile propaganda by the leading Gujarati newspapers against NBA, according to Patkar and Sangvai (2006), only underlined the legitimacy of the issues raised by it and strengthened doubts about the project. There were also a few newspapers like *Gujarat Mitra, The Times of India (Gujarati), Kachchmitra, Janmabhoomi* and *Gujarat Times* which questioned the claims of the government and defended the rights of the Adivasis in the Narmada valley. Journalists who worked for the English newspapers showed more professionalism in covering environmental and displacement issues.

One Gujarati weekly, *Abhiyan*, wrote about the contrast between poor people's struggle against the dam and the government-sponsored pro-rich campaign for the dam which became an eye-opener for the middle class and the intelligentsia in Gujarat. The English newspapers like *The Times of India* and the *Indian Express* have exposed the tall claims made by the government about the benefits of the dam

(Patkar & Sangvai, 2006). However, poorly made canals, salination, waterlogging and ingress of the sea, and irregular supply of drinking water have not been given due coverage.

The government and the pro-dam supporters have used advertising to obfuscate the issues raised by NBA. These advertisements which were malicious and defamatory were carried by some newspapers even though they made questionable claims about the benefits of the dam and disparaging remarks against the opponents. The Supreme Court which was hearing the Narmada case in 1997 had expressed displeasure over a series of pro-dam advertisements that attempted to malign the movement against big dams.

Although localized protests were occurring all along the Narmada valley, wider public attention to the struggle of NBA was drawn through a spectacular event called the 'rally for the valley' held between 29 July and 4 August 1999, in the Narmada valley. The rally was organized after the Booker Award-winning writer and thinker Arundhati Roy wrote an essay titled 'The Greater Common Good' in the *Frontline* (22 May 1999) and *Outlook* (24 May 1999) magazines analysing the economic, political, social, cultural and environmental factors associated with the irrigation and power projects in the valley. It was the first comprehensive report on the projects in the Narmada valley where she had spent several months talking to different stakeholders, examining records and piecing together details of the livelihood of the Adivasis facing eviction.

Even though a lot had appeared in the press about the Narmada valley projects it was this cover story that presented a comprehensive picture of the destruction of the Narmada valley and its impact on the lives of the tribal people. The essay written with literary flair and abundant statistics gave a big boost to the Narmada movement and the anti-dam resistance in the country. Roy's declaration in the essay that the big dams are to a nation's 'development' what nuclear bombs are to its military arsenal and that they are both 'weapons of mass destruction' (Roy, 1999, p. 29) was fiercely debated by the anti- and pro-dam groups throughout the country. The essay which was a well-researched and well-argued case against big dams in India brought hundreds of people across the country to the Narmada valley to stand in solidarity with the Adivasis who were facing displacement without proper compensation, resettlement and rehabilitation. At the end of her essay, she appealed to the readers to join the rally.

In response to her appeal, more than 400 persons from all over the world and from all walks of life came to the valley to take part in the rally. The contingent of rallyists included journalists, researchers, students, scientists, economists, artists, architects, religious charitable groups, Gandhians, activists from people's struggles and voluntary agencies from rural areas who responded to Arundhati Roy's invitation to join the rally and see things for themselves. Representatives of international environmental groups including Friends of the Earth and Greenpeace participated in the rally. The rally that remains the biggest rally ever held in the Narmada valley attracted the attention of national and international media. Nearly 50 media persons from India and abroad arrived in the valley to cover the rally. It was for the first time that such a rally of supporters was held. The rallyists were joined by thousands of Adivasis when they reached the Narmada valley.

The event received massive coverage in the national newspapers but much of it was focused on the event itself rather than on the issues the event was attempting to highlight. Among the English language newspapers, *The Hindu* provided comprehensive and balanced coverage whereas the coverage in *The New Indian Express* was one-sided and negative. *The Hindu* provided detailed information to the readers about the Narmada valley projects from the planning stage to the status of construction till 1999. The paper presented a meaningful debate on the issue by giving adequate coverage to opposing views on the question of big dams. Besides correspondents, experts and activists debated the benefits and the environmental effects of the dam. One of the issues seriously debated was the problem of resettlement and rehabilitation. A majority of the reports in *The Hindu* indicated that rehabilitation of all those displaced by the SSP was almost an impossibility as there was no land available to be distributed. The newspaper provided a forum for public debate not only on the issues in the valley but also on the question of the long-term consequences of the large irrigation dams.

In contrast to *The Hindu*, the coverage in *The New Indian Express* was directed at belittling and discrediting the movement itself. NBA was dubbed 'militant', 'obstinate' and 'unreasonable'. The participants in the rally were described as 'merrymakers', 'city dwellers' and 'romantic environmentalists'. They were also accused of indulging in a sexual orgy on the bank of the Narmada.

The coverage in *The New Indian Express* began with an article by one of its correspondents criticizing NBA for the course of action it was taking. The very first article with the headline 'All set for NBA's "rally for the valley" in Indore' began this way,

> The first time some of us heard about the NBA, we thought of Michael Jordan. But the Narmada Bachao Andolan has nothing to do with claiming hoops, all they want is justice for the dispossessed in the 'big dam' projects but what works against them is their militancy. (Thayil, 1999d, p. 9)

NBA was branded as a militant movement although there had been no violent incidents in any of the protests held previously. There had been no violent incidents in which NBA was involved in its then 13-year-old struggle (Sharma, 1999). NBA has always adopted Gandhian methods of protest. Its activists have held protest marches with their hands tied to emphasize the non-violent nature of their struggle. Despite the fact that NBA has always used such peaceful methods of protest, its leaders and supporters have been harassed, attacked and jailed repeatedly (Gadgil & Guha, 1995). There was no reference in the report to any action of NBA that could be considered as militant. The article quoted a supporter of NBA as saying, 'We will immerse ourselves in the water, we will use non-violent methods to achieve our objective.' To this statement of the supporter, the correspondent wrote, 'Suicide by drowning seems pretty violent in any case.'

Since violent struggles do not enjoy public support, describing a movement as militant can create negative opinions among the people. No mention was made about the fact that NBA leaders and the villagers in the submergence zone had been beaten up and arrested by the police when they tried to drown themselves in the river in 1994. The leaders of NBA had argued that was the only way left for them, as the government had never heard their pleas. The article argued that many of the supporters of NBA had no idea about its objectives. Referring to the inability of some of the schoolteachers to take part in the rally the article said 'But that has not stopped the Medha Patkar Group from going great guns at the schools'. The article presented NBA as an organization fighting for a wrong cause and those supporting it as a group of ignorant people. The very first report about the rally negatively presented NBA's cause.

In another article (Prasannarajan, 1999b), a correspondent made personalized comments on NBA leaders and the rally leader Arundhati Roy. It said, 'It was the river-rafting novelist as a rainy revolution's pin-up girl. It was Arundhati Roy, the famous waif from the banks of the Meenachai, as the flower child of the Narmada. It was fiction garlanded by choreographed reality' (Prasannarajan, 1999a, p. 1). The whole article was a sensationalized account of what dress Roy and NBA supporters wore, what they ate and what they talked for six days in the valley. 'For seven nights and six days, city-slick radicalism sang hum sub ek hai (We are all togther) with bucolic solidarity, and the Narmada didn't give a damn to the bachao-barking invasion,' the article said pointing at the supposedly pointless struggle and questioning the seriousness of the rallyists. A picture carried with the article showed Roy as an enchantress. The article also conveyed an impression of some weird sexual orgy being indulged in by NBA when it said, 'Condoms, crocodiles and shivlingams provided unsolicited adjectives to river yatra—things so distant from Roy's anger and sorrow.' The paper that had once described Roy as a writer who had brought international recognition to English writing in India had now found her pursuing a wrong cause.

The paper published two of the letters that came in response to the article (12 August 1999). One was from Shripad Dharmadhikary of the NBA and the other was from economist and writer Devaki Jain. The editor's note carried with the letters betrayed the newspaper's excitement over the controversy created by the article. It said, 'A front-page report in The New Indian Express has set passions rising faster than Narmada's waters.' What was apparent in the note was a strong defence of the article indicating editorial opposition to NBA.

In his response to the article, NBA's Shripad Darmadhikary said,

It is in very bad taste, misrepresents the facts, gives misleading impressions, and is highly defamatory in parts.... The remarks in the article are not based on facts and damage the image and good standing of the Andolan. One paragraph in the article states 'in the din and darkness, nobody heard or saw the response of the Shivalingam. And the diyas have already travelled quite a distance in the river, as if they are running away from the pornography of the andolan.'

What does your correspondent mean by this remark? What pornography has the NBA indulged in? This remark is obnoxious, highly defamatory, causing immense damage, and certainly in bad taste. Another statement which precedes the one above: 'When body fluid achieved metaphoric harmony with the river water in Maheshwar, did Shiva, the presiding deity of the temple in the ghat, laugh? Used condoms, illuminated by a hundred diyas in the Narmada, in the shadow of Maheshwar's revered Shivalingam? The remarkable loudspeakers of the NBA gave answers in the language of a less-than-erotic revolution.'

What 'body fluid', please? And where were the condoms to be illuminated by diyas? This particular paragraph conveys a graphic image of the Maheshwar ghat littered with condoms—a totally false and highly misleading pictures. Again, obnoxious and in very, very bad taste. Again, highly damaging to the Andolan. There are other such remarks and indeed, the article as a whole conveys an impression of some weird sexual orgy being indulged in by the Narmada Bachao Andolan. (*The New Indian Express*, 9 August 1999, p. 9)

As stated in the letter, the article was indeed in very bad taste and written with malice to defame NBA. In response to the letter, the author of the article Prasannarajan defended what he had written and argued 'I thought only dams could damage the *andolan*, not a report that defied Dharmadhikary's mind'. The newspaper produced mostly negative stories on the 'rally for the valley'.

Devika Jain in her letter said,

I am troubled, if not shocked, to find that apart from not signaling the emergency in the valley, no mention is made of the extraordinary, informed, the collective will of the masses that was almost tangible or the foreboding of mass death in the villages that will soon be submerged. It is a pity to trivialise the mass struggle in the Narmada valley by personalising it either into Medha's war or Arundhati's gimmick, city-slicking or anti-growth madness. Attention should have been called to the state of 13000 hectares of forest land and 40000 hectares of rich cultivated land.... Attention should be drawn to what is being traded off by neglecting the struggle, rather than to the picturesque language and titillating titles that we see in Prasannarajan's report. It would be important to see the implication of neglecting this particular andolan in relation to the rest of the social movements in India, which have given public policy in India a human face and enabled it to learn from stake-holders other than the traditional power lobbies. (*The New Indian Express*, 9 August 1999, p. 9)

The letter pointed out the way environmental movements are reported by newspapers which tend to focus more on personalities rather than on the cause (Guha, 1992). The controversial claim of the article that used condoms were strewn around on the bank of the Narmada became the topic of a daily column on the editorial page of the newspaper (10 August 1999). The column argued that if the condoms had been used that would put a question mark on the seriousness and commitment of the agitators. 'Somehow condoms and agitators have a habit of going hand in hand. In the early days of the students' agitation in Assam used condoms were found all over the place' (Dutt, 1999, p. 8) said the column questioning the morality of those involved in social movements. The rally was described as a strong campaign for the condom. *The New Indian Express* was not only trying to discredit NBA but also maligning all social movements by portraying the activists as those who had questionable morality and motives.

It is important to note that no other newspaper reported any such happening during the rally. Thoughtfulness seemed to have given way to sensationalism. Most of the statements made by NBA were followed by sarcastic remarks. For example, when NBA told journalists about the developments in the valley, the remark that followed was 'The stories we were told on the way were bizarre, to say the least'. The bias in coverage was also made clear by the fact that a majority of the reports were loaded with opinions. While *The Hindu* threw light on different aspects of the issue *The New Indian Express* appeared fixed on the leader of the rally Arundhati Roy. She became the focus rather than the issue. The newspaper trivialized and obscured the real questions that ought to have been discussed during the 'rally for the valley'. The fact that NBA was leading a mass struggle in the valley for more than a decade was completely ignored. Arundhati Roy and Medha Patkar dominated the news stories in *The Times of India*. This reflects a tendency among the newspapers to strongly associate mass struggles with popular personalities and celebrities. The entire movement was trivialized and marginalized through images that emphasized frivolity, outlandishness, militancy and deviance while understating the environmental consequences of building large dams. Thus, the protestors were made the issue rather than the things about which they were protesting. Such images of protestors in the media play a significant role in shaping the perception of the public about a movement. The paper tried to divert public attention away from the root cause of the social conflict. Protest actions and events were described as theatre spectacles rather than as part of a democratic struggle over issues of the rights of the people.

Newspapers' support to the construction of big dams was evident in the coverage given to the Supreme Court's decision on 18 October 2000, allowing the construction of the Sardar Sarvar dam, which had been suspended for more than four years following a court order. Almost all newspapers welcomed the court's decision. Their editorials advised NBA to accept the verdict, give up agitation and concentrate its attention on rehabilitation measures. Patkar's criticism of the verdict was described as negative and irrational. The whole issue was seen as a conflict between Patkar and the Government of Gujarat reflecting a tendency of the newspapers to equate movements with the personalities of their leaders thereby reducing the issue to the level of personality clash (Guha, 1992).

Even while some newspapers appreciate the work of NBA they strongly favour the big dams. In an editorial with the headline 'The Narmada Valley project marches on' a day after Prime Minister

Narendra Modi dedicated the Sardar Sarovar dam to the country (17 September 2017) *The Economic Times* strongly defended the project dismissing all objections to the building of the big dams.[2] The editorial said,

> Submergence displaces people, mostly poor, sinks cropped land, and kills off wild fauna and flora. Yet, India must build large dams, to harness the monsoons' bounty that drains away. The sum total of benefits across space and time from such dams would far outweigh the costs. But the costs are borne by a relatively small number of people, over a short period of time.
>
> A striking feature of the Narmada project has been that those whom it displaced received compensation, not everyone nor in full measure. Yet, thanks to the valiant efforts of the Narmada Bachao Andolan, a norm was established that project oustees must be rehabilitated and compensated. (*The Economic Times*, 2017)

The editorial reflected the general attitude of the newspapers towards big dams. The newspaper does not want the construction of large dams stopped even when there is ample evidence to show that displaced persons are neither given compensation nor resettled. It believes that only a few people are affected for a short period, contrary to the reality that millions of people have been displaced and generations of people have suffered the consequences of displacement. Interestingly, the editorial praises NBA for helping establish a norm for compensation and rehabilitation even though it brushes aside the fundamental questions about the environmental consequences of large dams.

Media Trial on 'Foreign Money'

Although NBA does not accept foreign funds or even government funds, there have been allegations that the organization has received foreign money. On media accusation about foreign funds, Medha Patkar (personal communication, 6 March 2019) says,

> Foreign money became a big issue in the media because we started opposing and questioning the system. We did not even take the

[2] https://economictimes.indiatimes.com/blogs/et-editorials/the-narmada-valley-project-marches-on/

money associated with our foreign awards. Otherwise, we would have had 55 lakh dollars from Right Livelihood Award (1990) and 60 lakh dollars from Goldman Prize (1992). If we had that money we would have easily carried on our work with the interest alone. But we refused to touch that money. Two Swedish activists came here to inform us and invite us to receive the Right Livelihood Award. We had a discussion throughout the night with three hundred representatives on whether to accept or not to accept the award. Baba Amte joined us early in the morning. Although some people said the money had no colour and that we should accept it, we decided overwhelmingly not to take the money. If we get the foreign money not only we will be accused but we will also be confused about mobilizing resources and the activist character of the movement will also get changed. The whole culture gets transformed. Even for lifting a bag, someone will ask for money.

Despite repeated clarifications by NBA some newspapers continued to write about foreign money being used for agitation in the Narmada valley. Legal actions launched against Patkar have not deterred the NBA from following the path of Satyagraha.

Even when Patkar received the Green Ribbon Award for Best International Political Campaigner by the BBC, media went about alleging that she was receiving foreign money again, even though the award did not have any financial component. Like Patkar, other leading environmental activists have also been accused of receiving foreign funds.[3] Patkar argues that even if there is foreign funding of non-governmental organizations and movements, the government or the media have no moral authority to question anyone because the government itself receives foreign funds for its various needs and media also receive foreign direct investment. NBA had to prove that it did not receive foreign money because the media had conducted a trial and had declared it guilty. *The Pioneer* newspaper published a story making a false charge against NBA that it had received foreign money. When NBA sent a reply refuting the charges the newspaper refused to publish it. (Medha Patkar, personal communication, 5 March 2019).

---

[3] The leader of the movement against Kundankulam Atomic Power Plant in Tamil Nadu S. P. Udaykumar (2012) was accused of using foreign fund with the motive of obstructing India from meeting its energy needs.

In the year 2000 the *Indian Express* newspaper that supported dam construction and questioned NBA's campaigns then, published an advertisement issued by V. K. Saxena, a pro-dam campaigner and supposedly the president of the Ahmedabad-based National Council for Civil Liberties (NCCL), attacking Medha Patkar personally and NBA (D'Souza, 2002, pp. 133–135). The half-page advertisement had appeared in *The Indian Express* on 10 November 2000 (p. 5) with the title 'True face of Medha Patkar and her NBA'. At the bottom of the advertisement, a line said, 'space donated by a patriot'. The first accusation it made was 'NBA is passing on confidential documents related to projects of national importance to the foreign people'. As 'proof' an 'email message' purportedly sent by NBA to two persons in Switzerland was produced. On the face of it the 'proof' of the email appeared to be false because it was handwritten. The email was related to Maheshwar dam project which was pushed with foreign funding without socio-economic and environmental appraisal. The email sent to the Swiss representatives said, 'I am enclosing the (confidential) risk analysis document that we have prepared'. The NCCL did not explain how a document prepared by NBA itself became a document of national importance. The second accusation made was that NBA was 'supporting itself through *hawala* transactions'. The advertisement displayed a thanking letter and a receipt showing that the Lok Samiti had received ₹40,000 by cheque from the Lalbhai Group of companies[4] but did not refer to money being brought in from abroad. It was a transaction within India. There was no proof of any hawala transaction.

Medha Patkar says V. K. Saxena who worked for the Adani Group as CEO of a collaborative project, gave a cheque of ₹40,000 to Lok Samiti, a non-political and non-religious people's organization founded by Sarvodaya leader Jayaprakash Narayan, as a contribution towards *jeevan shalas*, schools for tribal children in Maharashtra and Madhya Pradesh run by NBA since 1992 (personal communication, 6 March 2019). Since there was no registered trust then to run the schools, NBA collaborated with Lok Samiti to run the schools and donations were received through Lok Samiti. When Patkar and 400 others were in jail for 14 days, V. K. Saxena offered the cheque of ₹40,000 issued by the Lalbhai Group to the Lok Samiti. The trustees

---

[4] www.narmada.org.archive/ie/20010413

of the Samiti told him to wait until Patkar and others were released from jail. But he insisted that they take the money and give a receipt and a thanking letter for giving the cheque even though the cheque got bounced. In reply to an RTI application by Lok Samiti the Syndicate Bank said that the account did not exist. The receipt and the thanking letter were used to show that NBA was involved in the *hawala* transaction. NBA was also presented as an organization that was working with the sole objective of halting India's progress. While NBA had never relied on foreign funds, it had not even accepted money associated with foreign awards. It had to write to foreign agencies asking them not to provide financial assistance to environmentally destructive projects in India, no financial assistance had been sought for NBA from any foreign agency. NBA's struggle and reconstruction activities are carried out with voluntary donations within India, and support in kind by farmers.

Medha Patkar had complained that the advertisement was based on false accusation and the imputations made in it affected her reputation causing harm to the movement (*The Times of India*, 9 July 2018). She filed a defamation case against V. K. Saxena who in turn filed two defamation cases against her; one for making derogatory remarks against him during a panel discussion in a television channel in April 2006 and another for issuing a defamatory press statement in relation to the fake cheque presented to Lok Samiti and false advertisement. *The Indian Express* published an apology about the advertisement. Saxena published a few more advertisements with accusations against Patkar. (*Outlook*, 8 December 2017). The cases are still being heard in the court. Patkar alleges that it was this Saxena who organized an attack on her when she went to attend a peace meeting at Sabarmati Ashram in April 2002.

On 9 July 2018, NBA sent letters to the newspapers bringing to their notice that a report[5] by the news agency Press Trust of India on the defamation case was completely lopsided as it was not based on even minimum investigation into the allegations. NBA requested the newspapers not to fall prey to the tactics of the corporate-prone politics which was all out to defame and harass activists who question the dominant development paradigm.

---

[5] http://www.ptinews.com/news/9864944_Defamation-charges-framed-against-Medha-Patkar

According to Patkar (personal communication, 4 March 2019), the PTI reporter who covered the court proceedings put out only the government version of the case. She says,

> I spoke to the chief of the PTI and told him that the reporter did not speak to me or any worker of the NBA before writing the report. Even when I tried to speak to the reporter to explain certain details of the case the reporter would not listen to me at all. Several stories have been planted against the Narmada movement to create adverse public opinion. Whenever fake media coverage comes up we usually keep quiet, but at times it becomes necessary for us to clarify and respond to make sure that the reporter or the head of the institution knows what the facts are and how the report is far from truth.

Two issues that relate to the media are important here. First, a newspaper allowed publication of an advertisement that attacked Medha Patkar and NBA. The question is whether a newspaper should allow a person to buy space only to make false allegations against an individual or an institution. Is it not the responsibility of the newspaper to ensure that no defamatory advertisement is published? *The Indian Express* which had been carrying on a campaign against NBA later apologized for publishing such an advertisement.[6] Second, a news agency that sells news to hundreds of newspapers throughout the country sent out a report that was one-sided and biased toward pro-dam groups. If the news agency sends out a report without looking into the key aspects of a case it is likely to prejudice the readers who are going to read the story in different newspapers. Both the newspaper and the news agency had not acted with responsibility. Even as the trial was going on, a section of the media tried to declare NBA guilty of using foreign money for its campaign.

Personality-centric Coverage

There is a tendency among the media to focus more on personalities leading social movements rather than on the issues that need to be explained to the people. Most of the environmental movements are

---

[6] https://icrindia.wordpress.com/2022/11/12/Medha-Patkar-vs-v-ksaxena

identified with personalities who lead them. When a leader becomes the face of the movement it is only natural that media attention is focused mostly on the leader. One view is that when well-known personalities get associated with movements, the magnitude of the problems they talk about gets magnified. More than the personalities wanting to get all the media attention, it is the media that try to identity entire movements with them to attract public attention.[7] Moreover, for journalists, the easiest way to report about environmental movements is to follow the events in which well-known personalities take part or to seek their opinions on key developments. Like many other movements, the movement in the Narmada valley has become synonymous with its leader Medha Patkar.

Medha Patkar, as the face of NBA, has been the centre of media debate on the issues related to the Narmada valley. She has also been criticized for creating a situation in which Medha is NBA and vice-versa when there have been other tribal leaders who have contributed to the movement against the Narmada valley projects (Omvedt, 2004). Nepal (2009, p. 27) says, 'Most of the time, the young leaders feel neglected despite their hard struggles because of media coverage of senior leaders. Young, aspiring leaders of the movement feel psychologically depressed as their names do not figure in the media coverage'. When asked about these criticisms Patkar says that she has requested media persons several times not to write reports focused only on her (personal communication, 5 March 2019). She has often spoken about media focusing too much attention on her. NBA has always tried to avoid the individual-centric approach or exaggerated role for any one person but the media have often seen the entire movement as a struggle between Medha Patkar and the chief minister of Gujarat (Patkar & Sangvai, 2006). Patkar maintains that it is a movement of the Adivasis and the media projection of only one individual as the leader of the movement is not fair to those activists who have kept up the spirit of the movement for decades.

---

[7] Panduranga Hegde (2010, p. 272) says that although the Chipko movement was essentially a women's movement, the media projected it as a movement led by Sunderlal Bahuguna and Chandi Prasad Bhatt. This according to him created a rift leading to emergence of two streams within the movement.

T. V. Jayan, who has written about the Narmada movement, says to shift the focus away from the leader, journalists sometimes try to quote several other lesser-known leaders but the time and space constraints do not allow that (personal communication, 11 September 2020). When a reporter tries to quote more than one person on the same issue in the same story, the subeditor on the desk cuts out the quote from a lesser-known person. When there is no space constraint and long stories are allowed to be written, quoting sources other than the leaders becomes a possibility. Quoting activists other than the leader in a story is important because it tells the readers that the environmental struggle is not a single person's show, but a collective effort.

The media tend to often quote those persons who are articulate and coherently explain issues. The views and experiences of the common people coping with displacement and struggling to live on are almost absent. Journalists who work under constraints of time and resources find it hard to go to the remote parts of the valley and report because of which they depend on the more articulate representatives of NBA. But to make a report comprehensive and authentic journalists must get the views, experiences and facts from all stakeholders. While most journalists want to quote mostly Patkar in their stories there have been a few journalists who have travelled to the places where the project-affected people live to tell their stories.

Patkar takes the example of two journalists from *The Hindu*—Meena Menon and Gargi Parsai—who wrote a series of stories that represented the voice of the people of the Narmada valley, not just of Patkar (personal communication, 5 March 2019). Expressing her admiration for the two journalists who presented issues with perspectives in their stories, Patkar says,

> They had a different kind of sensitivity. Even in media conferences, journalists would always focus on well-known activists. So, I had to speak the most. If I told them to let the five persons sitting next to me speak, they would look here and there and run away. These two women would listen to several not-so-well-known activists. They would get the views of the Adivasis. That would make a lot of difference. They would travel to the interiors of the tribal villages to get their news stories. They found news away from NBA

office and its key activists. These journalists helped us, at times, understand what the views of the Adivasis were.

The *Frontline* gave massive coverage to the movement for several years bringing in-depth analysis. The stories were not focused on one or two individuals leading the movement but on the impact of displacement on the livelihoods of the people and the environment.

Just as the movement is not individual-centric, its campaigns are also not directed at any individual. Targeting any individual will only lead to aggressive counterattacks and will strengthen opposition to the movement. At times, media have presented NBA's struggle as the one directed at some individuals despite Patkar and other leaders repeatedly denying it. It is a struggle that questions policies, approaches, priorities and attitudes of politicians, bureaucrats and corporate houses rather than questioning individuals. But the personality-centric media coverage of the developments in the Narmada valley continues.

Lack of Issue Orientation

Media may give space and time when there is an intense mass struggle or brutal attack on agitators by the state or when legal battles are fought in the court of law. While agitations and oppressive actions do get into the editorial space of media frequently, there is no sustained coverage of the fundamental arguments, perspectives and constructive programmes of NBA.

When the Supreme Court lifted the ban on construction of the Narmada dam in October 2000 some newspapers celebrated it as if a major hurdle in the way of development of the country had been removed. But they had not captured the mood of the people resisting the dam project. Patkar broke down while addressing a press conference in Delhi after the court rejected the pleas of the Adivasis. But when she returned to Barwani, thousands of people gathered in a hall and declared that the real struggle had just begun and that they would not allow the Supreme Court to give the clearance. The mood of NBA activists got changed and there was a renewed spirit to fight on until justice was done. The media did not capture any of these moments. Newspapers report events but fail to capture the processes that happen between the events. According to Patkar, between the two fasts or protest demonstrations, there is so much happening but that does not get reported in media.

In 2006 when NBA had a 21-day fast on the Madhya Pradesh–Gujarat border 700 journalists from all over the country landed there. As *jal samadhi* (death by drowning) had been announced journalists were there expecting the unfolding of a great event. Once those events were over, journalists were nowhere to be seen for several months. The intensity of the struggle will not be the same all the time. The spirit of the masses will also not be the same all the time. Patkar explains,

> The year 2017 was something special in the life of the NBA as people were on the streets throughout the year. Protests and programmes were going on throughout the year. Many of these events were reported by the media. Continuing with that is neither possible nor necessary always. There will be phases of struggle to be matched with phases of reconstruction. There are phases of political challenges vis-à-vis dialogue and phases of a hundred percent unity vis-a-vis some divisions as a result of people taking different positions. Events and processes do not always happen as per the desire of the Andolan leadership.
>
> Sometimes different issues have come before the NBA. For example, the women who are a major strength of the Narmada movement got involved in the struggle against liquor. Even as the NBA was planning to focus on the architecture of reconstruction, a new challenge of the river dying has come up. When there are such struggles media tend to assume that the movement has run out of steam even though the movement continues to raise environmental issues and the resulting consequences. The moment major events are out of sight most of the journalists are also out of sight. But there are a few journalists whose attention to our struggle is not connected to only the events we organise. They investigate our vision, strategies and strengths. (Personal communication, 6 March 2019)

There have been many phases of the movement but the media have looked for only events that are typically associated with a movement paying little attention to the work it has been involved in beyond the issue of displacement.

According to Ashutosh Sen, a multimedia journalist reporting for both print and web-based media from Barwani where NBA's office is located, the local media go beyond events while reporting issues in the Narmada Valley (personal communication, 6 March 2019). *Naidunia*, a Hindi newspaper known for accuracy and balance, is one paper that consistently provides news and analysis about the issues in the Narmada valley even when there are no major events. Sen says the paper has carried several in-depth stories analysing the processes that have led to the destruction of the ecology in the valley. The *YouTube* channels like *Dabang India News, Bharath News Live, India Update News* and *Naidunia* have been frequently reporting about sand mining and industrial activities in the valley that have led to the depletion of water in the Narmada river. 'All those promises about providing water to the water-scarce areas were false promises which should be explained to the people because the project has been built with the taxes they pay', Ashutosh says. He is of the view that only the coverage in national media is event-oriented whereas the local media report frequently on issues affecting the people throughout the year although there is higher coverage during the mega events like rallies and week-long fasts.

In recent days, Ashutosh has been writing frequently on the depletion of water in the Narmada river. Sand mining and industrial activities along the river have greatly contributed to the reduction in the quantity of water that flows in the Narmada. He feels it is necessary to explain to the people of Gujarat that the promise of providing water to the water-scarce areas in their state was a promise that could never be fulfilled.

Although big dams give rise to the problems of displacement of population, submergence of forests, waterlogging and salination, siltation, and increase in the possibility of earthquake, the media coverage rarely focuses on the consequences of these problems in the long run. Medha Patkar and the activists of NBA feel that the media coverage of the issues in the Narmada valley has been inadequate despite their best efforts to explain them to media persons. The coverage continues to be sporadic and focused on events that have dramatic elements.

Alternative Media

While NBA has made efforts to see the problems in the valley reported in the mainstream media it has also used alternative communication channels to reach out to the people both in the valley and outside. One news agency that has helped the movement explain and interpret the situation in the valley to the people through Hindi newspapers is the Sarvodaya Press Service (SPS). The agency, founded by Mahendrabhai, a veteran Sarvodaya leader, has served as a source of strength for the Narmada movement as it has disseminated written accounts of the struggles of the project-affected people through 200 Hindi dailies and magazines. It has played a key role in gaining support for the movement. The SPS which receives articles, opinion pieces and reports on issues affecting the people from writers, journalists, activists and citizens, selects three articles and sends them to the newspapers in the form of a bulletin. Started in 1960, SPS has been posting the bulletin every Friday to newspapers in 17 states covering issues related to development, human rights, discrimination against Dalits and women. In contrast to the nongovernmental organizations that have the heavy infrastructure, sources of funding and administrative setup, the SPS works on a shoe-string budget with employees rendering only honorary service. With a low subscription fee and with a humble honorarium received from the Gandhi Peace Foundation, the SPS has been able to sustain its operations for six decades.

When writer-activist Arundhati Roy received the Man Booker Award she distributed the prize money of ₹1.5 crore among 50 media and social organizations including SPS which received ₹2 lakhs. Medha Patkar has also routed many of her articles in Hindi through SPS. Since those who write for the press service are also activists, the reports it sends are based on the direct experience on the ground. Some of the highly regarded newspapers of the Hindi belt like *Deshbandhu,*

Jan Morcha, Dainik Bijnore Times and *Dainik Madhya Pradesh* often carry articles from the SPS (Dogra, 2016). While journalists from the national media mostly report from district centres, those who write for the SPS travel to the remote rural areas and present the voice of the people. The Narmada movement that has spread to the remotest corners of Madhya Pradesh and Maharashtra has greatly benefited from this rare kind of grassroots journalism.

Wall posters and handbills are often used in villages to mobilize people for rallies and demonstrations. *Narmada Samachar* is a bulletin about the programmes of NBA. Street plays, songs, puppet shows are organized with the involvement of the village youth. Well-known playwrights, painters, poets, film artists and theatre personalities have presented ecological issues associated with the projects in the Narmada valley through their works. They have reached people in different parts of the country telling them how the Adivasis in the valley have been evicted before making proper plans for their rehabilitation and resettlement.

Independent filmmakers who made documentaries on the social and ecological consequences of dam projects in the Narmada valley helped the anti-dam campaign reach social organizations and academic institutions in different parts of the world. They presented the problems associated with dam building to the audiences who had very little understanding of the consequences of big dam projects. Ananda Patwardhan, a well-known documentary filmmaker who has made several films mainly dealing with human rights, made 'A Narmada Diary' in 1995. The film documented people's resistance to the building of the Sardar Sarovar dam and how the state and the elites showed insensitivity towards the displacement of the poor people. It was the first documentary to present a comprehensive picture of how the livelihood of poor people is affected by the construction of big dams. The film, distributed by the CSE, had worldwide viewership contributing significantly to the international support NBA received. However, because of the film's criticism of the government and the Narmada projects, Doordarshan refused to broadcast it despite the fact that it had won a national award (Chapman, 2007).

Kaise Jeebo Re (How do I survive) is another documentary film that tells the story of the ruthlessness of the state and the callousness of the engineers that led to the displacement of Gond tribes not once but three times by the same dam. The Bargi dam, one of the 30 big dam projects in the Narmada valley, was completed in 1989 displacing more than a lakh people. The film made by Anurag Singh and Jharana Jhaveri in 1997 poignantly shows how the Gonds, thrown out of their forests that sustained them for generations ended up in the slums of Jabalpur as they were not rehabilitated and resettled as promised. The film powerfully conveys the arguments against big dams highlighting the significance of the Narmada movement. What the film portrayed was a pointer to what was to happen to the people facing displacement by the Sardar Sarovar dam 700 km downstream Bargi dam.

Franny Armstrong's documentary *Drowned Out* made over three years and released in 2002 captures the impact of the Sardar Sarovar dam on the livelihood of a folk doctor of Jalsindhi village in Madhya Pradesh and the struggle of NBA through rallies, demonstrations, hunger strikes to get justice for the displaced persons. The documentary features writer-activist Arundhati Roy and NBA leader Medha Patkar who explain how the government went ahead with the project even though it had failed to fulfil its promise of giving land for land and resettling and rehabilitating displaced persons.

Although there are other documentaries on the Narmada movement, these three documentaries helped NBA explain to the stakeholders and the audience that the project was destructive and that resettlement and rehabilitation mostly remained on paper. They have helped explain NBA's point of view and the false claims of the dam builders and their supporters. These documentaries have been screened in schools, colleges, universities and the villages in the Narmada valley. When the film *Drowned Out* was screened at Jalsindhi village with the help of a generator (as there was no electricity in the village), one year after its completion, the villagers saw moving images on the screen for the first time.[8] These films, also screened at seminars, workshops and consultative meetings, helped NBA seek support for the struggle of the Adivasis in the Narmada valley.

[8] https://www.spannerfilms.net/cinema_jalsindhi

The youngsters working with NBA manage social media and have helped change the perspectives of the people over time. Talking about NBA using social media to reach out to people and admitting her lack of familiarity in handling the social media, Patkar says,

I have sought the password for my Facebook account only today. Two of my colleagues have it. I came to know that I don't have a separate id. They have been putting my page on their pages. This is not proper. Many people and also people on Facebook ask me why there have been no inputs, no reports for a long time. My Facebook page which my colleagues were putting up on their pages has a good readership. I have something new every day to share. Since live recording is also possible I think we must use it. At times I have decided to have my own separate id and share information on my own on my Facebook page but have not been able to attain such independence due to heavy workload. My Twitter account is also being handled by my colleagues. (Personal communication, 5 March 2019)

Saurav Rajput who assists the NBA with social media says that information is being put out with regular frequency on social media and that the response has been encouraging, barring a few comments that cross the limit of decency in criticizing the movement (personal communication, 4 March 2019).

Identifying the necessity and also the limitations of social media, Patkar says,

You are compelled to be on social media because otherwise, you will fall behind. You will not know what is happening across the country and the world. But beyond a limit, it kills your creativity. It simply consumes a lot of your time. When my own friends prepare a WhatsApp group, the conversation becomes unstoppable. When I attended Gandhi Vigyan Sammelan in which over 200 senior Gandhians participated there was a WhatsApp group. All small things were being discussed. People were saying that my speech was good and they were asking where I was going, what I was planning to do, and so on. Something that we always plan in a face-to-face meeting became a thing of faceless communication. Once you open it, a lot of time goes into it. We cannot do that. I also think it is like a double-edged sword. There are advantages and disadvantages. Certain things that are never reported in mainstream media can be seen on social media. (Personal communication, 5 March 2019)

Although NBA finds it very difficult to keep pace with social media, it has become necessary to use them to communicate about events and developments in the valley.

One of the limitations of WhatsApp, according to Patkar, is that it reaches only friends and supporters who are already convinced and committed to conserving the environment but there is a need to reach out to the others who need to be educated about human consequences of what they think as development. Even those who are on the email list are also supporters of the movement. Social media do not provide depth but they can be used to get people interested in issues written about in newspapers.

Reflecting Emerging Realities

Contrary to the criticism that the Narmada movement is mostly supported by the educated urban middle class (Omvedt, 1999, 2004), there is overwhelming support by the common people (Kothari, 1999) because they are worried about basic needs of food, clothing and shelter. Patkar says (personal communication, 6 March 2019),

> If you meet *rickshawwallahs*, peasants, *chaiwallahs*, labourers and shopkeepers throughout the country you will know that they have been staunch supporters of our struggle. They empathise with us and say the movement is appreciable and a must. There is a minority that tries to use media to build opinions in favour of questionable projects.

She asserts that the movement is broad-based and has the support of most of the media and the common people.

She says,

> Actual social space is not matching with media space. There is a contradiction. Media do not necessarily represent the people, just as politicians fail to do it. Media are full of ads and exciting news about

religion and other emotional issues. This diverts the attention of the people from the real issues leading to a huge loss of youth energy. No movement can grow and expand unless the young people start asking questions and show concern towards the problems that are going to affect them in the future. Media have the responsibility of helping young people channelize their energies towards pressurizing the political class to adopt a model of development that is sustainable in the long run and just too.

She says that people tend to get carried away by the claims of the corporations made through the media that they are protecting the environment whereas, in reality, they are doing exactly the opposite. Patkar points out that when the Coca-Cola company, which extracts water from the ground, claims that it is recharging groundwater, the corporate media simply take their claim to be true. She says that the media that promote the interests of the corporate houses are unable to educate the youth about the threats to their own future.

The media that have been reporting mostly about issues of displacement have overlooked other issues that are emerging in the Narmada valley. There has been a drastic reduction of water in the Narmada which is a real cause for concern. Several activists in the valley express the view that it is the result of a combination of factors including climate change that has caused erratic rainfall, illegal mining and industrial activities throughout the valley. There is an industrial corridor covering hundreds of kilometres which is going to disturb the ecology of the Narmada valley. The scarcity of water and floods are affecting the livelihood of the people living upstream and downstream of the SSP. Since the water is stored until the beginning of the Monsoon for power generation, when the rains arrive, there is flooding above the dam and when the water is released from the dam, floods consume villages downstream.

Around 6,000 families of fishermen have become jobless because of the dam. After the Monsoon rains are over and the water level dips, the seawater comes up to 60 km into the river. This is going to pose a serious threat to the river ecosystem. The linking of Narmada with Kshipra, Mahi, Parwati, Gambhir, Kali Sindh and Chambal rivers is going to pose a serious threat to the environment. The pipeline that has been laid between the rivers has already caused enough damage and the linked rivers flow only during the monsoon and nearly dry up later. There is already irrefutable proof that the dams in the Narmada valley have caused irreversible damage to the ecosystem and that they have not delivered what was promised.

The damage caused to the environment in the Narmada valley and its effect on the livelihoods of the people is becoming more and more visible now but the media have not given serious attention to the issues that remain after the completion of the dam. According to Patkar, many journalists tend to think that since the dam is complete it is a closed chapter. Dwindling water flow in the Narmada and drying up of tributaries after the Monsoon have caused a lot of concern among the people in the valley. Resettlement and rehabilitation of the project-affected people before the submergence of their homes and lands was a condition that the Supreme Court order had imposed while allowing the raising of the height of the dam. But these conditions have not been fulfilled. NBA activists say that the problems that follow the completion of dam construction and the non-realization of the promised benefits need to be the focus of media coverage.

According to Patkar (personal communication, 6 March 2019) in recent years, a new generation of activists and journalists who have been witnessing the consequences of big dams have started covering the Narmada movement. They have realized that resettlement and rehabilitation of the displaced persons have not happened even after generations. There appears to be some realization among a few newspapers that big dams have been a disaster. They have expressed the view that the big dams are no solution to the problems of irrigation and energy. *The Daily News and Analysis* (DNA) carried an editorial on 20 May 2019, with the title 'Dry states—Maha, Guj show why big dam policy has not worked' and stressed the need to look for alternatives. The editorial echoes the long-held position of NBA about big dams.

Questions are justifiably being raised over the Narmada Valley Project's very reason for existence—to irrigate farms in Kutch, Saurashtra, and North Gujarat, which remains unfulfilled. As can be expected, the state governments are supplying drinking water through tankers, a normal routine at this time of the year. Clearly, something needs to be said about the policy of promoting large dams, as is evident in the case of both Gujarat and Maharashtra, which has not yielded commensurate benefits. Instead, a shift towards micro-irrigation projects must be prioritised. States such as Telangana have shown the way, having implemented a large scheme to rejuvenate its tanks, something that has been found wanting in Maharashtra and Gujarat. Sadly, in a period of election-related theatrics, real issues like the water crisis and acute shortage of stored water have been swept under the carpet.[9]

That the promised benefits have not been fulfilled seems to have dawned on the newspapers. Micro-irrigation projects are being promoted as possible ways of mitigating the irrigation problems.

The Hindustan Times in its editorial[10] on 19 September 2017 put forth a very strong argument against big dams stressing the need to rethink the 'big dams' model of development. The human and environmental costs, it said, were far higher than the promised benefits. Coming down heavily on the dismal record of resettlement and rehabilitation of the displaced person in India, the editorial elaborated on what it means to be losing one's land and home.

This is, of course, not counting the fact that the land that tribal communities and others have occupied for centuries is not just something that can be measured in acres and rupees. The cost of history and memory that lies inland and ancestral property can never be reimbursed.

The newspaper had gone beyond compensation and into the history and memory that lie in the land of ancestral property. A newspaper closely looking into the human and social cost of the dam is a reflection

9 https://www.dnaindia.com/analysis/editorial-dna-edit-dry-states-maha-guj-show-why-big-dam-policy-has-not-worked-2750973

10 https://www.hindustantimes.com/editorials/it-is-time-to-rethink-the-big-dams-model-of-development/story-Q8aMISORnsxIr6o8MjuHEP.html

of understanding a problem beyond the economics of dam construction and its benefits.

Conclusion

Media coverage of the environmental and livelihood issues in the Narmada valley has been a mixed bag of fairness and negativism. NBA does not go after the media and does not believe in organizing events only to grab media attention. But the media covered the movement only when some events were organized. Newspapers were largely supportive of the movement in the 1980s and early 1990s but turned more hostile later. At some crucial times when the movement was ignored by the media, breakthroughs came from some perceptive journalists. While the national English newspapers were broadly neutral, most of the Gujarati newspapers and some Hindi newspapers were critical of NBA, many a time unfairly. Since a majority of the beneficiaries of the SSP are the people of Gujarat, newspapers in the Gujarati language echoed the voice of the government that was pushing the project through without implementing either the Narmada Water Disputes Tribunal (NWDT) order or the Supreme Court order about resettlement and rehabilitation. Some newspapers framed the Narmada movement as an 'anti-national' and 'anti-development' movement conspiring to harm India's development.

One of the English newspapers, *The New Indian Express*, tried to belittle and ridicule the movement, in the late 1990s, as if it was a fad of the urban middle class but changed its stance in the 2010s and began supporting it. While some newspapers covered different aspects of the Narmada project generating political debate about community rights over natural resources, others reported the claims of the government and industry. The coverage was more on the economics of compensation and benefits rather than on the social and cultural dimensions of displacement. In most newspapers, reporting was event-oriented and personality-oriented. Patkar admits that she has been the focus of media coverage and says that media should listen to the other activists to get a wider perspective. There were exceptions of newspaper reporters going to the remote Adivasi villages to understand the problems from the people at the grassroots level and presenting them with perspectives. Even though newspapers expressed sympathy towards the displaced persons for not being fully compensated, rehabilitated and resettled, no newspapers called for a halt to the construction of the dam. In the view of NBA activists, there has generally been a decline in coverage in recent years. They feel that the movement does not receive the kind of coverage it used to receive until 2000. Nevertheless, there have been some indications that at least some newspapers, if not all, have lately realized that the big dams are not the permanent solutions to the problems of irrigation and energy and that other options should be explored.

CHAPTER 8

Environment and the Media

The Media Discourse on Kerala–Kodagu Floods

India has been experiencing extreme weather events at a greater frequency in recent years. Heat waves and floods are the most common of these events. They are usually referred to in media as 'natural' disasters despite the ample evidence available to link them to anthropogenic activities. Disasters are symptoms of the recklessness with which the resources have been used for decades. Disasters make big news not only because of their magnitude but also because of the issues they throw up for public debate. When media report about disasters, they seem more concerned with death counts than longer-term effects on economic and social life (Benthall, 1993). Studies have shown that the media have not paid adequate attention to the link between extreme weather events and the environmental factors (Hopke, 2020; Painter et al., 2020). Those media which have journalists specializing in environmental reporting carry detailed accounts of extreme weather events and try to relate them to environmental factors on the basis of scientific evidence. However, it is also important to note that covering a massive disaster needs a coordinated effort by a team of reporters.

Unprecedented rains battered Kerala and the Kodagu district in Karnataka in August 2018, leading to floods and landslides. In the heaviest rains in nearly a century, hundreds of people lost their lives and nearly a million people had to be evacuated to safety. People lost their homes, land and property valued at thousands of crores of rupees. Thousands of relief camps were set up for the flood victims with financial and material aid coming from different parts of the country and the world. By the second week of August, the flood situation had worsened and landslides were reported in several regions. The National Disaster Response Force (NDRF) sent its battalions to the worst affected areas. The state of Kerala experienced the worst floods since 1924 that affected 14 districts and claimed 483 lives. As many as 3,274 relief camps were opened at various locations to accommodate over 1.2 million flood victims. As much as one-sixth of the population of Kerala was directly affected by the floods and landslides. Massive rescue and relief operations were launched. The Government of India declared the floods in Kerala as the 'calamity of a severe nature'.

Kodagu, the smallest district in Karnataka with a population of 5.5 lakhs as per the 2011 Census, is geographically contiguous with Wayanad which was one of the worst affected districts in Kerala. The floods and landslides in Kodagu claimed 16 lives and affected 200 villages. The district received the highest-ever rainfall of 1,675 millimetres in August, breaking the 1931 record of 1,569 millimetres (Sharma, 2018). Over 1,200 houses collapsed, forcing nearly 7,000 people to take shelter in 51 relief camps. This extreme weather event shocked the citizens, bureaucrats and politicians but not the ecologists who had been warning about the possible consequences of degradation of the Western Ghats.

How was the disaster reported in media? What aspects of the disaster received greater media attention? What were the possible causes of the floods and landslides the media focused on? Did newspapers link the disaster with climate change? How were they framed? How educative was the coverage in terms of understanding the environmental factors that possibly led to the unprecedented floods and landslides? These are the questions that need to be answered to understand the media role in reporting environmental issues associated with disasters.

In order to find answers to these questions a content analysis of coverage of floods and landslides in Kerala and Kodagu was carried out. For the purpose of content analysis four major English newspapers and four Kannada newspapers were selected. All issues between 9 August and 4 September 2018 were selected for analysis. The flood caused by heavy rains that lashed Kerala and Kodagu began to be reported in newspapers from 9 August 2018. Although there were no more floods and landslides by the last week of August media continued to carry reports and articles continued to appear some more days. Media reports could hardly be seen after 4 September. The English newspapers selected for content analysis were *The Hindu, The Times of India, The New Indian Express* and the *Deccan Herald*. Three of the four English newspapers selected for the study have a wide readership[1] in Kerala and Kodagu. Only *Deccan Herald* has a readership mostly confined to Karnataka, although it has readers in Wayanad and Kasaragod districts of Kerala.

The four major Kannada newspapers selected for analysis— *Prajavani, Kannada Prabha, Vijaya Karnataka* and *Samyukta Karnataka*—have readers[2] throughout Karnataka and also in parts of Kerala. All items that appeared about the floods and landslides were counted and the reports, articles and editorials that referred to the environmental and natural causes were analysed. Some of the reports and editorials that had appeared in the old issues of newspapers have also been examined to understand the media portrayal of environmental issues over the years. A qualitative analysis of the content was also carried out to understand how facts and opinions about the disaster were presented and framed.

Heavy rains began causing floods on 9 August and continued to pound Kerala–Kodagu for the next two weeks. Floods and landslides

---

[1] According to the Indian Readership Survey 2019, *The Hindu, The Times of India, The New Indian Express* and *Deccan Herald* had the readership of 52.26 lakh, 152.36 lakh, 18.46 lakh, and 12.43 lakh, respectively. The *Deccan Herald* had a readership of 12.43 lakh as per the Indian Readership Survey 2017.

[2] According to the Indian Readership Survey 2019, *Prajavani, Kannada Prabha* and *Vijaya Karnataka* had a readership of 71.77 lakh, 26.62 lakh and 79.10 lakh, respectively. The circulation of *Samyukta Karnataka*, according to its editor, was 1.7 lakh in August 2019 but readership figures are not available.

destroyed homes, paddy fields, plantations and livelihoods of lakhs of people and the media were full of stories on rescue and relief operations. Although rains receded by the last week of August, the newspapers continued to report on relief operations, causes and consequences of the unprecedented disaster. Since the purpose here was to examine how the media covered floods and landslides in Kerala–Kodagu, news about floods and landslides reported from districts outside Kodagu and states outside Kerala were not counted. Journalists, activists, experts and the affected people were also interviewed in Kerala and Karnataka to know their perception of media coverage of floods and landslides.

At the time of a disaster, media are expected to play a crucial role in providing timely and accurate information that can be of immense value in rescuing people and in getting immediate assistance. They have the responsibility of avoiding sensationalism and social division while delivering vital information to the affected communities. They not only have the responsibility of reporting what has happened but also have the duty to explain the causes so that measures are initiated to prevent such massive disasters in the future. Although the media coverage of the floods in Kerala and Kodagu was initially very low, it increased by several folds as the gravity of the situation became more visible.

The Coverage

When heavy rains were reported by the end of the first week of August 2018 the national media had not yet gauged the enormity of the floods in Kerala and Kodagu. Therefore, while the local media were full of reports about floodwaters inundating the low lying areas, the gravity of the floods was not reflected in the national media coverage. Former Union Minister and Member of Parliament from Kerala Shashi Tharoor (2018) tweeted on 15 August 2018, that

> The flood situation here in Kerala is really bad. The national media coverage has been grossly inadequate compared to the gravity of the situation here. It is a sad reflection of the truism that the farther you are from Delhi the less you matter in today's India.

However, as the situation worsened the national media and the regional media began covering the floods with their correspondents spread across Kerala and Kodagu.

As can be seen in Figure 8.1, the number of stories about floods in Kerala and Kodagu increased dramatically from 15 August, reaching a maximum of 184 stories on 20 August and declining on the following days as rains receded. Although heavy rains began on 8 August, for the next one week media had not yet realized how massive the floods were. Shashi Tharoor's tweet that the media had not paid adequate attention to the issue appeared to be true as there was a sharp increase in the number of stories about floods only after 15 August. The newspapers were slow in responding to the enormity of the disaster. What he said about the supposedly Delhi-based newspapers was true of even newspapers the South. Between 19 and 21 August, the stories of floods and landslide occupied nearly 40 per cent of the total space in newspapers, with several stories appearing on the front page. As the floods receded in the last week of August, the number of stories in the newspapers declined. Stories and pictures about houses surrounded by the floodwaters, collapse of houses and buildings, landslides on hill slopes, bridges washed away and people carrying babies, the sick and the old filled the pages of newspapers. As indicated in the news stories, several journalists from each newspaper covered the loss of lives and property, rescue and relief operations. There were stories of heroism, humanism, compassion, brotherhood and collective efforts amid devastation showing the great resilience of people. There were also elements of rumour, exaggeration and sensationalism in coverage which is not unusual in reporting a disaster of such massive magnitude.

While reporters on the ground produced such stories, there were also stories on what caused massive floods and landslides. The sources in these stories were scientists, environmentalists and the affected people.

During the period between 9 August and 4 September, news about floods and landslides accounted for 8.27 per cent of news carried in the newspapers (Table 8.1). Kannada newspapers provided

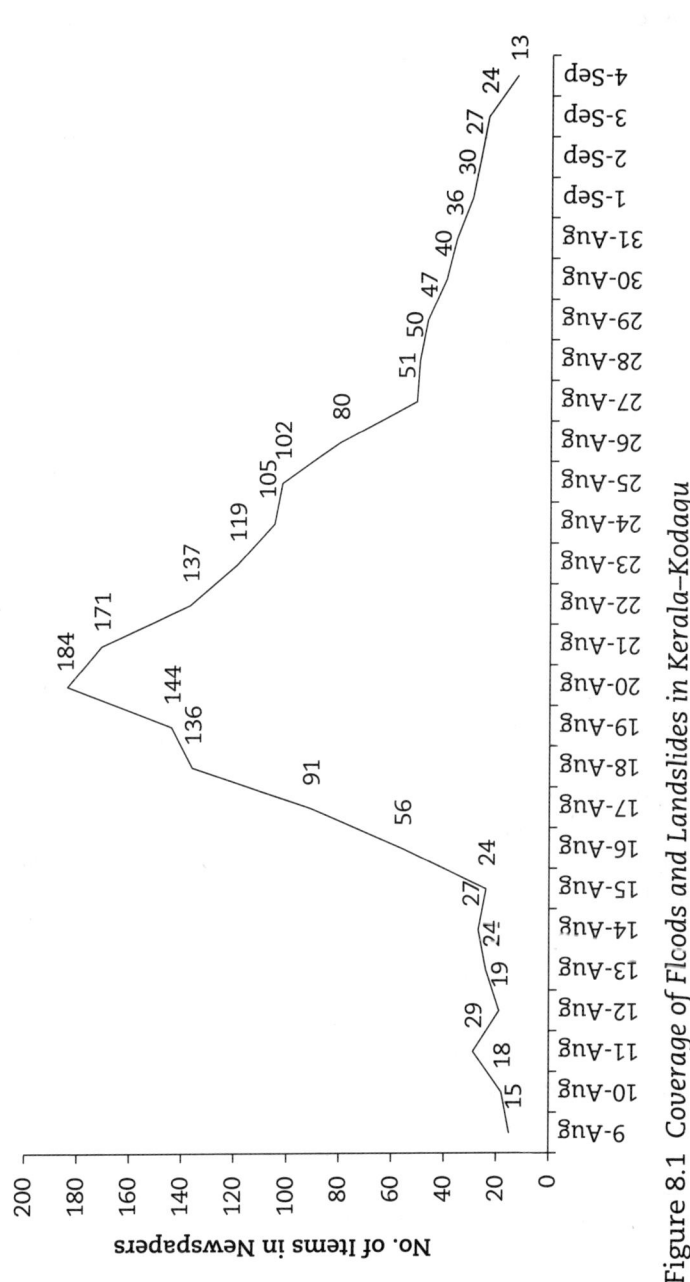

Figure 8.1 Coverage of Flcods and Landslides in Kerala–Kodagu

Table 8.1 *Coverage of Floods, Landslides and Their Causes*

Newspaper	All Items	No. of Items on Floods and Landslides	% of Items	Items on Causes	% of Items on Causes
The Hindu	3,618	230	6.36	9	3.91
The Times of India	2,538	241	9.50	8	3.32
The New Indian Express	2,754	224	8.13	12	5.36
Deccan Herald	3,321	225	6.78	14	6.22
Prajavani	2,457	250	10.18	12	4.80
Vijaya Karnataka	2,106	219	10.40	13	5.94
Kannada Prabha	2,646	239	9.03	7	2.93
Samyukta Karnataka	2,322	171	7.36	6	3.51
Total	21,762	1,799	8.27	81	4.50

higher coverage (9.22%) to the disaster as compared to the English newspapers (7.22%). The Kannada newspapers *Vijaya Karnataka* and *Prajavani* gave the highest coverage to the disaster. However, there were no significant differences between Kannada and English newspapers. A significant positive correlation was found among all newspapers. The coverage reached its peak between 15 and 24 August. Of all the items carried by the newspapers, as many as 4.50 per cent were about the causes that led to floods and landslides. Various environmental factors that possibly led to the disaster were discussed in those stories.

Except for a slight variation in the number of items, there was no significant difference between English and Kannada newspapers about identifying the causes of the disaster. Among the English newspapers, the *Deccan Herald* had the highest percentage (6.22%) of items that discussed factors that led to the disaster. *The Times of India* had the lowest per cent of stories on the causes. Of the four Kannada newspapers, it was *Vijaya Karnataka* which had the highest per cent of stories about anthropogenic activities responsible for heavy rains and landslides. In *Kannada Prabha,* less than 3 per cent of the stories on the disaster referred to the causes. The dominant opinion expressed in the newspapers was that it was environmental degradation that led to the disaster in Kerala and Kodagu.

Causes of Floods and Landslides

Although the newspaper pages were filled with stories about loss of life and property and rescue and relief operations of a massive scale, there were also reports, articles and editorials about the causes of the disaster. Several environmental factors came up for discussion in the newspapers even as the rescue and relief operations were going on. Deforestation, mining, tourism, roads, industries, urbanization and climate change were the major factors that were frequently mentioned in the reports, articles and editorials on the disaster (Figure 8.2).

Deforestation appeared as the major cause in all the 81 items that the newspapers carried about the causes of floods and landslides. Every report, article and editorial written about the causes of the disaster found destruction of the forest and conversion of forest land for non-forest purposes as the major contributor to the disaster.

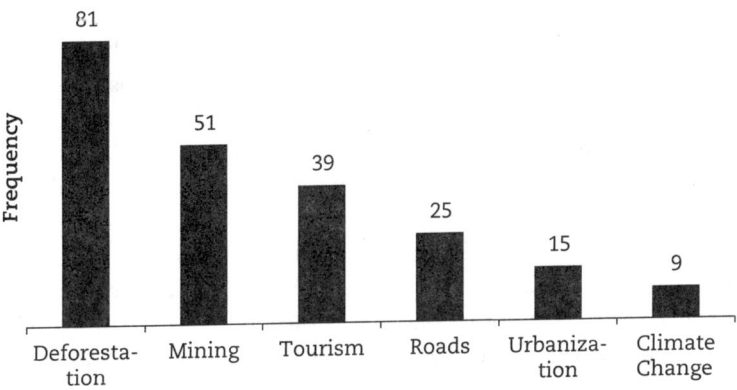

Figure 8.2 *Causes of Floods and Landslides in Newspapers*

The forest cover had decreased by 20 per cent in the Idukki district and by 11 per cent in Wayanad district in the last one decade (Padma, 2018). The loss of forest cover as shown in newspapers caused floods and landslides in these most heavily forested districts of Kerala affecting the lives of lakhs of people. In Kodagu, the evergreen forests had declined to 27.14 per cent in 2018 from 40.47 per cent in 1973 because of unchecked tree felling and expansion of coffee plantations.[3] In several areas, monoculture of a specific type of tree, especially teak had replaced wild varieties of trees that could have helped prevent floods. According to environmentalists replacing wild trees with silver oak in the coffee plantations, led to large scale erosion. As quoted in newspapers, they argued that native trees were very essential in coffee plantations to prevent erosion and landslides. In Kodagu, massive landslides had happened in Mukkodlu, Galibeedu, Kalur, Monnangeri and Madapur villages where large-scale deforestation had taken place in the last two decades.

Mining in the Western Ghats region, including sand mining in rivers and streams in Kerala and Kodagu became the second most often cited cause (51). Dunes and sandbanks that had acted as barriers to flooding had been removed causing degradation of rivers. Reports said that illegal mining had been continuing because of the nexus among politicians, contractors and bureaucrats. Besides mining, the encroachment of the banks of rivers and streams caused the inundation of towns and big cities.

According to the newspaper reports and articles, the pressure of tourism had a serious impact on the ecologically sensitive areas. Tourism that accounts for 10 per cent of Kerala's GDP was the third most frequently mentioned cause (39) of floods and landslides. Resorts and homestays for the tourists were constructed on hills by clearing forest and flattening the land on slopes. In some places, to accommodate the rising number of tourists, buildings had been constructed by creating artificial hills. Reports in newspapers gave details about how coffee plantation owners had created artificial lakes on the top of the hills to attract tourists for their homestays

---

[3] https://www.coorg.com

and to water the coffee plants during the summer. They said that the promotion of tourism in the ecologically sensitive areas had led to an increase in construction activities, many of them illegal. In Kodagu alone, there were an estimated 4,000 homestays, out of which only 404 had been registered.[4]

Construction of unscientific roads that cut through the hills of the Western Ghats was mentioned in 25 of the 81 newspaper items as another contributor to the landslides. Besides violating rules of road construction, many roads had been constructed in areas where they should have been built, claimed the sources quoted in the news reports. On the roads in the Western Ghats, vehicles were permitted to carry up to a maximum of 16.2 tonnes but most of the trucks were allowed to carry up to 30 tonnes that could weaken the stability of the hills.

Unplanned urbanization was mentioned as another factor that caused floods and landslides in 15 newspaper stories. Residential houses, public and commercial buildings that had come upon unstable hill slopes and on natural drainage systems had led to floods and landslides. In several reports, the flooding of the Kochi airport built on the paddy fields and wetlands by the side of the Periyar river was cited as an example of poor planning.

Of all the causes of this extreme weather event the least mentioned was climate change. Only in 11 per cent of the stories on the factors responsible for the disaster referred to climate change. National and international leaders were blamed for not making sincere efforts to reduce greenhouse gases despite being signatories to international agreements. The sources quoted in the news stories argued that apart from posturing in the international fora, India had done virtually nothing to reduce greenhouse gases. Changing weather patterns because of global warming were blamed for the unprecedented rains. Although newspapers cited climate change as a serious threat, many of the reports referred to the disaster as a natural occurrence. Painter et al. (2020) say that while newspapers in the developed countries often link

[4] http://www.coorgnews.in/general-news/karnataka-make-online-registration-homestays-compulsory/

extreme weather events to climate change only a small per cent of the stories in newspapers in China and India blame climate change for such events. While the newspapers in the developed countries have environmental and climate change correspondents, such specialization does not exist in most of the Indian newspapers. Since the level of awareness about climate change in India is very low among the people and journalists it is less often mentioned as a possible cause (Nagesh Hegde, personal communication, 14 October 2018).

Newspapers also carried stories about rumours, unscientific theories and sensational claims concerning the cause of floods and landslides. Some headlines blamed unusually heavy rains for everything and described the floods as 'monsoon mayhem', 'monsoon's macabre dance', 'rain havoc', 'nature's fury', 'apocalypse', 'nature's curse' and 'dance of death'. One of the causes of the disaster in Kodagu that people started talking about was the earthquake of low intensity measuring 3.4 on the Richter scale that was recorded on 8 July 2018. Even before the scientists examined the evidence and established the link between the earthquake and landslides, politicians and the plantation lobby started blaming the earthquake for all landslides. The media too put out stories about the possible effect of the earthquake on landslides. A preliminary analysis by the National Geophysical Research Institute revealed that there was no such link.

The Times of India (2 September 2018, p. 4) carried a report titled 'What Triggered Floods, Landslides in Kodagu—Quake or Cloudbursts?' While experts were still analysing the causes of the disaster, the newspaper declared that they were clueless. The newspaper claimed that the newly established seismograph centre at Galibeedu in Kodagu had 'reportedly' recorded tremors. The director of the National Institute of Seismology who dismissed the argument that earthquake had caused the floods and landslides was also quoted but only towards the end of the report. Instead of the scientist's view, it was the rumour that occupied a large part of the report. The report was an attempt to blame natural factors for the disaster and to spice up the false news.

Kannada Prabha (24 August 2019) carried a front-page report ('Quake Was Not the Cause of the Disaster') that quoted the director of the National Centre for Seismology Dr K. Gehlot as saying that the landslides in Kodagu were not related to the low-intensity earthquake of 9 July. The prominence given to this story assumed significance in the context of rumours being spread about the causes of the disaster. The report also quoted the scientist who said in his letter to the Karnataka government that the landslides may have been caused by deforestation and digging on the slopes of hills. Vasanth Kodagu, a journalist based in Somwarpet town of Kodagu district, says that those persons who had built resorts and buildings for homestays were probably involved in creating this rumour because they did not want to be blamed for cutting down trees and hill slopes (personal communication, 3 September 2018). According to him local politicians who had invested in the resort business kept the rumour mill running. These rumours were posted in social media, and from there, they were picked by some journalists. The rumours had also created a fear among the people of the district that another earthquake might hit the district.

A report in the *Deccan Herald* (25 August 2018, p. 5) with the headline 'Scientists Try to Pin Down a Cause for Landslides, Rule Out Quake' gave scientists' view along with the opinions of the people residing in Kodagu. A false message which claimed that the 9 July tremors were caused by an earthquake was getting circulated. It also said that the tremors had loosened the earth and that another earthquake was a possibility. By giving the version of the scientists and the opinion of the scientists the *Deccan Herald* report attempted to dispel rumours and fears.

Environmental Factors in Focus

Before the floods began to be reported in the media *The Hindu* had stressed the need to prepare for the challenge of changing monsoon trends. An editorial titled 'Welcome Clouds' (*The Hindu*, 9 August 2018, p. 8) discussed the prediction of the Indian Meteorological Department regarding the monsoon of 2018 coming true after two months of rains but cautioned about the effects of climate change. It said, 'the forecast is optimistic, but changing monsoon trends are a challenge' as the rainfall had altered in terms of intensity and variations across regions. Heavy rains were reported from the Western Ghats region in Kerala and Karnataka in the second week of August.

The editorial pointed at the environmental factors that had affected the rainfall causing death and destruction in several states. The newspaper stressed the need to pay attention to climate change as an environmental issue because it could cause floods as well as droughts.

Even before the worst was to come to Kerala, the *Deccan Herald* wrote a hard-hitting editorial (*Deccan Herald*, 13 August 2018, p. 10), which said that the floods and landslides were the results of the decades-long assault on the Western Ghats. The editorial titled 'Kerala's Disaster Is Partly Man-made' said that the excessive rainfall in Kerala could have been a sign of climate change.

The newspaper said while examining the causes of the disaster:

Kerala's vulnerability to floods may also have increased because of the rise in sea levels, induced by climate change, and especially because its rivers are short. But when the waters recede and people go back home, some lessons will also have to be carried home. It is the assault on the ecologically sensitive Western Ghats, which has continued for decades, which made it difficult to contain the impact of rains. Human habitations and the construction of houses and roads etc, and the destruction of forest have reduced the capacity of the earth to absorb rainwater

It blamed the governments and the politicians for allowing such assaults leading to nature hitting back. It said it was a lesson for other states. Several readers wrote letters to express their agreement with the editorial. They pointed out that as the editorial had rightly said, environmental degradation was the major cause of the disaster.

The Times of India (20 August 2018, p. 4) carried a report titled 'Nature Hits Back: Landslides, Floods Due to Mining, Tourism', which said that illegal sand mining, deforestation and infrastructure development activities had made Kodagu vulnerable to landslides and floods. The report quoted forest and wildlife conservationists who had been witness to the decline of the forest cover. Coffee growers and residents said that the trees had been felled for resorts and coffee cultivation. The nexus among local politicians, revenue officials, police and senior bureaucrats had led to plundering of the green gold in Kodagu (Kanathanda, 2018).

In its editorial titled 'Kerala's Sorrow', *The Times of India* (20 August 2018, p. 10) saw floods and landslides in Kerala and Kodagu as natural calamities but warned about encroachment into the Western Ghats. Referring to the Uttarakhand floods of 2013, Srinagar floods of 2014, and Chennai floods of 2015 the editorial argued that the chaotic urban development that constricted wetlands and riverbeds had choked river flows. Although the editorial played down the role of environmental factors it called for bold, short and long-term green measures despite the possibility of popular resistance. Another editorial titled 'Misplaced Pride' (*The Times of India*, 23 August 2018) urged the Central government to accept foreign assistance for relief and rehabilitation. All newspapers saw no reason for rejecting the offer of help by foreign countries.

An article in *Kannada Prabha* (19 August 2018) on the editorial page identified six causes of the disaster: Construction of resorts on hills, deforestation, commercialization of land, sand mining, removal of natural trees in the forest, and encroachment of rivers and streams. It suggested that the only way to prevent such disasters in the future was to halt the unchecked assault on nature.

The *Deccan Herald* (21 August 2018, p. 5) published a report titled 'Rapacious Development Begot Kodagu Its Doomsday: IISc Experts'. It said, quoting the scientists at the Indian Institute of Science (IISc), Bengaluru, that large-scale destruction of natural vegetation in the name of development in the last four decades was the major cause of floods and landslides. The damage that was done in the previous four decades had begun to show results according to a professor at the Centre for Ecological Studies, IISc. The vegetation not only held the topsoil intact but also retained rainwater to be released later (Kaggere, 2018). All the landslides according to the expert had happened wherever vegetation had been cleared for road, agriculture and other purposes. Wherever there was forest, there was hardly any surface run-off and water had percolated into the ground.

Vijaya Karnataka (21 August 2018) carried a banner headline on page 2, raising the question 'Did man's meddling with nature cause Kodagu's disaster?' Heavy rains were not new to Kodagu and Kerala but the amount of damage they caused was unprecedented, the report said, referring to the views and experience of the people who had witnessed rains over several decades. The contention of scientists and environmentalists that excessive pressure on natural resources and unsustainable development had led to the disaster was presented with several questions which had no ready answers. A column authored by a well-known thinker of Karnataka expressed the same view on the same day. There were several reports on the same day that emphasized man-made causes for the disaster.

Prajavani (22 August 2018, p. 5,) produced a report ('Massive Rains Wrought by Deforestation') based on the opinions of scientists at the IISc in Bengaluru. The scientists claimed that landslides had taken place only in those areas where deforestation had taken place, and resorts had been built. The report also provided statistics about the conversion of forests for commercial purposes. That the scientist had warned about a possible disaster in Kodagu was highlighted as a testimony to the government's apathy over such warnings.

A report in the *Deccan Herald* on 25 August 2018 showed that India had recorded the highest number of deaths due to landslides, a majority of which were triggered by mining (Ray, 2018a). Poor construction practices, road building, quarrying, hill cutting and deforestation had led to increased landslide hazard. The report presented the issue in the global context.

Samyukta Karnataka had a full-page article titled 'An Appeal to Mother Cauvery' (*Samyukta Karnataka*, 26 August 2018, p. 13) on the violence man had committed against nature in Kodagu. The article was in the form of a confession made to River Kaveri asking her to pardon those who had acted as the owners of nature. A strong view that the disaster in Kodagu was man-made and that the so-called development was self-destructive was put forward. It was more an emotional appeal than an analysis based on factors that led to the disaster. Although *Kannada Prabha* wrote three editorials on the floods and landslides, none of them talked about the environmental factors that caused the disaster. All of them were about the loss of life, damage to property, rescue operation, relief work and on preparedness for such disaster in the future. However, it carried articles explaining the perspectives of the scientists and environmentalists on the causes of the disaster.

Vijaya Karnataka also carried five editorials, none of which had anything to say about the causes of the disaster. Three editorials saw the disaster as only nature's fury and stressed the need to speed up the relief work by making use of the aid. One of the editorials was about the United Arab Emirates offering aid of ₹700 crore for the relief work in Kerala. The other editorial urged the state governments to take adequate measures to ensure that heavy damage was not caused to property and that lives were not lost.

Prajavani came up with a front-page report on 28 August examining the possibility of ponds on the hills causing landslides. According to the report the hills caved in as they could not withstand the weight of the artificial lakes built by the planters to irrigate their coffee plantations. These unscientifically and illegally built ponds with an average weight of 900 tons had caused the landslides. Big planters had bigger ponds causing landslides in the coffee estates of their neighbours. Two edit page articles on the same day presented facts to show that 'development' was the biggest man-made disaster. They questioned the development model that India had been pursuing but felt that Indian had come too far on the path of destructive development.

Samyukta Karnataka (18 August 2018, p. 6) in its hard-hitting editorial 'Karnataka–Kerala: The Curse of Rain' quoted the aphorism attributed to Mahatma Gandhi 'nature provides for everyone's need but not for a single man's greed' and said that the floods and landslides in Kodagu were the results of looting of the Western Ghats. According to the editorial, deforestation, conversion of paddy fields into housing colonies, raising ginger crop in the forested land were the main contributors to the disaster. The editorial found a direct link between the disaster and the degradation of the environment in the Western Ghats.

The New Indian Express carried an article on 19 August 2018, which expressed concern about India not learning from past disasters. The article said:

Year after year India witnesses, discusses and pushes past disasters, and frequently disasters acquire the hues of a sequel. Every disaster is painted as if it is all nature's fault. Yes, the trigger is always a kind of black swan event—the rains in Kerala, the flash floods in Kashmir, the downpour in Chennai or the record rains in Mumbai. Every event is aggravated by criminal neglect of ecological tenets.

An expert group which looked into the July 2005 disaster that left over 500 dead pointed out that there were clear man-made reasons for the floods. These included changes in land use, occupation of floodplains, erosion of mangrove setbacks, siltation of rivers and water bodies, and indiscriminate disposal of solid waste, topped by crumbling infrastructure and systems. The findings of Mumbai would resonate with those in Chennai, Bengaluru, Gurugram, or any metropolis. Man-made interventions clearly worsen a natural event. (Aiyer, 2018, p. 9)

The article was categorical that it was the ecological degradation that caused floods and landslides. It saw a pattern in the occurrence of floods: Mumbai in 2005, Assam and Bihar in 2007, Kosi-Bihar in 2008, Andhra Pradesh and Karnataka in 2009, Ladakh in 2010, Assam in 2012, Uttarakhand in 2013, Jammu and Kashmir in 2014, Uttar Pradesh, Bihar, Odisha in 2011, Chennai in 2015, Gujarat in 2017 and Kerala in 2018. Every disaster according to it had a predictable course. It also highlighted the fact that committees that made recommendations after studying those floods had not been implemented.

The New Indian Express published two reports on 20 August based on interviews with researchers, geologists, forest officials and environmentalists (Bhardwaj, 2018; D'Souza, 2018). A research paper published by two researchers at the University of Mysore had predicted that changes in land use in the ecologically sensitive region of Kodagu could cause landslides. The rapid rise in population and economic activities had led to the construction of buildings and roads causing a serious threat to the fragile hills. According to forest officials, geologists and environmentalists, the landslides in Kodagu were caused by the rampant conversion of lands in the Western Ghats followed by decreased vegetation. They welcomed the decision of the Karnataka government to temporarily halt land conversion in the Ghats region. The two reports show the efforts the newspaper made to find out the causes of the disaster in Kodagu and to make people aware of the consequences of environmental degradation.

Even as Kodagu was reeling under floods and landslides, a report in *The New Indian Express* (17 August 2018) showed that lessons had not yet been learned about how nature had responded to the 'developmental' activities in the Western Ghats. The general manager of the South Western Railways had confirmed that the plan to go ahead with the Mysuru-Kushalnagar-Madikeri railway line had not been shelved despite stiff resistance from Kodavas and environmentalists. The report pointed out that the project estimated to cost ₹2,600 crore would fall into the 'negative rate of return' category with an expected loss of a minimum of 5.65 per cent. The authorities wanted to go ahead with the project that was not only environmentally destructive but also economically unviable. *The Hindu* also carried a report (17 August 2018) in which environmentalists argued that the railway line cutting through the hills would be destructive to Kodagu. The report said that the massive felling of trees in the district had already caused drought and change in the rainfall pattern.

The *Deccan Herald* carried an analytical article ('Behind Kodagu Disaster: Unabated Tree Felling') written by a retired chief conservator of forest, Karnataka, which said that the landslides were the direct consequences of deforestation (Singh, 2018). Even though Kodagu district lost 30 per cent of its tree cover in 40 years, tree felling had not stopped. Tree felling permitted with the condition of compensatory afforestation had not worked as the forest departments had been successful in only growing monoculture of teak and acacia. The argument was that once the forest was lost it was lost forever. The author opposed the laying of a railway track through Kodagu and across the Western Ghats to link Ankola with Hubballi. Over the years, the article said, natural drainage systems had been disturbed due to increasing urbanization. Referring to the floods it said whenever there was heavy downpour, water did not find enough space to flow and that caused flooding. The article suggested that no natural drains be disturbed while planning residential layouts.

Amidst the description of the floodwaters marooning entire cities the newspapers also had quotes from the victims who believed that it was because of man's encroachment of the floodplains of rivers that the disaster of this magnitude happened. It was a tragedy waiting to happen. A 79-year-old resident who witnessed the water forcing its way through the fields exclaimed 'River has reclaimed its lost self' (Anandan & Praveen, 2018).

There were a few articles in newspapers that rejected any link between anthropogenic activities and the disaster. An article titled 'Should Kodavas Live in Darkness Even Now' (*Vijaya Karnataka,* 23 August 2018, p. 2) rejected the views of scientists who had said that environmental degradation was a major contributor to the disaster. It argued that the floods and landslides were not man-made but caused by natural factors. Even though geologists had rubbished the rumour that there was a link between the low-intensity earthquake of 9 July 2018 and the disaster that happened a month later, the article saw a link between them and questioned whether scientists had studied the problem. It went to the extent of asking a question like 'if deforestation reduced rains why were there heavy rains this year?' (*Vijaya Karnataka,* 23 August 2018, p. 2). A strong case for the promotion of tourism and infrastructure development in Kodagu was presented criticizing those who were seeing the district as ecologically sensitive.

One of the difficulties a journalist constantly encounters is uncertainty and counterclaims about the cause of an environmental catastrophe. While most of the scientists and environmentalists said that the disaster in Kodagu was mostly man-made, an Australia-based geologist Lychettira G. Machaiah argued that it was a rare but natural occurrence. *The New Indian Express* (31 August 2018) carried a report based on the views of this geologist who claimed that the calamity was due to unprecedented rains and not because of deforestation or mining. The geologist said,

> Landslides in Kodagu are due to unprecedented rain in Pusjhapgiri Range and nearby region. What has happened to Kodagu is a natural calamity and not a man-made disaster. It is bizarre how some politicians and overnight ecology experts blame the same old timber mafia, sand mafia, forest encroachment, and planters' mafia as the cause for this disaster. Due to excess rainfall, the clay soil and laterite stone under the earth create a cave that starts to store water. And excess, unprecedented rain will result in their collapse, accompanied by a sound of breaking of earth's plates. Western

Ghats have a history of over 10 crore years and these disasters are natural to occur once in an occasion. (*The New Indian Express*, 31 August 2018, p. 2)

According to him, only the floods in the Harangi basin were probably induced by the conversion of wetland and construction of housing layouts on the river bed. He rubbished the claims of ecologists and geologists that deforestation had caused the disaster.

An article in *The New Indian Express* on 26 August 2018 explained how the pressure of urbanization on the environment had caused floods in Kerala. It said,

The hills are demolished to fill the low lands and ponds and paddy fields are filled to build apartments and shopping malls. This is not a natural urbanisation. Urbanisation puts environmental pressure on the city and its catchment area. In Kerala, the urbanisation is spread all over the state. There is no method for this madness. It is very rare to find a planned layout in any Kerala cities. There are rarely any public parks, other than the ones that were built before Independence. Green space does not even figure in city planning. The entire state is one large haphazard city built on either side of national and state highways, filled with militant people who would not yield an inch of their precious land to expand the roads. Is there any surprise that when the flood came, it affected the entire state? (Neelakantan, 2018, p. 3)

Unplanned urbanization in Kerala was cited as a major reason for the floods in articles and reports of newspapers. They also pointed out how real estate lobbies succeeded in encroaching forested land and public spaces affecting the drainage systems that existed.

A report in *The Hindu* on 18 August described the floods in Kerala as a massive disaster made worse by a fragile flood management system (Anandan & Praveen, 2018). The report stressed the long-term comprehensive plan for disaster management as the eco-sensitive Western Ghats were prone to degradation. In a report titled 'Halt Land Conversion in the Western Ghats Immediately' (*The Hindu*, 19 August 2018, p. 8), an activist of Sahyadri Sanchaya, an organization fighting for the protection of the Western Ghats, was quoted as saying that the calamity had happened because of the exploitation of the Ghats beyond their carrying capacity. Both government and private projects had caused considerable damage to the ecosystem, according to him. The infrastructure projects had caused the disaster as they were executed without paying attention to slope the protection mechanism.

The *Deccan Herald* (23 August 2018, p. 8) carried an article titled 'Kerala Floods: Global Warming in Action' by a former senior vice-president of the World Bank which linked the floods and landslide in Kerala and Karnataka to global warming.

The article said,

> Three factors are turning hazards of nature into full-blown catas-trophes. The first is the growing exposure of people in harm's way due to population increase and urbanisation, as we have seen on the western coast of India. The second is the greater vulnerabil-ity of people because of the destruction of the environment and natural defences, which hurt the poor the most. The third reason is that because of relentless emissions of heat-trapping greenhouse gases (especially carbon dioxide from fossil fuels like coal), our planet is now one degree Celsius hotter than before the Industrial Revolution. With that, the rate of evaporation from the ocean increases, warmer air holds more vapour, and more intense rainfall and deadly flooding follow.

The article argued that global warming was responsible for the floods and that the higher rate of evaporation from a warmer climate con-tributed to more intensive precipitation and rain (Thomas, 2018). Reduction in the use of coal in power generation, transport and agri-culture was recommended as a means of bringing down carbon dioxide emission levels. The article presented the issue in the global context and called upon the countries of the world to cut carbon emissions as per the Paris Agreement. Articles of this nature are important to bring pressure on the government to take effective steps to prevent global warming.

Two weeks after the floods and landslides in Kodagu, *The Hindu* carried an article that said that landslips were a result of both natural and man-made causes (Rao, 2018). The article said 'the hand of man through deforestation and concretisation, the wrath of the rain clouds, and an earthquake may have played a part in the immense devastation seen in Kodagu district this month' (p. 3). While the tremor of 9 July 2018 was cited as one of the factors that caused landslips, a geologist of the Geological Survey of India (GSI) who was quoted in the article said that stronger earthquakes contributed to landslips but the impact of tremor in Kodagu had to be examined. Experts in geology, disaster management, and geophysics who were quoted in the article said that the disaster was man-made. Road construction without adequate retaining walls, lack of drainage, clearing of vegetation, diversion of Bengaluru–Mangaluru traffic through Kodagu, and unscientific construction of houses on slopes were the major contributors to the landslips. Pointing out how the human activities in the district had contributed to the disaster the article said Talacauvery, which is surrounded by natural forests, received the most rains but had the least number of landslips, whereas relatively dense habitations along the Madikeri-Sampage road saw the most number of landslides.

According to the Forest Survey of India's State of Forest Report, Kodagu had lost 88 sq. km of forests since 2007 and moderately dense and open forests, many of which fall under private ownership, had also decreased by 654 sq. km since 2015. The article also quoted the Coorg Wildlife Society, a collective of citizens who have been fighting against 'unnecessary' development projects, which had found out through RTI queries that more than 2,800 acres of paddy fields, coffee plantations and highlands were converted into residential layouts, sites, commercial complexes and resorts between 2005 and 2015. The article was the first in *The Hindu* that provided a comprehensive picture of what had happened in Kodagu. It gave statistical details about landslip-prone areas, natural factors and human-induced factors.

A report in *The Hindu* on 2 September 2018 said that the planters in the coffee-growing areas criticized the scientists for blaming homestays and water bodies atop the hills for landslips. The report highlighted how a serious environmental issue was being rejected by the planters. While many newspapers reported climate change as a factor causing excessive rain in Kodagu and Kerala, two newspapers—*The Times of India* and *Kannada Prabha*—carried a report that blamed the 'Somali jet' effect for excessive rains. The Somali jet streams are winds that originate near Madagascar off the southeast coast of Africa which is a dry surface and head towards the Western Ghats. This particular cause for excessive rains was played down by the other newspapers because the phenomenon required more scientific analysis for drawing conclusions.

The *Deccan Herald* highlighted the problem of unsegregated waste accumulating at the relief centres. It was feared that the large amount of plastic waste generated at relief centres would become a breeding ground for mosquitoes (Kulkarni, 2018). Much of the relief material came in plastic bags and bottles including drinking water. It was one environmental crisis leading to another.

The newspapers brought into focus environmental causes for the disaster in Kerala and Kodagu through interviews with scientists, environmentalists and the victims providing diverse views. Out of the 23 editorials carried in the selected newspapers between 9 August and 4 September as many as 14 were about rescue and relief operations whereas nine were about the causes of the disaster. Significantly, all the editorials about the causes of the disaster cited environmental degradation as the major contributor.

Veerendrakumar, chairman and managing director of the Mathrubhumi Printing and Publishing Company Limited[5] that publishes Malayalam daily *Mathrubhumi*, a newspaper with a pro-environment policy, believes that the devastation in Kerala and Kodagu was entirely man-made (personal communication, 18 September 2018). Climate change according to him is the major contributor to the extreme weather events that have happened in recent past. The newspapers and magazines of the Mathrubhumi group, he says, have been writing regularly about the need to make concerted effort to reduce greenhouse gases. 'If urgent steps are not taken through international initiatives to check rising global temperature, this earth is going to be

[5] The Mathrubhumi Group publishes 16 editions of its daily newspaper, including 10 in Kerala and six outside Kerala. It also brings out 11 magazines and owns Mathrubhumi TV and an FM radio channel.

uninhabitable,' he argues. The media in Kerala, he says, have not only provided complete and balanced coverage of the floods and landslides but were also critical of the development model that has led to the destruction of the Western Ghats. According to him, writing about the environmental degradation in the Western Ghats when a tragedy takes place is not enough but there should be a sustained campaign to create awareness among the people as well as politicians.

Balakrishnamurthy, a retired professor at Adishankara College in Kaladi and a member of the Kerala River Protection Council, whose house in Aluva had four feet of water for over five days, says while the newspapers did an exemplary job of reporting the floods from all over Kerala their analysis of the environmental factors that led to the disaster lacked depth and sincerity (personal communication, 21 September 2018). He feels the newspapers did not do much when deforestation and sand mining were going on for decades. According to him despite scientific evidence linking extreme weather events to climate change, the politicians and the media have not taken the issues seriously. Girish, a medical store owner in Aluva, who lost medicines worth ₹50 lakh as waist-deep water remained in his shop for over five days, is of the view that media failed to provide timely information (personal communication, 21 September 2018). If they had provided information in time, he feels, a lot of property could have been saved. With regard to whether the media discussed the environmental causes of the floods, he says they did, but they should have paid greater attention to them in the previous years. He thinks there is no use talking about the causes after the disaster has destroyed the livelihoods of millions of people. He wants media to raise the level of awareness among the people, bureaucrats and politicians through a sustained campaign based on scientific data.

Colonel Muthanna of the Coorg Wildlife Society says that media could have played a much more active role in covering the environmental factors about the landslides and floods in Kodagu (personal communication, 24 September 2018). Excessive and uncontrolled tourism, according to him, is beyond the carrying capacity of the district. He says that a study needs to be carried out to examine the carrying capacity of the district and geophysical factors behind the landslides and floods.

The mining lobby wields so much power that it has ensured that sand mining is not blamed for the floods. The sand provides a kind of cushion to the pressure created by the flowing water in rivers but with the removal of sand from the river bed the water flows with full force. Natural control of floodwaters did not take place. He is of the view that journalists are not well-informed about the issues related to environmental degradation. He feels it is necessary to conduct workshops to bring the attention of the journalists to the environmental issues of the district. He is unhappy that coffee planters are being unfairly blamed by the media for the environmental problems of the Kodagu district. The coffee planters, according to him, started homestays as their income from coffee started dwindling. He wants the media to consider several aspects before arriving at conclusions.

Brigadier M. A. Devaiah who also works with the Coorg Wildlife Society says that the media in Kerala did a tremendous job of pushing the politicians to action to such an extent that politicians of all parties took part in the relief and rescue operations (personal communication, 24 September 2018). Unlike Kerala, the politicians in Karnataka were accusing each other of not doing anything in Kodagu. Devaiah says,

> Media became a platform for mudslinging. They should not allow themselves to be part of the political blame game instead they should focus on creating awareness about the environmental issues in the district. Media have the power to change people's attitudes towards the environment and they should focus on moulding the opinion of the people.

Devaiah did not see a balanced and informed debate in media about factors responsible for the disaster but firmly believes in the power of the media in influencing the opinions of the people.

An activist and a planter in Somwarpet taluk of Kodagu district Pudiyathanda Ganapathy who was a victim of the floods and landslide, says:

> We are entirely responsible for what Kodagu has become today. We cut down the forest, converted land with full abandon, constructed roads and buildings unscientifically. Some people are blaming

nature because of their ignorance. It has tolerated all our atrocities all these years and has just now hit back. Of course, the rains that would fall in one month fell in a week. That caused the floods but the loss of life and property happened because of the damage done to the environment. I was happy to see some newspapers produce analytical reports about the environmental degradation in Kodagu that led to the tragedy of this scale. But, in general, media were unable to go to the depth of the issues. (Personal Communication, 10 September 2018)

He believes that the media did not raise their voice loudly when illegal resorts were coming up and encroachment of the forest was going on for decades. When environmentalists were raising those issues, the media were looking the other way, but they woke up only when floods and landslides claimed over a dozen people.

The government officials who were involved in rescue and relief activities are of the view that the media were of immense help in providing timely information to the people. The deputy tahsildar of Idukki in Kerala Mini Joseph who was in charge of relief centres says that the media not only provided a balanced coverage but also tried to identify what had led to such unprecedented floods (personal communication, 19 September 2018). According to her, environmental factors rather than dam management were responsible for the floods and landslides.

Devassy Pulikkal, an environmental activist in Ernakulum who worked as a volunteer during the rescue operations does not believe in the explanation provided by the officials in Kerala about the management of dams but strongly argues that deforestation was the major reason for the floods (personal communication, 19 September 2018). He contends that officials who mismanaged dams and did not release water in time contributed to the disaster becoming a massive one unseen in history. He believes the media remained blind to environmental degradation happening in the Western Ghats for decades.

T. V. Jayan who wrote editorials and articles on the disaster, in *The Hindu Business Line*, says that journalists believe that many of the environmental problems are man-made (personal communication,

11 September 2020). According to him, the floods and landslides were a result of the state's failure to strike a balance between development and environment which was evident in media coverage. The media had written about deforestation, mining, land conversion and unchecked tourism in the Western Ghats but the politicians and bureaucrats did not pay adequate attention to the seriousness of the problem, he says.

What emerges from the content analysis of newspapers is that they made attempts to explain the environmental factors that had led to the devastation in Kerala and Kodagu. Though there were differences among the newspapers about the major causes of the disaster, there was unanimity that it was man-made. That kind of unanimity, excluding a few articles, is necessary to make people aware of their responsibilities towards nature. Activists and officials do not appear to be completely happy with media coverage although they acknowledge that they did a commendable job of providing reliable information at the time of the disaster. While climate change was not often discussed as a major cause of floods in newspapers, environmental activists and the affected persons say that it was a major contributor to the extreme weather events.

The Debate on the Degradation of the Western Ghats

Protection of the Western Ghats, which are one of the eight top biodiversity hotspots of the world, has been at the centre of the environmental debate in India. The Ministry of Environment and Forests, Government of India, set up a panel to frame a comprehensive policy for the protection of the Western Ghats. The Western Ghats Ecology Expert Panel (WGEEP) headed by Madhav Gadgil, a well-known ecologist and former head of the Centre for Ecological Sciences, IISc, Bengaluru, submitted its report in 2011. The panel recommended that 64 per cent of the Western Ghats be declared as an ecologically sensitive area. Strict curbs on mining, quarrying and use of land for non-forest purposes were recommended to protect the Ghats. It also recommended setting up of Western Ghats Ecology Authority (WGEA) and involving *gram sabhas* in the decision-making process. The recommendations of the panel were criticized for being excessively environment-friendly and not in tune with ground realities. None of the six states in the Western Ghats region—Kerala, Tamil Nadu, Karnataka, Goa, Maharashtra and Gujarat—agreed with the recommendations because they felt that their economies would be affected if development activities were restricted in the ecologically sensitive areas.

The Ministry of Environment and Forests then appointed a working group in 2012 to advise the government on the recommendations of the WGEEP. The High-Level Working Group (HLWG) headed by K. Kasturirangan, former chairman of Indian Space Research Organization (ISRO), in its attempt to address the concerns of the people about development in the Western Ghats region, watered down the regulatory regime that was proposed by the WGEEP. The ecologically sensitive area in the Western Ghats was limited to 37 per cent or 60,000 sq. km spread across the six states. The HLWG prohibited mining, quarrying and sand mining but allowed diversion of the forest with extra safeguards. It also banned construction of buildings beyond 20,000 sq. m, thermal power projects and polluting industries. The Ministry of Environment and Forests accepted the HLWG report and asked the six states to submit their response. The state governments are yet to submit their final response despite several extensions of deadlines.

The reports of the two panels, popularly known as the Gadgil Committee Report and the Kasturirangan Committee Report came up for public discussion in the wake of floods and landslides in Kerala and Karnataka. An attempt is made here to analyse how the reports were debated in media even as they were covering floods and landslides in August 2018.

All newspapers reported Madhav Gadgil's statement in Panaji, Goa, on 20 August 2018, that the floods and Landslides in Kerala were man-made (Sinha, 2018). He categorically said that Kerala and Karnataka experienced the worst kind of floods and landslides as a result of ignoring his report on the Western Ghats. He cautioned that what had happened in Kerala could happen in Goa if precautions were not taken on to ensure that no further damage was caused to the ecology of the Western Ghats. Pointing to the inactions of the state governments, Gadgil said, 'The governments have been lax on implementing environmental norms. The Central government is bending over backward to make sure the National Green Tribunal (NGT) does not function properly'.

By giving wide coverage to Gadgil's statement the newspapers had brought the attention of the government to the destructive activities in the Western Ghats that had contributed to the floods and landslides. While some newspapers buried Gadgil's statement in the inside pages, others highlighted it on the front pages. The Kerala government, like other state governments, had opposed the implementation of the recommendations of the panel. According to him while the magnitude of rainfall in Kerala during August 2018 was not exactly unprecedented, the kind of floods witnessed in the state had never been experienced before. Illegal quarries and unauthorized construction on river beds were the major contributing factors to the disaster. *Kannada Prabha* carried a brief report of Gadgil's warning that what had happened in Kerala would also happen in Goa at the bottom of page 9 while political leaders visiting Kodagu received prominent coverage. *Vijaya Karnataka* too carried a single-column story of Gadgil's warning to Goa.

Vijaya Karnataka (19 August 2018, p. 5) carried a report based on the opinions of the experts who had been studying various aspects of the Western Ghats ('What Do Experts Say on Kerala–Kodagu Disaster'). The report strongly argued that if the recommendations of the Gadgil committee had been implemented in their entirety there would not have been a disaster of such magnitude in Kerala and Kodagu. Highlighting the key recommendations of the report it said mining, quarrying, using land for the non-forest purpose and construction of tall buildings should not have been allowed. The Gadgil report had proposed to empower the local people by making their participation mandatory in the decision-making process with regard to the use of natural resources. This key aspect of the report did not receive due attention in media. Large parts of Idukki, Wayanad and Kodagu that come under ecologically sensitive areas as per the panel report have suffered the worst. The Kerala government came in for heavy criticism for rejecting the Gadgil panel report. An ecologist was quoted as saying that there had been rains of more intensity in the past but they had not caused floods of this kind as there was forest cover. The depletion of forest cover was cited as the major reason for landslides in Kerala and Kodagu.

The demand by an environmentalist, who had been a member of the Western Ghats Task Force, that reports of the panels headed by Gadgil and Kasturirangan be implemented was also highlighted. By quoting the chief minister of Karnataka who claimed that 90 per cent of the disaster was caused by nature's fury and only 10 per cent of it was man-made the newspaper report presented a contrast between political perception and the perception of the environmentalists. It also indicated through the CM's statement that despite the disaster claiming so many lives and causing unprecedented destruction in Kerala and Kodagu there was no possibility of either Gadgil's report or Kasturirangan report being implemented. On 21 August 2018, Kasturirangan himself was quoted as saying that Kerala–Kodagu floods and landslides were caused by excessive exploitation of natural resources, deforestation, soil erosion and climate change. Based on his statement the newspaper carried a lead story on 21 August titled 'man-made disaster'.

While several environmental groups, scientists and activists demanded implementation of the Gadgil and Kasturirangan panel reports in the wake of the disaster in Kerala and Kodagu, opposition to the implementation of the reports came from people living in the Western Ghats region and their political leaders. Zoning off of the ecologically sensitive areas where no development activity would be allowed became the main bone of contention between the opposing groups. Groups vigorously opposing the inclusion of their villages under ecologically sensitive areas argued that it was impractical to implement the recommendation in a densely populated state like Kerala (Ananda & Praveen, 2018).

Even as the rains were causing floods in Kerala and Kodagu, there were reports of protests against the implementation of the Kasturirangan report ('Demand for Kerala-type Revised Kasturirangan Report', *Prajavani*, 14 August 2018, p. 3). The protestors in

Theerthahalli of Shivamogga district of Karnataka alleged that the report was unscientific as it depended on satellite surveys for identifying ecologically sensitive areas. They were also quoted as expressing the fear that if the report was implemented, it would place a severe restriction on developmental activities in the Western Ghats region and deny access to their own land. Another report that appeared in newspapers was about the claims of well-known environmentalist Kalkuli Vittala Hegde who blamed the government departments and NGOs for the degradation of the Western Ghats. Hegde termed Gadgil report as unscientific and rejected any link between the construction of resorts in the Western Ghats region and the landslides. He also claimed that floods and landslides were being used as an excuse to impose Gadgil report on the people living in the region. Landslides, according to him, had taken place even where there was a thick forest. By carrying these reports newspapers allowed public debate on the causes of the disaster.

A report in *The Hindu* on 22 August said that the Government of Karnataka had written to the Central government opposing the implementation of the Kasturirangan report (Khajane, 2018). The Karnataka government's position was that declaring 1,576 villages along the Western Ghats as falling under ecologically sensitive areas would restrict development activities in the villages. The Centre had asked the state governments of Karnataka, Kerala, Maharashtra, Goa, Gujarat and Tamil Nadu for their views on the ecologically sensitive areas for issuing a final notification based on the report of the Kasturirangan panel. All of them were opposed to the implementation of the panel's recommendations.

Newspapers continued to carry reports of political groups staging a protest against the implementation of the Kasturirangan report. Protests intensified as the Karnataka state was preparing to submit its revised recommendations on the demarcation of ecologically sensitive areas (ESAs) by 25 August 2018. Activists opposed the report as the ESA status would impose restrictions on civic amenities and rights of the people to collect minor forest produce in as many as 1,553 villages in Karnataka. The report also said that many poor farmers would lose their land if the report was implemented.

The Times of India (23 August 2018, p. 6) report with the headline 'Kodagu Mayhem Turns Focus Back on Kasturiranga Report' said that the major political parties in Karnataka were in no mood to accept the Kasturirangan report. The report quoted politicians from different political parties saying that implementation of the report would affect the livelihood of people in 33 taluks. However, the report argued that protecting ESAs would go a long way in preventing Kodagu-like disasters (Moudgal, 2018).

Prajavani (25 August 2018, p. 5, 'Opposition to Kasturirangan report: Ruckus in Front of the Minister) reported a confrontation between ex-soldiers and the political representatives of the district in front of the union minister on the issue of implementation of the Kasturirangan report. While the ex-soldiers who demanded implementation of the Kasturirangan report argued that deforestation was responsible for landslides, the Member of Parliament representing Kodagu and two MLAs argued that the demand for the implementation of the Kasturirangan report was a conspiracy to create more problems to the people of Kodagu. The latter demanded that the Kasturirangan report should not be implemented, contending that the claims about deforestation causing landslides were false. The report showed that political leaders were refusing to see any man-made factors as causes of landslides.

However, *Prajavani*'s view was that these protests were uncalled for. In an editorial titled 'No Politics: Listen to the Scientists' *Prajavani* (28 August 2018, p. 6) came down heavily on the state governments for ignoring the reports of Gadgil and Kasturirangan panels. It said when the people wanted implementation of the Kasturirangan report, political leaders were opposing it. It cited the instance of the people of Kodagu requesting the Union Minister Nirmala Seetharaman during her visit to the district to implement the Kasturirangan report whereas the legislators of the district were opposing it. The editorial, supporting the implementation of the Kasturirangan report, said:

The Western Ghats spread across five states including Kerala and Karnataka have unique biodiversity. The Ghats are home to 49 thousand plant species and 91 thousand animal, bird, and insect species. In Karnataka, they are spread over 20, 668 kilometers. It is shameful that Karnataka is scuttling the efforts of the central government in implementing the Kasturirangan report to save such unique Ghats. To save the biological world in the forests, surrounding as many as 1576 villages in 33 taluks, it is necessary to declare them as belonging to ecologically sensitive areas. If the report is implemented, mining and red category industries will be banned to conserve biodiversity in the region. But there is no proposal to evict people from these villages. There is a provision to build roads and to promote ecotourism. Despite this, people's representatives are opposing the implementation of the report. The state government has succumbed to their pressure. This is not right. The flood experienced in Kerala and Kodagu should be a lesson for us. (*Prajavani*, 28 August 2018, p. 6)

Prajavani took a firm stand on the Kasturirangan report and urged the governments to implement it while the public discourse lacked such clarity. The newspaper argued that people's fears about the consequences of the implementation of the report were unfounded. An edit page write-up with the headline 'If the earth is angry who will give protection?' was supportive of the editorial stance of the newspaper on the issue. It was observed that opposition to the implementation of the Kasturirangan report by politicians and some organizations was unfortunate.

The New Indian Express (22 August 2018, p. 2) in a report with the headline 'Environmentalists Decode Reasons behind Flood in Kodagu, Kerala' stressed the need for implementation of Gadgil and Kasturirangan reports and provided a detailed account of the claims made by environmentalists about the causes of the disaster in Kerala and Kodagu. Overexploitation of natural wealth, overuse of pesticides which render the surface soil soft, resorts and homestays built on hill slopes, encroachments of lakes, streams and buffer zones of rivers and weakening of the environmental laws were cited as the reasons for the disaster. An article in the same paper dated 26 August argued that influential lobbies joined together to defeat the purpose of the Gadgil panel report (Neelakantan, 2018). Politicians who had votes at stake, the article said, vilified the report with vengeance. It referred to the

Kasturirangan report as the watered-down version that was accepted in principle by the government. Although *The New Indian Express* wrote three editorials on floods and landslides in Kerala and Kodagu, none of them examined the environmental factors for their cause barring one editorial (*The New Indian Express,* 23 August 2018) in which there was a suggestion that the disaster was not natural but man-made.

There were very few reports in newspapers about the demand for implementation of the Gadgil report. On 23 August 2018, the *Deccan Herald* also reported that groups of environmentalists in the Chikkamagluru district of Karnataka urged the Central government to implement the Madhav Gadgil Committee report. According to them, the floods and landslides in Kodagu were the results of forest encroachment, mining, construction of resorts and homestays and clearing of forests to create coffee estates.

In an editorial titled 'Trouble in the Hills: On Western Ghats Ecology', *The Hindu* (25 August 2018, p. 8) demanded a public consultation on Gadgil and Kasturirangan reports to work on sustainable development plans. The editorial said,

> The catastrophic monsoon floods in Kerala and parts of Karnataka have revived the debate on whether political expediency trumped science…. The State governments that are mainly responsible for the Western Ghats—Kerala, Karnataka, Tamil Nadu, Goa and Maharashtra—must go back to the drawing table with the reports of both the Gadgil Committee and the Kasturirangan Committee, which was set up to examine the WGEEP report. The task before them is to initiate correctives to environmental policy decisions. This is not going to be easy, given the need to balance human development pressures with stronger protection of the Western Ghats ecology. The issue of allowing extractive industries such as quarrying and mining to operate is arguably the most contentious. A way out could be to create the regulatory framework that was proposed by the Gadgil panel, in the form of an apex Western Ghats Ecology Authority and the State-level units, under the Environment (Protection) Act, and to adopt the zoning system that is proposed. This can keep incompatible activities out of the Ecologically Sensitive Zones (SEZs).

Endorsing parts of the reports that restrict developmental activities in eco-sensitive regions the editorial argued that all proposals for new dams should be rejected. The newspaper was clear that no dam construction should be allowed in the sensitive Western Ghats region. It wanted sustainable development with public consultation. The editorial called for a moratorium on quarrying and mining in the sensitive zones echoing the recommendations of the two expert committees on the Western Ghats.

The Hindu published an article by Madhav Gadgil (30 August 2018, p. 9, 'A People's Campaign to Rebuild Kerala') which said that beyond material loss there was massive loss of natural, human and social capital for which no estimates were available. He argued that the short-sighted attempts in building man-made capital had ignored the degradation of natural, human and social capital. He emphasized the need to identify the causes of the disaster.

The article brought the attention of the readers to the fact that the disaster was the result of several factors including flouting of laws, ignoring serious degradation of human capital in terms of health and employment, continually discarding scientific knowledge and advice and erosion of social capital. He argued that to maintain the health of the ecosystems, local communities must be given the right to decide what development they want and what kind of conservation method would be appropriate for their environment. Contrary to the notion that the Gadgil report took away the rights of the people living in the Western Ghats, Gadgil argued that local bodies at the level of the ward, panchayat, and town would be empowered to decide the use and regulation of biodiversity resources. Most media have ignored this recommendation which should have been discussed to dispel people's fears about the report.

T. V. Jayan who wrote editorials and articles in *The Hindu BusinessLine* about the landslides, says that the Kasturirangan report is a watered-down version of the Gadgil report (personal communication, 11 September 2020). Gadgil's report according to him is more democratic and inclusive in the sense that it gives a lot of authority to the *gram sabhas* (village councils) rather than to the state and Central governments to decide on what happens to their environment. Both the state governments and the centre did not want to give that kind of power to the *gram sabhas*. They made use of the fears that people had about the implementation of the Kasturirangan report. Most people had not read the report and they were incorrectly informed about the consequences of its implementation. Jayan says there would have been some inconvenience caused to the people living in the Western Ghats region in the short run, but they would benefit from it in the long run. Despite newspapers writing about the necessity to implement the report, opposition to it continued as it turned into a political issue with every party trying to project itself as the champion of the people living in the Western Ghats region. One fear that was genuine and the one that the media missed was that the Kasturirangan report would take away the rights of the *gram sabhas* in violation of the 73rd amendment to the constitution.

A report in *The Times of India* with the headline 'Was Kodagu Disaster Natural or Man-made' presented the views of the environmentalists who observed that implementation of Gadgil report could have prevented the disaster in Kodagu (Shrinivasa, 2018, p. 3). Of the several measures recommended by the Gadgil panel scrapping of the controversial Gundia hydel power project in Hassan district and ban on inter-basin diversion of rivers in the Western Ghats had a special mention. 'Compared to the Gadgil report, the Kasturirangan report had some exemption on human interventions but politicians are not even willing to implement the Kasturirangan report,' an environmentalist was quoted as saying.

In a report titled 'Karnataka Throws Spanner, Ghats Notification Lapses for 3rd Time', the *Deccan Herald* (25 August 2018, p. 1) came in support of the Central government's notification about the implementation of recommendations of the Kasturirangan report. It was critical of the Karnataka government which wanted to come out of the legal regime while the other states sought a reduction in the area marked as ecologically sensitive areas in the draft notification. The report argued that the implementation of the Kasturirangan report as per the Gazette notification was very much necessary in the wake of floods and landslide in Kerala and Karnataka (Ray, 2018b).

While some reports in other newspapers highlighted the questions raised by the opponents of the Kasturirangan report, the *Deccan Herald* was clearly in favour of its implementation to save the Western Ghats. The newspaper's editorial dated 13 August 2018 (*Deccan Herald*, 13 August 2018, p. 10, 'Kerala's Disaster Is Partly Man-made') highlighted the key aspects of the Kasturirangan report and the long-term benefits of implementing it. The *Deccan Herald* (16 August 2018, p. 4) carried a news story (Kasturirangan panel report detrimental to state: Rai) in which a former cabinet minister of Karnataka had said that the Kasturirangan report was against the interest of the people of the state. He had appealed to the Central government not to issue the notification that specified ESAs where construction activity could not take place. The newspaper was balanced in its coverage but gave space to opposing views.

Vijaya Karnataka (28 August 2018, p. 3) carried a report 'If the Western Ghats Are Not Protected There Is No Future for Five States', in which experts had opined that if the Western Ghats were not protected the future of the five states—Kerala, Tamil Nadu, Karnataka Maharashtra and Goa—was threatened. It said the disaster in Kerala and Kodagu could have been prevented had Kasturirangan panel recommendations been implemented. It blamed the states for refusing to give a response to the notification issued by the Central government about protecting the ESAs in the Western Ghats. A column written by a noted filmmaker and environmentalist Suresh Heblikar also argued that preserving the Western Ghats was very crucial to prevent floods and landslides in Kerala and Karnataka.

Newspapers, in general, were for the implementation of the Gadgil and Kasturirangan panel reports as indicated in articles and reports. But some groups of people in the Western Ghats and political parties have been opposing the implementation of the reports. Newspapers and the governments have been expressing contrasting views on the reports. One of the strong voices in favour of the implementation of the Gadgil panel report was M. P. Veerendrakumar of the Mathrubhumi group. He was of the firm view that Gadgil panel's report should have been implemented in letter and spirit (personal communication, 18 September 2018) to protect the Western Ghats and that there was no need to appoint Kasturirangan panel. He felt that ecologically sensitive areas should not be touched and argued that Kasturirangan panel's recommendations were inadequate for protecting the Western Ghats. The Mathrubhumi group is known for its pro-active role in the conservation of the environment. A decade ago it was in the vanguard of the struggle against Coca Cola water plant at Plachimada in Kerala and campaigned relentlessly to ensure that the plant, which was extracting water from the ground causing depletion and contamination of the groundwater, was closed down. The views of Veerendrakumar as reflected in the publications and the television channels of the Mathrubhumi group are in contrast to those held by the United Democratic Front (UDF) and Left Democratic Front (LDF), which have rejected the reports of both Gadgil and Kasturirangan panels.

Nagesh Hegde says that the newspapers did not do enough to educate people about the long-term benefits of accepting the Gadgil and Kasturirangan reports (personal communication, 9 August 2021). Since the reports have not been translated into Kannada, he says, the newspapers should have taken up the responsibility of translating the key recommendations of the panels in the form of articles to dispel people's fears about them. According to him, Kerala has accepted the Kasturirangan report partially because of the informed debate over it through media leading to a consensus. But that has not happened in Karnataka.

The editor of the *Star of Mysore* and *Mysuru Mitra* K. B. Ganapathy, who hails from Kodagu, is of the view that the media lack a comprehensive understanding of the complexity of the issues related to the implementation of the Gadgil and Kasturirangan reports (personal communication, 10 December 2018). He feels the media have not been able to make people understand the contradictions and limitations involved in implementing the report. He wants the Gadgil report implemented as it empowers local people to have their say in decision-making about the use of resources for development. He is critical of the Central government for accepting the Kasturirangan report and at the same time planning construction of a four-lane road to Kannur in Kerala cutting across Kodagu and also a railway line connecting

Kadagu with Mysore and Thellissery. These projects, he believes, are going to cause irreparable damage to Kodagu's ecology. He faults the media for not educating the people about the two reports and the need to save the Western Ghats.

Col Muthanna of Coorg Wildlife Society believes the debate about Gadgil and Kasturirangan reports is not going to be of any use (personal communication, 23 September 2018). He says that the media had failed to convince the people about the necessity of making some sacrifices to save the Western Ghats. Balakrishnamurthy of the Kerala River Protection Council, who was a victim of the floods in Aluva in Kerala, says if the recurrence of the disaster is to be prevented the destruction of the Western Ghats has to stop at once and the media should bring pressure on the state governments to accept Gadgil's report (personal communication, 21 September 2018). He is unsure if the media are committed to the views they have expressed about saving the Western Ghats.

Pudiyathanda Ganapathy who lost his agricultural land and nine cattle in floods and landslides in Kodagu, says Gadgil panel report should be implemented in total even if it is going to cause his own displacement (personal communication, 10 September 2018). He says the ecology of the Western Ghats should be protected at any cost. According to him, the protests against the Kasturirangan report were the results of the misreading of the report and a misleading campaign by the vested interests who are going to benefit from unregulated construction activity in the district. He feels the newspapers gave too much publicity to the protests of the people instead of highlighting the benefits of accepting the Gadgil report. Even as some organizations continue to protest against the implementation of the report he strongly argues that they are wrong. Very few people have come openly in support of the implementation of the report.

Most of the reports, articles and editorials in newspapers were in favour of notification of the Kasturirangan report so that ecologically sensitive areas were protected. Scientists and environmentalists whose opinions were presented in the newspapers expressed concern over the state governments refusing to accept the report. There was a demand for implementation of Gadgil's report which they felt was necessary to check environmental degradation in the Western Ghats region with the involvement of the local people. For the newspapers protecting the Western Ghats was more important than the profits that would come from mines, dams, industries and tourism. Newspapers rarely take such a position on matters related to the environment.

Conclusion

Floods are the most common weather events that have been occurring frequently in India in recent years. The unprecedented heavy rains leading to floods and massive landslides in Kerala and Kodagu in August 2018 were a massive challenge to the media. They had to report the devastation, rescue and relief operations and at the same time focus on the factors that had caused the disaster of that magnitude. Except for the initial delay in seeing the gravity of the flood situation, media coverage was unparalleled in its scale. The coverage increased dramatically from 15 August 2018 reaching a peak on 20 August and declining on the following days as rains receded.

While the disaster and the dramatic events of rescue and relief operations were covered with details there were also reports, articles and editorials on the possible causes of the disaster. Although Kannada newspapers gave greater coverage to the disaster there were no significant difference between the English and Kannada newspapers in identifying the causes of the disaster. Deforestation as the cause of the disaster appeared in all stories that referred to the causes. Mining and tourism were also the other major factors that were frequently mentioned in the news stories. Tourism as a cause of the disaster may look curious, but it must be seen in the context of tourism being a major economic activity in both Kerala and Kodagu. Hotels, resorts, homestays, roads and ponds have been constructed on top of the hills and on mountain slopes posing serious threat to the fragile ecosystem in the Western Ghats. Construction activity due to tourism has also meant felling trees, increasing the possibility of landslides. Unscientific roads that cut through the mountain slopes and unplanned urbanization were cited as the other two reasons for the landslides. Only a small per cent of the stories referred to climate change as a factor causing heavy rains.

Although scientists and environmentalists frequently talked about the broader issue of climate change in their seminars and discussions, it was not given as much importance as the other causes. Infrequent references to climate change as a key factor leading to unprecedented rains may be due to journalists' preference for generic phrases rather than referring to the specific problem of climate change. In their study of newspaper coverage of two extreme weather events in India—Chennai floods and heat wave in Andhra Pradesh in 2015—Painter et al. (2020) found that Indian journalists were often interested in examining the question of possible link between extreme weather events and climate change but they used generic phrases to describe the link. The general lack of awareness about the link between extreme weather events and climate change could be a reason for climate change not prominently figuring in the news stories. There were a few reports that produced conflicting opinions about the causes of the disaster while a majority of them pointed at man-made factors. The right time to make people aware of the cause of environmental destruction is when people have just suffered from it. The newspapers appear to have done that job well, barring a few cases of rumours and sensationalism. Much of the newspaper analysis of causes of the floods and landslides was in development vs environment frame.

Although newspapers generally favoured implementation of the Kasturirangan panel's recommendations for the conservation of the Western Ghats, they also carried reports of the claims of groups and individuals who rejected the report arguing that it would prevent development and pose a serious threat to the livelihood of the forest dwellers. Nevertheless, the dominant view in newspapers was that the floods and landslides in Kerala–Kodagu were man-made and that conservation of Western Ghats was crucial to prevent the occurrence of such disasters in the future.

CHAPTER 9

Conclusion

Environmental Degradation as a Human Rights Issue

Environmental protection and human rights are being seen as interconnected issues only in recent times. For a long time, the ideas of human rights did not figure in the debate on environmental issues. Several countries have made laws that recognize the link between the environment and human rights, even though the United Nations itself has not yet officially recognized environmental rights as human rights. Much of the demand for formal recognition of the environmental rights as human rights has come from indigenous people who have borne the brunt of the so-called human progress. Communities which were once self-reliant have been pushed to desperate situations as their ecosystems have been severely damaged, depriving them of the minimum resources for their very existence. Millions of people around the world have been forced to live a life without adequate water, food, shelter, education, health and sanitation (Kothari & Patel, 2006).

Environmental rights primarily mean unrestricted access to natural resources that include land, shelter, food, water and air.[1] They also mean ecological rights, political rights, collective rights of indigenous communities and the right to information. Protecting environmental

[1] https://www.foei.org/what-we-do/environmental-rights-human-rights

rights is a complex one, as it requires measures by the government to regulate corporate entities, trade and investment.

As nations push for economic growth, the questions on control over land, water, forests and minerals have become important. While the indigenous communities are asserting their traditional rights over natural resources the governments and corporations want to have unrestricted access to them, claiming that that is necessary in the 'national interest'. In several parts of the world, people are facing the threat of forced displacement, pollution, violence, denial of access to natural resources, militarization and intimidation. Even as indigenous communities are resisting threats to their livelihoods, they are being subjected to repressive actions of the state and corporations. Environmental activists who have been raising questions on these forms of violence have also become the victims of intimidation from state agencies as well as dominant political groups and vested interests.

The demand for environmental justice has grown in recent decades, especially in the context of the poor and marginalized communities increasingly becoming the victims of extreme weather events that are now being linked to climate change. The concept of environmental justice,[2] which sees environmental problems from the perspective of civil rights, has four components according to Capek (1993): People have the right to information about their situation, the right to be heard, the right to compensation for the harm caused to them and the right to democratically participate in deciding their future. Environmentalism in recent decades has made environmental justice a part of its discourse as it began to focus more on justice and equity (Hannigan, 2006). Adivasis in India have often alleged that these rights have been denied to them for decades. Climate justice is an issue that has come up before climate negotiations at the United Nations, although radical demands for specific actions have repeatedly been sidelined (Roberts et al., 2018).

---

[2] The concept that began to be used in the 1980s refers to seeking justice for those communities that are affected disproportionately by the impact of environmental degradation. The principle is that 'all people and communities are entitled to equal protection of environmental and public health laws and regulations' (Bullard, 1996, p. 445).

There are no specific norms about recognizing the right to a healthy environment as a human right. An international agreement that came close to recognizing a healthy environment as a human right came in the form of Principle 1 of the United Nations Conference on Human Environment held in Stockholm, Sweden, in 1972. The Stockholm declaration says that 'Man has the fundamental right to freedom, equality and adequate conditions of life, in an environment of a quality that permits a life of dignity and well-being and he bears a solemn responsibility to protect and improve the environment for present and future generations' (UNESCO, 1999). Several proposals made at the conference for a clear reference to environmental human rights were rejected.

Environmental rights as human rights began to be discussed worldwide when Chico Mendez, a Brazilian environmentalist, launched a struggle for the conservation of rainforests in the Amazon and the human rights of peasants and indigenous peoples in the 1980s. Mendez, who was a rubber tapper and a trade union leader organized a movement against deforestation, road paving and cattle ranching, which had begun to pose a serious threat to the livelihood of rubber tappers. After six attempts on his life, he was assassinated by a rancher on 22 December 1988.[3] Although Chico Medes did not have any formal schooling, he wrote countless letters to the authorities and signed articles in the newspapers *Folha do Acre* and *A Gazeta* (Rodrigues, 2007, p. 139). He argued that the rights of the people were being violated and that the destruction the Amazon forests would seriously threaten the lives of indigenous people. A section of the media began recognizing environmental rights as human rights and started paying serious attention to the greenhouse effect (Revkin, 1990). The ranchers' purpose of silencing Chico's voice was defeated as it went global (Saxena, 2013). After the death of Chico, an extractive reserve, covering nearly a million hectares was created in his name to ensure the sustainability of the resources in the Amazon forests. Despite these measures, there has been no legislative recognition of the right to a

[3] When he wrote to the authorities about threat to his life, the press and politicians dismissed it as an attempt to get his name in the newspapers (Rodrigues, 2007, p. 143).

healthy environment as a human right (Correa, 2010). Chico remains an inspiration for many environmentalists and tribal activists who are fighting to save the forests in India.

Recently, the Brazilian government launched a virtual war against Brazil's indigenous people by deciding to expand agriculture into their territories (Phillips, 2019). If their lands are not protected, they are likely to face genocide and the entire communities of uncontacted tribes could be wiped out. The Brazilian and international media widely covered the issue and argued that indigenous people were the best guardians of the natural world and that there is enough evidence to show that they manage their environment better than anyone else.

Principle 1 of the Declaration of United Nations Conference on Environment and Development held at Rio de Janeiro in 1992 says 'Human beings are at the centre of concerns for sustainable development. They are entitled to a healthy and productive life in harmony with nature'. The term 'right' was dropped from the Rio Declaration and the principle adopted there was less suggestive than Principle 1 of the Stockholm declaration. The idea of generic human right to an adequate or healthy environment has failed to garner general international support (Handl, 2012). At the Rio summit, as many as 1,400 NGOs participated in negotiating alternative treaties and stressed treating environmental issues as human rights issues. Affected people, activists, academicians, intellectuals, NGOs and other civil society organizations began working towards creating awareness among the people and politicians about the violation of people's right to a healthy environment. The demand of the environmental groups from different parts of the world to move towards formulating a global human rights treaty did not receive the expected response.

Seven years after Chico Mendes was assassinated, a well-known Nigerian environmental activist who led the Movement for the Survival of the Ogoni People (MOSOP) against environmental degradation caused by Royal Dutch Shell Company, was executed. Ken Saro-Wiwa campaigned non-violently for enforcement of environmental regulations on the foreign petroleum companies operating in the area where the Ogoni people lived. His execution on 10 November 1995, by the military dictatorship of Sani Abacha on the false charges of murdering four Ogoni chiefs attracted worldwide condemnation by governments and human rights organizations.

Human rights groups around the world brought pressure on their governments to intervene and impose economic sanctions against Nigeria (Klein, 2000). Sanctions and diplomatic pressures did not have any effect. The media in several countries helped mobilize international support for him but could not prevent his execution. The outraged human rights groups held worldwide protests against Shell Oil and gave a call for boycotting the company. Nigeria was suspended from the Commonwealth of Nations for over three years for executing Saro-Wiwa. The Ogoni Bill of Rights which Saro-Wiwa had drafted asserted the right of the Ogoni people on their land. He was posthumously honoured with Goldman Environmental Prize and Right Livelihood Award. The international media, especially *The Guardian* and *The Washington Post* reported his struggle, the illegality of his trial by the military tribunal and the violation of the rights of the Ogoni people bringing the issue to the attention of the world community. However, the struggle of the Ogoni people for justice and their demand for cleaning up of the Niger delta that followed Saro-Wiwa's execution was ignored by a large section of the mainstream media. His children took to journalism not only to tell their own stories but also the stories of the people who have suffered the way the Ogoni people have suffered (Gianotti, 2018). Even after democracy was restored in Nigeria in 1999 information about oil pollution continues to be blocked and the rights of the Ogoni people continue to be ignored (Ukpong, 2018). Saro-Wiwa's execution remains a classic case of violation of human rights linked to a nexus between the government and a multinational corporation. The media played a key role in internationalizing the impact of pollution on the community of the Ogoni people. Although the media cover the dramatic and violent events related to the rights of the indigenous peoples, what follows, in the long run, is usually ignored (Whitten-Woodring, 2009).

The World Summit on Sustainable Development (WSSD) which was held in Johannesburg in September 2002 stressed the importance of human rights and fundamental freedoms in achieving sustainable development. The WSSD plan emphasized the importance of public participation in environmental decision-making. The United Nations Declaration on the Rights of Indigenous Peoples (UNDRIP) adopted by the General Assembly in 2007 established a universal framework of minimum standards for the survival, dignity and well-being of the indigenous peoples of the world. This is the most comprehensive international instrument on the rights of indigenous peoples that expands the scope of existing human rights standards and fundamental freedoms as they apply to the specific situation of indigenous peoples.

Article 29 of the UNDRIP says, 'Indigenous peoples have the right to the conservation and protection of the environment and the productive capacity of their lands or territories and resources. States shall establish and implement assistance programmes for indigenous peoples for such conservation and protection, without discrimination'.[4] As per the Article the states have an obligation to make sure that without the prior and informed consent of the indigenous peoples no hazardous materials are either stored or disposed of in their territories.

In the UNDRIP declaration and other declarations, human rights have been conceived as those that are inherent, inalienable and universal (Watts, 2018). Rights being inherent mean that they are the birth rights of all human beings and people enjoy them simply by their human existence. There is nothing like a sovereign or superior authority granting these rights to the indigenous people. Inalienable right means that people cannot agree to give them up or have them taken away from them. The rights of the individuals are not derived from the state. They are *universal* as they do not just apply to individuals as 'citizens' or groups but to all persons.

The Supreme Court of India has expanded the scope of Article 21 of the constitution, which guarantees the right to life to include the right to a clean and healthy environment giving it the status of a fundamental right (Shankar & Bindal, 2012). It has said that any disturbance caused to air, water and soil, which are necessary for life would be hazardous to life within the ambit of Article 21.[5] A person

---

[4] http://www.unesco.org/new/en/indigenous-peoples/sustainable-development-and-environmental-change/undrip-sd-cc/
[5] *M. C. Mehta vs Kamal Nath* (1997) 1 SCC 388.

whose environmental right has been violated under this Article can seek justice under Article 32[6] and Article 226.

Despite several court judgements and documents that have defined the rights of citizens, journalists still run into difficulty trying to define the term 'human rights'. Many journalists feel the term is vague and difficult to interpret. Because so many different ideas are included within the category, there has been a tendency to focus more on civil and political rights, ignoring violations of economic, social and cultural rights (Ennals & Skogly, 1988, p. 130). Economic, social and cultural rights do not easily fall into a breaking news format. Poor health services, lack of water, deprivation of livelihood and inadequate education are issues that are difficult to be sold to editors concerned with budgets and advertising revenue.

Press freedom, which is a fundamental right in several countries, is under attack in recent years. There has been a steady decline in respect for press freedom in the world press freedom Index prepared by Reporters Without Borders (RSF). According to RSF governments are becoming more authoritarian, corporations are becoming more commercial and fundamentalist groups are becoming more aggressive.[7] On the press freedom index, India ranked 142nd among 180 countries in 2020.

Media have the ability to influence policy decisions concerning human rights by making them the agenda through sustained coverage. The media can 'disseminate human rights information, mobilize human rights NGOs, strengthen popular participation in civil society, promote tolerance and shine a light on government activity' (Apodaca, 2007, p. 151). The media and human rights NGOs are 'helpful to each other in the fight against human rights violations' (Burns, 2002, p. 33). The NGOs serve as monitors and sources of information for human rights stories. Former chairman of the NHRC Justice Balaksrishna, had said on 19 December 2013, that the commission took 300 cases *suo moto* based on media coverage and information provided by the NGOs (Business Standard, 2013).

[6] *Subhash Kumar vs State of Bihar* (1991) 1 SCC 598.
[7] (https://rsf.org/en)

The NGOs use global media to highlight human rights abuses, which in turn will shame abusers to put an end to their attitude (Cmiel, 2004). Besides, the NGOs have used documentaries to depict the conditions of people who have been denied human rights (Okafor, 2006). Although human rights issues are newsworthy, the media have given very little attention to them (Metzl, 1996; Ovsiovitch, 1993).). Studies have indicated that human rights as a concept often fails to be used as a subject in the headings of media stories. Media often point to human rights indirectly, but that is problematic because they do not enhance comprehension of human rights in the right perspective.

Media continue to see human rights as those that are related to war and conflicts. Because of a lack of comprehensive knowledge of human rights instruments, journalists fear being labelled as 'politically biased' if they frame their news stories as stories of human rights violations (Nwankwo, 2011, p. 19). Lack of comprehensive knowledge about human rights may lead to ignoring violations that the journalists may have come across in their own neighbourhood or region. Even though Indian journalism has, in the past, played the role of a watchdog, human rights have not encompassed environmental human rights which have been given a 'backseat' (Acharya, 2010, p. 42). Western journalists tend to think that human rights violations happen only in third world countries and therefore overlook the violations that happen right around them (International Council on Human Rights Policy, 2002). Space constraints may be a limiting factor for the media in covering human rights issues in-depth (Prabhash, 2005; Schimmel, 2009). The pressure on media to attract readers and to give priority to topical and controversial issues often leads to a lack of comprehensive coverage of human rights violations (Heinze & Freedman, 2010). Many of the environmental issues may not appear to be topical and may not attract readers' attention as issues involving human rights.

Denial of Information Right

Information regarding environmentally destructive activities in eco-logically sensitive areas is hardly available in the public domain. The right of citizens to know about the possible harm that the industries can cause has not always been given its due importance. Principle 10 of the Rio Declaration in 1992 led to the adoption of a convention on Access to Information, Public Participation in Decision-making and Access to Justice in Environmental Matters (Aarhus Convention) in 1998. Although the convention came into effect in 2001 there has been no significant change on the ground. Instead of using a rights-oriented language, the convention requires states only to 'ensure' that the public has access to information even though it draws on notions of international human rights law.[8] Despite such efforts, information about several controversial industrial projects is still not available to the public and is considered an official secret.

The Official Secret Act in India has often been used to deny information and to act against those who write about the harmful consequences of 'development' projects. Journalists have often faced the threat of being punished for violating the Act. Although there has been a demand for scrapping of some of the provisions of the Act no concrete steps have been taken. The Act is being more frequently used now than before. Iron curtains have been raised around the dams, mines and industrial projects in order to prevent journalists from reporting on the questions raised against them. One industry that has been protected from media coverage is the nuclear industry. Very little information is available about the health hazards of building, operating and decommissioning nuclear plants.

A section of the media has presented the denial of information about the effects of radiation on human health as a violation of human rights. In the year 1959, the International Atomic Energy Agency (IAEA) and the World Health Organization (WHO) signed an agreement that bars WHO from reporting diseases caused by nuclear radiation. Article 3 of this agreement states 'Whenever either organization proposes to initiate a programme or activity on a subject in which the other organizations has or may have a substantial interest, the first party shall consult the other with a view to adjusting the matter by mutual consent' (cited in Narain, 2015, p. 114). This agreement

[8] www.humanrights.is/en/humnrights-concepts-ideas-and-fora/human-rights-in-relation-to-other-topics/human-rights-and-the-environment

effectively suppresses information about nuclear accidents. When the Chernobyl nuclear accident took place in 1986, the WHO suppressed the information about its effect because of this agreement. Protest against this agreement began on 26 April 2007, 21 years after the Chernobyl accident happened. The WHO was accused of keeping the health consequences of the disaster hidden.

According to the Japanese media, it was this agreement that prevented the WHO from taking stock of the effects of radiation in 2011. They have also reported about the signing of a memorandum of cooperation by IAEA, Fukushima authorities and Fukui Prefectures that had a confidentiality clause (Narain, 2015). The clause makes it binding on the parties to consider anything as confidential if any one of them has classified it as confidential.

Japanese media have seen it as a violation of the right to information vital for protecting lives. Even while the Indian nuclear programme has seen the addition of new reactors in the recent past information about the effects of radiation is hardly accessible. At the same time, the media have been criticized for distorting facts about cancer-related deaths in atomic energy hubs in the country. The Indian media reported that an RTI enquiry had revealed that between 1995 and 2014 as many as 2,600 had died of cancer in these hubs (Narain, 2015). However, the Department of Atomic Energy (DAE), which rejected these figures, argued that not more than 152 people had died due to cancer-related causes.

While some media have expressed concerns about the safety norms in nuclear power plants the dominant view is that nuclear energy is necessary to overcome the energy crisis and in the process if some people are affected that should not be the reason why the nuclear option should be rejected. Despite evidence to show that nuclear radiation causes cancer, it is seldom seen as a violation of human rights. When protests were held against Kudankulam Nuclear Power Project in Tamil Nadu the coverage in media, both national and regional, ignored the issue of risks to human lives posed by the nuclear power plants (Basu, 2012). Several newspapers, especially those in Tamil, and television channels were in favour of the projects despite questions about their safety. Some of the newspapers and television channels produced stories about the harmful effects of radiation with statistics and interviews of victims.

Nagesh Hegde says that much of the information about a nuclear hazard is kept in secrecy and a journalist runs the risk of attracting action under the provisions of the Official Secrets Act (personal communication, 14 October 2018). Very little information about the effect of nuclear radiation on the environment and human health is available in the public domain.

Narasimha Adi and Ashok Hasyagar, the two journalists who have been writing about the environmental consequences of Kaiga nuclear power plant in Uttara Kannada district of Karnataka, argue that people have the right to know if radiation from the plant is causing cancer (personal communication, 27 February 2019). Both of them have written stories about the increasing incidence of cancer in the villages around the Kaiga plant. For them, the denial of information about the long-term health risks of the plant is a violation of human rights. They have given human rights angles to their stories although readers do not always perceive the issues related to the Kaiga plant from the same angle. The nuclear establishment in India continues to deny any link between rising cancer cases and the Kaiga plant. Comparative studies between cancer cases in Kaiga area and another area, which is geographically and culturally similar, have not been carried out. People's right to know about the possible effects of radiation on health has not been universally recognized.

Displacement as a Human Rights Violation in Media

Development projects have displaced millions of people around the world. The acquisition of land on a big scale took place in the mid-19th century for the construction of railways (Sarkar, 2010). There were protests and court cases that led to changes in plans culminating in the Land Acquisition Act 1894. The Act survived until 2013 when the Right to Fair Compensation and Land Transparency in Land Acquisition, Rehabilitation and Resettlement Act came into effect. The land acquisition process was so callous that rehabilitation and resettlement came as an afterthought with scant regard for the rights of the people who lost their land and common property resources leading to the loss of their livelihood (Tumbe, 2018). An estimated 60 million people have been displaced by development projects in India since independence (Verma, 2016) and 40 per cent of them are Adivasis who constitute 8.6 per cent of the India's population as per 2011 census (Nadimpally et al., 2019). That there are no up-to-date authentic figures available is itself an indication as to how seriously the problem of displacement has been addressed. Some people who have been repeatedly displaced by one project after the other ultimately end up in the slums on the periphery of big cities (Roy, 1999).

The construction schedule of large dams in most cases does not synchronize with the relocation of the people (Mathur, 2013). Lakhs of people have been displaced by the rising water levels of dams before they are given compensation and relocated. Writer and activist Arundhati Roy who wrote an essay titled 'The Greater Common Good' in the *Frontline* (2 May 22–24 June 1999) and *Outlook* (24 May 1999) magazines presented the issue of displacement as an issue of human rights violation. She presented the dehumanizing conditions created by development-induced displacement. People had been thrown out of their homes without their consent and with no proper rehabilitation and resettlement. Several communities had lost their land, forest and other common property resources essential for their livelihood. Roy's essay brought into sharp focus how the development projects in India had enormous consequences on the social, economic, political and cultural rights of the displaced persons. Her description of big dams as the weapons of mass destruction emphasized the violation of the right to livelihood of the tribes who have been the worst victims of displacement. She said (Roy, 1999, p. 29),

> Big Dams are to a Nation's 'Development' what Nuclear Bombs are to its Military Arsenal. They're both weapons of mass destruction. They're both weapons Governments use to control their own people. Both Twentieth Century emblems that mark a point in time when human intelligence has outstripped its own instinct for survival. They're both malignant indications of civilization turning upon itself. They represent the severing of the link, not just the

link—the understanding—between human beings and the planet they live on. They scramble the intelligence that connects eggs to hens, milk to cows, food to forests, water to rivers, air to life and the earth to human existence.

Roy put forth a forceful argument in defence of the right of the people to have access to natural resources that is essential for their very survival. The essay was published at a time when the agitation against big dams led by Narmada Bachao Andolan (NBA) had suffered a setback with the Supreme Court permitting rising of the height of the Sardar Sarovar dam from 80 m to 85 m. The stay on construction during the previous four years had reduced the visibility of the movement, as there were few demonstrations or mass actions. The media interest had failed to notice the quiet processes through which NBA was educating the people in the valley about their rights. Her involvement in the Narmada movement and her views on the consequences of big dams evoked appreciation and criticism from journalists, scholars and politicians. Following the rally in which over 400 people took part, displacement by big dams became an issue of debate in newspapers. Some of those who wrote on the issue argued that forced displacement was a violation of human rights. In an article, Madhav Menon (1999), a member of the Law Commission, wrote in the *Deccan Herald* on 7 August 1999:

> Protest, dissent, civil disobedience, and direct action within limits are legitimate methods of influencing the decision making process of the government in a democracy. Given the condition and the predicament of thousands of helpless tribals displaced by avoidable large dams and similar projects essentially serving the urban middle class, it is only natural for public-spirited citizens to question the so-called development projects adopted by the ruling classes. More so when they virtually endanger the basic rights of those unfortunate project displaced citizens who have no voice in policymaking affecting their lives and livelihood.

The article strongly defended the Narmada movement in the broader context of human rights. Development-induced displacement is often viewed in terms of the economics of compensation ignoring the human rights angle.

According to Medha Patkar, media in India have not paid attention to displacement as a human rights violation. She explains her experience with media persons:

> Every time we tried to explain to the media about how displacement had been depriving the Adivasis of their livelihood and destroying their community and culture, their focus would still be on the cost and benefits of dam building. Many of them would actually believe the false claims made by the government about the benefits. The violation of the rights of the people cannot be understood if the journalists attend only press conferences and events. They should travel to the Adivasi villages and see for themselves the impact of the dam on their lives. They need not believe what we tell them. They should discover on their own how the rights of the Adivasis are violated. Is it not a violation of human rights when Adivasis are forced out or their homes in the forests and ordered to live in rows of small tin-sheet sheds? Adivasis have refused to move into those sheds which were fabricated elsewhere, brought on trucks, and erected in places with no water and no common property resources. A few journalists have travelled extensively in the Adivasi villages and have produced reports written with a human rights perspective. (Personal communication, 5 March 2019)

The very development paradigm, according to her, is violative of the right to life of the people which can be understood when journalists see projects like dam building in the broader context of equality, equity and justice. 'Displacing people from their environment means you are disconnecting them from their land, forests and rivers without which they cannot live. Displacing Adivasis from their forest is like throwing fish out of water,' Patkar says. She wants journalists to see such displacement from a human angle, not from the angle of providing only compensation and resettlement package. Despite the fact that millions of people have been displaced and continue to be displaced, violation of their rights has not been a subject of the mainstream media debate.

While displacement by big dams has received some attention of the media, climate change-induced displacement is yet to be seen as a threatening problem. Representatives of people from several countries who face the threat of the consequences of climate change met at Girdwood of Alaska state in the United States from 1 to 4 October 2018, and adopted a declaration on climate-forced displacement. The islands, delta and the arctic ecosystems from where the representatives had come were facing the extreme impacts of climate change. They call it a 'crisis', not a 'change' and demand immediate measures to lower the global temperature. Rising temperatures, rising sea levels, flooding, landslide, erosion, ocean acidification, storms and other disasters threaten their very existence.

Expressing the consequences of climate change, they said,

> We are deeply alarmed by the accelerating climatic devastation brought about by unsustainable development and natural events. We are experiencing profound and disproportionate adverse impacts on our cultures, lands, human and environmental health, human rights, spirituality, well-being, traditional systems and livelihoods, food systems and food security, local infrastructure, economic viability, and our very survival as First Peoples and Indigenous Peoples of the world.[9]

The declaration called upon the Conference of Parties (COP) to the United Nations Framework Convention on Climate Change (UNFCCC) and its decision-making bodies to consider the rights of the climate-displaced people as a matter of urgent concern. The media ignored the convention and the declaration, although climate change has been the agenda of several international summits. The rights of the people living on the islands in the Pacific Ocean, Bangladesh, Alaska, Washington, Louisiana did not matter much to the media. While the convention received coverage only in the local media, in Alaska the issue the convention was raising was not even considered newsworthy by several national and international media. The Indian media ignored the issue indicating that issue of climate change has not been on the agenda of the mainstream media despite the fact that a large number of people in the country are going to be affected by a rise in seal levels. In 2020, 1.4 crore people were displaced by climate disasters and 4.5 crore people are estimated to be displaced by 2050

---

[9] https://www.uusc.org/wp-content/uploads/2018/09/Declaration.pdf

in India (*The Economic Times*, 2020). This is a clear indication for the media to pay serious attention to the issue of climate change and to bring pressure on the politicians to act with all seriousness towards reducing greenhouse gases.

Rohin Kumar, who has been a keen observer of media coverage of climate change, says when journalists have a poor understanding of what climate change is, they would not understand what climate justice is (personal communication, 20 May 2021). That, according to him, explains why climate-induced displacement is not seen in the larger context of human rights and climate justice. He says Greenpeace has been trying to bring the justice perspective to climate change coverage by explaining the key issues in simple ways with facts and figures and making them available to journalists. Greenpeace has been able to mobilize reporters to do in-depth stories on climate-induced displacement. Even though climate change is generally not disputed in India, there is still a section of the media, which thinks that the responsibility is only on the developed countries. In its response to the sixth assessment report of IPCC predicting global temperature increase beyond 1.5 degree benchmark in the next two decades, the Government of India said that it was a 'clarion call for the developed counties' (King, 2021). The media coverage of the report broadly reflected the government response but also called for immediate steps to be taken in India.

Community Rights and the Media

The industry–media nexus is said to be a major cause of media silence on environmental issues affecting the health of the people. Several big industries, besides directly owning media and investing in them, pump in crores of rupees of advertising revenue to the newspapers. As the media mainly depend on the advertising revenue for their very survival, they would either not carry stories that would harm the interest of the advertisers or relegate them to an insignificant space (Herman & Chomsky, 1988). Many of the environmental struggles in India, as elsewhere, have been against big corporations, which wield enormous political influence on the media agenda through their advertising money. When there are conflicts between corporate interests and community interests the media have the responsibility of ensuring that the rights of the communities are not violated.

Environmental organizations working in mining areas have often raised questions about violations of human rights by the mining companies. Holding protests and speaking in national and international fora about the impact of the mining activities on the livelihood of communities living around the mining areas have been subjects of intense debate in media. One of the issues widely debated in the Indian media was the 'offloading' of a policy advisor for Greenpeace India, Priya Pillai, by the Indian immigration authorities when she was about to board a flight to London on 11 January 2015. She was travelling to the United Kingdom to make a presentation before a group of parliamentarians about the violation of human rights by the UK-based ESSAR group.[10] The Hindalco and the ESSAR group had started a joint venture company named Mahan Coal Ltd to open a coal mine in Mahan in Madhya Pradesh.

Greenpeace had argued that Mahan was home to the oldest and largest surviving Sal forest in Asia and that opening of a mine there had the potential of displacing the tribal communities from the forests. It would not only destroy the forest on which the tribals were living but also pollute air and water, threatening their livelihood. The purpose of Priya Pillai's visit to the UK was to speak about violations of environmental laws to the British parliamentarians so that they brought pressure on the UK-based ESSAR group to fall in line with the legal regime in India. The Indian authorities argued that Pillai's visit to the UK had the potential of degrading the image of India in the eyes of the foreign nations. They also said that her interaction with the British MPs would work against India's economic development and harm the national interest. This has generally been the charge made against environmental activists and the NGOs that raise questions on the violation of the environmental law by big corporations. The Delhi High Court rejected the arguments of the Indian authorities

---

[10] *Priya Parameshwaran Pillai vs Union of India and Ors*, 12 March 2015 (https://indiankanoon.org/doc/64486862/)

and declared that preventing Priya Pillai from visiting the UK was against her fundamental right.

The Indian media were divided on the issue though a majority of them saw a potential threat to the lives of tribal communities in Mahan. They argued that there could be different views on what constitutes development but preventing a Greenpeace employee from travelling abroad and talking about the effects of mines was uncalled for (Subramanian, 2015). However, the focus of media was not on whether the environmental rights of the people were being violated but on the right of an Indian citizen to travel abroad. The destruction of sal forests, displacement of tribes and the threat of pollution were not debated at all.

Some newspapers saw the decision to 'offload' an activist anti-democratic and urged the government to be more tolerant towards 'alternative voices'.[11] The *Deccan Herald* in an editorial[12] (Why was Pillai put on watch list?) on 13 January 2015 said,

> The government's barring of Greenpeace-India campaigner Priya Pillai from boarding a flight to London lays bare a deepening anti-democratic streak in its approach to alternative voices, dissenting opinion, and activism. By silencing opinion and putting citizens on blacklists and watch lists, the government is acting unconstitutionally. It is only shaming itself....

The Indian Express in its editorial on 14 January 2015, said:

> The social sector should be seen as a partner in the process of development, not a political adversary paid in dollars to lobby for alien agendas and foment dissatisfaction in the countryside. Lobbying and activism are legitimate acts. The government's response should be to negotiate. The puerile alternative of offloading inconvenient people mars the image of confident maturity that India is trying to project.[13]

[11] https://www.bbc.com/news/world-asia-india-30808797
[12] https://www.deccanherald.com/content/453324/why-pillai-put-watchlist. html
[13] https://www.bbc.com/news/world-asia-india-30808797

Though the government action came in for severe criticism the environmental rights of the tribes on whose behalf the Greenpeace campaigner was going to speak was hardly the focus of such criticism. The Indian media were generally sympathetic to Greenpeace. By projecting the government's action as a state-civil society conflict, the media had given the benefit of doubt to Greenpeace (Vardhan, 2015). The editorial page articles in several newspapers came to the support of Greenpeace which could not be interpreted as the support for the tribal community's opposition to the coal mine. That the rights of the tribal community were facing threat because of mining was hardly the focus of media. Many mines across the country are located in the regions where most tribes live and violation of their right to a clean and healthy environment does not make news in the mainstream media whereas social media provide bits and pieces of information though they lack comprehensive analysis.

One of the struggles that remains a major milestone in the history of the environmental movement in India has been the struggle of a village panchayat in Kerala against the international cola giant Coca-Cola. In March 2000 a Coca-Cola plant was commissioned at Plachimada in the Palakkad district of Kerala to produce Coca-Cola, Thums Up, Fanta, Limca, Maaza, Kinley Soda and Sprite. The Hindustan Coca-Cola Beverages Pvt. Ltd (HCCB), a subsidiary owned by the Coca-Cola that produces Coca-Cola, was given a licence to install a motor to draw water. But the company sank six borewells and began extracting millions of litres of water illegally (Shiva, 2004). The villagers discovered that the groundwater level had gone down to 500 feet from 150 feet because of the extraction of 1.5 million litres of water per day. The company had not only extracted a huge quantity of water from the ground but had also polluted it (Konikkara, 2019). Although the villagers had started complaining about water pollution six months after the plant was opened, organized protests began in April 2002. The protests by the Dalits and Adivasis against the HCCB continued until the plant was shut down.

Media coverage of the struggle not only helped mobilize people but also significantly contributed to its successes. Water pollution caused by the Coca-Cola plant was framed as an issue of violation of human rights by the media. The British Broadcasting Corporation (BBC), *Mathrubhumi* daily and the *Outlook* magazine presented investigative stories about wells drying up and water turning toxic because of the sludge dumped by the Coke plant in the nearby area.

In July 2003, a journalist from the BBC visited the villages around the plant to investigate whether the sludge passed off to the farmers as fertilizer by the HCCB and the water in the nearby wells were contaminated. A lab at the University of Exeter in London to which the journalist had sent the samples found high levels of cadmium and lead in the sludge. High levels of other heavy metals like nickel, chromium and zinc were also found in the sludge. Cadmium and lead were also found in the sample of water collected from a well. While cadmium, which is classified as carcinogenic is toxic to the kidney and liver, lead is harmful to human development and the nervous system.

The BBC reported on 25 July 2003, in its Radio 4 *Face the Facts* programme that carcinogens were found in the waste (Bijoy, 2006). It showed with ample evidence that there was groundwater depletion and contamination of water in the wells that threatened the livelihood and lives of the people. *Janaveedhi*, a human rights organization, had come out with equally revealing facts a year before the BBC report. However, the BBC report got the attention of national and international media. The environmental group Greenpeace shared the findings of the University of Exeter with the Kerala State Pollution Control Board (KSPCB) and the media. The BBC report hit the headlines in the Kerala media. The KSPCB, which not only confirmed the BBC Report but also found higher levels of chemical and metals in the samples, ordered the company to stop supplying the waste, recover it, and store it safely in the plant site.

In April 2005, The High Court of Kerala ordered Purumatty panchayat under which Plachimada falls to issue a licence to the company to extract five lakh litres of water a day. However, the panchayat rejected the company's application twice (Ninen, 2005). Following the high court order, the *Outlook* magazine published a two-page story in May 2005 titled 'Don't Poison My Well'. The magazine got the water from the well of an Adivasi woman living close to the Coke plant tested at a lab in Chennai accredited by the Department of Science and

Technology, Government of India. The lab report said that the water was highly acidic and could not be used for consumption, cooking, washing or agriculture (Anand, 2005). The magazine argued that the toxic waste from the plant posed a serious threat to the people who consumed groundwater. Curiously on 6 June 2005, the magazine carried a six-page rejoinder from the HCCB which rubbished the story and presented results from different labs that showed total dissolved solids at levels far below the permissible limits. There was no response from the magazine to the claims of the company. The international cola giant had effectively silenced the magazine on the issue that involved the lives of the Adivasis.

The Malayalam daily *Mathrubhumi* which carried on a campaign on behalf of the affected people for over three years called upon the people to boycott Coca-Cola. The newspaper described how the Adivasi women had to walk 5 km to fetch drinking water when truckloads of soft drinks came out of the Coca-Cola plant. The company filed a ₹50 lakh defamation case against the newspaper. The reports in the newspaper presented water contamination caused by the Coca-Cola company as an issue of human rights violation.

Even as the struggle against the Coca-Cola company was intensifying, the World Water Conference was held at Plachimada between 21 and 23 January 2004. The conference adopted a declaration titled 'Plachimada Declaration' that asserted the right of the local community to use and conserve water. The declaration said, 'The right to conserve, use and manage water is fully vested with the local community. This is the very basis of water democracy. Any attempt to reduce or deny this right is a crime' (Shiva, 2004). Reports in media highlighted the key demands of the declaration focusing on the harm the plant was going to cause to the lives of the Adivasis.

Mathrubhumi gave human rights angle to all major stories about the plant in all publications of the group. The chairman and managing director of *Mathrubhumi* group M. P. Veerendrakumar, a writer, thinker and politician, said,

> For the first time in history, a village panchayat successfully fought against a powerful multinational corporation like Coca

Cola and forced it to close down one of its manufacturing units. Mathrubhumi stood solidly with the Adivasis who were the major victims of water depletion and contamination caused by the company. It is a crime if the water is used for commercial gains at the cost of generations of humanity. We campaigned against the company rejecting all offers of inducements. We refused to carry their advertisements. We wanted people to boycott Coca Cola products and switch to tender coconut. The right of access to safe drinking water was being violated by the company as it had polluted the groundwater with chemicals and heavy metals. The defamation case the company had filed against us was dismissed by the court as the reports in our newspaper were based on facts. It was a clear case of violation of human rights and we wanted to defend human rights at any cost. (Personal communication, 18 September 2018)

Veerendrakumar, who was also president of the Indian Newspapers Society, was of the firm view that media should treat pollution caused by industries as violation of human rights. As the chairman of the Mathrubhumi group and as a politician he not only carried on a campaign against the cola major but was also involved in organizing the World Water Conference at Plachimada.

The BBC, *Outlook* and *Mathrubhumi* presented the issue of water depletion and contamination as an issue of human rights violation and helped the movement of the Adivasis in Plachimada get national and international attention. While the BBC and *Mathrubhumi* stood by their reports, *Outlook* allowed the company to offer a six-page rebuttal of its own reports and remained silent after that.

One of the few environmental movements in India that has succeeded in defending the religious, communitarian and individual rights of the Adivasis has been the Niyamgiri movement. The movement began in 2003 when the UK-based mining company Vedanta Resources sought clearance to mine bauxite, a raw material for aluminium, on the Niyamgiri Hills considered sacred by the Dongria Kondhs who believe that their deity Niyamraja rules the mountains (Borde & Bluemling, 2020). When the media began reporting about the movement, international agencies like the Amnesty International, Survival International and ActionAid took interest in it. The protests organized by these advocacy groups were widely covered in the national and international media. Media framing of mining on the Niyamgiri Hills as violation of the rights of the Adivasis helped the movement gain support from several organizations and activists. Niyamgiri Suraksha Samithi (Niyamgiri Protection Committee), which has been carrying on the struggle, has always argued that the hills are tied to their religion, their identity and their survival (Chandrashekhar, 2017). Among the Dongria Kondhs, felling trees on mountain tops is a taboo and a sign of disrespect to their supreme deity.

A turning point to the movement came when the *Time* magazine published an article in which a comparison was made between the Na'vi featured in *Avatar*, the 2009 Hollywood blockbuster and the Dongria Kondhs living on the Niyamgiri Hills (Thottam, 2010). The article quoted an advertisement issued by an international network of activists supporting the Kondhs' cause in the 8 February issue of *Variety*, a film trade journal. The advertisement said '*Avatar* is fantasy … and real. The Dongria Kondh tribe in India are struggling to defend their land against a mining company hell-bent on destroying their sacred mountain. Please help the Dongria' (cited in Thottam, 2010).

The activists not only drew a parallel between Na'vi and Dongria Kondhs in their advertisement but also protested in front of Vedanta's office in London by painting themselves in blue to resemble the Na'vi in Avatar and holding the placards that said 'save the real Avatar tribe' (Borde & Bluemling, 2020). These dramatic protests were very widely reported in national and international media sensitizing the people not only to the threats the Kondhs were facing but also to the threats the indigenous people were facing around the world. According to Rana (2020), the 'symbolism of humans fighting with indigenous people for mineral rights is an apt metaphor for the Niyamgiri movement'.

After the Ministry of Environment and Forests banned mining in Niyamgiri Hills in August 2010, the Odisha government questioned the action of the central government in the Supreme Court. In a landmark judgement on 18 April 2013 The Supreme Court said mining on the Niyamgiri Hills could be allowed only if the *gram sabhas* (village councils) permitted it. All 12 *gram sabhas* selected by the Odisha government for referendum unanimously voted against mining. Following the decision of the *gram sabhas* the Ministry of Environment and Forests banned mining on the Niyamgiri Hills. It was for the first time that a green referendum had been held in India. In 2016 the Odisha government moved to the Supreme Court again seeking review of the decision of *gram sabhas*, but the appeal was rejected (Singh, 2018). Even though the ban on mining stays, the troubles are not yet over for the Dongria Kondhs as they are being arrested and harassed for their alleged association with Maoists (Sahu, 2017a). The attempts to acquire their land continue.

Rath (2019, pp. 228–230), who conducted a survey in Niyamgiri Hills, found that a great majority (76%) of the people believed that media were biased against the movement. They were also not satisfied (62%) with the media coverage of the movement in the Hills. While the national and international media gave wide coverage to the movement, the media in the state were biased against the movement. Since the mining project was being promoted by the Odisha government, it is possible that the media were reflecting the view of the government rather than seeing the movement from the point of view of the rights of the Adivasis. This appears similar to what the Gujarati newspapers did with regard to the Narmada movement discussed in Chapter 8. Newspapers did not want the construction of the dam to be halted even when the displacement persons were resettled.

While the media as institutions may be lacking in their commitment to protecting the environmental rights of the people there have been efforts by individual journalists to report issues from the rights perspective. Some of them have also been part of community organizations working towards preserving the democratic rights of the people. They have presented environmental struggles from the perspective of environmental justice. Darryl D'Monte, the founder-president of the International Federation of Environmental Journalists, was involved in the civil liberties movement in the 1970s. He was one of the few environmental journalists who rose to higher positions in the editorial hierarchy of newspapers. He became the resident editor of *The Indian Express* and *The Times of India* in Mumbai. Human rights remained the central focus of his writings on environmental issues (Sharma,

2019). Even when he began conducting research for a book in the 1980s on the impact of rapid economic growth on the environment, his commitment to protecting human rights did not weaken a bit (D'Monte, 2010).

Keya Acharya, an says when a journalist presents a problem in the context of a community the story is given a human rights angle (personal communication, 12 September 2020). Many journalists in the mainstream media, according to her, do not see an issue from the point of view of a community. Pollution of a river or a water body is a violation of the right of a community to have access to safe drinking water. Understanding community rights requires field-based reporting and deeper analysis of the livelihoods of the people. Human rights as generally written about in media do not encompass environmental human rights which have been given a 'backseat' (Acharya, 2010, p. 42).

Environmental activist Panduranga Hegde feels that serious environmental issues will not get the immediate attention of the government unless they are framed as human rights issues (personal communication, 26 February 2019). He says,

> When the survival itself becomes a question for the people who have been victims of environmental degradation and displacement, it is important to treat it as a human rights issue. In much of the media coverage of environmental issues, the human rights angle is missing. Any development that leads to contamination of air, water, and soil, the basic needs of mankind, violates human rights. I am amazed that the media have not been seeing air pollution as a violation of human rights.

Muralidhar Khajane says that he has given human rights angle to the environmental stories he has written (personal communication, 26 June 2019). In his view, environmental problems are more often referred to as controversies and disputes in media which is not fair to those who are affected by environmental degradation. 'When the lives of people are at stake it is certainly a violation of human rights. Since the lives of lakhs of Adivasis are affected by mining and deforestation it is important to see them as equal citizens who are entitled to the right to life', he says.

According Nagesh Hegde, the entire issue of the environment is connected to human rights (personal communication, 12 October 2018).

> Nuclear radiation, air pollution, and water pollution pose a serious threat to the lives of people who may not be aware of it. People have the right to know about the food they eat, the air they breathe, and the water they consume. The right of access to information is often denied. It is the responsibility of the media to highlight such denial of rights.

Many of the articles he wrote for *Prajavani* and the *Sudha* weekly presented issues from the point of view of human rights.

Environmental and human rights activist Vidya Dinker says that the rights perspective is often missing in environmental stories. Journalists do express empathy and sympathy with their suffering but they may focus more on human interest angle rather than on the human rights angle (personal communication, 5 May 2021). According to her, journalists who are so much a part of an unequal society do not see human rights as a major issue:

> The journalists usually carry the superior and unequal kind of mind frame. So, they will respond to suffering and try to document it, but they are weak in positioning it as an issue of rights. They do not see it as a problem because there is so much of inequality in society and so entrenched, and even journalists grow up with the feeling that they live in an unequal world and inequality is okay. If a person living in a slum does not get proper water, it does not hit a journalist as very wrong because they carry inherent prejudices. There are some people who are meant to suffer, a woman has to suffer discrimination and a farmer has to struggle to protect or sell his crop. It does not seem inherently wrong because inequality is accepted as part of the society. They have to question themselves and their own perceptions but that does not happen with most of them. There is some hope with some younger journalists but they constitute a very small percentage of the journalistic community. We have to go a long way because inequity is in our minds and hearts.

In Vidya's perception there is normalization of violation of human rights to such an extent that journalists do not see it as a serious issue at all. A high level of sensitivity is needed, according to her, to understand and interpret issues from the rights' perspective. Her argument primarily emphasizes that the issues of environmental rights cannot be addressed without questioning the practices that perpetuate social injustices.

Journalists and activists are of the view that the media should attempt to present environmental issues from the perspective of human rights and justice. They feel that media should respect the right to a healthy environment and that journalists should be sensitized towards environmental issues so that they will be able to understand and analyse issues in the context of human rights. They believe that periodic orientation programmes and workshops are necessary to help journalists understand violations of environmental regulations from the point of view of the livelihood rights of the marginalized sections of the society.

Conclusion

Even though Indian environmentalism is largely about social justice, the Indian media rarely present environmental degradation in human rights frame. The demand for environmental justice has grown in recent decades as more and more people have begun to experience the consequences of environmentally unsustainable projects and climate change. Despite the worldwide debate on violation of human rights, there have been no clear and binding norms with regard to environmental rights. The people who are affected by the development projects hardly have any access to information, which is human right. Much of the information concerning development projects is kept in secrecy and very little is available in the public domain. Media too have no free access to information, which is essential to keep the people well-informed about how they are going to be affected by the so-called development projects. Although human rights violations are newsworthy, media have given very little attention to them.

Despite the fact that dams and other development projects have displaced an estimated 60 million people, media coverage of mass displacement and the consequent problems has been very limited. Development-induced displacement is often presented as an issue of compensation and resettlement but not as an issue of justice and human rights, even though displacement leads to homelessness, landlessness, marginalization and food insecurity.

Media have the responsibility of creating awareness among the audiences about violations of their environmental rights. When peaceful advocates of environmental causes are harassed, intimidated, criminalized, attacked and even killed, and their right to life and physical integrity is violated, it is important for the media to play the watchdog role and expose the perpetrators of violence. The rights of the communities to have access to natural resources that are necessary for their very survival are not adequately highlighted in environmental stories. While the media have defended the freedom of expression of the environmental activists, they have not given due coverage to the questions activists have raised about violation of the environmental rights of the Adivasis.

That the human rights angle given to environmental stories can greatly contribute to the success of environmental movements is shown in the way the Plachimada and Niyamgiri movements were covered by the media. Human rights defenders have often come together in solidarity with the victims of environmental degradation and have tried to present environmental issues in justice and rights angle. Environmental rights are yet to be recognized by states as human rights even though organizations of the indigenous people in different parts of the world have been campaigning for such recognition. Journalists too have been reluctant to use environmental justice and rights frame for their stories. Unfortunately, in India, as in countries across the world, environmental regulations are being further diluted to the advantage of industrial corporations. Even though media have carried stories of environmental degradation, their voice against the weakening of the environmental law that has far-reaching consequences on the livelihoods of the marginalized people has been very feeble.

Appendix: Persons Interviewed

- Ms Medha Patkar, environmental activist and leader of the Narmada Bachao Andlolan, Barwani, Madhya Pradesh
- Mr M. P. Veerendrakumar, Member of Parliament and Chairman, Mathrubhumi Printing and Publishing Company Ltd, Kozhikode, Kerala
- Mr Nagesh Hegde, senior environmental journalist and former Assistant Editor, *Prajavani*, Bengaluru
- Mr Panduranga Hegde, environmental activist and leader of the Appiko movement, Sirsi, Uttara Kannada district, Karnataka
- Mr T. V. Jayan, Senior Deputy Editor, *The Hindu BusinessLine*, New Delhi
- Mr K. S. Dakshina Murthy, Associate Editor, *The Federal*, former editorial consultant, *Deccan Herald* and *The Hindu*, Bengaluru
- Mr Manohar R. Yadavatti, Zonal Editor, *Hindustan Samachar*, Bengaluru
- Mr Umapathy D., senior journalist and columnist, former special correspondent, *Kannada Prabha*, *Vijaya Karnataka*, *Prajavani*, New Delhi
- Mr K. G. Vasuki, special correspondent, *The Pioneer*, Bengaluru
- Ms Keya Acharya, independent journalist and President of Forum of Environmental Journalists in India, Bengaluru
- Mr K. Giriprakash, Associate Editor, *The Hindu BusinessLine*, Bengaluru
- Mr Shivananda Kalave, independent environmental journalist and columnist, Sirsi, Uttaraka Kannada district, Karnataka
- Ms Vidya Dinker, environmental and human rights activist and President, Indian Social Action Forum, Mangalore
- Ms Poornima R., senior journalist and former editor, *Udayavani*, Bengaluru
- Mr Muralidhar Khajane, Deputy Editor, *The Hindu*, Bengaluru
- Mr B. S. Nagaraj, independent journalist and contributor to *ThePrint*, former special correspondent, *The Indian Express*, New Delhi

- Mr Hunaswadi Rajan, Group Editor, *Samyukta Karnataka*, Bengaluru
- Mr Mohit Rao, special correspondent, *The Hindu*, Bengaluru
- Ms Meera Bhardwaj, special correspondent, *The New Indian Express*, former Doordarshan News correspondent, Bengaluru
- Mr Leo Saldanha, Coordinator, Environmental Support Group, Bengaluru
- Mr Narasimha Adi, senior journalist, Sirsi, Uttara Kannada district, Karnataka
- Mr Devramji, farmer and NBA activist, Khaparkhed village, Dhar district, Madhya Pradesh
- Mr Waheed Mansoor, farmer and NBA activist, Chikalda village, Dhar district, Madhya Pradesh
- Mr Ashok Hasyagar, Chief Editor, *Janamadhyama*, Sirsi, Uttara Kannada district, Karnataka
- Mr Asutosh Sen, multimedia journalist, Barwani district, Madhya Pradesh
- Mr Saurav Rajput, volunteer, NBA, Barwani, Madhya Pradesh
- Brg M. A. Devaiah, Coorg Wildlife Society, Napoklu, Kodagu district, Karnataka
- Col Muthanna, Coorg Wildlife Society, Napoklu, Kodagu district, Kerala
- Mr Balakrishnamurty, retired professor of history, Sree Sankara College, Kalady, and member, Kerala River Protection Council, Aluva, Kerala
- Mr Pudiyathanda Ganapathy, planter and social activist, Somawarapet, Kodagu district, Karnataka
- Ms Mini Joseph, Deputy Tahsildar, Idukki, Kerala
- Mr K. B. Ganapathy, Editor in Chief, *Star of Mysore and Musuru Mitra*, Mysore
- Mr Rohin Kumar, media specialist, Greenpeace India, Bengaluru
- Mr P. S. Sadananda, Editor, *Loka Dwani* daily, Sirsi, Uttara Kannada district, Karnataka
- Mr Ramnath Shenoy, State Bureau Chief, Press Trust of India, Bengaluru
- Mr Devassy Pulickal, environmental activist, Ernakulam, Kerala
- Dr Kamalaksha Shenoy, radiation oncologist, AJ Hospital, Mangalore
- Dr H. M. Somashekarappa, professor of nuclear physics, Mangalore University, Mangalore
- Dr R. Vasudeva, professor of forest biology, College of Forestry, Sirsi, Uttara Kannada district, Karnataka

References

Acharya, K. (2010). Writing about the birds and the bears. In K. Acharya & F. Noronha (Eds.), *The green pen: Environmental journalism in India and South Asia* (pp. 38–44). SAGE Publications.

Ader, C. R. (1995). A longitudinal study of agenda-setting for the issue of environmental pollution. *Journalism and Mass Communication Quarterly, 72*(2), 300–311.

Adiga, S. (2017). *Environmental issues and the press in Dakshina Kannada: A study* [PhD thesis, Kuvempu University].

Adiga, S., & Poornananda, D. S. (2012). GM crops and the press: The Bt brinjal controversy in English and Kannada newspapers. *Media Watch, 3*(2), 34–43.

Aiyer, S. (2018, 19 August). Kerala floods: India's disaster déjà vu. *The New Indian Express*, p. 8.

Ajay, A. (2018). Role of technology in responding to disasters: Insights from the great deluge in Kerala. *Current Science, 116*(6), 913–918.

Akhileshwari, R. (1989). Environment and the media. *Vidura, 26*(3), 11–13.

Albrecht, S., & Mauss, A. (1975). Environment. In A. Mauss (Ed.), *Social problems as social movement*. Lippincott Co.

Althoff, P., Greig, W., & Stuckey, F. (1973). Environmental pollution control attitudes of media managers in Kansas. *Journalism Quarterly, 50*(4), 666–672.

Anand, S. (2005, 16 May). Don't poison my well. https://www.outlookindia.com/magazine/story/dont-poison-my-well/227376

Anandan, S., & Praveen, M. P. (2018, 18 August). Trial by water: How Kerala is coping with an extraordinary natural disaster. *The Hindu*, p. 9.

Anderson, A. (1991). Source strategies and the communication of environmental affairs. *Media, Culture & Society, 13*(4), 459–476.

Anderson, A. (1993). Source media relations: The production of the environmental agenda. In A. Hansen (Ed.), *The mass media and environmental issues* (pp. 51–68). Leicester University Press.

Anderson, A. (2017). Source influence on journalistic decisions and news coverage of climate change. In M. Nisbet (Ed.), *Oxford research encyclopaedia of climate science*. Oxford University Press.

Apodaca, C. (2007). The whole world could be watching: Human rights and the media. *Journal of Human Rights, 6*(2), 147–164.

Archibald, F. F. (1996). *How environmental reporters on daily newspapers construct news of the environment* [Unpublished PhD dissertation, University of Georgia].

Asian Mass Communication Bulletin. (1998, 30 November). Asian Federation of Environmental Journalists Code of Ethics, p. 2.

Assadi, M. (2002). Kudremukh: Of mining and environment. *Economic & Political Weekly*, *37*(49), 4898–4901.

Atkin, E. (2018, 25 July). The media's failure to connect the dots on climate change. The New Republic. https://newrepublic.com/article/150124/medias-failure-connect-dots-climate-change.

Atwater, T., Salwen, M., & Anderson N. B. (1985). Media agenda setting with environmental issues. *Journalism Quarterly*, *62*(2), 393–397.

Babu, Sheshu. (2019, 20 March). Darryl D'Monte: A journalist of people and environment. https://countercurrents.org/2019/03/darryl-dmonte-a-journalist-of-people-and-environment/

Bansal, S. (2018, 29 August). Learning from Malayaoam TV news channels. https://www.livemint.com/opinion/lufALAx4Pp6bdruveV2wJ/

Basu, N. (2012, 18 December). Kudankulam's nuclear holy cow. http://asu.thehoot.org/research/special-reports/kudankulam-s-nuclear-holy-cow-6497

Beder, S. (1998). *Global Spin: The corporate assault on environmentalism*. Green Books.

BEDROC. (2011, 2 May). The end of days for endosulfan. http://www.bedroc.in/?q=content/end-days-endosulfan

Beharriell, R. H. (1992). *The environment and the mass media: A study of Canadian daily newspaper editors* [PhD thesis, University of Toronto].

Bendix, J., & Liebler, C. M. (2010). Environmental degradation in Brazilian Amazonia: Perspectives in U.S. news media. *Professional Geographer*, *43*(4), 474–485.

Benthall, J. (1993). *Disasters, relief and the media*. I. B. Tauris & Co.

Bezbaruah, S. (2004, 16 February). Govt panel confirms pesticides in soft drinks, emphasises strict norms for drinking water. https://www.indiatoday.in/magazine/controversy/story/20040216-govt-panel-confirms-pesticides-in-soft-drinks-emphasises-strict-norms-for-drinking-water-790587-2004-02-16.

Bhardwaj, M. (2015, 4 November). Luxury resort in Kudremukh draws conservationists ire. *The New Indian Express*, p. 1.

Bhardwaj, M. (2018a, 20 August). It was a man-made disaster waiting to happen, say experts. *The New Indian Express*, p. 5.

Bhardwaj, M. (2018b, 30 November). Activists appeal to CM H D Kumarswamy for MM Hills temple sanitization project. *The New Indian Express*, p. 3.

Bhardwaj, M. (2019, 27 March). Heat takes a toll on this caged leopard in Bengaluru. *The New Indian Express*, p. 3.

Bhat, P. (2018, 30 July). Lawyer, activist Ajit Nayak murdered in Uttara. https://www.thequint.com/news/india/lawyer-activist-ajit-nayak-murdered-in-uttara-kannada

Bhat, P. (2019, 18 November). Hundreds protest as Kaiga nuclear plant expansion threatens Western *Ghats*. https://www.thenewsminute.com/article/hundreds-protest-kaiga-nuclear-plant-expansion-threatens-western-ghats-112497

Bidwai, P. (1987, 3 January). The Kaiga story. *Economic & Political Weekly*, *22*(1–2), 16–17.

Bijoy, C. R. (2006). Kerala's Plachimada Struggle: A narrative of water and governance rights. *Economic & Political Weekly, 41*(41), 4332–4339.

Biswas, N. B. (2009). *A content analysis of the trends of the newspaper coverage of environment in India* [PhD thesis, Assam University, Guwahati]. http://hdl. handle.net/10603/94329

Borde, R., & Bluemling, B. (2020). Representing indigenous sacred land: The case of the Niyamgiri movement in India. https://doi.org/10.1080/104557 52.2020.1730417

Bowman, J. S., & Hanaford, K. (1977). Mass media and the environment since the Earth Day. *Journalism Quarterly, 55*(l), 160–165.

Boykoff, M. (2011). *Who speaks for the climate? Making sense of media reporting on climate change.* Cambridge University Press.

Brechin, S. R., & Kempton, W. (1994). Global environmentalism: A challenge to the postmaterialism thesis? *Social Science Quarterly, 95*(2), 245–259.

Brookes, S. K., Jordan, A. G., Kimber, R. H., & Richardson, J. J. (1976). The growth of environment as a political issue in Britain. *British Journal of Political Science, 6*(2), 245–255.

Brown, J. D., Bybee, C. R., Wearden, S. T., & Straughan, D. M. (1987). Invisible power: Newspaper news sources and limits of diversity. *Journalism Quarterly, 64*(1), 44–54. https://doi.org/10.1177/107769908706400106

Bullard, R. D. (1996). Symposium: The legacy of American apartheid and environmental racism. *St. John's Journal of Legal Commentary, 9*, 445–474.

Burns, L. (2002). *Understanding journalism.* SAGE Publications.

Business Standard. (2013, 19 December). Media role in promoting human rights culture important: Balakrishnan. https://www.business-standard.com/article/news-ani/media-role-in-promoting-human-rights-culture-important-balakrishnan-113121900361_1.html

Capek, S. M. (1993) The 'environmental justice' frame: A conceptual discussion and an application. *Social Problems, 40*, 5–24.

Caramel, L. (2014, 30 June). Besieged by the rising tides of climate change, Kiribati buys land in Fiji. *The Guardian.*

Carson, R. (1962). *Silent spring.* Houghton Miffin.

Centre for Science and Environment. (2014). *Bhopal gas tragedy after 30 years.*

Chandrashekhar, A. (2017, 4 August). The anatomy of a fake Surrender: A movement against bauxite mining in Odisha's Niyamgiri Hills and the state's efforts to circumvent it. https://caravanmagazine.in/vantage/odisha-bauxite-mining-fake-surrender-niyamgiri.

Chapman, G., Kumar, K., Fraser, C., & Gaber, I. (1997). *Environmentalism and the mass media: The North-South divide.* Routledge; Chelsea Green Publishing Company.

Chapman, J. (2007). India's Narmada dams controversy. *Journal of International Communication, 13*(1), 71–85. http://dx.doi.org/10.1080/13216597.2007.9 674708

Cmiel, K. (2004). The recent history of human rights. *The American Historical Review, 109*(1), 117–155.

Coastal Digest. (2014, 30 December). Sullia shuts down protesting Kasturirangan recommendations. http://www.coastaldigest.com/sullia-shuts-down-protesting-kasturirangan-panel-recommendations?page=5

Cobb, R. W., & Elder, C. D. (1972). *Participation in American politics: The dynamics of agenda-building*. Allyn and Bacon.

Cohen, B. (1963). *The press and foreign policy*. Princeton University Press.

College of Social and Applied Human Sciences. (2019, 12 November). Gandhi, environmentalism and the World Today: Hopper lecture 2019 with Ramachandra Guha (video). https://www.youtube.com/watch?v=ptDOZ2mt6xQ

Comfort, S. E. (2020). Journalism as an advocacy tool: Negotiating boundaries of professionalism in the 20th-century american environmental movement. *Journalism & Mass Communication Quarterly, 97*(4), 1080–1100.

Commoner, B. (1971). *The closing circle*. Bantam.

Corbet, J. B. (1992). Rural and urban press coverage of wildlife: Conflict, community and bureaucracy. *Journalism Quarterly, 69*(3), 929–937.

Correa, M. S. (2010). Environmental Journalism in Brazil's elusive hotspots: The legacy of Euclydes Da Cunha. *The Journal of Environment and Development, 19*(3), 318–334.

Cotgrove, S. F., & Duff, A. (1981). Environmentalism, values land social change. *British Journal of Sociology, 32*(1), 92–110.

D'Monte, D. (1985). *Temples or tombs? Industry versus environment: Three controversies*. Centre for Science and Environment.

D'Monte, D. (2010). Foreword. In K. Acharya & N. Noronha (Eds.), *The green pen: Environmental journalism in India and South Asia* (pp. xi–xv). SAGE Publications.

D'Souza, D. (2002). *The Narmada dammed: An inquiry into the politics of development*. Penguin.

D'Souza, V. (2018, 20 August). Research by UoM two years ago predicted landslides in Kodagu. *The New Indian Express*, p. 5.

David, S. (2001, 23 July). Strange illness afflict Kerala villagers, pesticide suspected behind menace. https://www.indiatoday.in/magazine/living/story/20010723-strange-illnesses-afflict-kerala-villagers-pesticide-suspected-behind-menace-773870-2001-07-23

Davis, A. (2013). *Promotional cultures: The rise and spread of advertising, public relations, marketing and branding*. Polity Press.

Deccan Herald. (2003, 6 August). Manufacturers trash charges, seek probe, p. 1.

Deccan Herald. (2013, 14 March). Radiation from Kaiga causing cancer. https://www.deccanherald.com/content/318962/radiation-kaiga-causing-cancer.html

Deccan Herald. (2015, 9 June). Kaiga radiations not cause for cancer: Study. https://www.deccanherald.com/content/482597/kaiga-radiations-not-cause-cancer.html

Deccan Herald. (2018, 13 August). Kerala's disaster Is partly man-made, p. 10.

Deccan Herald. (2018, 21 August). Rapacious development begot Kodagu its doomsday: IISc experts, p. 5.

Deccan Herald. (2018, 23 August). Kerala Floods: Global warming in action, p. 8.

Deccan Herald. (2018, 25 August). Karnataka throws spanner, Ghats notification lapses for 3rd time, p. 1.

Deccan Herald. (2018, 25 August). Scientists try to pin down a cause for landslides, rule out quake, p. 5.

Deccan Herald. (2018, 27 August). Behind Kodagu disaster: Unabated tree felling, p. 8.

Deccan Herald. (2018, 1 December). Protest against implementation of Kasturirangan report. https://www.deccanherald.com/protest-against-implementation-705945.html

Dennis, E. E. (1991). In context: Environmentalism in the system of news. In C. L. LaMay & E. E. Dennis (Eds.), *Media and the environment* (pp. 55–66). Island Press.

Denzin, N. K. (1978). *The research act: A theoretical introduction to sociological methods.* McGraw-Hill.

Detjen, J. (1991). The traditionalist's tools (and a fistful of new ones). In C. L. LaMay & E. E. Dennis (Eds.), *Media and the environment* (pp. 91–101). Island Press.

Detjen, J. (1995). *Environmental news: Where is it going?* A talk delivered at the University of Tennessee, Knoxville on 18 September.

Devschooluea. (2016, 14 October). *Ramachandra Guha: The three waves of environmentalism in India* (Video). https://www.youtube.com/watch?v=vnKprWbTNPc&t=2471s

Dhawan, R. (2000). The wealth of nations revisited. *Seminar, 492*, 15–19.

Dogra, B. (2016). For the love of Gandhi's ideas. http://asu.thehoot.org/media-watch/regional-media/for-the-love-of-gandhis-ideas-9677

Donohue, G. A., Tichenor, P. J., & Olien, C. L. (1973). Mass media functions, knowledge and social control. *Journalism Quarterly, 50*, 652–659.

Downs, A. (1972). Up and down with ecology: the issue attention cycle. *The Public Interest, 28*(3), 38–50.

Down to Earth. (2002, 15 July). Endosulfan conspiracy. https://www.downtoearth.org.in/coverage/endosulfan-conspiracy-38732

Dunlap, R. E., & Van Liere, K. D. (1984). Commitment to the dominant social paradigm and concern for environmental quality. *Social Science Quarterly, 65*(4), 1013–1028.

Dunlap, R. E., & Scarce, R. (1990). The polls: Poll trends, environmental problems and protection. *Public Opinion Quarterly, 55*, 651–656.

Dunwoody, S., & Griffin, R. J. (1993). Journalistic strategies for reporting long-term environmental issues: A case study of three superfund sites. In A. Hansen (Ed.), *The mass media and environmental issues* (pp. 22–50). Leicester University Press.

Dutt, B. (2014). *Green wars: Dispatches from a vanishing world* (Kindle Paperwhite edition). https://www.amazon.in/Green-Wars-Dispatches-Vanishing-World-ebook/dp/B00KLBIH0S

Dutt, B., Garg, K. C., & Bhatta, A. (2013). A quantitative assessment of the articles on environmental issues published in English-language Indian dailies. *Annals of Library and Information Studies, 60*(3), 219–226.

Dutt, N. (1999, 10 August). Time out: Case for the condom. *The New Indian Express*, p. 8.

Eckholm, E. P. (1982). *Down to earth: Environment and human needs*. The International Institute for Environment and Development.

Einsiedel, E. (1988). *The Canadian press and the environment*. [Paper presentation]. Paper presented at the XVIth Conference of the International Association for Mass Communication Research, Barcelona, Spain, 24–29 July.

Einsiedel, E., & Coughlan, E. (1993). The Canadian press and the environment: Reconstructing a social reality. In A. Hansen (Ed.), *The mass media and environmental issues* (pp. 134–149). Leicester University Press.

Ekwurzel, B., Frumhoff, P. C., & McCarthy, J. (2012). Climate uncertainties and their discontents: Increasing the impact of assessments on public understanding of climate risks and choices. *Climatic Change, 108*, 791–802.

Ennals, M., & Skogly, S. (1988). Human rights and the media. In A. Eide & S. Skodgly (Eds.), *Human rights and the media* (pp. 125–135). Norwegian Institute of Human rights.

Entman, R. M. (1993). Framing: Toward clarification of a fractured paradigm. *Journal of Communication, 43*(4), 51–58.

Filler, L. (1976). *The muckrakers*. Pennsylvania State University Press.

Finnegan, W. (2020, 7 May). Environmental activism goes digital in lockdown— but could it change the movement for good? https://theconversation.com/ environmental-activism-goes-digital-in-lockdown-but-could-it-change-the- movement-for-good-137203

Fisher, C. (2015). The advocacy continuum: Toward a theory of advocacy in journalism. *Journalism, 17*(6), 677–693.

Fishman, M. (1980). *Manufacturing the news*. Random House.

Foster, J. B. (1999). *The vulnerable planet: A short economic history of the environment*. Monthly Review Press.

Foster, J. B. (2009). *The ecological revolution: Making peace with the planet*. Monthly Review Press.

Freedman, E. (2011). Environmental Journalism in Kyrgyzstan and Kazakhstan: Reporting scarce amid environmental and media problems. *Applied Environmental Education & Communication, 10*(2), 126–134.

Freeman, M. (2002). *Human rights*. Polity Press.

Friedman, S. (2015). The changing face of environmental journalism in the United States. In A. Hansen & R. Cox (Eds.), *The Routledge handbook of environment and communication* (pp. 144–157). Routledge.

Friedman, S. M. (1991). Two decades of the environmental beat. In C. L. LaMay & E. E. Dennis (Eds.), *Media and the environment* (pp. 17–28). Island Press.

Frome, M. (1998). *Green ink: An introduction to environmental journalism*. University of Utah Press.

Gadgil, M., & Guha, R. (1992). *The fissured land: An ecological history of India*. Oxford University Press.

Gadgil, M., & Guha, R. (1995). *Ecology and equity*. Penguin.

Gadgil, M., & Guha, R. (2007). Ecological conflicts and the environmental movements in India. In M. Rangarajan (Ed.), *Environmental issues in India* (pp. 85–428). Pearson.

Gadgil, M. (2018, 30 August). A people's campaign to rebuild Kerala. *The Hindu*, p. 9.

Gamson, W., & Modigliani, A. (1989). Media discourse and public opinion on nuclear power: A constructionist approach, *American Journal of Sociology, 95*(1), 1–37.

Gans, H. J. (2004). *Deciding what's news: A study of cbs evening news, nbc nightly news, newsweek and time*. Northwestern University Press.

Ghosh, S., & Thankurta, P. G. (2016). *Sue the messenger: How legal harassment by corporate is shackling reportage and undermining democracy in India*. Paranjoy.

Gianotti, Z. (2018). Ken Saro-Wiwa: A continuing struggle over oil. https://www. scu.edu/environmental-ethics/environmental-activists-heroes-and-martyrs/ ken-saro-wiwa.html

Gitlin, T. (1980). *The whole world is watching: Mass media in the making and unmaking of the new left*. University of California Press.

Goffman, E. (1974). *Frame analysis: An essay on the organization of experience*. Cambridge University Press.

Gooch, G. D. (1996). The Baltic Press and the environment: A study of the coverage of environmental problems in Estonian and Latvian newspapers 1992–93. *Geoforum, 26*(4), 429–443.

Gottlieb, R. (2005). *Forcing the spring: The transformation of the American environmental movement*. Island Press.

Greenberg, M. R., Sachman, D. B., Sandman, P. M., & Salomone, K. L. (1989). Risk, drama and geography in coverage of environmental risk by network TV. *Journalism Quarterly, 66*(2), 267–276.

Greenslade, R. (2009, 10 December). Reporting is different from journalism and it's the latter we need to protect. https://www.theguardian.com/media/ greenslade/2009/dec/10/newspapers-pressandpublishing

Gregory, R. (1972). Conservation planning and politics. *International Journal of Environmental Studies, 4*, 33–39.

Griffin, R. J. (1995). Impacts of information subsidies and community structure on local press coverage of environmental contamination. *Journalism and Mass Communication Quarterly, 72*(2), 271–284.

Grundmann, R., & Scott, M. (2014). Disputed climate science in the media: Do countries matter? *Public Understanding of Science, 23*(2), 220–235.

Guha, R. (1989). *Unquiet woods: Ecological change and peasant resistance in the Himalaya*. Oxford University Press.

Guha, R. (1992). Coming of age. *Critique, 1*(5), 23–24.

Guha, R. (2000). *Environmentalism: A global history*. Oxford University Press.

Guha, R. (2008, 27 March). The rise of fall of Indian environmentalism. https:// ramachandraguha.in/archives/the-rise-and-fall-of-indian-environmental-ism.html

Guha, R. (2014). *Environmentalism: A global history*. Penguin.

Guruvitch, M., & Levy, M. (1985). Introduction. In J. A. Anderson (Ed.), *Mass communication review yearbook 5*. SAGE Publications.

Hachten, W. P. (1992). *The world news prism*. Iowa State University.

Hall, S., Critcher, C., Jefferson, T., Clarke, J., & Roberts, B. (1978). *Policing the crisis: Mugging, the state, and law and order*. Macmillan.

Handl, G. (2012). *Declaration of the United Nations conference on the human environment* [Stockholm Declaration, 1972, and the Rio declaration on environment and development, 1992]. http://legal.un.org/avl/pdf/ha/dunche/dunche_e.pdf

Hannigan, J. (2006). *Environmental sociology*. Routledge.

Hannigan, J. A. (1995). *Environmental sociology: A social constructionist perspective*. Routledge.

Hansen, A. (1990). Socio-political values underlying media coverage of the environment. *Media Development, 37*(2), 4–6.

Hansen, A. (1991). The media and the social construction of the environment. *Media, Culture and Society, 13*, 443–458.

Hansen, A. (1993). Greenpeace and press coverage of environmental issues. In A. Hansen (Ed.), *The mass media and environmental issues* (pp. 150–178). Leicester University Press.

Hansen, A. (2010). *Environment, media and communication*. Routledge.

Hansen, A. (2011). Communication, media and environment: Towards reconnecting research on the production, content and social implications of environmental communication. *The International Communication Gazette, 73*(1–2), 7–25.

Hansen, A. (2015). Communication, media and social construction of the environment. In A. Hansen & R. Cox (Eds.), *The Routledge handbook of environment and communication* (pp. 25–38). Routledge.

Hansen, A. (2020). Sources, strategic communication, and environmental journalism. In D. B. Sachsman & J. M. Valenti (Eds.), *Routledge handbook of environmental journalism* (pp. 38–51). Routledge.

Hardin, G. (1978). The tragedy of the commons. *Science, 162*, 1241–1252.

Harrison, S. (2013). Climate change, uncertainly and risk. In S. Weintrobe (Ed.), *Engaging with climate change: Psychoanlytic and interdisciplinary perspectives* (pp. 227–238). Routledge.

Hegde, N. (2015, 12 March). Tadadiya kadala tadiya kadadalu tudita. *Prajavani*, p. 6.

Hegde, P. (2010). The Chipko and Appiko movements. In K. Acharya & F. Noronha (Eds.), *The green pen*. SAGE Publications.

Heinze, E., & Freedman, R. (2010). Public awareness of human rights: Distortions in mass media. *The International Journal of Human Rights, 14*(4), 491–523.

Herman, E. S., & Chomsky, N. (1988). *Manufacturing consent: The political economy of the mass media*. Vintage.

Hestler, A. (1973). Theoretical considerations in volume and direction of international news flow. *Gazette*, *19*(4), 239–247.

Hindustan Times. (2003, 9 August). Pepsi, Coca-Cola issue ads denying pesticides claim. https://www.hindustantimes.com/india/pepsi-coca-cola-issue-ads-denying-pesticides-claim/story-4TbF1Jj4bjbGd14hz76xKK.html

Hobsbawm, E. (1994). *The age of extremes*. Cambridge University Press.

Hochberg, L. (1980). Environmental reporting in boomtown Houston. *Columbia Journalism Review*, May/June, 71–74.

Hoffman, L. H. (2006). Is internet content different after all? A content analysis of mobilizing information in online and print newspapers. *Journalism and Mass Communication Quarterly*, *53*(1), 58–76.

Hopke, J. E. (2020). Connecting extreme heat events to climate change: Media coverage of heat waves and wildfires. *Environmental Communication*, *14*(4), 492–508. https://doi.org/10.1080/17524032.2019.1687537

Howenstine, E. (1987). Environmental reporting: shift from 1970–82. *Journalism Quarterly*, *64*(4), 842–846.

Hoynes, W., & Croteau, D. (1989). *Are you on the nightline guest list?* Fairness and Accuracy in Reporting.

Hungerford, S. E., & Lemert, J. B. (1973). Covering the environment: A new 'Afghanistanism'? *Journalism Quarterly*, *50*(3), 475–482.

Inglehart, R. (1977). *The silent revolution: Changing values and political style among western publics*. Princeton University Press.

Iqbal, M. (2021, 14 May). Twitter revenues and usage statistics (2021). https://www.businessofapps.com/data/twitter-statistics/

International Council on Human Rights Policy. (2002). *Journalism, media and the challenge of human rights reporting*.

Ismail, N. A. M. (2018, 28 August). Pravahadondige banda sullu suddiya mhapura. *Prajavani*, p. 7.

Iyengar, S. (1991). *Is anyone responsible? How television frames political issues*. University of Chicago Press.

Iyengar, S. (2010). Framing research: The next steps. In B. Schaffner & P. Sellers (Eds.), *Winning with words: The origins and impact of political framing* (pp. 185–191). Routledge.

Jackson, D. (1991). Who speaks for the land? In C. L. LaMay & E. E. Dennis (Eds.), *Media and the environment* (pp. 135–146). Island Press.

Jadhav, M. H. (2015). *A study of the coverage of environmental news in Indian mass media with particular reference to Marathi and English daily newspapers* [PhD thesis, Savithribai Phule Pune University, Pune].

Jaffrelot, C., & Ganesh, V. J. (2020, 19 December). India has to meet climate change mitigation targets, it needs to take decisive action now. https://indianexpress.com/article/opinion/columns/walk-the-green-talk-7110490/

Jarrell, M. L. (2007). *Environmental crime and the media: News coverage of petroleum refining industry violations*. LFB Scholarly Publishing LLC.

Jogesh, A., & Painter, J. (2013). Country studies: India. In J. Painter (Ed.), *Climate change in the media: Reporting risk and uncertainly* (pp. 98–107). I. B. Tauris & Co.

Joshi, S. (1999). Liberalising pollution. https://www.downtoearth.org.in/coverage/liberalising-pollution-20084

Joshi, S. (2001, 28 February). Children of endosulfan. https://www.downtoearth.org.in/coverage/children-of-endosulfan-15838https://www.downtoearth.org.in/coverage/children-of-endosulfan-15838

Joshua, A. J., Paul, A., Anooj, T. V., Narayan, B., Dheeraj, D., Tumarada, K., & Vipin, M. G. (2006). *Effects of endosulfan on human beings* [Bachelor's dissertation, NITK, Calicut]. http://www.indiaenvironmentportal.org.in/files/Effect_of_endosulfan.pdf

Kaggere, N. (2018, 21 August). Rapacious development begot Kodagu its doomsday: IISc experts. *Deccan Herald*, p. 6.

Kanathanda, M. A. (2018, 20 August). Nature hits back: Landslides, floods due to mining, tourism. *The Times of India*, p. 5.

Kannada Prabha. (2018, 19 August). Kodagu floods: Rescue operations continue, p. 8.

Kannada Prabha. (2019, 24 August). Quake did not cause the disaster, p. 1.

Kappan, R. (2020, 23 May). Dramatic drop in Uttara Kannada's forest cover: Study. https://www.deccanherald.com/state/top-karnataka-stories/dramatic-drop-in-uttara-kannada-s-forest-cover-study-840870.html

Kariel, H. G., & Rosenvall, L. A. (1984). Factors influencing international news flow. *Journalism Quarterly*, *61*(3), 509–516.

Keating, M., & Gallon, G. (1997). Three decades on the green beat. *Alternatives Journal*, *23*(1), 111–121.

Kerala Sastra Sahitya Parishad. (1984). *Science as social activism: Reports and papers on the people's science movement in India*.

Khajane, M. (2018, 22 August). Karnataka says 'no' to Kasturirangan report. *The Hindu*, p. 3.

Khanna, G. N. (1993). *Global environmental crisis and management*. Ashish Publishing House.

Khoshoo, T. N., & Moolakkattu, J. S. (2009). *Mahatma Gandhi and the environment: Analysing Gandhian environmental thought*. The Energy Resources Institute.

Killingsworth, M. J., & Palmer, J. S. (1992). *Ecospeak: Rhetoric and environmental politics in America*. Southern Illinois University Press.

King, S. (2021, 10 August). Climate report a 'clarion call' for rich nations to cut emissions: India. https://strugglerking.com/climate-report-a-clarion-call-for-rich-nations-to-cut-emissions-india-india-news/

Klein, N. (2000). *No logo*. Flamingo.

Klein, N. (2019). *On fire*. Penguin Books. Kindle Edition.

Kolappan, B. (2012, 5 March). I am not affluent enough to fund any organisation in India: German national. https://www.thehindu.com/news/national/tamil-nadu/i-am-not-affluent-enough-to-fund-any-organisation-in-india-german-national/article2961107.ece

Konikkara, A. (2018, 6 October). How social media was vital to rescue efforts during the Kerala floods. https://caravanmagazine.in/vantage

Konikkara, A. (2019, 16 March). Nearly 15 years after Coca-Cola plant shut down, Plachimada's fight for Rs. 216 crore in compensation continues. https://caravanmagazine.in/communities/coca-cola-plachimada

Koop, F. (2020). Environmental journalism in Latin America. In D. B. Sachsman & J. M. Valenti (Eds.), *Routledge handbook of environmental journalism* (pp. 283–291). Routledge.

Korse, K. (2019, 8 February). Stop monkeying around. https://www.deccanherald.com/opinion/main-article/stop-monkeying-around-717281.html

Koshy, J. (2020, 19 June). Gains from coal mine auction uncertain. https://www.thehindu.com/sci-tech/energy-and-environment/gains-from-coal-mine-auction-uncertain/article31873354.ece

Kothari, A. (1991). The Press and Jan Vikas Sangharsh Yatra. *The Economic & Political Weekly*, *26*(19), 1207–1209.

Kothari, A. (1999). An open response to Gail Omvedt's open letter to Arundhati Roy. http://www.narmada.org/debates/gail/ashish.response.html

Kothari, A. (2014, 2 January). Revisiting the legend of Niyamgiri. https://www.thehindu.com/opinion/op-ed/comment-on-niyamgiri-and-fight-between-dongria-kondh-tribal-group-and-vedanta/article6745650.ece

Kothari, A., & Patel, A. (2006). *Environment and human rights*. National Human Rights Commission.

Kovarik, B. (2020). The rise of environmental journalism in Asia, Africa and Latin America. In D. B. Sachsman & J. M. Valenti (Eds.), *Routledge handbook of environmental journalism* (pp. 52–69). Routledge.

Kraemer, R., Whiteman, G., & Banergee, B. (2013). Conflict of astroturfing in Niyamgiri: The importance of national adivasi networks in anti-corporate social movement. *Organization Studies*. https://doi.org/10.1177/0170840613479240

Kriesi, H. (1989). New social movements and the new class in the Netherlands. *American Journal of Sociology*, *94*(5), 1078–1116.

Krishna, S. (1996). *Environmental politics*. SAGE Publications.

Kulkarni, C. (2018, 28 August). After floods, plastic from relief centres a new threat. *Deccan Herald*, p. 1.

Kulkarni, M. (2014). MRPL faces massive protest from villagers for causing pollution. https://www.business-standard.com/article/companies/mrpl-faces-massive-protest-from-villagers-for-causing-pollution-114101100574_1.html.

Kumar, K. J. (1996). Mass media and environmental awareness: A research perspective. *Vritta Vidya*, April, 11–13.

Kundu, C. (2018, 20 August). Fact check: Now fake news floods Kerala. https://www.indiatoday.in-fact/check/story/kerala-floods-fake-nes-fact-1319187-2108-08-20

Kwansah-Aidoo, K. (2001). The appeal of qualitative methods to traditional agenda-setting research. *Gazette: International Journal for Communication Studies*, *63*, 521. https://doi.org/10.22230/cjc.2003v28n1a1340

Kwansah-Aidoo, K. (2003). Events that matter: Specific incidents, media coverage, and agenda-setting in a Ghanaian context. *Canadian Journal of Communication*, *28*, 43.

Lacey, C., & Longman, D. (1993). The press and public access to the environment and development debate. *The Sociological Review*, *41* (2), 207–243.

Lakoff, G. (2010). Why it matters how we frame the environment. *Environmental Communication: A Journal Nature and Culture*, *4*(1), 70–81.

Lang, G. E., & Lang, K. (1983). *The battle for public opinion: The president, the press and the polls during watergate*. Columbia University Press.

Lazarsfeld, P. F., & Merton R. K. (1948). Mass communication, popular taste and organized social action. In L. Bryson (Ed.), *The Communication of Ideas* (pp. 95–118). Harper and Row.

Leiserowitz, A., & Thaker, J. (2012). *Climate change in the Indian mind*. Yale Project on Climate Change Communication, Yale University.

Lemert, J. B. (1981). News context and the elimination of mobilizing information: An experiment. *Journalism Quarterly*, *61*(2), 243–249.

Lemert, J. B., & Larkin, J. (1979). Some reasons why mobilizing information fails to be in letters to the editor. *Journalism Quarterly*, *56*(3), 504–512.

Lemert, J. B., Mitzman, B., Seither, M., Cook, R., & Hackett, R. (1977). Journalists and mobilizing information. *Journalism Quarterly*, *54*(4), 721–726.

Lewis, M. W. (1992). *Green delusions: An environmental critique of radical environmentalism*. Duke University Press.

Lidskog, R., & Waterton, C. (2018). The anthropocene: A narrative in the making. In M. Bostrom & D. J. Davidson (Eds.), *Environment and society: Concepts and challenges* (pp. 25–46). Palgrave Macmillan.

Lippmann, W. (1922). *Public opinion*. Macmillan.

Lowe, P., & Morrison, D. (1984). Bad news or good news: Environmental politics and the mass media. *The Sociological Review*, *32*(1), 75–90.

Lytle, M. H. (2007). *The gentle subversive: Rachel Carson, silent spring and the rise of the environmental movement*. Oxford University Press.

Maitra, S. (2014). Social-conscience of post-linearization urban India. In S. Batabyal (Ed.), *Environment, politics and activism: The role of media* (pp. 59–77). Routledge.

Martinez-Alier, J. (2002). *The environmentalism of the poor: A study of ecological conflicts and valuation*. Edward Elgar.

Mathur, A. (2006). (Ed.). *The Indian media: Illusion, delusion and reality*. Rupa & Co.

Mathur, H. M. (2013). *Displacement and resettlement in India: The human cost of development*. Routledge.

Mattelart, A. (1980). *Mass media, ideologies and the revolutionary movement*. The Harvest Press.

Mazoomdar, J. (2006). Media and environmental issues. In A. R. Mathur (Ed.), *The Indian media: Illusion, delusion and reality* (pp. 150–165). Rupa & Co.

McCallum, D. B. (1991). Communicating about environmental risks: How the public uses and perceives information sources. *Health Education Quarterly, 18*(3), 349–361.

McClellen, S. (1992). Gearing up for green coverage. *Broadcasting, 122*(22), 14–16.

McCleod, J. M., Becker, L. B., & Byrnes, J. E. (1974). Another look at the agenda setting function of the press. *Communication Research, 1*, 14–21.

McClure, R. D., & Peterson, T. E. (1978). Setting the political agenda: Print vs network. *Journal of Communication, 26*, 23–28.

McCombs M. E., & Shaw, D. L. (1972). The agenda setting function of mass media. *Public Opinion Quarterly, 36*, 172–187.

McQuail, D. (1994). *Mass communication theory*. SAGE Publications.

McQuail, D. (2005). *McQuail's mass communication theory*. SAGE Publications.

Menon, M. (1999, 7 August). Taking a liberal view: Justice beyond the Supreme Court. *Deccan Herald*, p. 10.

Mercado, M., & Chavez, M. (2020). Environmental journalism in Spain. In D. B. Sachsman & J. M. Valenti (Eds.), *Routledge handbook of environmental journalism* (pp. 234–245). Routledge.

Metzl, J. F. (1996). Information technology and human rights. *Human Rights Quarterly, 18*(4), 705–746. https://doi.org/10.1353/hrq.1996.0045

Miller, N. (2001). *Environmental politics: Interest groups, the media, and the making of policy*. Taylor & Francis.

Mishra, M. (2020). Environmental journalism in India: Past, present and future. In D. B. Sachsman & J. M. Valenti (Eds.), *Routledge handbook of environmental journalism* (pp. 291–305). Routledge.

Misra, S. S., & Joshi, S. (2017, 13 January). Tracking decades-long endosulfan tragedy in Kerala. https://www.downtoearth.org.in/coverage/health/for-a-good-night-s-sleep-57314

Mohan, N. (2018, 30 August). Kerala flood coverage: Malayalam news channels set an example in the media world. https://www.exchange4media.com/media-tv-news/kerala-flood-coveragemalayalam-news-channels-set-an-example-in-the-media-world-91804.html

Mohan, R. (2019, 4 October). Madhya Pradesh villagers displaced by Sardar Sarovar Dam wait in tin sheds for new life. https://www.thehindu.com/society/madhya-pradesh-villagers-displaced-by-sardar-sarovar-dam-wait-in-tin-sheds-for-new-life/article29596657.ece

Mohanty, R. (1995). *Environmental movement in the context of development: A sociological study of the movement against the Narmada valley project* [Unpublished PhD thesis, Jawaharlal Nehru University].

Moser, S. C., & Dilling, L. (2007). *Creating a climate for change: Communication climate change and facilitating social change.* Cambridge University Press.

Motta, B. H. (2020). The education needs of future environmental journalists. In D. B. Sachsman & J. M. Valenti (Eds.), *Routledge handbook of environmental journalism* (pp. 113–122). Routledge.

Moudgal, S. (2018, 23 August). Kodagu mayhem turns focus back on Kasturirangan report. *The Times of India*, p. 6.

Nadimpally, S., Venkatachalam, D., & Fatima, A. (2019). Eviction of tribals: Forced displacement and its links with poor health. https://thewire.in/rights/supreme-court-eviction-tribals-displacement

Narain, S. (2003, 31 August). We the regulators. https://www.downtoearth.org.in/blog/we-the-regulators-13397

Narain, S. (Ed.). (2015). *Environmental history reader.* Centre for Science and Environment.

Narain, S. (2017). *Conflicts of interest: My journey through India's green movement.* Penguin Random House India.

Neelakantan, A. (2018, 26 August). Destructive catharsis of restoration. *The New Indian Express*, p. 3.

Nepal, P. (2009). How movements move? Evaluating the role of ideology and leadership in environmental dynamics in India with special reference to the Narmada Bachao Andolan. *Hydro Nepal Journal of Water Energy and Environment*, *4*(4), 24–29.

Nerli, R. B., & Ghagane, S. C. (2018, 2 November). Cancer incidence around Karwar (Kaiga Nuclear Plant) needs further research rather than spread false information. http://www. jscisociety.com

Neuzil, M. (1996). *Mass media and environmental conflict: America's green crusades.* SAGE Publications.

Neuzil, M. (2008). *The environment and the press: From adventure writing to advocacy.* Northwestern University Press.

Newslaundry. (2019, 8 August). *Media rumble: Climate change in Indian media* (Video). https://www.youtube.com/watch?v=Yqs8WD1i5Gw&t=134s

Nicodemus, D. M. (2010). Mobilizing information: Local news and the formation of a viable political community. *Political Communication*, *21*(2), 161–176. https://doi.org/10.1080/10584600490443868

Ninen, S. (2005, 19 June). The Plachimada saga. *The Hindu*, p. 12.

Nirmala, T. (2019). *Newspaper coverage of environmental issues in Tamil Nadu* [PhD thesis, Anna University, Chennai]. http://hdl.handle.net/10603/303415

Nisbet, M. C., & Newman, T. P. (2015). Framing, the media, and environmental communication. In A. Hansen & R. Cox (Eds.), *The Routledge handbook of environment and communication* (pp. 325–338). Routledge.

Noelle-Neumann, E. (1974). The spiral of silence: A theory of public opinion. *Journal of Communication*, *24*, 43–51.

Nwankwo, V. C. (2011). *The role of media in promoting human rights: An analysis of the BBC documentary 'Chocolate: The bitter truth'* [Master's thesis, Roehampton

University]. https://munin.uit.no/bitstream/handle/10037/3500/thesis. pdf?sequence=1&isAllowed=y

Okafor, F. U. (2006). From praxis to theory: A discourse on the philosophy of African law. *The Cambrian Law Review, 37*, 37–48.

Olausson, U. (2009). Global warming, global responsibility? Media frames of collective action and scientific certainty. *Public Understanding of Science, 18*(4), 421–436.

Omvedt, G. (1999). An open letter to Arundhati Roy. http://www.narmada.org/debates/gail/gail.open.letter.html

Omvedt, G. (2004). Struggle against dam or struggle for water? Environmental movements and the state. In R. Vora & S. Palshikar (Eds.), *Indian democracy: meanings and practices.* SAGE Publications.

Oreskes, N., & Conway, E. M. (2010). *Merchants of doubt.* Bloomsbury Press.

Outlook. (2017, 8 December). NBA opposes every developmental project in India: KVIC Chief alleges in court. https://www.outlookindia.com/newsscroll/nba-opposes-every-developmental-project-in-india-kvic-chief-alleges-in-court/1205340

Ovsiovitch, J. S. (1993). Human rights coverage in the media: A quantitative content analysis. http://search.proquest.com/docview/304046052

Padel, F. (2014, 14 July). The Niyamgiri movement as a landmark of democratic process. https://vikalpsangam.org/article/the-niyamgiri-movement-as-a-landmark-of-democratic-process/

Padhi, R., & Negi, R. S. (2018, 6 January). Kalingnagar, where development is threatening a way of life. https://thewire.in/rights/kalinganagar-development-threatening-way-life

Padma, T. V. (2018, 3 September). Mining and dams exacerbated devastating Kerala floods. https://www.nature.com/articles/d41586-018-06145-2

Painter, J. (2013). *Climate change in the media: Reporting risk and uncertainly.* I. B. Tauris & Co.

Painter, J., & Ashe, T. (2012). Cross-national comparison of the presence of climate scepticism in the print media in six countries, 2007–10. *Environmental Research Letters, 7*(4), 1–8.

Painter, J., & Gavin, N. T. (2015). Climate skepticism in British newspapers, 2007–2011. *Environmental Communication,* 1–21.

Painter, J., Osakab, S., Ettingerb, J., & Waltonc, P. (2020). Blaming climate change? How Indian mainstream media covered two extreme weather events in 2015. *Global Environmental Change, 63*(2020), 102119. https://doi.org/10.1016/j.gloenvcha.2020.102119

Pandey, K. (2019, 9 April). Finally, both BJP and Congress manifestos talk climate change. https://www.downtoearth.org.in/news/general-elections-2019/finally-both-bjp-and-congress-manifestos-talk-climate-change-63913

Parveen, H. (2016). A study of the coverage of environment and sustainable development in Indian English dailies. *IMS Manthan-The Journal of Innovations, 6*(2), 80–86.

Patel, J. (1995). *Narmada project.* Evictions and Displacement in South Asia: Towards Pre-emptive Action (EDSA:TPA).

Patel, J. (2018, 21 August). Republic TV, NY Times share Kodagu, Karnataka landslide as that from Kerala. https://www.altnews.in/republic-tv-ny-times-share-kodagu-karnataka-landslide-as-that-from-kerala/

Patkar, M., & Sangvai, S. (2006). The Narmada movement and the media: The efforts, the experience and hope. In A. Mathur (Ed.), *The Indian media: Illusion, delusion and reality* (pp. 166–180). Rupa & Co.

Phadke, M. (2018, 2 August). How a small protest in Thoothukudi turned into an explosive cocktail. https://theprint.in/india/governance/how-a-small-protest-in-tamil-nadu-turned-into-an-explosive-cocktail/90850/

Phillips, D. (2019, 2 January). Jair Bolsonaro launches assault on Amazon rainforest protections. https://www.theguardian.com/world/2019/jan/02/brazil-jair-bolsonaro-amazon-rainforest-protections

Pinto, S. (2014, 3 April). Western Ghats manifesto seeks public hearings on Gadgil, Kasturirangan reports to avoid politicization. *The Times of India,* p. 3.

Planning Commission of India. (1975). *The Fourth Five-Year Plan.*

Pohjenen, M. (2014). Tracking the long tail of climate change. In S. Batabyal (Ed.). *Environment, politics and activism: The role of media* (pp. 39–56). Routledge.

Poornananda, D. S. (2008). Claims-makers and frames of environmental news in the Indian Press. *Mass Communicator, 2*(3), 31–40.

Poornananda, D. S. (2017). Development-induced displacement and the print media in Karnataka. *Journals of Media and Social Development, 5*(1), 5–44.

Powers, M. (2018). *NGOs as newsmakers.* Columbia University Press.

Prabhash, J. (2005). Mediated rights: Media, women and human rights in India. *The Indian Journal of Political Science, 66*(1), 53–74.

Prajavani. (2018, 14 August). Demand for Kerala-type revised Kasturirangan report, p. 3.

Prajavani. (2018, 22 August). Massive rains wrought by deforestation, p. 5.

Prajavani. (2018, 25 August). Opposition to Kasturirangan report: Ruckus in front of the Minister, p. 5.

Prajavani. (2018, 28 August). No Politics: Listen to scientists, p. 6.

Prakash, C. G. (1997, 12 February). Parisara Matthu Rajakarana. *Prajavani,* p. 5.

Prasad, P. (2019, 12 December). 1.09 crore trees cut in five years: Environment ministry in Parliament. https://www.news247plus.com/post.php?id=2695&title=109-crore-trees-cut-in-last-five-years-Environment-Ministry-in-Parliament

Prasannarajan, S. (1999a, 7 August). Narmada is elsewhere: When the valley waited for the river child. *The New Indian Express,* p. 1.

Prasannarajan, S. (1999b, 7 August). Narmada is elsewhere: When the valley waited for the river child. *The New Indian Express,* p. 3.

Press Council of India. (2007). *Annual report (April 01, 2007 to March 31, 2008).* http://presscouncil.nic.in/OldWebsite/AR_COMPENDIUM/Annual%20-Report-07-08.pdf

Ragi Kana. (2018, 28 June). Was Gandhi an environmentalist? Mr. Ramachandra Guha-Part 3 (Video). https://www.youtube.com/watch?v=V7oVoWe3qK0

Rai, M. (1999). *Parisara Chaluvalligalu*. Prasaranga, Kannada University.

Raj, S. R. (2017). People's movement in Odisha: An assessment. *Indian Journal of Public Administration, 63*(2), 265–283.

Rajagopalan, P. K. (2017). Kasanur Forest Disease. https://ncdc.gov.in/WriteReadData/linkimages/File683.pdf.

Rajan, S. R. (2014). A history of environmental justice in India. *Environmental Justice, 7*(5),111–121. https://doi.org/10.1089/env.2014.7502

Rakesh, K. M. (2018, 14 August). 'Do not donate' hate messages in Kerala. *The Telegraph*. https://www.telegraphindia.com/india/do-not-donate-hate-messages-in-kerala/cid/1310177

Ramesh, R. (2004, 4 February). Soft-drink giants accused over pesticides. https://www.theguardian.com/world/2004/feb/05/india.randeepramesh

Rana, S. (2020, 27 March). Niyamgiri movement: Questioning the narrative of development politics. https://feminisminindia.com/2020/03/27/niyamgiri-movement-questioning-narrative-developmental-politics/

Rao, M. (2018, 23 August). Kodagu landslips a result of natural and man-made causes. *The Hindu*, p. 3.

Rath, P. K. (2019). *Media and mass movements role of print media case study of mass protest movements about POSCO Niyamgiri and Utkal alumina* [PhD thesis, Central University of Orissa]. http://hdl.handle.net/10603/288936

Ray, K. (2018a, 25 August). India tops the world in landslide deaths. *Deccan Herald*, p. 8.

Ray, K. (2018b, 27 August). Karnataka throws spanner, Ghats notification lapses for 3rd time. *Deccan Herald*, p. 1.

Rebello, R. L. (2018). Sarvodaya Press Service: Development and social feature service. www. doccentre.net/docsweb/RWH-dw/sps_indore.doc

Redclift, M. (1986). Redefining the environmental issues in the south. In J. Sestron (Ed.), *Red and green: The new politics of the environment*. Pluto Press.

Reese, S. (1990). The news paradigm and the ideology of objectivity: A socialist at the *Wall Street Journal*. *Critical Studies in Mass Communication, 7*, 390–409.

Reinert, M. (2020). Environmental journalism in France at a turning point. In D. B. Sachsman & J. M. Valenti (Eds.), *Routledge handbook of environmental journalism* (pp. 203–210). Routledge.

Revkin, A. (1990, 17 June). Chiko Mendes: The man who tried to save the Amazon rain forest. https://www.latimes.com/archives/la-xpm-1990-06-17-op-385-story.html

Roberts, J., Pellow, D., & Mohai, P. (2018). Environmental justice. In M. Bostrom & D. J. Davison (Eds.), *Environment and society: Concepts and challenges* (pp. 233–256). Palgrave Macmillan.

Rodrigues, G. (2007). *Walking the forest with Chico Mendes*. University of Texas Press.

Rosenbaum, W. A. (2019). *Environmental politics and policy.* SAGE Publications.

Rosenblum, M. (1979). *Coups and earthquakes: Reporting the world for america.* Harper & Row.

Roshco, B. (1975). *Newsmaking.* University of Chicago Press.

Roy, A. (1999). The greater common good: The human cost of big dams. *Frontline, 16*(11), 4–29.

Roy, A. (2014). *Capitalism: A ghost story.* Haymarket Books.

Roy, B. (2021, 7 January). The paradox of India's energy transition. https://www.thehindubusinessline.com/opinion/the-paradox-of-indias-energy-transition/article33521959.ece

Rubin, C. T. (1994). *The greed crusade: rethinking the roots of environmentalism.* Free Press.

Rubin, D. M., & Sachs, D. P. (Eds.). (1973). *Mass media and the environment.* Praeger.

Sachsman, D. B., & Valenty, J. M. (2015). Environmental reporters. In A. Hansen & R. Cox (Eds.), *The Routledge handbook of environment and communication* (pp. 154–157). Routledge.

Sadashiva, M. S. (2018, 15 December). Karwar says no to expansion of Kaiga atomic power plant. https://www.deccanherald.com/state/karwar-says-no-proposed-708408.html

Sahay, A. (2020, 3 December). Bhopal gas tragedy: 36 years on, survivors still wait for justice. https://www.hindustantimes.com/india-news/36th-bhopal-gas-tragedy-anniversary-mere-lip-service-ritual-says-survivor/story-xZh0C-UOb5181D0V9jOm1aK.html

Sahu, P. R. (2017a, 6 May). Battle for Niyamgiri: Odisha police story on Adivasi girl accused of being Maoist does not add up. https://scroll.in/article/836756/battle-for-niyamgiri-odisha-polices-story-on-adivasi-girl-accused-of-being-maoist-does-not-add-up

Sahu, P. R. (2017b, 22 March). As POSCO exits steel project, Odisha is left with thousands of felled trees and lost livelihoods. https://scroll.in/article/832463/as-posco-exits-steel-project-odisha-is-left-with-thousands-of-felled-trees-and-broken-job-promises

Samyukta Karnataka. (2018, 18 August). Karnataka–Kerala: The curse of rain, p. 6.

Samyukta Karnataka. (2018, 26 August). An Appeal to mother Cauvery, p. 13.

Sandman, P. M., Sachsman, D. B., Greenberg., & Gochfeld, M. (1987). *Environmental risk and the press.* Transaction Books.

Sangomla, A. (2018, 28 May). After a 23 year long battle, Tamil Nadu's Sterlite plant finally shuts down. https://www.downtoearth.org.in/news/governance/tamil-nadu-govt-orders-permanent-closure-of-sterlite-plant-in-tuticorin-60676

Sardesai, R. (2004). Drawing the Ram-rekha. *Seminar, 533.* http://www.india-seminar.com/2004/533/533%20rajdeep%20sardesai.htm

Sarkar, S. (2010). Land acquisition for the railways in Bengal, 1850–62. *Studies in History*, *26*(2), 103–142.

Save the Western Ghats Movement (k.n.).Report of the Save the Western Ghats Movement and Conference. http://www.savethewesternghats.org/pdfs/SWG%20Movement%201987-88%20Official%20handbook.pdf

Saxena, S. (2013, 27 December). 25 years after death, Chico Mendes lives in to save Amazon. https://www.downtoearth.org.in/news/-25-years-after-death-chico-mendes-lives-in-to-save-amazon-43116

Scheufele, D. A., & Tewksbury, D. (2007). Framing, agenda setting, and priming: The evolution of three media effects models. *Journal of Communication*, *57*(1), 9–20.

Schimmel, N. (2009). Media accountability to investigate human rights violations. *A Journal of Social Justice*, *21*(4), 442–447.

Schmid-Petri, H., Adam, S., Schmucki, I. & Häussler, T. (2017). A changing climate of skepticism? The factors shaping climate change coverage in the US press. *Public Understanding of Science*, *26*(4), 402–417.

Schoenfeld, A. C. (1980). Newspapers and environment today. *Journalism Quarterly*, *57*(3), 456–462.

Schoenfeld, A. C., Meier, R., & Griffin, R. (1979). Constructing a social problem: The press and the environment. *Social Problems*, *27*(1), 54–60.

Scott, A. (1990). *Ideology and the new social movements*. Unwin Hyman.

Seetharaman, G. (2018, 18 April). The story of one of the biggest land conflicts. No mine now, but is it all fine in Niyamgiri. https://economictimes.indiatimes.com/vedanta-ltd/stocks/companyid-13111.cms

Sengupta, A. (2018). Narmada Bachao Andolona: The longest living Gandhian satyagraha. https://www.nationalheraldindia.com/opinion/the-longest-gandhian-satyagraha-over-narmada

Sethi, A., & Jebraj, P. (2011, 11 December). High court clearance for DB power coal mine in Chhattisgarh. https://www.thehindu.com/news/national/High-Court-stays-clearance-for-DB-power-coal-mine-in-Chhattisgarh/article13422969.ecepower-coal-mine-in-Chhattisgarh/article13422969.ece

Sethi, M. (2015). *Development in the era of globalization*. Himanshu.

Sethunath, K. P. (2019, 11 April). Greens for Western Ghats to be south India water tower. https://www.deccanchronicle.com/nation/current-affairs/110419/greens-for-western-ghats-to-be-south-india-water-tower.html

Shankar, U., & Bindal, S. (2012). Right to environment and right to development: A judicial conundrum. *Christ University Law Journal*, *1*(1), 49–68.

Sharma, K. (2002, 9 April). Gujarat and freedom of the press. *The Hindu*, p. 10.

Sharma, K. (2019, 19 March). D'Monte, a passionate journalist who lived by his convictions, left a lasting legacy. https://indianexpress.com/article/opinion/columns/goodbye-darryl-5632792

Sharma, P. (2018). Kodagu's tragedy. *Frontline*, *35*(18). https://frontline.thehindu.com/cover-story/article24801277.ece

Sharma, S. (2014a). Politics of body spectacle. In S. Batabyal (Ed.), *Environment, politics and activism: The role of media* (pp. 114–133). Routledge.

Sharma, S. (2014b). Indian media and the struggle for justice in Bhopal. *Social Justice, 1/2*, 135–136. https://www.jstor.org/stable/24361595

Shaw, D. L., & McCombs (1977). *The emergence of American political issues: The agenda setting function of the press.* West Publishing Company.

Shiva, V. (2004, 13 May). Building water democracy: People's victory against Coca-Cola in Plachimada. https://zcomm.org/zcommentary/building-water-democracy-peoples-victory-against-coca-cola-in-plachimada-by-vandana2-shiva/

Shrinivasa, M. (2018, 1 September). Was Kodagu disaster natural or man-made. *The Times of India*, p. 3.

Sigal, L. V. (1973). *Reporters and officials: The organisation and politics of news-making.* Heath.

Singh, A. (2017, 31 January). Punjab has a cancer train. Few political parties talk of the disease. https://www.ndtv.com/india-news/punjab-has-a-cancer-train-few-political-parties-talk-of-the-disease-1654354

Singh, B. K. (2019, 27 August). Behind Kodagu disaster: Unabated tree felling. *Deccan Herald*, p. 8.

Singh, R. K. (2021, 26 March). India to double down on coal projects amid climate warnings. https://www.bloombergquint.com/business/india-to-double-down-on-coal-projects-amid-climate-warnings

Singh, V. (2018, 23 April). Odisha's Niyamgiri Hills and its people are still under threat. https://thewire.in/rights/odishas-niyamgiri-hills-and-its-people-are-still-under-threat

Singh, V. (2021, 8 February). Green revolution and a harvest of cancer. https://www.dailypioneer.com/2021/state-editions/green-revolution-and-a-harvest-of-cancer.html

Sinha, A. (2018, 20 August). Kerala tragedy partly man made: Madhav Gadgil, expert who headed Western Ghats report. https://indianexpress.com/article/india/kerala-floods-rains-disaster-western-ghats-report-5314873/

Sitaraman, S. (1996, 15 April). By book or by crook. https://www.downtoearth.org.in/coverage/by-book-or-by-crook-25719

Smith, H. W. (1992). *Strategies of social research.* Holt, Rinehert and Winston.

Smith, J. (2006). *What do greens believe?* Granta Books.

Snells, G. F. (2009, 8 December). Reporting is now a commodity but journalism isn't. https://hightalk.wordpress.com/2009/12/08/reporting-is-now-a-commodity-but-journalism-isnt/

Soley, L. C. (1992). *The news shapers: The sources who explain the news.* Praeger.

Soroka, S. N. (2002). Issue attributes and agenda-setting by media, the public, and policymakers in Canada. *International Journal of Public Opinion Research, 14*(3), 264–285.

Spuy, A. V. D. (2008). Mirror, mirror upon the wall: Is reality reflected at all? https://globalmedia.journals.ac.za/pub/article/viewFile/38/73

Sreejith, K. (2014, 9 June). I lost but Palakkad's people won. https://magazine. outlookindia.com/story/i-lost-but-palakkads-people-won/290915

Sridhar, A. (2021). Dignifying Indian environmentalism. *Seminar, 744,* 15–18.

Stevenson, R. L., & Cole, R. R. (1982). Some thoughts on the future content analysis. *Gazette, 30,* 167–176.

Stocking, H., & Leonard, J. P. (1990). The greening of the press. *Columbia Journalism Review, 29,* 37–44.

Subramanian, S. (2015). India's war on Greenpeace. https://www.theguardian. com/world/2015/aug/11/indias-war-on-greenpeace.

Sudhir, T. S. (2018, 28 August). Kerala's news channels show hot to cover a disaster responsibly. https://qz.com/india/1364531/kerala-floods-asianet-manorama-beat-english-news-channels/

Taleb, B. A. (2004). *The bewildered herd: Media coverage of international conflicts and public opinion.* iUniverse Inc.

Tankovska, H. (2021, 4 May). Twitter-statistics & facts. https://www.statista. com/topics/737/twitter/

Taylor, N., & Nathan, S. (2002). How science contributes to environmental reporting in British newspapers: A case study of the reporting of the global warming and climate change. *The Environmentalist, 22,* 325–331.TED. (2020, 18 August). *Here's how to use social media to combat climate change | Gia Chinchilla* (Video). https://www.youtube.com/watch?v=o8UL3zeZ-bM

Tharoor, S. (2018, 15 August). The flood situation here in Kerala is really bad. The national media coverage has been grossly inadequate compared to the (Image attached). https://twitter.com/shashitharoor/status/1029728827755 257856?lang=en

Thayil, S. (1999a, 9 August). Narmada Bachao Andolan: A hefty, single-minded bull. The *New Indian Express,* p. 9.

Thayil, S. (1999b, 10 August). When the Baba met 'Saraswati' on the banks of river Narmada. *The New Indian Express,* p. 9.

Thayil, S. (1999c, 11 August). The many layers to truth in the tally for the valley. *The New Indian Express,* p. 9.

Thayil, S. (1999d, 30 July). All set for NBA's 'Rally for the Valley' in Indore. *The New Indian Express,* p. 9.

The Economic Times. (2017, 18 September). The Narmada Valley project marches on. https://economictimes.indiatimes.com/blogs/et-editorials/the-narmada-valley-project-marches-on/

The Economic Times. (2020, 18 December). Over 4.5 crore people in India will be forced to migrate from homes by 250 due to climate disaster. https:// economictimes.indiatimes.com/news/politics-and-nation/over-4-5-crore-people-in-india-will-be-forced-to-migrate-from-homes-by-2050-due-to-climate-disasters/articleshow/79797117.cms

The Hindu. (2003, 7 August). No more soft drinks in parliament. https://www. thehindu.com/todays-paper/no-more-soft-drinks-in-parliament/arti-cle27789164.ece

The Hindu. (2013, 16 November). Protest against Kasturirangan report turns violent in Kottiyur. https://www.thehindu.com/news/national/kerala/protest-against-kasturirangan-report-turns-violent-in-kottiyur/article5354804.ece

The Hindu. (2018, 1 June). MRPL discharging chemical into water body, say activists. https://www.thehindu.com/news/cities/Mangalore/mrpl-discharging-chemical-into-water-body-say-activists/article24050985.ece

The Hindu. (2018, 9 August). Welcome Clouds, p. 8.

The Hindu. (2018, 17 August). Rail link to Kodagu, Thalasserry: Projects not dropped, say officials, p. 2.

The Hindu. (2018, 19 August). Halt land conversion in the Western Ghats immediately, p. 8.

The Hindu. (2018, 25 August). Trouble in the hills: On Western Ghats ecology, p. 8.

The Hindu. (2021, 18 January). Climate urgency: India and the world. https://www.thehindu.com/brandhub/climate-urgency-india-and-the-world/article33600024.ece.

Thekaekara, T. (2015, 17 July). Blindly ahead. *The Hindu BusinessLine*, p. 8.

The New Indian Express. (1999, 9 August). Postcards from the edge of the river: Dazed and confused, p. 9.

The New Indian Express. (1999, 9 August). Postcards from the edge of the river: Trivial pursuit, p. 9.

The New Indian Express. (2003, 8 August). Pesticide residues: Pepsi, Coke sales hit, p. 3.

The New Indian Express. (2018, 21 June). Cancer cases up near Kaiga plant: Study. https://www.newindianexpress.com/states/karnataka/2018/jun/21/cancer-cases-up-near-kaiga-plant-study-1831251.html

The New Indian Express. (2018, 17 August). Mysore-Kodagu railway line gets green signal, p. 2.

The New Indian Express. (2018, 22 August). Environmentalists decode reasons behind flood in Kodagu, Kerala, p. 2.

The New Indian Express. (2018, 23 August). Landslides, floods in Kodagu: A wake-up call, p. 8.

The New Indian Express. (2018, 31 August). Kodagu floods natural: Geologist, p. 2.

The New Indian Express. (2020, 20 December). Kasturirangan report: It's friction between eco-balance, livelihood. https://www.newindianexpress.com/states/karnataka/2020/dec/20/kasturirangan-report-its-friction-between-eco-balance-livelihood-2238721.html

The Pioneer. (2019, 27 April). Activists urge Delhiites to think about environment while casting vote https://www.dailypioneer.com/2019/state-editions/activists-urge-delhiites-to-think-about-environment-while-casting-votes.html.

The Times of India. (2003, 13 August). Coke, Pepsi sales hit due to pesticide allegations. https://timesofindia.indiatimes.com/business/india-business/coke-pepsi-sales-hit-due-to-pesticide-allegations/articleshow/128768.cms

The Times of India. (2010, 16 June). Cancer on the rise in Kaiga. https://timesofin-dia.indiatimes.com/city/hubballi/cancer-on-the-rise-in-kaiga-area/article-show/6055749.cms

The Times of India. (2012, 8 January). Cancer expert allays fears of villagers near Kaiga https://timesofindia.indiatimes.com/city/hubballi/cancer-expert-allays-fears-of-villagers-near-kaiga/articleshow/11408568.cms

The Times of India. (2018, 9 July). Defamation charges framed against Medha Patkar. https://timesofindia.indiatimes.com/india/defamation-charges-framed-against-medha-patkar/articleshow/64919062.cms

The Times of India. (2018, 20 August). Nature hits back: Landslides, floods due to mining, tourism, p. 4.

The Times of India. (2018, 20 August). Kerala's sorrow, p. 10.

The Times of India. (2018, 23 August). Misplaced pride: Centre must accept foreign assistance to Kerala. Aiding people in distress knows no borders, p.10.

The Times of India. (2018, 23 August). Kodagu mayhem turns focus back on Kasturirangan report, p. 6.

The Times of India. (2018, 2 September). What triggered floods, landslides in Kodagu—quake or cloudbursts? p.4.

The Times of India. (2021, 17 April). Most environmental cases in SC against govts, finds thinktank. https://timesofindia.indiatimes.com/city/delhi/most-environmental-cases-in-sc-against-govts-finds-thinktank/article-show/82108560.cms

The Tribune. (2003, 6 August). *Soft drink giants refute findings.* https://www.tribuneindia.com/2003/20030806/main3.htm

Thomas, V. (2018, 21 August). Kerala floods: global warming in action. *Deccan Herald*, p. 8.

Thottam, J. (2010, 13 February). Echoes of *Avatar*: Is a tribe in India the real-life na'vi? http://content.time.com/time/world/article/0,8599,1964063,00.html

Thurow, L. (1980). *The zero sum society: Distribution and possibilities for economic change.* Basic Books.

Tichenor, P. J., Donohue, G. A., Olien, C. N., & Bovers, J. K. (1971). Environment and public opinion. *Journal of Environmental Education, 2,* 38–43.

Triandafyllidou, A. (1996). Green corruption in the Italian press: Does political culture matter? *European Journal of Communication, 11*(3), 371–391.

Tripathi, S., & Singh, N. K. (1988, 31 October). Narmada valley development project controversy acquires a sharper edge. https://www.indiatoday.in/maga-zine/special-report/story/19881031-narmada-valley-development-project-controversy-acquires-a-sharper-edge-797826-1988-10-31

Tuchman, G. (1972). Objectivity as strategic ritual. An examination of newmen's notion of objectivity. *American Journal of Sociology, 77*(4), 660–679.

Tuchman, G. (1973). Making news by doing work: Routinising the unexpected. *American Journal of Sociology, 79*(1), 110–131.

Tuchman, G. (1978). *Making news. A study in the construction of reality*. The Free Press.

Tumbe, C. (2018). *India moving: A history of migration*. Penguin.

Udaykumar, S. P. (2012, 12 March). The Koodankulam struggle and the 'foreign hand'. *Economic & Political Weekly*, *47*(12). https://www.epw.in/journal/2012/12/commentary/koodankulam-struggle-and-foreign-hand.html?destination=node/126302.

Ukpong, C. (2018, 10 November). Remembering Ken Saro-Wiwa 23 year after brutal killing by Nigerian govt. https://www.premiumtimesng.com/features-and-interviews/295004

UNESCO. (1999, 24 September). Declaration of Bizkaia on the right to the environment. https://unesdoc.unesco.org/ark:/48223/pf0000117321

Valiverronen, E. (1992). *Environmental controversies: The role of experts and legitimation of science in the debate on forest damages in Finland*. Paper presented to IAMCR Conference, 16–21 August, Sao Paulo, Brazil.

Vardhan, A. (2015, 18 June). Seductions of the green savior. http://asu.thehoot.org/media-practice/seductions-of-the-green-saviour-8389

Varma, K. (1988). The myth of editor's freedom. *Countermedia*, *1*(5), 17–19.

Varna, M. (2020). *Media and environmental issues in the western ghats* [Unpublished PhD thesis, Kuvempu University].

Vasuki, K. (2019). Kaiga nuclear power plant expansion sparks stir. https://www.dailypioneer.com/2019/india/kaiga-nuclear-power-plant-expansion-sparks-stir.html.

Venkat, V. (2016, 10 August). The story of Kudankulam: From 1988 to 2016. *The Hindu*, p. 11.

Verma, M. K. (2016). Development induced displacement, SEZs and the state of farmers in India: Some insights from recent experiences. *NHEC Journal*, *15*, 24–48. https://nhrc.nic.in/sites/default/files/nhrc_journal_2016.pdf

Vijaya Karnataka. (2018, 19 August). What do experts say on Kerala–Kodagu disaster, p. 5.

Vijaya Karnataka. (2018, 21 August). Did man's meddling with nature cause Kodagu's disaster? p. 2.

Vijaya Karnataka. (2018, 23 August). Should Kodavas live in darkness even now, p. 2.

Vijaya Karnataka. (2018, 28 August). No future for the five states if the Western Ghats are not protected, p. 3.

Wang, Z. (1991). The Chinese mass media: Environmental coverage. *Interaction*, *9* (1–2), 94–118.

Watts, J. (2018, 9 March). UN moves towards recognizing the human right to a healthy environment. *The Guardian*. https://www.theguardian.com/environment/2018/mar/09/

Weaver, D. H., & Wilhoit, G. C. (1986). *The American journalist: A portrait of US news people and their work*. Indiana University Press.

Weber, T. (1987). *Hugging the trees: The story of the Chipko movement.* Viking-Penguin Inc.

Whitney, D. C., Fritzler, M., Jones, S., Mazzarella, S., & Rakow, L. (1989). Geographic and source biases in network television news 1982–1984. *Journal of Broadcasting and Electronic Media, 33*(2), 159–174.

Whitten-Woodring, J. (2009). Watchdog or lapdog? Media freedom, regime type, and government respect for human rights, *International Studies Quarterly, 53*, 595–625.

Wiebe, C. D. (1973). Mass media and man's relationship to his environment. *Journalism Quarterly, 50*(3), 427–432.

Wilkins, L. (1987). *Shared Vulnerability: The media and American perceptions of the Bhopal disaster.* Greenwood Press.

Wilkins, L., & Patterson, P. (1987). Risk analysis and construction of news. *Journal of Communication, 37*(3), 80–92.

Wilkins L., & Patterson, P. (1990). Risky business. Covering slow-onset hazards and rapidly developing news. *Political Communication and Persuasion, 7*(1), 11–24.

World Commission on Environment and Development (WCEP). (1987). *Our common future.* Oxford University Press.

World Resources Institute. (1989). *The crucial decade: The 1990s and the global environmental challenge.*

Yadav, K. P. S. (2017, 12 May). Lies, damn lies and endosulfan. https://www.downtoearth.org.in/indepth/lies-damn-lies-and-endosulfan-11070

Young India. (1928, 20 December). The evil of industrialism. https://www.mkgandhi.org/voiceoftruth/industrialism.htm

Zachariah, M., & Sooryamurthy, R. (1994). *Science for social revolution.* SAGE Publications.

Zwerdling, D. (2009, 11 May). In Punjab, crowding onto the cancer train. https://www.npr.org/templates/story/story.php?storyId=103569390

About the Author

D. S. Poornananda is Professor, Department of Journalism and Mass Communication at Kuvempu University in Karnataka. He primarily teaches development communication, environmental communication and communication theory. He has an MA in journalism from University of Mysore; an MS in television, radio and film from Syracuse University, New York; and a PhD from Mangalore University. He was a Fulbright Scholar at Syracuse University during 1997–1998. He was a Visiting Fellow at Volda College in Norway during 2001. Development communication, environmental communication, political economy of media and film studies are areas of his interest. He has worked on research projects related to rural television, panchayat raj system, development-induced displacement and media use in a tribal community.

Index

newspaper report
  Journal of the Scientific Society,
    147
newspapers
  Abhiyan, 208
  A Gazeta, 279
  campaign against the Coca-Cola
    Company, 129
  Dainik Jagran, 104
  decreased forest cover, 244
  Folha do Acre, 279
  Gujarat Samachar, 207
  implementation of Gadgil and
    Kasturirangan panel reports,
    272
  Indian Express, 208
  Madhava Gadgil's statement in
    Panaji, 263
  Malayala Manorama, 141
  Mathrubhumi, 129, 297
  selected for analysis in Kannada,
    238
  The Hindu, 118
  The Pioneer, 119
  The Times of India, 208
newspapers managements, 131
nuclear power plant
  cancer risk, 145–51

objectivity, 74
  adherence, 74
  arguments on existence, 80
  concept, 74
  criticisms against, 74
  environmental reporting, 76
  journalists, 75
Official Secret Act, 285
Ogoni Bill of Rights, 281
Our Common Future, 10

Panduranga Hegde
  Appiko movement, 26
pesticide industry
  claims, 144

Pesticides Manufacturers and
  Formulators Association of India
  (PMFAI), 141
Plantation Corporation of Kerala
  (PCK), 140
politically biased, 284
political reporting
  balance, 93
Prajavani, 84, 91
  Bhopal Gas Tragedy, 114
  Cogentrix Energy Inc., 115
  Dakshina Kannada, blocking
    stories, 116
  management standing by its
    journalists, 116
  Nagesh Hegde, 114
  stand on Kasturirangan report, 268
press freedom, 283
pro-establishment and pro-industry
  bias, 103
  Leo Saldanha's views, 103
  Rohin Kumar's view, 104
pro-government bias, 104
  Dainik Bhaskar, 108
  Giriprakash's views, 106
  Kudankulam nuclear power plant,
    105
Project Tiger, 7, 15
protection of Western Ghats, 262
public interest litigation (PIL), 37

Real Estate Regulatory Authority
  (RERA), 65
report
  Deccan Herald, 247, 250
  Forest Survey of India's State of
    Forest, 257
  Gadgil Committee Report, 263
  Kannada Prabha, 246
  Kasturirangan Committee Report,
    263
  Madhav Gadgil report, 158
  Prajavani, 250
  Rapacious Development, 249